Ex-foliations

Electronic Mediations

Katherine Hayles, Mark Poster, and Samuel Weber, *Series Editors*

Ex-foliations

Reading Machines and the Upgrade Path

Terry Harpold

Electronic Mediations 25
University of Minnesota Press
Minneapolis • London

Permission to reprint previously published and trademarked material is found
on pages 331–32. Every effort was made to obtain permission to reproduce
material in this book. If any proper acknowledgment has not been included here,
we encourage copyright holders to notify the publisher.

Published by the University of Minnesota Press
111 Third Avenue South, Suite 290
Minneapolis, MN 55401-2520
http://www.upress.umn.edu

LIBRARY OF CONGRESS CATALOGING-IN-PUBLICATION DATA
Harpold, Terry.
  Ex-foliations : reading machines and the upgrade path / Terry Harpold.
    p.   cm. — (Electronic mediations)
  Includes bibliographical references and index.
  ISBN 978-0-8166-5101-6 (hc : alk. paper)—ISBN 978-0-8166-5102-3
(pb : alk. paper)
  1. Reading machines (Data processing equipment).   2. Electronic books.   I. Title.
  TK7887.8.R4H37 2009
  070.5'797—dc22   2008018610

Produced by Wilsted & Taylor Publishing Services
Copyediting by Nancy Evans
Design and composition by Yvonne Tsang

Printed in the United States of America on acid-free paper

The University of Minnesota is an equal-opportunity educator and employer.

15 14 13 12 11 10 09   10 9 8 7 6 5 4 3 2 1

For Jeanne, who reads ahead

I believe in calling a spade a spade—not a personalized
earth-moving equipment module; and a multi-dimensional
spade, by gum, a hyper-spade—not a personalized earth-moving
equipment module with augmented dirt access, retrieval and
display capability under individualized control.
                    —Theodor Holm Nelson, *Dream Machines* (1974)

In our time, a machine has nothing whatever to do with a tool.
There's no genealogy from the spade to the turbine. The proof of this
is that you can quite legitimately call a little sketch that you make
on this paper a "machine." Nothing else is needed. You have simply
to have an ink capable of carrying current in order that this should
be a very efficient machine. And why shouldn't it be conductive?
The mark is already in and of itself a conductor of sensual pleasure.
                    —Jacques Lacan, *L'Envers de la psychanalyse* (1969–70)

Contents

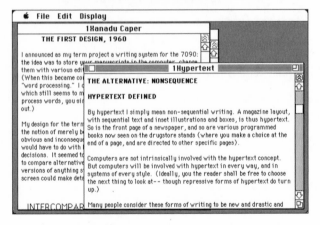

FIGURE 0.01. *Top:* A 3½-inch, 400K Macintosh floppy disk containing Theodor Holm Nelson's *Literary Machines* ("the first hypertext edition" [1987], in OWL Guide format). Collection of the author. *Bottom: Literary Machines* running under Mac OS 6 (1990).

Read Me First

0.01 Much of the theory of new media of the 1980s and 1990s concerned objects that have become difficult to access in their original forms ▶6.29.* This *medial-historical* fact of new media studies limits our understanding of claims made about these objects in the first two decades of the discipline. Accelerating technical and conceptual changes in the digital field also make it harder to estimate those objects' significance for future developments.

0.02 Any field of study so tightly bound to media technics as is new media studies will generate revised and contested versions of its tenets as those technics are changed. Even so, the emphases and tenor of debate in this field have shifted, in some cases very substantially, in ways that bear directly upon the field's earliest claims to originality and importance. The unrestrained enthusiasm of criticism of the first wave of digital literature seems now overly optimistic or naïve.▶N0.01 New textual methods and operations of reading that were proclaimed by some—decried by others—as portents of a late age of print seem now not so new and perhaps less scandalous.▶N0.02 Some have moved easily into the idioms of contemporary literate culture, or were discovered to be already a part of it, as Ted Nelson proposed more than

---

*Each paragraph in this book is labeled in a numeric sequence that identifies the chapter and position of the paragraph in that chapter: 0.01 (above) is the first paragraph of chapter 0, the book's introduction; 7.73 is the seventy-third paragraph of chapter 7, also the last paragraph of the main text. Cross-references (links) between paragraphs are in the form ▶6.29, directing the reader in this case to paragraph 6.29, the twenty-ninth paragraph of chapter 6. Links to illustrations and footnotes are labeled slightly differently: ▶Figure 0.01 for the first figure of chapter 0, ▶N7.55 for note 55 of chapter 7, and so on. In deference to page-oriented citation conventions, pages in the book are numbered in Roman or Arabic series. Entries in the index, however, are keyed to paragraph, figure, and note numbers.

four decades ago. Others have lost their shock value and possibly their relevance, as media appear to have moved away from textual and narrative emphases toward systems of visual spectacle: the immersive landscapes of console video games and Massively Multiplayer Online Role-Playing Games (MMORPGs); the aggregate still and moving images and programmed interactions of Web-based documents; and the increasing photorealism and animation of the graphical user interface (GUI), to which most of us have adapted with cheerful readiness, forgetting that there was ever an alternative ▶ 7.43. ▶N0.03

0.03 The supposed shift from *text* and *narrative* to *spectacle* (or *play* or *interaction*—all of these terms need to be better defined than they have been and I will try my hand at each) has elicited as much debate, pro and con, as did the "end of books" when it was proclaimed (a little prematurely) by enthusiasts of hypertext fictions in the early 1990s ▶ 6.01. I have already stated, if briefly, my position in these debates (Harpold 2005, 2008); this book several times elaborates on that position, but I am less interested in doing that than in backing up and reconsidering a history that might orient new versions of our discussions of where we have been and where we are now. Clearly, some qualities and operations of the objects that most engage our attention as new media scholars have changed, but I think it would be premature (again) to state with confidence what those changes represent for the present or future of the screen, or for our teaching and research in relation to these things, without some retrospection. We are entering a period that promises to resolve our misgivings about media through convergences, but only, as Anne Friedberg has observed, at the price of a strict technical determinism (digitalization erases differences between media, as Friedrich Kittler has proposed), and a suppression of specific qualities of media, namely of print and digital texts, that demonstrate that the feedback systems by which they are related to and distinguished from one other are complex and irregular (Kittler 1999; Friedberg 2006, 238). Understanding the qualities of a moving field, and not only being swept along by its currents, requires conscientious investigation of its precursors and, equally as significant, of the inertias and atavisms that persist within it. Among the chief reasons why much of this book is devoted to systems and hypertexts of the first wave (and print texts and mechanical devices for reading them decades and centuries older than that) is that I do not think we understood them very well the first time or that we have discharged our responsibilities to them. In this respect, *Ex-foliations* joins with other recent scholarship in the field in emphasizing the merits of returning to what seems at first like old and familiar territory.[N0.04]

0.04 *Conceits of the upgrade path.* Returning is not easy. Storage media degrade over time, becoming unreliable or unusable. Computer hardware falls out of favor or is superseded by faster/bigger/better instruments. Operating systems (OSs) are rewritten for new technologies and may no longer support older media, peripherals, or programs.[N0.05] Programs themselves fall out of favor or are replaced by versions that may not be fully backward-compatible. Documents created in proprietary formats or that rely on specific OS or program features become difficult or impossible to access if those features are no longer supported. When these documents can be converted to a more accessible format, this almost always results in changes of attributes of the original.[N0.06]

0.05 Because technical innovation in popular computing is driven more by the allure of expanding markets than by something so quaint as a sense of responsibility to historical continuity, commercial discourses of the upgrade path will inevitably promise consumers new and more satisfying interactions, and encourage them to see the older ones as outmoded or no longer relevant.[N0.07] The conceits of the upgrade path are tightly bound to ideologemes of the marketplace and the fantasies of progress they induce. Even when the crassest aspects of their pressure can be resisted, more subtle evolutions will determine how we interpret the operations of texts created with older systems when we are still able to run them. Larger or more colorful screens will change visual attributes of the text; faster microprocessors will accelerate its responses, perhaps to the point of no longer being reliable (a common problem with legacy computer games); changes in the idioms of the GUI will influence our estimation and even our comprehension of older ones. Consequently, program traits that once made perfect sense in their context and programmers' ingenuity in working within and against limitations of hardware and software may go unnoticed or seem perverse (▶ 6.28, Harpold 2008). It is not necessary to track every change in the conditions of reading in order to grasp salient differences between how a work signified then and how it may signify now. But it seems advisable at least to register these differences where that can be done, and to attend to what they might reveal of the historical arc of our reading.

0.06 All things being equal, the most straightforward solution to this problem is to keep around hardware and software of the period in which a work was released and to run it only on that machine. Then one is able to review the work in circumstances that approach as closely as possible to those when it was still new. But all things are not equal, and there are a number of reasons this approach is often impractical, to which I will return shortly.

0.07 A generally more viable solution is software and hardware emulation or virtualization. An *emulator* duplicates features of one computing system using the resources of another so as to imitate behaviors of the first system as closely as possible. Programs that can be run under emulation do not conflict with the host system because they are aware only of the emulated system, and this makes emulators particularly useful for isolating and running software that is incompatible with the host system's architecture. *Virtualization* is a more general term in computer science, but in this context it usually refers to platform virtualization, a technique for creating one or more *virtual machines* that may be run concurrently with the operating system of a *host machine*. Because virtualization does not emulate low-level hardware—the virtual machines and the host share those resources—it is the better solution for running legacy or incompatible software that has the same basic hardware needs as the host OS: a virtual Windows 95 machine running on a modern Windows computer, a virtual Windows XP machine on an Intel-based Macintosh, and so on.

0.08 The image on the bottom in ▶Figure 0.01 was created using an emulator that reproduces a circa 1990 Macintosh Plus on modern Mac OS systems.[N0.08] It shows several windows of one of the first commercial hypertext programs, OWL International's Guide for Mac OS.[N0.09] Released in 1987 and distributed on a 400K floppy disk, this software was designed for Macintosh computers of the period, combining monitor and central processing unit (CPU) in one housing, a 9-inch, 512 × 342 pixel CRT monochrome screen, a maximum of 4 MB of RAM, and running on an 8 MHz Motorola MC68000 processor. All of these attributes have long since been superseded: in 2008, Apple computers are based on multiple Intel microprocessors, have a dramatically different hardware footprint, and run an OS incompatible with the Macintosh Plus and Guide.[N0.10] With a little luck and cautious jiggery—the file conversions required are tricky, because modern Macintoshes have no floppy drive and haven't been able to read 400K disks for a decade—it is possible to emulate a system that can run this more than twenty-year-old software. Guide's unique "folding" link scheme and interactive cursor can be studied now only in this way.▸N0.11

0.09 More significant than its example of the methods of an early hypertext program is the text of this Guide document. Theodor Holm (Ted) Nelson's book *Literary Machines* (1987b, 1990a) is one of the most important statements of modern hypertext theory. Scholars cannot ignore it; I cite it often in this book. Surprisingly, the 1987 Guide edition of *Literary Machines* is the only digital hypertext created from Nelson's early self-published writings. My somewhat worse-for-wear floppy disk appears to be a rare thing; I've tried unsuccessfully for years to locate another; Nelson doesn't own one.▸N0.12 The only object that applies methods of digital hypertext to one of the most influential documents of the discipline ceased to be readable except under emulation more than a decade ago.

0.10 The ability of emulation and virtualization methods to preserve or resurrect legacy software makes them invaluable for historical research on new media. Many scholars working in preservation and archive studies are convinced that they are essential to future efforts to safeguard digital media for future access.▸N0.13 I have used them extensively in the preparation of this book.▸N0.14 But these methods are limited in several important respects. Writing software that duplicates the myriad interactions of hardware and software is an exceedingly difficult task, and emulators are often buggy and incomplete in their support of the systems they reproduce.▸N0.15 Many are hobbyist projects created by enthusiasts of programs designed for an obsolete system, most often, games; they may be less interested in reproducing the complete behavior of the OS than in supporting those features needed by their favorite programs. Emulation projects usually lack the support of—or are actively opposed by—the publishers of the emulated systems, who wish to maintain control over their intellectual property even when it is no longer in use. Terms of agreement for the use of software often prohibit the decompiling or reverse-engineering required to document behaviors of deprecated systems. More generally, the legality of emulation and the distribution of orphaned software ("abandonware") remains unclear under prevailing interpretations of the Berne Convention and the Digital Millennium Copyright Act of 1998.▸N0.16

0.11   When they are well-supported commercial endeavors, emulators and legacy software are no less subject than other programs to the vicissitudes of the marketplace and the consequences of evolving hardware and software standards. At some point maintaining backward compatibility with legacy software is no longer fiscally or technologically advantageous for OS publishers, and the software will be orphaned if another solution is not found. For example, versions of Mac OS X up through 10.4 ("Tiger") include a compatibility layer, essentially a limited emulator, called "Mac OS Classic," that enables users to run Mac OS 9 software concurrently with OS X. Running in Classic can be cumbersome, but it is a workable solution for users who need access to programs designed for Mac OS 9 and earlier, including some of the most significant new media fictions and art of the 1990s created in Storyspace, HyperCard, and SuperCard. (Options for running these programs on Windows machines are inferior or simply unavailable.) Apple's decision to end support for Classic with the release of OS X 10.5 in 2007 means that these programs cannot be run on a modern Macintosh computer. Users who want to run them must maintain older Macintoshes for that purpose or a new emulator that runs Mac OS 9 under Mac OS X 10.5 must be created. (None exists at present.) But that solution might mean postponing the inevitable: any emulator that runs only on a specific platform may itself become obsolete if it is not modified when the platform is changed. For this reason, some proponents of emulation as an archival solution have argued for the creation of generalizable, platform-independent emulation. The technical challenges presented by such a project are considerable (Bearman 1999; Granger 2000).

0.12   For the teacher and researcher, the obstacles to the conscientious study of new media's technical history are increased by her reliance on the institutions of her profession. Maintaining old computer systems in good working order is a time-consuming and often expensive endeavor requiring significant technical expertise and ingenuity. Replacement parts and intact and legal copies of legacy OSs and application software can be difficult to find. Again, all things being equal, this is what the scholar should do, but doing it on her own, or perhaps in collaboration with a small group of researchers or students, is often not practicable. An institutional framework that draws in part on existing IT support would be more efficient in many respects, but there are several reasons why this is unlikely at most universities. Under pressure to remain current in their technology offerings, universities update or discard obsolete computers and software as quickly as their budgets allow. Funding for maintenance of "outdated" equipment is likely to be even more limited than the usually inadequate sums allocated to maintenance of new equipment. At state-funded institutions in the United States, accounting procedures and software licenses often restrict reallocation of older equipment and software, requiring that they be handed down to the next poorer department, cannibalized for parts, or inventoried into black holes from which they rarely return. Classroom and laboratory space at such institutions is usually at a premium, and must be cleared of systems that do not serve instruction or new research projects. Enterprise solutions and authentication schemes that have been implemented to deal with burgeoning tech support issues are usually incompatible with older systems. The greater susceptibility of some older OSs to malware (viruses, Trojans, spyware, etc.) and the lack of up-to-date antivirus software for them may result in their outright banning from active networks. IT staffs' preference for uniform hardware and software configurations leaves the researcher working in a minority or discontinued operating system to her own devices.

0.13 Institutions of the university that are explicitly charged with archival responsibilities may be no more helpful. For budgetary reasons, libraries are often unable to purchase multiple copies of "non-productive" software like new media fiction and games—if they purchase them at all—so that some may be kept out of circulation to ensure their future availability. The physical plants of most university rare books and preservation departments are ill-equipped to house generations of ancient CPUs and peripheral devices. So long as computer hardware, operating systems, and user interfaces are thought of as (only) information appliances and not as (also) historical and cultural *machines* in the broadest sense, it will be difficult to make the case that their varieties should be archived by academic institutions for the purposes of genealogical research. ▶N0.17

0.14 These problems are not new to the digital field. Parchment and paper were once as precious as hard disk space and RAM are now, and were conserved and reused with parsimony. Manuscripts and printed pages have always been subject to loss or reckless destruction (biblioclasm is the rule, not the exception [Battles 2004]). The archival preservation of emergent or minor genres and of materially or formally unusual printed texts has always been inconsistent (Bright 2005; Drucker 1995); and literary translation and intermedial adaptations are capricious and contested arts in all media situations. The technologies of writing have always predetermined in some ways the fate of the written; technologies of reading have always shaped our possible relations to the lettered object, and the media historian has always had to work against the regressions and stumbling advances of her objects of study.▸N0.18

0.15 *Historiation.* The pace of change of operations of digital texts and their associated visual forms, most notably, the evolution of the GUI in the last three decades, touches on a more general historical characteristic of the digital text I will term *historiation*. In chapter 2, I define this as a form of recollection activated by visible traits of the reading surface. It is typical of reading in every medium, but its effects are especially marked in the dynamic textual fields of digital media. In this context, *textual* should be taken to indicate the broadest possible spans of language's material supports, including determinate structures activated by obvious traits of the textbase and its particular parsings; others of a more general and culturally shared nature, which depend on systems of citation and connotation; and contingent structures *sui generis* that are activated by a specific reading by a specific subject that cannot be easily repeated or categorized. Historiation is in this sense the medial basis of a reader's mnemonic relation to the text's surfaces. It marks a subjective dimension of reading—bound to the text's concrete, objectively present graphemic and structural characteristics—that is typical of our encounters with the complex surfaces of modern texts (Drucker 1996; McGann 2001; White 2005).

0.16 To the degree that it describes an aspect of the reader's engagements with the reading surface, historiation is distinguished from a concept such as "interactivity" by its emphasis on the unconscious determinisms of these engagements. Drawing on Jacques Lacan's concept of language's "insistence" —which applies to any form of language (textual, graphic, gestural, etc.)— I will argue that reading takes form at the join of constellations of signifiers—the text, as an immanent, if complexly and inconsistently activated field—with a history that is repeated and *insists* there: an archive, individual and cultural, recollected by the reader. Historiation is shaped by her memory, aware and unaware, of prior encounters with other texts, and is elicited by traits of the text presented to her in the present. In the most literal sense imaginable (and imagining, *seeing* an emerging shape, is decisive here), the patterns of the present reading surface determine how it will be parsed and how its orders of meaning will be enframed in relation to a system of texts that is unique to the *hic et nunc* of a given reading encounter. These are not the only aspects of the digital text whose interpretation is so oriented, but in the era of the GUI they are those most clearly directed by it ▶ 7.49. As I will show, reading machines, analog and digital, whose influences may be detected in the behaviors of the modern GUI, have been concerned with exchanges of textual elements and the signature effects of reading they sustain, characteristic of historiated reading.

0.17 These forces—the effects of the upgrade path and the dimension of historiation in the reception of new media—bear on operations of reading from the computer screen in such ways, I propose, as to *involve* the reader in formal and material systems of the screen. ("Involve": figures of the circuit and of circulation will return repeatedly in my discussion, prompted by contours of textual volumes that appear to require circumnavigations of one kind or another.) In that she is an interpreter of these texts, the reader is a subject of historiation; historiation is one of the conditions of her engagements with the reading machine. I come to this term independently of N. Katherine Hayles's exploration in *Writing Machines* "of what the print book can be in the digital age" (2002, 9). In focusing on the *reading* machine, I do not mean to reify readerly intentionality (namely, "a machine with which one reads"), or to minimize the role of dynamisms of print and screen texts highlighted by Hayles. I conceive of the reader's engagement with texts as basically heteronomous in its most decisive operations, in that the reader is less free than she knows, even though the determinisms of her reading cannot be entirely accounted for. Reading, because it is one of the most constrained of the vicissitudes of language, is more machinic than intentional. Since Turing and Lacan, Friedrich Kittler suggests, it could not be responsibly *symbolized* in any other way ▶ 2.51.

0.18 The effects of historiation are aggregative and noncommutative; their products will be inconsistent and hostage to the hazards of reading and the contingencies of the reader's memory of reading. These points of departure for her (re)imaginings of the texts' expressive surfaces are necessarily multiple and open to future revisions, some of which may become part of a sociolect of reading, while others will persist only in the trails within a more local and intimate store. In chapter 4, I introduce the second major neologism of the book, in the term *ex-foliation,* meaning a loosely grouped set of procedures for provisionally separating the layers of the text's surfaces without resolving them into distinct strata or hierarchies, with the aim of understanding their expressive concurrencies. Since it must be bound to the reader's recollections and anticipations of other significant surfaces ▶ 2.24, ex-foliation will be opportunistic, even capricious, in its address of surface-work. It implies no methodological responsibility, because it accepts a disjunction between the signifiers it isolates (they are immanent to the text or its performances) and the signifieds it derives from or articulates in response to those signifiers (the signifieds are a *historical* effect of historiation, specific to the reader). It does not discover the basis of historiation.

0.19 *Map of this text* ▶ 1.03. Chapters 1 and 2 investigate circuits of Vannevar Bush's and Ted Nelson's early models of the hypertext archive, Memex and Xanadu. In relation to these "entangled" archival trajectories, I introduce the concept of historiation to describe the reader's (chiefly visual) engagements with their structure—which occurs always, I propose, in terms of her memories and anticipations of meanings marked on the surfaces from which she reads. Of significance in this context are the unrepresentable crises on which, as Freud discovered, subjective structures of memory are founded. I show that the urgencies of Bush's and Nelson's projects for improved archivy were bound to specters of nuclear annihilation, overpopulation, and environmental devastation characteristic of the historical periods in which the projects emerged. Memex and Xanadu, albeit with different emphases and models of textual form, undertook to contain the effects of imagined crisis on archival practice. The broader significance of hypertext's vexed relations to technics of memory lies in its orientation of figures of absolute oblivion within the reading situation.

0.20 Elements of Bush's reworked desk drawer and Nelson's evolutionary lists prefigured a join of textual structure to technics of media. Front-end forms of the trail ▶ 1.39 and the twingle ▶ 2.54 keep Memex from devolving into a banal variant of cinema and the Xanadu workstation from devolving into an "interactive" version of television. I begin chapter 3 with Michael Joyce's observation that "hypertext is the revenge of the word on television" (1993b). A celebrated author of print and digital fictions, he could not have meant by this a complete repossession of territory lost by the letter to the contours of the screen; his own work demonstrates that its allures are too charged to be likely to be abandoned. In any case, the screen is also a surface for writing, and writing now takes place in a culture of screens. The "television" Joyce decries might be rendered in words and letters as equally as pictures; what counts is the degree of a flattening or narrowing of unruly signifiers. An inconsistent intersection of inward-directed circuits with outward-directed field effects was a basic feature of Memex. Nelson's conception of the docuverse as an unbounded exteriority decentered Bush's archive but did not surrender its clanking, clattering machinery.

0.21 In the domain of the reading machine, textual structure installs feedback loops that orient our understanding of graphemes in terms of their form, not their reference. The reading machine does not concern itself with the meaning of the mark, only with its presentation on the reading surface. Even when that front-end function is linked to database-driven back-end functions, the manner in which the mark is presented to us enforces a distinction between the mark's potential references and the substance of its presentation, which may in turn sustain or evoke other references. Drawing on terminology coined by Jean-Gérard Lapacherie, I describe four categories of *grammatext* characteristic of the reading surfaces of literary hypertexts, video games, and classic and modern GUIs. Attention to these typographemic traits of the screen, independent of linguistic function, opens critical reading to material bases of historiation.

0.22 Backward glances verging on nervous atavism are a trait of every medial shift, but appearances of the page and codex on-screen seem especially freighted with the effects of nested and embedded textual surfaces. In chapter 4, I discuss an important class of objects I term *perforated* texts, in which a literal or figured opening in the page or screen is marked. I describe a variety of such texts (artist's books, children's literature, graphic novels, video games, and avant-garde multimedia) and the role in them of a real limit to the recursivity of such openings. *Reading is, before it can be anything else, surface-work.* Perforated texts represent, I argue, varieties of a crisis of surfaces that reading represses and memorializes, and that rereading, especially close, critical reading, must repeat. This is the domain of ex-foliation. The ancestry of human-computer interface design in human factors science and cybernetics has left that discipline unprepared to interrogate these operations of reading; its emphasis is on diagnosing inefficiencies or ambiguities and reshaping user interfaces to defined, if evolving, conventions of program behavior. Literary-theoretical approaches to the digital field, while open in principle to aesthetic understanding, have too often been limited by their abstractions of program and interface and their emphases on narrative and mimetic operations. I conclude this chapter by proposing that the material and grammatextual lessons of the codex, above all those of aberrant or eccentric codices, may be applied to objects of the digital field, in the expectation that *the specific mediality of the digital sign will be expressed most clearly in the outliers of new media design practices.* I examine in detail one such outlier, Elliott Peter Earls's classic multimedia work *Throwing Apples at the Sun* (1996). Earls's text is, I conclude, an exemplary collection of surfaces bordered by the most frank fictions of disclosure, which it openly and gleefully subverts.

0.23 Chapters 5 and 6 offer close readings of classic hypertext fictions by Shelley Jackson and Michael Joyce. I use Jackson's *Patchwork Girl* (1995a, 1995b) as a case study for a critique of the use of the term *lexia* as a synonym for the unit of hypertext reading, coincident (in this use) with segments of the textbase. The term, I argue, was misappropriated from the writings of Roland Barthes, whose concept of the lexia is virtual and illocutionary, a dynamic form sustained by the reader's active parsing of a textual corpus (her "structuralist activity"). I propose, however, that Barthes's original sense of the term is applicable to expressive structures of hypertext fiction, with some modifications of its meaning in keeping with distinctive medial traits of hypertext. The second half of chapter 5 undertakes this in the example of the graphically and textually evocative opening nodes of *Patchwork Girl*.

0.24 Michael Joyce's *Afternoon, a Story* (1987, 1989, 1990, 1992a, 1992b, 1998b, 2001a, 2001b, 2007) has been described by Robert Coover as the "granddaddy of hypertext fiction" (Coover 1992).[N0.19] Though it is unclear which fictions Coover meant to be *Afternoon*'s prospective grandchildren, one must take seriously the family romance anticipated by this now-famous designation. Its effects are evident everywhere in the theory, criticism, and pedagogy of hypertext, in which *Afternoon* serves as a privileged model and counter-model: included in every course reading list, alluded to in every critical discussion, ranged among the most serious challenges of the digital text to regimes of print, or offered (more recently) as the limit-case that illustrates how hypertexts of the 1990s are something we have left behind. My emphasis in chapter 6 is on a problem that this legacy presents to historical analysis: there is more than one *Afternoon*; Mac OS and Windows versions of the text differ notably in their visual presentation and reading apparatus. Critics have rarely made note of these differences, though they have meant that some claims made about this seminal work are applicable only to its versions on one or the other of the two computing platforms. *Afternoon*, I conclude, represents a telling example of the conceits of the upgrade path and the need for programmatic, historically and grammatextually sensitive readings of the user interfaces of even the most familiar of digital texts.

0.25 *Ex-foliations* closes with an examination of early modern and twentieth-century reading machines proposed by Agostino Ramelli, a sixteenth-century engineer, and constructed by Daniel Libeskind, a twentieth-century architect. I describe also a third machine constructed by the pataphysician Juan-Esteban Fassio, imaginatively descended from Ramelli's wheel but custom-fitted to assist in reading Raymond Roussel's masterful twentieth-century revision of the codex *Nouvelles Impressions d'Afrique* (*New Impressions of Africa*, 1932). These devices, I observe, activate looping, multidimensional circuits of textual intercomparison, and project the printed page into complex field geometries.

0.26 In chapter 7, I contrast these reading machines with comparable but impoverished systems of the modern GUI. In these I find evidence of a canny foreclosure of the real bases of historiation that the analog machines seem to admit more openly. As a reading surface, the primary function of the screen as it is presently constituted—that is, of all the widgets, menus, buttons, icons, and so forth that compose the avatars of knowledge on the screen—is to protect the user from the very quality of the screen that is unreadable.

0.27 Here, historiation—in all of its medial and subjective specificity—traverses the upgrade path and crosses the barest alibi of the interface. The screen in the modern form of and on our desktops *screens* us from something that the page also obscured, but seems to have done so less effectively, less consistently. In the opaque substance and material inertias of the page and its avatars, we are reminded again and again of a real limit of reading that the reading machine is propped upon. The screen, in contrast, presents its surface as the thinnest of coverings of a navigable space that remains open to our entry and departure. It presents us with an *imaginarized symbolic* that appears immune to perturbations introduced by media's real attributes. That those perturbations will be felt is inevitable; we have only to wait for our reading to catch up to them.

1.

"A Future Device for Individual Use"

Why is a raven like a writing desk?
—The Mad Hatter to Alice, in Lewis Carroll,
Alice's Adventures in Wonderland (1865)

1.01 "Let me introduce the word 'hypertext,'" writes Theodor Holm Nelson in 1965—it is his first published paper on this subject and the first occurrence of the term in print ▸N1.01—

> to mean a body of written or pictorial material interconnected in such a complex way that it could not conveniently be presented or represented on paper. It may contain summaries, or maps of its contents and their interrelations; it may contain annotations, additions and footnotes from scholars who have examined it. Let me suggest that such an object and system, properly designed and administered, could have great potential for education, increasing the student's range of choices, his sense of freedom, his motivations, and his intellectual grasp. Such a system could grow indefinitely, gradually including more and more of the world's written knowledge. (Nelson 1965, 96)

1.02 He adds in a footnote,

> The sense of "hyper-" used here connotes extension and generality; cf. "hyperspace." The criterion for this prefix is the inability of these objects to be comprised sensibly into linear media, like the text string, or even media of a somewhat higher complexity. (Nelson 1965, 98)

1.03 Hypertext is, then, first a practice of composition: hypertexts comprise other textual objects. Among these, Nelson proposes, may be summaries and maps, annotations, additions, and footnotes. These are not all of a hypertext's possible parts (their kinds will proliferate in the subsequent design literature) but they are sufficient to mark from its inception the liminality of the hypertextual. Maps and summaries describe, contain, and displace; conceptually and procedurally, they operate at or beyond the boundaries of objects they gather and abstract. (A map whose extension is coterminous with the territory it represents would be something . . . more *and* less . . . than a map.[N1.02]) The relations of annotations, additions, and footnotes with regard to texts they mark are more varied (Genette 1987), but they too operate within a system of enclosure: complete maps or summaries of those texts would include them.

1.04 In Nelson's initial formula, hypertext begins by being spread over the gamut of prior and possible textual practices as a boundary phenomenon: joined to and depending on existing habits of writing and reading—especially those derived from print and marked by its discontents—and reaching beyond them, into conjectural habits of a new technical regime, more fluid, more varied, and more extensive than its precursors. What distinguishes *hyper*texts from the others, suggests Nelson, is the manner in which they combine their parts and represent this combining: hypertexts include other texts more *sensibly* (that is, more rationally, but perhaps also more perceptibly) than they may include . . . yet other texts. Hypertexts differ in qualities of their effects; they do something more or else; they present and *re*present in ways other texts cannot. This formal and referential play—something more than recursion and self-citation, and less than antinomy—has contoured the hypertext imaginary from the beginning. Nearly four decades after its introduction, Nelson's neologism retains all the methodological and performative ambiguities of its first use.[N1.03]

1.05 "The simplest way to define hypertext," software usability guru Jakob Nielsen proposes in *Multimedia and Hypertext,*

> is to contrast it with traditional text like this book. All traditional text, whether in printed form or in computer files, is sequential, meaning that there is a single linear sequence defining the order in which the text is to be read. First you read page one. Then you read page two. Then you read page three. And you don't have to be much of a mathematician to generalize the formula which determines what page to read next. (Nielsen 1995, 1)

1.06 *Hypertext is a kind of text inconveniently realized in print.* In 1991, Nelson suggested that this is its most general trait: "The best current definition of hypertext, over quite a broad range of types, is 'text structure that cannot be conveniently printed.' This is not very specific or profound, but it fits best" (253). Such a definition raises two stumbling blocks for a theory of hypertext's difference from other textual forms. First, there is the awkwardness of a negative economic model: how little convenient must the printing of a text or texts be to be judged *in*convenient, in order to merit a hypertextual approach? Second, what assumptions regarding textual operations are encoded in the choice of a restricted category of texts—letterforms set in parallel lines on facing leaves, bound in the center, and so on: Nielsen's "this book" or *this book* ▶0.02—as the normative model, from which something called hypertext seems to depart?

1.07 No one is compelled to read a book in the way that Nielsen claims. Readers seldom read any but a relatively small and banal category of texts (assembly instructions, travel directions, shopping lists) with so fixed and programmatic a method. Even in these cases, one can foresee skipping over items in a list or taking them out of turn because of changing conditions of use, or, perversely, just to see what might come of it.▶N1.04 Beginning and seasoned readers alike treat print's presumed rules of engagement with equal impertinence: they begin and end where they please; they read against prescriptions of sequence and integrity, out of whimsy or boredom, or to save time (Barthes 1973). It is probably true that readers do not skip every which way and at any level of granularity—narrative enforces some principles of order, hierarchy, and completeness, if it is to make sense (Ryan 2001b); the most fractured lyric forms require minimal syntactic integrity, or else they are unordered lists; Nielsen is at least partly right in observing that the physical regimes of the codex tend to induce predictable patterns of reading, if only because it is difficult to work around those regimes. But none of these orientations of reading is absolute, and none applies equally or consistently to all readers or all situations of reading.

1.08 Even when readers elect to read a printed text in the order of its lines and pages, they will also parse its paratextual regimes: formal, graphemic, and material traits that direct the pursuit of sequence without being fully absorbed into it.▶N1.05 These may be multiplied over the text's surfaces and involutions: the title; the running foot or head; the page number; the choice of paper stock, typefaces, and page layouts; binding methods (and faults in binding); typographical errors, stains, folds, and tears; an earlier reader's marginalia. All, as Jerome McGann has observed, are *marked* in our readings, which may potentially engage every characteristic of the text's surfaces. The consequences of the visible and material language of the page will extend beyond the serial procedures of the letter and the line, to include structures and scansions those procedures activate but do not limit (McGann 1993, 2001). One reads any printed book in constant, if not always conscious, relation to structures and orders, cycles and epicycles that are bound complexly and inconsistently to its material form and that exceed its serial systems. ►N1.06

1.09 In addition, we must consider the suppleness and adaptability of printed surfaces. Whole traditions of typographic and bibliographic practice such as the artist's book depart openly from received practices of the page and codex. In many printed texts, a degree of procedural difficulty and material resistance—that is, of some *inconvenience* that print and paper may manifest—is essential to their method. Rather than representing outliers of practice, these traditions have operated across and within print culture from its inception, anticipating and advancing its development and diversity. ►N1.07

1.10 The "traditional" sequences of the page invoked by Nielsen can be defined as such only in contrast to the persistence of disorderly practices of paper and ink. Repression of the variety of those practices—reflected in much of the critical literature of new media in the most naïve descriptions of what may be accomplished with the printed surface—has resulted in a systematic blindness in that literature to the actual and potential expressiveness of print. I would not now go so far as to endorse McGann's proposal that the codex's hypermedia powers exceed those of the digital text (2001, 168), but it is clear that those powers are greater than is often acknowledged. ►N1.08

1.11   By "hypertext," I simply mean non-sequential writing. A magazine layout, with sequential text and inset illustrations and boxes, is thus hypertext. So is the front page of a newspaper, and so are various programmed books now seen on the drugstore stands (where you make a choice at the end of a page and are directed to other specific pages).

Computers are not intrinsically involved with the hypertext concept. But computers will be involved with hypertext in every way, and in systems of every style . . .

Many people consider these forms of writing to be new and drastic and threatening. However, I would like to take the position that hypertext is fundamentally traditional and in the mainstream of literature. (Nelson 1990a, 1/17)

1.12 Hypertexts are all around us, familiar and even unremarkable; like Molière's bourgeois gentleman, we may be pleased to discover we have been writing and reading in a peculiar mode all our lives.[N1.09] They represent the general economy of textual operations, a fact that has been hidden to varying degrees, Nelson suggests, by the inefficiencies of analog media.

> The inner structure of literature has been that of documents, each with an owner/creator, which quote and refer to one another in an ever-growing snowball. And when I say "documents," I mean not just written objects, but movies, symphonies, lab reports—any human production of text or pictures or audio or other media, any package of information.
>
> The connections among documents may not be apparent. But every book refers to others, explicitly and implicitly; every movie has connections to what came before. Sometimes these connections are visible, sometimes they are not. But they are always there.
>
> Literature has always been interconnected. But in the past we could not see many of the connections, and could not follow them instantly. The new interactive hypermedia make it possible to show and follow these connections electronically. (1997, 53–54)[N1.10]

1.13 The displacement from the document to *literature* avoids the pitfalls of equating hypertext and just-plain-text with corresponding non-serial and serial reading habits, or basing their difference on attributes of the printed page and a presumed transformation of them in the digital field. (Though this is a canny displacement: the document is at best a procedural fiction; Nelson's is a system of literature(s), not of documents ▶ 2.07.) But the assertion that hypertext is a general form of text raises further difficulties, invoking new ambiguities and linkages in the prefix: *hyper*-text as text's liberated potential; *hyper*-text as text's over-excited, pathological mode (Birkerts 1994; Heim 1993).

1.14   Consider a future device for individual use, which is a sort of mechanized private file and library. It needs a name, and, to coin one at
random, "memex" will do. A memex is a device in which an individual stores his books, records, and communications, and which
is mechanized so that it may be consulted with exceeding speed and
flexibility. It is an enlarged intimate supplement to his memory. (Bush
1991a, 102) ►N1.11

1.15 The word "hypertext" is not found in Vannevar Bush's 1945 essay, "As We
May Think." But the research problem and the solution Bush describes appear to have provided an opening for a new scheme of textual practices, such
that critical or historical reflections on hypertext must always chain Memex
to Xanadu, Nelson's unrealized design for a global hypertext archive. ►N1.12
The conventional history of hypertext has, as Michael Joyce has wryly observed (2000, 242), the feel of latter-day Old Testament genealogies: prior
to and between Memex and the Xanadu SilverStand, there are generations,
begettings and further begettings, and nested loops of influence and diver-
gence. ►N1.13 I will repeat portions of that history here. My aim, however,
is not to emphasize continuities of design and thought that join Memex to
Xanadu, but to draw attention to a crucial turn that distinguishes Bush's
and Nelson's respective representations of textual systems. In Memex, these
are chiefly directed inward, though some of the device's operations hint at
other possibilities. In Xanadu and in hypertext schemes influenced by it,
textual systems are directed outward, and the interiority of the archive is
recast as a potentially unlimited extensivity. Analysis of these systems and
their significance for the contemporary digital field must take this turn into
account.

1.16 The passages in Bush's essay concerning Memex, among the best-known
of any he wrote in a distinguished career of academic research and public
service, describe the device as a sort of desk outfitted for the information
age (► Figure 1.01 and ► Figure 1.02).

In one end is the stored material. The matter of bulk is well taken
care of by improved microfilm. Only a small part of the interior of
the memex is devoted to storage, the rest to mechanism. Yet if the
user inserted 5000 pages of material a day it would take him hundreds of years to fill the repository, so he can be profligate and enter
material freely.

FIGURE 1.01. *Left:* Close-up of a Memex display screen. *Right:* Memex as office furniture. "Memex in the form of a desk would instantly bring files and material on any subject to the operator's fingertips. Slanting translucent viewing screens magnify supermicrofilm filed by code numbers. At left is a mechanism which automatically photographs longhand notes, pictures and letters, then files them in the desk for future reference" (Bush 1945b, 123). Illustration by Alfred D. Crimi (1945); reproduced with permission of Bob Crimi.

Most of the memex contents are purchased on microfilms ready for insertion. Books of all sorts, pictures, current periodicals, newspapers, are thus obtained and dropped into place. Business correspondence takes the same path. And there is provision for direct entry. On the top of the memex is a transparent platen. On this are placed longhand notes, photographs, memoranda, all sorts of things. When one is in place, the depression of a lever causes it to be photographed onto the next blank space in a section of the memex film, dry photography being employed. ►N1.14

There is, of course, provision for consultation of the record by the usual scheme of indexing. If the user wishes to consult a certain book, he taps its code on the keyboard, and the title page of the book promptly appears before him, projected upon one of his viewing positions. Frequently used codes are mnemonic, so that he seldom consults his code book; but when he does, a single tap of a key projects it for his use. Moreover, he has supplemental levers. On deflecting one of these levers to the right he runs through the book before him, each paper in turn being projected at a speed which just allows a recognizing glance at each. If he deflects it further to the right, he steps through the book 10 pages at a time; still further at 100 pages at a time. Deflection at the left gives him the same control backwards.

FIGURE 1.02. "Memex in use is shown here. On one transparent screen the operator of the future writes notes and commentary dealing with reference material which is projected on the screen at left. Insertion of the proper code symbols at the bottom of the right-hand screen will tie the new item to the earlier one after notes are photographed on supermicrofilm" (Bush 1945b, 124). Illustration by Alfred D. Crimi (1945); reproduced with permission of Bob Crimi.

A special button transfers him immediately to the first page of the index. Any given book of his library can thus be called up and consulted with far greater facility than if it were taken from a shelf. As he has several projection positions, he can leave one item in position while he calls up another. He can add marginal notes and comments, taking advantage of one possible type of dry photography, and it could even be arranged so that he can do this by a stylus scheme, such as is now employed in the telautograph seen in railway waiting rooms, just as though he had the physical page before him. (Bush 1991a, 102–3)

1.17 Alfred D. Crimi's illustration of the device's interior for the September 1945 publication of the essay in *Life* (▶ Figure 1.01) recalls traditions of the automata—Vaucanson's flapping, drinking, digesting duck, or Kempelen's chess-playing Turk, seated before his cabinet.▸N1.15 All the working parts are in full view and we can envision most of their movements, but it is not easy to see how they would operate as a whole. This is speculative design in its most persuasive form—as simple alibi for the imagination—with just a hint of conjuring, enough to make it all look as though it should function as described. The duck, after all, did not actually digest the grains it was fed; it stored up pre-softened droppings in its belly and dispensed them as required to give the appearance of defecating. And the Turk was operated by a man secreted away behind a false panel in the cabinet, working the machine's mechanical arm. The obvious gimmickry made little difference to audiences, who found the simulation of digestion or chess playing nonetheless fascinating. Memex, as Bush describes it and as Crimi has rendered it, has had that hold on audiences since 1945, even though—as will become clear—it is a figure of how such a machine might be imagined to operate rather than a prediction of how it could actually operate.▸N1.16

1.18 In the end, it is mostly a piece of furniture, where one sits, reads, and writes. The *Life* illustrations evoke another pictorial tradition, older but close to conditions Bush envisioned for his new kind of desk. The many paintings and illustrations of Saint Jerome reading are a prototype here (▸ Figure 1.03): deep in solitary thought, the reader is bent over a book, pressing a finger or a quill to the page. He is for the moment oblivious to the piles of papers and books surrounding him on tables, shelves, and windowsills, their disorder marking in inverse proportion the degree of his concentration (Clark 1977; Hanebutt-Benz 1985; Petroski 1999; Rice 1985). Memex facilitates sharing of information between users but (at least in its first incarnation) these exchanges are notably one-directional: the "operator of the future" works mostly alone in the corner of his lab; Memex is "intimate" in that sense of the word, too. It *involves* its user; the "trails" it builds from his reading—I will come to these shortly—are specific to the manner in which the device enables him to review a burgeoning archive composed of his and others' writings.▸N1.17

1.19 To achieve this, Bush assumes a modest improvement in technologies of microphotography, resulting in a nonetheless impressive reduction of paper originals. ("The Encyclopedia Britannica could be reduced to the volume of a matchbox. A library of a million volumes could be compressed into one end of a desk" [1991a, 93].) The archive's effective capacity is vast; an entire lifetime of research will not overrun it. Its physical dimensions are, however, strictly limited—Memex is a piece of furniture, not a library or a warehouse; Crimi's cut-away diagram reveals an interior that is partitioned and compact, a handy place for putting things away and bringing them out when they are wanted. In this regard it evokes an array of related storage spaces and practices associated with them: the closet, the cupboard, the strongbox, the trousseau, the casket, the wardrobe, the *Wunderkammer*—the public, private, and disciplinary enclosures and varieties of furniture-as-intimate-exteriority that Gaston Bachelard characterizes as the "organs of the secret psychological life" (1964)—though, strangely, Bachelard never included the desk among them (Kopelson 2004, xv).[N1.18] Or the scholar's cell, though that omission may be less surprising given the technical complexity of the cell: Bachelard prefers spaces with more uniform, atechnical interiors; he is not much interested in the automatisms of writing and reading typical of the apparatuses of the *studium*.

1.20 Consider, for example, Antonello da Messina's ca. 1475 painting of Jerome (▶Figure 1.03). The famous image, Georges Perec writes, is organized around a piece of furniture, and the furniture around a text. All that is peripheral to Antonello's depiction of Jerome's carrel—the "glacial architec-

ture" of the church; the distant landscapes visible through the window and vaulted corridors on the left and right; the lion, cat, birds, and potted plants that encode the image's complex allegorical system—is cancelled out, Perec says, by the inward pull of the desk and the open book at the painting's center. "They are there solely to lend scale to the piece of furniture, to enable it to be *inscribed* [*lui permettre de s'inscrire*]" (1974, 118). Perec exaggerates here; the painting's allegorical programs are not cancelled out, but they are certainly subdued by this visual centering on the desk and the page, and by the anachronistic traits of the furnishings, Jerome's garments, and the architecture that frames the carrel. Images in this tradition, Henry Petroski has observed, often represent the Doctor of the Church in trappings of the painter's era, presumably because this was thought to make the subject of the image more salient to the contemporary viewer (1999, 108). In this case the anachronism signals also a resituating of Jerome's cell to Quattrocentro contexts more concerned with the technics and responsibilities of reading than with the elevation of historical or religious figures who happen to read. This is the image's subtle textual logic, though no text *per se* can be read from it (we can't see what piece of scripture or profane literature Jerome is looking at): in a period of changing understanding of the textual bases of language ▶ 2.25, the painting can be seen to be mostly *about* reading

FIGURE 1.03. Three depictions of Saint Jerome reading. *Far left:* Antonello da Messina, *San Gerolamo nello studio* (*Saint Jerome in His Study*), ca. 1475. Oil on panel. Copyright The National Gallery, London. *Center:* Albrecht Dürer, *Der heilige Hieronymus in der Zelle* (*Saint Jerome in His Cell*), 1511. Woodcut. Photograph copyright 2008 Museum of Fine Arts, Boston. *Right:* Jerome dressed as an Augustinian canon in *La Vie, mors et miracles du glorieux Saint Jherome* (*The Life, Death, and Miracles of the Glorious Saint Jerome*), ca. 1515 (France, artist unknown). Image reproduced with the permission of L. Tom Perry Special Collections, Harold B. Lee Library, Brigham Young University.

(Jerome reading, Jerome as the model reader, how a model reader reads with his eyes and body). In operational terms, the cranking of Ramelli's, Libeskind's, and Fassio's reading wheels (▶7.02, ▶7.29) are not far off. Nor is the mechanical arm of Kempelen's Turk, representative of automatisms of such enclosures. In the second of Crimi's illustrations, the pull of such an enclosure is so powerful that the human operator is nearly cancelled out, appearing only as an accessory hand reaching in from outside the frame to annotate the screen (▶Figure 1.02).

1.21 These early modern depictions of the *studium* are still. The spaces they show must be almost entirely quiet, apart from the scratching of the quill, the rustling of papers from time to time, and perhaps the purring of the lion at Jerome's feet. In contrast, Bush's desk would be a noisy contraption. We can easily imagine it whirring and clicking as it labors, gears turning, the spools of film rolling and unrolling inside. From time to time, a noise, muffled, which is heard less and less often in an age in which beginnings and ends may be coterminous: the sound of the stub of a spool of film slapping against the lens housing. (Image subsystems of the digital reading machine are more effective at throwing up camouflage for the real stubs of their archival series: messages that reduce a limit to a misdirection "404 Not Found" or a static image that collapses every imagined interior of the machine to a blank surface: the "blue screens of death" ▶7.69.) Other aspects of this imagined scene are similarly retrospective: an enormous, open office, dozens of Memexes arrayed in neat rows under long banks of overhead fluorescent lights. They are staffed by busy researchers or their assistants, interior reels spinning, levers, keys, and lenses clicking. Each desk is far enough from the others to permit movement between them, but close enough to allow the hand-to-hand exchange of spools. Uniformed messengers run up and down the room's length to move the spools between desks at opposite ends, or to other offices like it. Or: a series of pneumatic tubes hanging from latticework bolted to the ceiling conveys the spools quickly to and from drop-baskets located at the side of each desk. The sound of the archive's furthest reach: *thunk*.

1.22 *Thought experiments.* "Only a small part of the desk" is taken up with the store of page images, "the rest to mechanism." This is not because Memex's reliance on optical-mechanical technologies results in the inefficient partitioning of its interior—most of the modern desktop computer is also devoted to input, output, and display operations. The mechanism, not the store, is the heart of the device.

1.23 Bush's leading role in analog computing technologies during the 1930s and 1940s may explain his emphasis on optical and electromechanical operations of Memex. Digital computing and magnetic data storage were in their infancy when he began to think about Memex in the early 1930s. In 1945, digital computing was still a relatively new field, and the importance of analog devices in the war effort, especially in antiaircraft fire control systems, greatly overshadowed the smaller contributions of the new digital devices. By the mid-1950s, however, these had begun to surpass analog computers in many situations in terms of their speed and generality, and the analog devices had begun to be consigned to a dwindling set of specialized laboratory tasks. By the end of the 1960s, computer science and engineering had for the most part transitioned to digital technologies. Bush's commitment to analog computation and simulation seems not to have flagged; the later designs for Memex incorporate some digital elements, but essential operations remain tied to analog systems (Burke 1991; Owens 1991).▶[N1.19]

1.24 One consequence of this is an irony seldom remarked upon by enthusiasts of Memex: no version of the device as described by Bush could have worked reliably in the workaday settings he envisaged for it. The fine tolerances it required would probably have made the device expensive to manufacture in quantity, particularly vulnerable to manufacturing faults, and prone to film misalignment and abrasion and mechanical breakdown. Typical levels of dust and other airborne contaminants found in laboratory environments could easily have crippled its sensitive optics. The extremely high speed microfilm spooling needed to advance through thousands or millions of page images in a timely fashion would have considerably magnified these problems. Moreover, the system's reliance on what is essentially a brute-force coding and retrieval scheme meant that the speed of searches must increase arithmetically as the size of the store increases, which would surely prove a disincentive to its use for very large collections of page images.▶[N1.20] Some kinds of useful searches (Boolean matches on multiple keycodes, for example) appear to be difficult or impossible in the proposed designs. How the user might retrieve keycodes she has forgotten or does not know is never addressed. There is no provision for remapping keycodes between different users' stores, and it is difficult to envisage how remapping could be implemented in a microfilm apparatus. When a spool is inserted into the desk, whose keycoding scheme will prevail, the owner of the host Memex or the creator of the spool? Bush does not say.

1.25 If Memex as Bush described it would not work as he described it, perhaps another Memex might have. Some of its complex electromechanical elements could be replaced with more fault-tolerant transistors. Other forms of data entry could supplement the keys and levers. More durable media for storing and retrieving the page images could be substituted for the fragile spools of film. A uniform or translatable keycoding scheme with support for Boolean matching could replace the purely idiosyncratic one proposed by Bush. His later designs for the device point in the direction of such improvements ▶ 1.45.

1.26 But Memex was always, above all, a thought experiment: that is—a reversal of that term seems justified here—an experimental application of a model of thought and its record. Bush is less interested in the engineering details than in forecasting the promise and heuristic of a new kind of mental furniture; everything else is there to lend it scale, to enable it to be *inscribed*. If that furniture also figures a limit-case of memory's representation, its familiar form (the desk as the privileged scene of mental labor) serves to pin memory's representation to something that appears easy to grasp. In comparison, the desktop computer with which I write these words—as I type they appear in a window that floats over another surface called a "desktop"—seems the more conjectural device. I press the keys, I see glyphs corresponding to them imprinted on the screen, I imagine that they will eventually be imprinted on a page. But between the keystroke, pixels, and the page it is harder to imagine intermediate processes that join them; those seem of a different order altogether, one composed of magnetic valences, electrical discharges, and more virtual things that exist only in the logic of a program; they are effected beneath or outside thresholds of my perception.

1.27 Memex's reliance on analog technologies must also result in a reification of writing and reading events and a degree of incommensurability—even irreversibility—of their effects. Despite (or because of) its function as an "intimate supplement" to the user's memory, documents archived in the device can be retrieved or transmitted to others only with another Memex. Crossing the desk's optical and spatial thresholds is not easily reversed;

page images recorded on microfilm will be too compact to read without the projector's magnifying lens and the display platens; whatever the coding scheme by which the images are marked for storage and recovery, these subsystems will rely upon the keyboard, levers, and spools. The conversion from paper to film results in copies equally as infrangible as the originals, and even more dependent than they on a specific condition of writing and reading that is not easily portable.

1.28 *Bijection.* We might have anticipated this orientation of the archive— toward, if not irreversibly an interior, then toward, somewhat irreversibly, a medial projection that implies an inside and an outside. Earlier in "As We May Think" (that is, before he introduces Memex), Bush speculates on the future direction of photography and its benefits to the laboratory worker. "The camera hound of the future," he proposes, will wear on his head a device "a little larger than a walnut" (▶ Figure 1.04).

Outfitted with a universal focus lens—it might have two lenses, so as to record stereoscopic images—the camera is controlled by a small bulb and cord threaded down the user's sleeve.

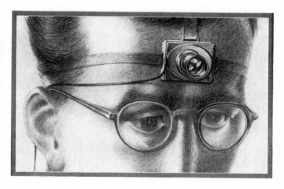

FIGURE 1.04. *Left:* The Cyclops camera. "A scientist of the future records experiments with a tiny camera fitted with universal-focus lens. The small square in the eyeglass at the left sights the object" (Bush 1945b, 112). Illustration by Alfred D. Crimi (1945); reproduced with permission of Bob Crimi. *Right:* "Peering through his automatic computing sight, the gunner swings his turret horizontally in a complete circle and vertically from the position shown here . . . to position in which the guns point straight down. The bullets feed into .50-cal. guns through the system shown in cutaway part of the drawing" ("Mechanical Brains" 1944, 66). Illustration by Alfred D. Crimi (1944); reproduced with permission of Bob Crimi.

A quick squeeze, and the picture is taken. . . . As the scientist of the future moves about the laboratory or the field, every time he looks at something worthy of the record, he trips the shutter and in it goes, without even an audible click. Is this all fantastic? The only fantastic thing about it is the idea of making as many pictures as would result from its use. (1991a, 91)

1.29 The lens of the "Cyclops camera"—the name appears to have been coined by *Life*'s editors—supplements the user's vision in much the way that Memex supplements his encounters with the written word: by bringing objects of perception directly into the archive—"in it goes, without even an audible click." The researcher must squeeze the bulb that opens and closes the shutter, but the transfer is nearly imperceptible, and the outward gesture is equivalent to an inward movement of vision. (Some forty years later, advocates of "direct manipulation" user interfaces ▶ 3.01 will term this seamless transposition the "put-that-there" event, thus collapsing an imaginary even more dispersed into a space even more compact [Bolt 1980].) The technology of "dry photography" is an adjunct to this structural condensation, reducing the transfer of images to the merest passage across a threshold marked by the film's surface.[▶N1.21]

1.30 *Seeing in a physical sense.* The squeeze of the bulb hidden in the researcher's pocket or in his hand—that portion of the mechanism is squirreled away from the outside in a fold ▶ 7.38 or enclosed in a fist[▶N7.28]—repeats a reflex already more intimate than a shutter opening and closing: the conscious batting of the human eye so as to register what is seen more clearly. And the camera does this with the greatest directness imaginable, because it is typical of the "new and powerful instrumentalities" Bush has celebrated a few pages earlier:

> Photocells capable of seeing things in a physical sense, advanced photography which can record what is seen or even what is not, thermionic tubes capable of controlling potent forces under the guidance of less power than a mosquito uses to vibrate his wings, cathode ray tubes rendering visible an occurrence so brief that by comparison a microsecond is a long time, relay combinations which will carry out involved sequences of movements more reliably than any human operator and thousands of times as fast. (1991a, 89)

1.31 "Seeing in a physical sense" reads like a description of optical or electronic phenomena, but in this context it surely carries also a specific epistemological valence. Recording "what is seen or even what is not" and doing it in less time and more reliably "than any human operator" suggests that these devices, including the Cyclops camera, operate in a visual field that is more fundamental than that of the human eye. The efficiency of the photographic image and its drawing of the spectator into identifying with the camera's eye, Walter Benjamin observed, are the bases of photography's stripping away of a contemplative relation to the image, of modern vision as a technic of reality-testing (1968a, 229) ▶ 7.43. Bush's enthusiasm for the thermionic tube and the cathode ray tube joins the unconscious of optics (Benjamin's term) to the atemporality of the stroboscopic images created by Harold Edgerton (one of Bush's students at MIT): bullets piercing apples, balloons, and playing cards, and milk droplets forming coronets as they splash (Jussim, Hayafas, and Edgerton 1987). These images of an invisible world captured only on camera were of surfaces traversed, cut, and pierced.

1.32 *Traveling shot.*▶N1.22 Other technics of vision may be signaled in the image of the camera. Crimi's *Modern Surgery and Anaesthesia* (1936), the first and only completed fresco of a series of five commissioned by the Works Progress Administration (WPA) for Harlem Hospital, shows seven surgeons and nurses observing or taking part in an operation on a patient heavily draped with surgery cloth.▶N1.23 Each is gowned, masked, and turned toward the center of the painting, so that only the eyes, the bridge of the nose, and one ear are visible, as in ▶ Figure 1.04. Though none wears eyeglasses, the surgeons' intense gaze, framed above and below exactly as the operator's gaze is by the upper and lower borders of the Cyclops image, is unmistakably the same. Because it is portrayed from a distance, the WPA mural demonstrates what can only be conjectured from the Cyclops image: the intimate, intentional connection of vision to action, of the gaze to gestures of pointing and grasping (scalpel, scissors, sutures) and writing (the anesthesiologist takes notes, his hand held in the position shown in ▶ Figure 1.02).

1.33 Whereas the fresco anticipates the user's relation to prosthetic vision, an illustration for a January 29, 1944, *Life* story on technologies of the air war, drawn by Crimi in his capacity as house artist for the Sperry Gyroscope Company, anticipates the logistical context of this relation (▶ Figure 1.04). Drawn in a "multidimensional" cut-away technique that Crimi would later

apply to other media (Crimi 1977; 1987, 150), the drawing shows an airman crouched in the lower ball turret of an Allied bomber, peering through
a gunsight. The image is centered on the airman's open eye, which looks
directly at the viewer.

> The gunner lines up his target with two vertical hairlines in the sight.
> The trick is to keep the enemy plane exactly framed within these
> lines, which are moved in or out by means of a range knob as the
> target approaches or recedes. As he follows the target in its course,
> the sight automatically makes deductions from this "tracking" pro-
> cess, which it translates into the relative course and speed of the tar-
> get. Taking this data, the range data and other factors like the weight
> of .50-cal. bullets, the gears and levers and circuits that make up the
> mechanical brain arrive with inhuman speed at an answer. (66)

1.34 Instead of spools of film (▶ Figure 1.01), a coiling gunbelt; mechanisms for
feeding syntagmatic units to the heart of the device are not much different,
and in each case the focus of action coincides with a visual focus. In the earlier illustration the totality of the prosthesis is especially clear: rounded and
foreshortened, the image seems to be viewed through a lens; it is as though
we are shown not only ourselves being seen by the gunner, but we are shown
this from inside the field of his gaze. "In it goes, without even an audible
click . . . the gears and levers and circuits that make up the mechanical brain
arrive with inhuman speed at an answer." Visual fields of the desktop and
the gun magazine cross in a space we may conjecture to have been constituted by the drawings of the camera and the ball turret; surely the uncanny
resemblance of the images indicates that the artist was interested in depicting a fundamentally logistic space proven by the roles of aerial reconnais-
sance and the "mechanical brains" behind the guns of the war, and that
this was also the optical condition of "thinking machines" predicted by the
editors of Bush's essay. Paul Virilio's critical genealogy of the ciné machine
gun, the parallel evolution of modern optics and modern aerial warfare, and
a concomitant "logistics of perception" fits this space very nearly (1984). It
differs only in the subjection of Memex's cinematic apparatus (central to
Virilio's argument) to the page image's residual evocation of the book.

1.35 Such crises of vision as these are more subtly folded into the optics of Bush's
laboratory of the near future, such that their disorienting influences are
masked. He expects the camera to do the work of vision-as-a-condition-

of-rememoration in the way that Memex will do the work of reading-as-a-condition-of-rememoration—that is, by means of a kind of vision capable of sifting out what is most important from the documents that pass over its surface, and then moving that data into the desk's inner orders. (How different can these labors be in a fundamentally optical-mechanical model in which any linkage of the text to other texts is also an optical-mechanical phenomenon? This is both the limitation of Bush's conception of reading and the path by which the trail reaches beyond equating memory with interiority, into other schemes of circulation.) That this, at least within the technical imaginary his editors mean to conjure, is a fundamental function of the whole of the armamentaria Bush describes is evidenced by the prominence given to the illustration of the Cyclops camera in the *Life* article. It appears there above the article's title ("AS WE MAY THINK / A TOP U.S. SCIENTIST FORESEES A POSSIBLE FUTURE WORLD IN WHICH MAN-MADE MACHINES WILL START TO THINK"), filling nearly half of the first page (1945b, 112). No other of Crimi's illustrations takes up more than one fifth of one column. Several are less prominent than advertisements for garters, breath mints, and hair tonic on the same page. The camera operates as the leading element of a chain of textual-graphic forms extending into a realm of popular consumerist anxiety and enthusiasms spinning outward from crises of the war ▶ 2.55.

1.36 It is in this context that the real basis of the archive, despite its repression in the figure of seamless conversion, returns from repression. In the example of this photomechanical phylactery we are already moving away from an interiority to a different order, or at least one with a different intensity in its partitioning and a more ambiguous commingling of the record with the technics of retrieval. The inward pull of Memex's model of storage and retrieval requires material procedures that cross the boundaries of the desk's enclosure—indeed, it cannot function without these procedures. To access the desk's imagined inside (the page images), the user may never dispense with its outside (the spools of film, the platens, the keys, the levers); the apparatus and the archive are always interleaved in this way, and the device's prejudicial interiority—mechanical, material, spatial—will be subtly drawn outward by aspects of its operation.

1.37 The specificity of the procedures required to cross from outside to inside and back shows why comparisons of Memex's scheme to twenty-first-century archival technologies—"a library of a million volumes" on a few

CD-ROMs or DVDs, or recorded in solid state memory, rather than packed into a desk drawer—are misleading. The later systems require a different translation from the photoreduction imagined by Bush: namely, the encoding of the grapheme (the glyph, the letter) and the pattern (the line, the paragraph, the page) into structured sequences of 1s and 0s; more precisely, of optical or magnetic valences. More so than microfilm, a human user cannot parse these records without a playback device that represents (re-presents) the document in simulacra: a page, a line, a glyph recreated on the screen in patterns of light and dark. In contrast, Memex's operations are activated and accessed via mechanisms whose actions begin by resembling the eye's operations: the user can easily visualize how the archive works (it sees "in a physical sense"); *that* is in fact a basis of Memex-as-thought-experiment. And the appreciable economies achieved by its methods are irreducibly spatial in a way that is easily grasped: Crimi's illustrations show us not just how the spools are stored, but that they are stored away in a magazine whose limits are well-defined; they can be removed from the store, transferred to another user, and so on. The space of the store is pragmatically ordered but, more important, it is imaginatively articulated. (The logic of the closet, cupboard, strongbox, etc. ▶ 1.19, until, like some topological curiosity— the film loop as Möbius strip; the desk as Klein bottle—the store turns itself inside-out.)

1.38 Crimi's illustrations *signify* on several registers support of this imaginary of storing-away or -up: desk drawer (the archive as enclosure), automaton (the archive as hidden mechanism), image (the archive as interiorized photology); put-that-there (the correlation of vision and action, the gaze as scalpel, the lens as bombsight). Which is not to say that these images constrain Bush's device to the limits of these forms—the cut-away view already implies a traversal of boundaries, the Cyclops camera and the concept of the trail more so. It would be more correct to say that they trace both those contours and potential crossings of them in an entanglement of inside and outside that is much older than either Bush's or Crimi's imaginations. Descartes thought the pineal gland the seat of the soul because only it, of the organs of awareness, stands at the site of bijection—the division of the outside from the inside—without being itself doubled. In lower vertebrates, the pineal gland functions as a primitive light receptor, and is thought to be the evolutionary precursor of the true eye. In birds and some mammals, it plays a little-understood role in migratory navigation. The Cyclops camera and the camera lens of Memex's desktop are versions of this third eye. Perhaps "versions" is too figurative a term: they *are* this eye, in the episteme that Bush's model repeats and (in a specifically post-photographic and post-Turing order) anticipates: vision not as it is actually experienced by its subject, imperfect, blurred by vicissitudes of the passage from the outside to the inside, but as it is conjectured to be: impersonal and objective, untouched by pathologies of desire and memory, transmedial without any alteration of its semiotic bases. Except that this structure of bijection articulates also in the other sense: the crossing of an interior and an extension that reaches beyond it is the principle of the archive's pathology, the foundation of its subjective character ▶ 7.43. ▶N1.24

1.39 All the gadgetry of Memex, Bush observes, is conventional apart from projected developments of existing technologies. The record's reduction and the ease with which it may be consulted are remarkable, but they are not the most important aspects of the device. More novel are the higher-level associative procedures it supports.

> This is the essential feature of the memex. The process of tying two items together is the important thing.
>
> When the user is building a trail, he names it, inserts the name in his code book, and taps it out on his keyboard. Before him are the two items to be joined, projected onto adjacent viewing positions. At the bottom of each there are a number of blank code spaces, and a pointer is set to indicate one of these on each item. The user taps a single key, and the items are permanently joined. In each code space appears the code word. Out of view, but also in the code space, is inserted a set of dots for photocell viewing; and on each item these dots by their positions designate the index number of the other item.
>
> Thereafter, at any time, when one of these items is in view, the other can be instantly recalled merely by tapping a button below the corresponding code space. Moreover, when numerous items have been thus joined together to form a trail, they can be reviewed in turn, rapidly or slowly, by deflecting a lever like that used for turning the pages of a book. It is exactly as though the physical items had been gathered together from widely separated sources and bound together to form a new book. (1991a, 103–4)

1.40 If we bracket for a moment the ambiguous orientation of the method by which they are gathered and retrieved, Memex's storage of page images does not appear to threaten the bounded interiority of the writing desk. Day-to-day operations of the device will reach outward, in the sense that film spools can be exchanged with users of other Memexes; the reliance on microfilm is expressly intended to allow this. And a degree of mobility on the user's part is still in keeping with the basic enclosure of the desk. Several pages before he introduces Memex, Bush envisages the future investigator moving within his laboratory: "his hands are free, and he is not anchored. As he moves about and observes, he photographs and comments. Time is automatically recorded to tie the two records together" (1991a, 95). He may even, Bush suggests, be connected "by radio" to his recorder when in the field or at home. So a certain orbit around the archive, connected by subtle threads of photographic film and radio voice, will allow the user to gain a little distance.

1.41 It is the trail that directs the device away from interiority more radically than any other of its features; the trail belongs, in point of fact, to a *textual* order that will ultimately invert that interiority. To trace this inversion and its significance, we must start with another ambiguity of the scheme described by Bush. The trail, strictly speaking, is not an annotation, transcript, or collation of the user's reading; it is, instead, a record of emergent structure. In order to repeat a reading, he or another user of Memex requires a copy of both the specific trail and the documents to which it refers.▸N1.25 How these two objects are exchanged is never made clear. (Is the trail recorded on the same spool as the document archive, somehow merged or interleaved with the keycodes? or must there be separate spools for page images and the trails that index them, as more than one trail may reference the same images?) In use, reading according to the trail—for the moment, let's put aside the seriality this entails—appears to be "exactly as though the physical items had been gathered together from widely separated sources and bound together to form a new book." But this can only be an operational conceit. "Binding" the page images, even temporarily—how? by recording snapshots of them on another spool?—would soon become cumbersome (a different spool of excerpts for every reading, including re-readings of earlier ones); it is difficult to see how further joining any item "into numerous trails" could be accomplished in this way without soon filling the desk or adversely affecting the efficiency of page retrieval.

1.42 Throughout the Memex essays, Bush fails to distinguish the trail (metadata) from the record (data), even as his descriptions of the device require that they be so distinguished. This is evident in the associationist model on which the device is based:

> [The mind] operates by association. With one item in its grasp, it snaps instantly to the next that is suggested by the association of thoughts, in accordance with some intricate web of trails carried out by the cells of the brain. It has other characteristics of course; trails that are not frequently followed are prone to fade, items are not fully permanent, memory is transitory. Yet the speed of action, the intricacy of trails, the detail of mental pictures, is awe-inspiring beyond all else in nature. (1991a, 102–3)

1.43 "Man cannot hope fully to duplicate this mental process artificially," Bush adds, "but he certainly ought to be able to learn from it. In minor ways he may even improve, for his records have relative permanency" (103). In comparison to those of the mind, Memex's trails "do not fade." The slippage from "the intricacy of trails" to "the detail of mental pictures" is not without precedent; it signals (although here its direction is reversed) a shift in the emphasis of his argument, from a concern for efficient storage and retrieval ("the detail of the mental pictures") to something markedly different, which is treated as a positive object in its own right. In the closing pages of "As We May Think," Bush illustrates the device's amazing utility with examples in which the ever-growing "mesh of associative trails" is consulted and amplified by its users (the historian, the patent attorney, the physician, the chemist). The mesh, he suggests, must be understood to be at least as important as the page images themselves. "The inheritance from the master becomes," Bush concludes on a triumphal note, "not only his additions to the world's record, but for his disciples the entire scaffolding by which they were erected" (105).

1.44 In this shift from an emphasis on the units of circulation to a more general, emergent circumstance in which the circulation is expressed and extended, Bush implicitly revises a methodological distinction he made sixteen years earlier in his first book, *Operational Circuit Analysis* (1929):►N1.26

> A **circuit** may be defined as a physical entity in which varying magnitudes can be sufficiently specified in terms of time and a single dimension. It thus involves movement of variation along a path. This is contrasted with the **field** problem in which there is variation with two

or three dimensions. Thus the analysis of the behavior of a speaking tube is a circuit problem, while a study of the production of sound in a room by a loud speaker is a field problem. (Bush 1929, 1)

Bush intends that Memex should be a servomechanism for reading, and the first design of the device is oriented chiefly by the circulation of units "in time and a single dimension." (The page images are not of "varying magnitudes," at least not in a material sense, but one could envisage devices like the spooling mechanisms for storing and moving around textual units of smaller granularity.[N1.27]) A *mesh* of associative trails, however, suggests the interplay of higher-dimension field effects that are not reducible to specified times and single paths. While they may be transmissible via a servomechanism for reading, it is unlikely that they could be contained by its enclosures or described by its movements.

1.45 Bush's increasing interest in such effects is evident in unpublished writings of the 1950s, in which he speculates on Memex's successor, called "Memex II" or "Memex Mark II," for which the trails assume priority over all other operations. The new machine will make use of promising new technologies of voice activation and recognition to extend the older interface of buttons and levers.[N1.28] Instead of microfilm, the new machine uses magnetic tape (still an analog technology):

> This is important, not merely because it will ultimately involve further compression in the volume necessary for the record, but more to the point because the magnetic record can be erased or added to almost instantaneously, without the sort of development and delay inherent in conventional photographic processes. It is essentially the equivalent of the system of dry photography . . . [used in Memex I], and in fact it is better for our purposes. (1991b, 167)

1.46 Some operations will dispense with spools and tapes altogether, having turned their functions over to the more efficient transistor. ("It will respond in a microsecond when activated, and will do so in precisely and specified manner [*sic*]" [170].)

1.47 As in the first version of Memex, trails may be created and extended by the user at will, but in Memex II this process is supplemented *by the device itself*:

For the machine remembers what it has been caused to do. Thus, when left to itself, stepping along some indicated trail, it will pause and explore a side trail if that has been its experience often when the trail was followed under orders. At an important bifurcation it will take the path that it has most frequently followed, and it can even give more weight to recent orders than to earlier ones, in making its decisions. Of course it can always be halted in its course and ordered to turn at will. Also it can be told, by another button, "de-emphasize that last trail you followed, and leave it as it was first introduced for I have finished with it." Then, too, trails, or parts of them, can be cancelled, as new material supersedes the old. One way of doing this is to project an item, place the new item on the recording platen, and cause a substitution, without removing codes. (1991b, 176)

1.48 Trails may now be shared to extents unforeseen in the first Memex (Oren 1991; Trigg 1991). Professional societies and publishing organizations, Bush predicts, will host libraries collecting users' trails and those created by in-house specialists, the descendants of the "trail blazers" predicted in the 1945 essays (1991a, 105).

One may then, under proper controls, dial by telephone directly into the memex of such a library, and use it from a distance, browsing about along trails, and transferring items of interest to the private store. . . . Many individuals may thus consult the library store simultaneously. When they meet on trails there will need to be special means provided so that they can pass one another. (1991b, 173–74)

1.49 Despite its basis in the first design, Memex II is in several respects a very different device. It is, first, more *intimate* than its predecessor. In the new design, the lenses behind the platens and worn on the researcher's forehead have, in effect, merged with the mechanism of archive: it watches, it learns, it is capable of seeing more of the user's habits than he is.[N1.29] A handier version of the desktop, a "light portable projection screen" outfitted with basic controls and connected to the main device by cables, can be used to track the user's responses to a book that has been inserted into Memex's memory. As he sits in an easy chair reading the book at his own pace and according to the ebb and flow of his interest, marking select passages he finds interesting or doubtful, Memex will watch and track his actions, and calculate where likely trails may be joined. On subsequent readings, it may alter the rhythms or sequence in which the text is displayed, anticipating his responses and incorporating them *a priori* into his next encounter with the text. "A book thus becomes controlled to reflect the interests," Bush writes, "and for that matter the personality, of the owner" (177).▶N1.30 And personalization may be more radical than this, as the user relies more on feedback loops of this kind:

> [The machine's] trails are formed deliberately, under full control of the user, ultimately in accordance with the dictates of experience in the art of trail architecture. This, in turn, remolds the trails of the user's brain, as one lives and works in close interconnection with a machine of scanned records and transistors. For the trails of the machine become duplicated in the brain of the user, vaguely as all human memory is vague, but with a concomitant emphasis by repetition, creation and discard, refinement, as the cells of the brain become realigned and reconnected, better to utilize the massive explicit memory which is its servant. (1991b, 178)

1.50 Supplementation has crossed into prosthesis—and even that term may not be sufficiently *personal* to capture this commingling of the inside and outside and the resulting thinning of layers between them. (But wasn't this already implied in the move from the "intricacy" of trails—which, whether neuronal or machinic, are formally no different—to the *hic et nunc* of the user's "mental pictures"?) Even so, a yet more intimate feedback loop can be imagined—after all, there are still those buttons and levers, and the eye and the camera lens will never coincide completely.

> Memex III may respond without this crudity of involving nerve systems which have no real part in cerebration. But this will have to wait until the psychologists and neurologists know far more than they do now, and until the advent of devices and instruments, of which the encephlograph [*sic*] is only a faint beginning, which can sense the activity of a brain without interfering with its action. (1991b, 182–83)▶N1.31

1.51 The spooling mechanism is still the heart of the device, but much of the gadgetry of the first design has been nearly abstracted away. (Only nearly: the shared trails of Memex II will be traversed by "rapid facsimile transmission over the telephone wires" [1991b, 173]. A global digital network is still decades away. Even so, the transmission of trail information by facsimile appears to mark a new level of distinction between the page images and trails that is not present in Memex I.) The treatment of the trail as a positive entity, manipulated and exchanged in much the same way as the page images, but also different in ways that are unclear, is one aspect of this idealization. Another is indicated by Bush's vague remark about Memex II users "meeting" and "passing" on trails. No aspect of the device seems to permit such crossings, except in the sense that two or more users following the same or different trails may possibly require the same document at the same time. Perhaps this is what Bush means? But the design of Memex II includes no server functions, only locally archived copies. Redundant, distributed storage of the kind fundamental to Xanadu or the World Wide Web is never addressed; the infrastructure it requires would have been difficult to envisage in the 1940s and 1950s. Near-simultaneous requests for access to the same document are possible, as in any print archive. But how this constitutes a "meeting" or a "passing" on trails remains unclear. Perhaps this abstraction is part and parcel of the shift toward increasingly immediate schemes of storage and retrieval (from film to magnetic tape, from levers to . . . thought); the later Memexes are in this respect less models for a new kind of mental furniture than tropes—for memory, for textual fields, for ill-defined points of contact between them, in the shape of furniture.

1.52 The concept of trail erasure and code reuse—". . . trails, or parts of them, can be cancelled, as new material supersedes the old. One way of doing this is to project an item, place the new item on the recording platen, and cause a substitution, without removing codes"—broadens the trail's import or, rather, brings forward an aspect of it that was only implied in earlier models. For in Memex II, trails not only encode the raw sequences of a user's reading, they may also identify directly temporal values of the sequence, mapping its units to an objective timeline. "The machine remembers what it has been caused to do": implied here is not only the recording of a collection based on a reading history, but—something new—*a direct recording of a collecting*, the incorporation with the collections of signs of its historical development. Nelson's "evolutionary list file" (ELF), in which every modification of the textbase is preserved and potentially repeatable, will carry this recording of a collecting to its extremity ▶ 2.35. ▶N1.32

1.53 Improved support for more flexible manipulations of page images, trails, and codes, and for possible formal crossings or overlaps of those elements,

indicates, moreover, a general entanglement of data and metadata. In the
· final analysis, the disassociation of the trail and the codes from the page
images is only a rhetorical conceit. In Memex II and III, trail and image
are treated as functionally homologous, each considered in its own right
and sustained according to closely related economies of manipulation and
transmission. This shift toward treating page image and trail equivalently (if
not, in the later designs, promoting the trail over the page image) will set the
stage for more radical abstractions of them in the work of Bush's successors.
There is nothing surprising in this equivalence: not all traits of document
structure are significant in every condition of reading. In some conditions,
however, each such trait must be. Any attempt to procedurally or conceptually isolate, remove, or alter traces of structure must alter other qualities of
the text that may be discernible only in its traversal. ▸N1.33

1.54   Every passion borders on the chaotic, but the collector's passion borders on the chaos of memories. More than that: the chance, the fate,
that suffuse the past before my eyes are conspicuously present in the
accustomed confusion of these books. For what else is this collection
but a disorder to which habit has accustomed itself to such an extent
that it can appear as order? (Benjamin 1968b, 60)

1.55 The archive compiled from everything that passes over the collector's desk
will include disciplined and undisciplined readings alike, always and in
their own way specific to the collector and the accustomed confusions of his
reading. These will be, necessarily, traced in patterns of the archive: those
he applies consciously and those—more individual—that are inscribed un-
consciously. (The paradox is that the latter may also be the most general
dimension of his reading: a collective unconscious—more concrete, more
textual, than an "archetype"—is traced in received practices of the national
tradition, the genre, the disciplinary emphasis, and so on.) Each of Bush's
designs for Memex undertakes to capture this *signature* of reading's history
in a concrete and repeatable form without constraining it to a predefined
sorting scheme that would strip it of its originality and specificity.

1.56 The pragmatic value of such a capture is that it may be exemplary: the order
that emerges from a reading history also distinguishes one object from another in a textual field. In the disarray of the collector's archive, a portion
of the labor required to reorder the archive in our way, to make it our own,

is already accomplished for us. There is never enough time to start from scratch; a prior history enables another to follow, even when it departs with as much vigor as the next reader can muster. This is the provocation of a previous reader's marginalia, or even our own from an earlier moment in our careers as readers: in the checks, crosses, underscores, and scribbles, we confront evidence of a scene of reading that has some cryptic relation to this one. We may surrender to some or all of its procedures and conclusions; we can refuse them, condemn the distraction, defend the privilege (the author's, but also ours) to a blank margin from which to begin anew, if such a thing were possible.[N1.34] Such three-party exchanges are oriented by something like the tendentious sadism of joke-work, in that someone must be pleased and someone must be the butt of the exchange. It is not always clear which plays which role.

2.

Historiations

Xanadu and Other Recollection Machines

Every history has two stories about it.
You either believe one or the other.
—Theodor Holm Nelson,
  The Future of Information (1997)

2.01 *All for one.* Nelson's Xanadu will advance abstractions of the Memex designs, resulting in more radical extensions of the archive. ►N2.01

> Making extra copies to keep track of changing work is simple, but cluttering and dumb. Instead suppose we create an automatic storage system that takes care of all changes and backtrack automatically. As a user makes changes, the changes go directly into the storage system; filed, as it were, chronologically. Now with the proper sort of indexing scheme, the storage facility we've mentioned ought also to be able to deal with the problem of historical backtrack.
>
> Think of it this way. An evolving document is really not just a block of text characters, Scrabble tiles all in a row; it is an ongoing changing flux. Think of its progress through time as a sort of braid or vortex.
>
> Think of the process of making editorial changes as retwisting this braid when its parts are rearranged, added or subtracted, and think then of successive versions of the document, at successive instants of time, as slices in this space-time vortex. (Nelson 1990a, 2/14–15)

2.02 This is no mere undo or auto-backup function: in Xanadu, each state of a document is the aggregate of its prior states; each change—addition, deletion, or reordering—is preserved and indexed independently. No instance of the document after its first saved state need be stored integrally, and displaying later instances requires (re)assembling them from fragments that may be dispersed throughout the network's address space (1990a, 2.14–15). The Xanadu "document"

> is not a physical unit; it may be assembled wholly or partly from other Xanadu documents; the contents of an individual document may be scattered throughout the docuverse; the document may have derivative copies throughout the network of servers; its only physical constraint is that a principal nucleus record must reside on its home server. (Nelson 1990a, 4/7) ►N2.02

2.03 How on-the-fly reconstruction of the document will be achieved on the lo-cal workstation remains unclear. Presumably, the system caches copies of document fragments (called "byte spans") retrieved from the network and displays them to the user in a composite form, in much the way a browser reconstructs Web pages from files it requests from different storage devices that may be in the same room or thousands of miles apart.►N2.03 No mat-ter, for that is a problem of procedure; operationally, distinctions between "original" and "copied" documents have no meaning in the Xanalogical store. They are, Nelson insists, only "windows" on a conceptually unified object, whose dispersed parts are *transcluded* in the screen presentation.

> Transclusion is what quotation, copying and cross-referencing merely attempt: they are ways that people have had to imitate transclusion, which is the true abstract relationship that paper cannot show. Trans-clusions are not copies and they are not instances, but the same thing knowably and visibly in more than one place. (Nelson 1999b, 8) ►N2.04

2.04 This distinctive here-and-many-thereness—it's difficult to envisage what it should *look* like on the back end, and that may be its decisive trait—is achieved by an addressing scheme breathtakingly simple in its method and maddeningly complex in its execution. Unlike, for example, the World Wide Web, in which documents are identified by combinations of absolute and relative machine and directory addresses, Xanadu presumes a write-once address space in which every byte span is uniquely identified. Addresses in this space are represented by multipart numeric sequences, called "hum-

bers" (for "humungous numbers") and "tumblers," from which it is possible
to calculate any span's position in relation to any other, and by arithmetical
operations to associate spans so as to merge or link them (1990a, 4/15–
40). Linking is bidirectional, multiply typed, and as granular as the user
requires: any addressable span may be linked to any other (page, paragraph,
line, grapheme, sound fragment, etc.); it may even be linked to spans that
have no assigned value. Links are, moreover, treated like other byte spans,
so a user's address space may include no "content" bytes, but only links to
other spans (1990a, 4/10). Duplication of the content of byte spans is allowed (that is how transclusion works), but all instances of a given piece of
data are treated within the address space as if they were the same object,
whatever their physical location. New transclusions may be defined at any
time; tumbler addresses will remain valid and accessible from anywhere in
the network, so long as the storage device remains connected to it (1990a,
4/19; 1998, 82–90).

2.05 This is very different from the method of the Web, in which a file's address
encodes the directory structure of a storage device (a server), whose address
depends on another scheme, namely, a human-readable string of characters
associated with a fixed IP (Internet Protocol) address assigned to that device.[N2.05] If the file is moved to another directory or to another device, its
previous address may no longer be valid, a phenomenon popularly known
as "link rot." In Xanadu's tumbler scheme, the directory structure of the
storage device, while of possible significance in matters of system overhead,
is otherwise irrelevant, because the tumbler address is unchanged when a
file is moved. This aspect of the tumbler scheme is of more than technical
significance: Xanadu conceptually pins the byte span when it is defined to a
signifier of an absolute origin:

> The leading digit "1" in tumbler addressing space has a special func-
> tion: it represents the entire universe of documents, or docuverse. Its
> use permits a uniform arithmetic across the docuverse, and uniform
> reference to spans of materials. Metaphysically, the leading 1 refers
> to a mythical Ur-document from which all others are descended.
> (Nelson 1987a, vi)

2.06 "All for one, one for all" (Nelson 1987a): the enormously complex computation required to implement a shared docuverse with minimal degrada-

tion of system performance as it grows—a reason (depending on whom one believes) for Xanadu's delayed birth or its quixotic futility (Nelson 1990a, 1992, 1998, 2002; Wolf 1995)—is directed to this end.

2.07 The Xanalogical document is thus complexly *temporal*—generated in real time by recombining its parts in a way that also encodes the history of each and of its prior instances—and it is *differential*: its uniform and unvarying nominal identity in the global store obscures the material fact that no portion comparable to a line, page, or frame—nothing much like a document in the pre-Xanalogical world—has to have a fixed location, even though nothing is ever out of place because everything has an address.

> A document consists of anything that someone wishes to store. It is designated by somebody to be a document; it may contain text, graphics, links, or window-links—or any combination of these—that the owner has created.
>
> By this convention, then everything in the system is a document and has an owner. No free-floating materials exist. Thus the Gettysburg Address is a document; "Jabberwocky" is a document; and a set of links between them, were someone to create it, would be a separate document.
>
> What this convention really does is stress the singularity of each document, its external and internal borders. Thus, we focus on the integrity of the "document" as we've known it. Evolutionary continuity is unambiguous. (Nelson 1990a, 2/29)

2.08 Under this regime, a "document" ("the 'document' as we've known it") is at best a notional term or a convention— a provisional suturing of dispersed units gathered by a specific frame. To that *specific framing* of the textbase certain privileges and obligations of ownership are bound; Xanadu's system of transcopyright, transpublishing, and microroyalties is based on the assumption that it may be repeated sometime in the future (Nelson 1999b). Because *framings* of other documents (1990a, 3/9), parts of documents, or links to parts or wholes can *be* a document, the document *qua* document exists only by virtue of having been brought together in a given moment by a given reading subject. (That subject need not be a person, of course; all sorts of automated schemes for collecting and linking byte spans are possible in this case. Proleptic reading bots of this kind were already an element of Bush's later designs for Memex ▶ 1.49.)

2.09 If, as Nelson insists, his design has the advantage of presenting the evolutionary continuity of texts in an "unambiguous" fashion, this can only be because the basis of that continuity is conceived of in *textual* terms, and only at a join of the back-end systems, which maintain the address space, with specific configurations of the front-end systems, which make continuity representable. Across this site of bijection ▶ 1.26, Xanadu orients into clusters or knots otherwise dispersed units of text, each with a history that pertains to it and the ensembles to which it may have belonged or may yet belong. Moreover, the user interface (UI) ▶ No.05 has to model the ways in which the reader finds herself carried forward by effects of those histories, generating—and, equally significant, *imagining*—new ensembles on the basis of new juxtapositions of elements of the reading surface. This is not a minor problem: how can the system sustain such interconnected tangles as its indexing scheme permits (and incorporate new tangles) and also present them to the user in a form that she can make sense of, without devolving them into a mere series of snapshots of document states?

2.10 *Grimper à l'arbre.* Near the beginning of his 1957 essay "L'Instance de la lettre dans l'inconscient ou la raison depuis Freud" ("The Instance of the Letter in the Unconscious, or Reason Since Freud," Lacan 1966, 493–530), Lacan reminds his reader of a diagram attributed to Ferdinand de Saussure: a tree (representing the signified, or concept), paired with its Latin name, *arbor* (in French, *arbre*, representing the signifier, or "acoustic image") (▶ Figure 2.01).

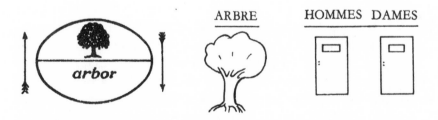

FIGURE 2.01. *Left:* Diagram of the sign, from Saussure's *Cours de linguistique générale* (1982 [1916]). Artist unknown. *Center:* Lacan's revision of the diagram. *Right:* Lacan's "more correct" version: facing lavatory doors labeled "Hommes / Dames" ("Gentlemen / Ladies") (Lacan 1957). Artist unknown.

2.11 The published versions of Lacan's text do not reproduce the diagram as it
appears in the 1916 and most later editions of Saussure's *Cours de linguistique générale*. Redrawn for his essay, Lacan's version is, moreover, altered
in several respects that he does not acknowledge. It is inverted, with the
signifier (ARBRE) placed above the signified (the drawing of the tree). The
original's oval frame has been removed, as have the arrows on the left and
right of the frame.

2.12 Lacan's reasons for making these changes may be guessed. His version of
the tree diagram follows by a couple of pages his introduction of the "algorithm" for the sign, S / s, "signifier over signified, 'over' corresponding
to the bar that separates the two levels"; the inverted tree doubles this relation and its prioritizing of the signifier. The algorithm, Lacan proposes,
"deserves to be attributed" to Saussure, "even though it is never reduced
strictly to this form in any of the numerous schemas in which it appears"
in the *Cours* (Lacan 1966, 497). His justification for this appears to be not
that this new formalization of the sign more accurately or—"reduction"
aside—more compactly represents its logic than versions in the texts attributed to Saussure, but that the legacy of the *Cours* permits such a revision.
Saussure's text is a "primordial publication for transmitting a teaching worthy of the name, that is, one that can only be stopped on its own movement"
(497). This, he says, legitimizes crediting Saussure with this fraction that
characterizes "in their diversity the schools of modern linguistics" (497).
Here, in fact, is a reduction effected by having credited the algorithm to
this *primordial* text: to collapse the whole of modern linguistics, presumably sequelae of the *Cours*, to a typographeme that appears in print for
the first time four decades later, in Lacan's text.[N2.06] The clockwork figure
to which he alludes, almost offhandedly, is crucial to this retroaction—
Lacan is calibrating a device that will be stopped only on its terms—but
this merely activates a general automatism that he has already put in place
by describing his fraction as an "algorithm," that is, as a textual expression that encodes a mechanism by which new readings may be constructed
from old.[N2.07]

2.13 When he introduces the tree diagram, Lacan does not attribute the original
to Saussure. He says only that it is the "classic" illustration of the sign's
functions, and faulty at that. But he must have expected that his readers
in 1957 and 1966 would know of its provenance and may even have rec-

ognized that he has altered its appearance. Perhaps his discretion signals an acknowledgment that the tree's origins are more vexed, more displaced, than is widely assumed. No matter: what is important is that, having attributed the algorithm to Saussure or a discourse derived from Saussure (the difference is also immaterial in this chain), Lacan is now free to reorient the tree accordingly, while still leaving open the possibility of further revisions. ►N2.08 By introducing the algorithm before the diagram and honoring the former and denigrating the latter, he has in effect doubled back on his appropriation of a ratio usually attributed to Saussure, appearing to discover its basis in sigils of his own devising. His removal of the frame and the arrows are further evidence of this retroaction, since their erasure disperses the suggestion of the original that the sign is an integral unit within which signifier and signified are mutually bound. By calling his unbound revision of the tree its "classic" illustration (Lacan 1966, 499), Lacan opens the image to circuitous operations of the pages of his text—in the journal *La Psychanalyse*, where the essay first appeared, and in *Écrits*, where it was most widely read—while emphasizing the persistence of the bar that divides the sign's two faces in both the algorithm and the diagram. The revised image of the tree has thus already firmed up the aporia that is its internal basis and fractured its borders—it is already, in other words, more a Freudian or Lacanian than a Saussurean tree.

2.14 This represents only the opening parry of the essay's revision of the Saussurean doublet. In place of the tree's "faulty illustration" (Lacan 1966, 499) of the sign, Lacan immediately proposes another "which can be considered more correct" (► Figure 2.01). This one shows the outlines of identical doors placed side by side, marked above "Gentlemen" and "Ladies" (499). "Simply by doubling the nominal type," he observes,

> by merely juxtaposing two terms whose complementary meaning [*sens*] would appear to have to reinforce each other—surprise is reproduced by the precipitation of an unexpected meaning [*sens*]. (499–500)

2.15 Doubles have begun to multiply in the most incongruous ways, and Lacan's explanation of this "contrived example" doesn't help much. He expands on the second diagram with a comic anecdote about a young boy and girl, brother and sister, who are seated facing each other in a train cabin. Looking out opposite windows as the train pulls into a station, each reads the sign over one of the lavatory doors on opposite platforms and mistakes it for the station's name. "'Look,' says the brother, 'we're at Ladies!' 'Imbecile!' his sister replies, 'Don't you see we're at Gentlemen'" (1966, 500).

2.16   Now, train cabins and station platforms are especially freighted zones in Freudian thought; they are common venues of events recounted in his joke and dream books; the specimen parapraxis of psychoanalysis occurs in such a space ▶ 2.69.▶N2.09 Lacan surely means to invoke these crossings (switches, rails, mechanical passages) in setting his elaboration on the signifier's "entrance" in the signified here (Lacan 1966, 500). The complexity of the scene shows that we are being conveyed beyond a simple dichotomy, and this is the context—literally, the textual situation—of the two illustrations: Saussure's doublet and Lacan's double doors are as little equivalent to each other as Lacan's tree and algorithm are to their graphic and conceptual precursors in the *Cours*. He means to effect another kind of relation—calling it "algorithmic" would not be far off the mark—between these objects. Coupled with the anecdote, the figure of the doors evokes a dramatically extended model of the signifier's "parallelism," in that the labels "Gentlemen" and "Ladies" condense multiple networks of meanings (honorific, anatomical, hygienic, etc.). Each is relationally activated, and the sense (*sens*, also the "direction") of each reaches beyond its nominative functions—which are finally not of much concern; that's the point of the joke.

2.17   Lacan's substitution of this elaborate syntagmatic series for Saussure's comparably simpler emblem of a tree opens all of these textual and graphic elements to new expressive effects. (Silently, Lacan has already interleaved the planes of their expression by flattening the space of the anecdote: whereas in the story the doors faced one another, in the diagram they appear side-by-side. As they must, if they are to be fitted to the printed page.) As a result, the signifieds of whatever these signifiers mark are shifted nearly out of the scene, off of the page, altogether. For the doors are not, as Saussure would understand this, the signifieds of the labels that appear above them. Unlike the drawing of the tree, they do not evoke a definite concept that we might associate with the words "Gentlemen" and "Ladies." What they are, in fact, are placeholders for relations of difference that they can only name indirectly, and only in the terms of a structure they effect by being placed before us in this way.

2.18 "It is in the chain of the signifier," Lacan observes a few pages later, "that meaning [*sens*] *insists*, but . . . none of the chain's elements *consists* in the signification it can provide [*dont il est capable*] at that very moment" (Lacan 1966, 502). Saussure's model of the sign is too bounded and too bilateral to capture these qualities of the chain. The "signifying factor" of language operates "polyphonically," and must be read on (at least) two axes, like a musical score.

> Indeed, there is no signifying chain that does not sustain—as if attached to the punctuation of each of its units—all attested contexts that are, so to speak, "vertically" linked to that point.
>
> Thus, if we take up the word *arbre* (tree) again, this time, not in its nominal isolation, but at the endpoint of one of these punctuations, we see that it is not simply because the word *barre* (bar) is its anagram that it crosses the bar of the Saussurian algorithm. (Lacan 1966, 503)

2.19 This anagram of the Saussurean password (by now, *arbre* has become that: the keyword of a semiological canon that Lacan means to implode) opens the floodgates.[▶N2.10] The paragraphs that follow are a bravura sequence of wordplay and allusions based, with increasing elaboration, on the word *arbre*, including references to botany, the Hebrew scriptures and the Christian cross (Tree of Knowledge, Tree of Jesse, etc.), higher mathematics and heraldry, the "tree" of the human circulatory system and *arbor vitae* of the cerebellum, alchemical terminology, Greek myth, Heraclitus's *Logos* and Heidegger's "Logos" (which Lacan had translated a year earlier), concluding with a masterfully dense coda comprising several lines of Paul Valéry's poem "Au Platane" ("To the Plane-Tree," Valéry 1957).[▶N2.11]

2.20 "When I make a word do a lot of work like that," as Humpty-Dumpty said to Alice, "I always pay it extra."[▶N2.12] The rhetorical aim of this performance may be guessed: to induce a kind of semiotic vertigo in the reader, via excesses of the tree's mutations. (If the double doors are less suited to this effect, it is because that diagram says too much in another way: it can only be taken as more correct because it "exaggerates . . . the incongruous dimension [of speech] that the psychoanalyst has not completely renounced" [Lacan 1966, 499].) But this rhetorical aim is not so different from its theoretical aim—how, for an account of the *agency* (*l'instance*) of the letter, could they be far apart? Viewed from the scintillating canopy of the plane tree, the 1916 diagram and its revisions are only props of a general program of ramifying *arbres*. "I need only plant my tree," Lacan observes of his own performance,

> in the locution: *grimper à l'arbre* [scamper up a tree], or even project onto it the derisive light that a descriptive context gives the word, *arborer* [hoist, unfurl], to not let myself be made prisoner in some kind of *communiqué* of the facts, however official it may be, and if I know the truth, to make it understood despite all the censures *between the lines* by the only signifier that my acrobatics can constitute across the branches of the tree. They may be provocative to the point of burlesque or only perceived by the well-trained eye, depending on whether or not I want to be understood by the many or the few. (Lacan 1966, 505)

2.21 On the one hand, the whole of the circuit from the earlier tree to the one on which Lacan performs his somersaults is the shrewdest of moves, as it tacks the apparatus of a new science of the signifier to a trunk springing from fertile soils absent from Freud's theory of language ("Geneva 1910, Petrograd 1920," Lacan 1966, 799). On the other hand, because Lacan means to Freudify Saussure and Jakobson as much as introduce their thought to the analyst's cabinet, a feedback loop of just this kind is the most direct means by which to achieve this revision. The linguists have—in general, linguistics has—no theory of desire, and therefore no way of accounting for clinical dimensions of speech that the analyst confronts on a daily basis with her patients (Mannoni 1969). And Freud is, even though his dream and joke books point beyond it, invested in a model of speech that distinguishes thing-presentations from word-presentations without quite recognizing that words may also be things (Van Haute 2003). Every branch in this canopy does not need to be grasped, every allusion does not need to be unpacked, to effect a mixing of these systems *in Lacan's text*: it is possible to put into motion automatisms solely on the basis of the series's opening term if it is properly engaged.▸N2.13 This is what the anagram *arbre-barre already* signals, in the most condensed form imaginable. (Literally *imaginable*: in a textual-graphic form projected before us, though it also elicits patterns of meaning whose effects are evident but unvisualizable.) We might consider the anagram to be implicit in the lower half of the 1916 tree, or to be the botanical tag for the species Lacan plants before our eyes. Like "Gentlemen / Ladies," it anchors an entire taxonomy it does not name outright.

2.22 Initiated by images (the tree diagrams; and the algorithm, which though composed of letters functions as a graphic condensation of cultural and disciplinary networks in the same way), these effects are activated *textually*—in the fullest sense of the term, in that they invoke all the resources of the surface on which are marked all the forms that surround them and that they evoke. (Barthes's lexia is activated in this way, as an inductive and connotative structure bound to a specific parsing of the textbase ▶ 5.03.) Lacan's arboreal acrobatics, if our eye and memory are well-trained, illustrate this principle. He has only to "plant [his] tree in the locution" and the reader is left by this "narrowing of the way," as he notes in his introduction to the essay, "no exit [*sortie*] other than the entrance [*entrée*], which I prefer to be difficult" (Lacan 1966, 493). Before she gets to the double doors, Lacan has projected for her the textual scope (*portée*) of a general scheme of access and departure, which she may choose (or not) to follow.

2.23 *Hopscotch.*

Assembling these patched words in an electronic space, I feel half-blind, as if the entire text is within reach, but because of some myopic condition I am only familiar with from dreams, I can see only that part most immediately before me, and have no sense of how that part relates to the rest. When I open a book I know where I am, which is

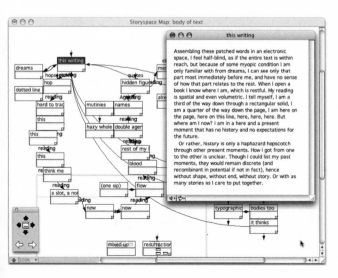

FIGURE 2.02. Shelley Jackson, *Patchwork Girl* {this writing}, 1st edition, Storyspace Reader 2.5 (2006), Mac OS X 10.4 (2007). Reproduced by permission of Eastgate Systems, Inc.

restful. My reading is spatial and even volumetric. I tell myself, I am
a third of the way down through a rectangular solid, I am a quarter
of the way down the page, I am here on the page, here on this line,
here, here, here. But where am I now? I am in a here and a present
moment that has no history and no expectations for the future.

   Or rather, history is only a haphazard hopscotch through other
present moments. How I got from one to the other is unclear. Though
I could list my past moments, they would remain discrete (and recombinant in potential if not in fact), hence without shape, without end,
without story. Or with as many stories as I care to put together.
(S. Jackson, *Patchwork Girl* {this writing})▸N2.14

2.24 *Historiation.* "Here, here, here": a reader's *textual* memory generates the
retrospective defiles of her reading and orients its possible futures. These
paths are robustly and inconsistently entangled and hard to imagine, though
they may be approximately represented; Lacan's elaborations on the 1916
tree are an example of this. Each moment of the reading encounter is the
inconsistent aggregate of other moments, stimulated—consciously and un-
consciously—by marks and patterns of marks (and relations of marks too
inchoate and variable to be qualified as "patterns") that evoke others and
thus generate meanings that are specific to the encounter. I propose to characterize these operations, which are bound to, and capable of anticipating
and generating new responses to, visual-textual traits of the reading surface,
by the term *historiation.*

2.25 My neologism draws on an internal circuit of Lacan's gymnastics in the
Saussurean canopy. Under the shadow of the cross, he proposes, the tree is
reduced

> to a capital Y, the sign of dichotomy—which, without the illustration
> that historiates armorials [*sans l'image historiant l'armorial*], would
> owe nothing to the tree, however genealogical it claims to be. (Lacan
> 1966, 504)▸N2.15

2.26 Multiple systems of reference are evoked here, but the allusion to the "historiated" initial is of particular significance. These large, often elaborately
colored and ornamented letters, sometimes containing scenes or figures,
were widely used in medieval illuminated manuscripts to mark a text's divisions, to signal its intertexts, and not infrequently to suggest parallel or

alternative interpretations of it. Scholars such as Michael Camille (2004) and Mary C. Olson (2003) have proposed that historiated initials and the related elaborations of margins and intercolumnal spaces of the manuscripts were the sign of a late medieval and early modern shift in the conception of written language, away from its being the record or cue for speech, and toward its being a domain in its own right, with distinctive formal conventions, principles of meaning, and practices of reception and interpretation ▶ 7.09.

2.27 Lacan links the initials to traditions of heraldry. Their canon, he suggests, has played a role in the "reduction" of the tree's symbolism, from its avatars in Hebrew and Christian thought, to the function of the capital Y as a "sign of dichotomy," presumably in the manner in which the field of a coat of arms is divided into three parts. (Though he may also mean the Y chromosome, as it differs from the X—of the cross—in marking sexual difference [Davis 1995, 228n6]; "dichotomy trees" are used in mathematical logic to describe schemes of progressive division into classes and subclasses that are graphed in Y-shaped forms.) *Sans l'image historiant l'armorial*, without the historiating image of the partitioned field of the heraldic symbol, he proposes, the Y would not serve as such a mark of division (Lacan 1966, 504).

2.28 As I read this passage, Lacan has skipped one or more links in this chain of associations, and then doubled back to mark them retroactively. The tree reduces itself (*se réduit*) to the figure of the capital Y. The Y gains its value as a sign of dichotomy, at least in part, from the history of heraldry, but in this respect "owes nothing to the tree, however genealogical it [the tree] claims to be" (504). Signifiers are flying fast and furiously, and other intertexts support this connection (sexual difference, mathematical logic), but Lacan has not, I think, carelessly juxtaposed the sign of dichotomy and the figure of the tree. Instead, he has demonstrated in this small turn the general potential of the series unleashed by the progressively more extended elaborations on Saussure's *arbre* and, before that, in the "correction" of the 1916 diagram with the story of a brother and sister arriving at a destination they do, and do not, understand.

2.29 Where Lacan leaves off and the reader takes up in this system is unclear, though this may be of little relevance, since an entangling and commingling of voices and positions sustained by these textual acrobatics represent one of their corrections of the "faulty illustration" that semiology has made its emblem ▶ 5.60. This much is clear: the concrete, visual and textual, form of Lacan's discourse invites the reader by a "narrowing of the way" (1966, 493) to locate one or more anchors—marks, images, key terms—on which she might base her comprehension of the system, and from which she may turn back to recollect others that resemble them ▶ 6.02. *She has only to read to articulate this process.*

2.30 This is where historiation will find its expressions on the complex surfaces of reading: on the one hand, in the traits (words, letters, images, even blanks) which in the most direct way extend a text's systems of reference. On the other hand, these traits are also the points of departure for subjective reimaginings of the text's significance—extensions in a more radical sense that depend on their insertion into a history of prior reading that recollects other signs and texts.▶N2.16 These operations are aggregative and noncommutative; the memory of reading in this way both potentiates and narrows the way ahead. They are not developmental or progressive, because the history of the reader *qua* reader is analogous to her history *qua* subject (Lacan 1966, 875): sensitive to the passage of time but not reducible to it, and marked by the lesser and greater oblivions of her forgetfulness.

2.31 *One for all.* Xanadu's versioning scheme is descended from an earlier design for document "intercomparison" that Nelson called "The Parallel Textface" (▶ Figure 2.03).

 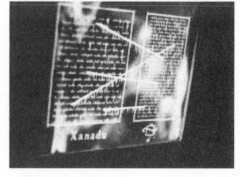

FIGURE 2.03. *Left:* Nelson's sketch of the Parallel Textface, showing in the right panel an expanded version of the text in the left panel. *Right:* A 1971 mockup. "Independent text pulls dependent text along. Painted streaks simulate motion, not icicles" (Nelson 1974). Images copyright 1974 Theodor Holm Nelson; reproduced by permission of Theodor Holm Nelson.

2.32 Illustrations of the Parallel Textface in Nelson's published writings in the 1970s and 1980s resemble in several respects Crimi's drawings of Memex's dual-screen setup (▶ Figure 1.02). But we must be careful to distinguish operations of the two conjectural systems; the line of descent between them that has become a part of new media mythology—encouraged in part by Nelson's acknowledgment of his debts to Bush—should be more tangled than it is. For one, Xanadu's logic of dispersal and provisional aggregation is more contingent on signature effects of reading than Memex's comparably well-behaved—though inconsistent—crossings of archival thresholds.

2.33 And the systems differ with respect to their temporal bases. Whereas Memex's screens show documents that the reader may connect ("on one transparent screen the operator of the future writes notes and commentary dealing with reference material which is projected on the screen at left . . ." ▶ Figure 1.02), the panels of the Parallel Textface show documents or portions of documents that have already been related in some way; in the canonical application of the system, they represent versions of the same document. The user of the Textface applies a lightpen to the screen to scroll the contents of one of the panels forward or backward. As it changes, so does the other:

> When links run sequentially, connecting one-after-the-other on both sides, the contents of the second panel are pulled along directly: the smooth motion in one panel is matched in the other. . . . The relationship may be reversed immediately, however, simply by moving the lightpen to the control pip of the other panel, whose contents then become the independent text.
>
> Irregularities in the links will cause the independent text to move at varying speeds or jump, according to an average of the links' connectivity.
>
> If no links are shown, the dependent text just stops. (Nelson 1974, DM 53)

2.34 More than two synchronized panels are permitted—intercomparison is always pairwise at the lowest level, but it may include series of pairs— and other configurations of the display are possible (Nelson 1974, DM 53; 1990a, 4/76). The only limit of their presentation is that base elements of the system should be clearly distinguished. Display of intercomparisons in the Textface should be, Nelson insists, "extremely simple from the user's point of view" (1974, DM 54).

2.35 "Inside," however, the system is "hairy" (1974, DM 54), an adjective that seems apt in both its vernacular and literal senses. The Textface is meant to be the front end of an information structure Nelson calls "zippered lists" and a corresponding file structure, "ELF" ("evolutionary list file").[►N2.17] A zippered list permits "permutation-invariant one-for-one inter-list entry-linking" of byte spans in multiple documents (Nelson 1965, 89); that is, the list indexes other lists—other versions of itself—which may include some of the same byte spans in different sequences (Nelson 1990a, 1/27). Links are made "sideways" (that is, not sequentially or hierarchically, unless the user so desires), and "no definite meaning is assigned to these entities or operations by the system; the user is free to let them mean anything he likes" (91). Links always occur in pairs (though, presumably, the content of one or both spans to which a link is applied may be undefined), and remain attached to the same spans even when linked lists are reordered (90). Linked spans must be paired to allow disambiguation of reordered lists in order to support backtracking. This requirement is the basis of the tumbler addressing scheme. Lists may contain or otherwise comprise other lists (transclusion), and linked lists may be of any length. More robust formal abstractions (linked byte spans containing only links, for example) are possible under this scheme, but are undefined.[►N2.18]

2.36 "The ELF may be thought of as a *place*, not a machine" (Nelson 1965, 91), though we must imagine it as a peculiarly hairy, scattered sort of place. (This rejection of the "machine" label is a typically humanist move on Nelson's part, because he is concerned that his scheme should empower users, not their devices or IT managers. One might counter that a place does function as a machine if locality is efficient in some way.) The technical challenge of implementing such a system is a consequence of its generality: no explicit structure must be imposed upon the data beyond that which the user stipulates, and she is free to reorient the system's representations of its structure. This is not the same thing as saying that the data space has no prior structure—zippered lists simply shift the insistence of structure away from requirements of the device toward those imagined by the user. Structure, multiple and fractious, will be discovered or retrieved from within the textbase (again, this ambiguous joining of interiority to another sort of projection) as the user revises its presentations so as to better figure the (dis)order of her mind ▶ 7.22.

> There is no *correct* way to use the system. Given its structure, the user may figure out any method useful to him. A number of different arrangements can be constructed in the ELF, using only the basic elements of entry, list, and link. Zippered lists may be assembled into rectangular arrays, lattices, and more intricate configurations. These assemblies of lists may be assigned meaning *in combination* by the user. (Nelson 1965, 92)

2.37 Real time and textual time cross in these assemblies, restless and entangled: that is the *subjective* efficiency of the Textface, and, more generally, of Xanadu's eversion of Bush's desktop and film store. The user of such a system will read zippered lists not so much in parallel—the parallelisms are only visual artifacts of the front-end—as backwards and forwards in time and side to side in the present, in an expanding series of relays. ("Series": that is perhaps too unilateral: Lacan's arboreal acrobatics would represent multiple filiations that are closer to the bramble I intend here ▶ 6.53.) The metaphor of the sliced braid ▶ 2.01 would seem to mark a pure synchrony that would isolate reading time from textual time—Saussure used a similar metaphor of cutting across a growing plant stem to distinguish the structure of a language (*langue*) from its development in time (Saussure 1982, 125). But the Xanalogical braid is, remember, dynamically constructed from dispersed fragments; some of these may belong to a different revision timeline or may even not yet exist. This suggests a more ambiguous and inconsistent relation of the text's temporal registers. This was implied perhaps in Memex's circuits, but the relentless seriality of the spooling mechanism and Memex's clunky support for random access must force the relation of synchrony to diachrony in Bush's device toward something more like coterminous episodes. In contrast, moments of the intercompared text are not only the outcomes of its development; it would be more correct to term them *presentings* of both its potential and abandoned developments. This is the peculiar dynamic of Xanalogical history: something of the global structure of the evolving textual braid will be efficient in each slice, each future anterior of what the text might have expressed and may yet express. Here, here, *here*.▶N2.19

2.38   Let me therefore frankly say that I have read all these; and storing up
in my mind very many things which they contain, I have dictated to
my amanuensis sometimes what was borrowed from other writers,
sometimes what was my own, without distinctly remembering the
method, or the words, or the opinions which belonged to each. (St.
Jerome to St. Augustine, describing his reliance on other authors in
his commentary on the Epistle to the Galatians, ca. 404 C.E.)▸N2.20

2.39 The classic topos of the scholar's carrel as a bounded enclosure, cell, or
garret, even when it may have had institutional or architectural validity,
was only ever an imaginary space. In his letters to Augustine, Jerome acknowledges that he read widely and borrowed freely. In most of the pictorial
tradition in which he is shown at work, this intertextual basis of his labor
is expressed by the clutter of papers and books that surround him, figures
of the vast canon of religious and secular texts he was the first to have mas-
tered. Antonello's depiction of the saint ▸ Figure 1.03 is less cluttered; the
openness of his reading has been transposed to allegorical elements of the
painting and, more abstractly, to borderless spaces beyond the arches and
windows where a few distant birds soar. This out-reaching condition is also
marked in *La Vie, mors et miracles du glorieux Saint Jherome*, where the
unknown artist shows us a landscape outside the window of Jerome's cell
▸ Figure 1.03. There, however, the reading scene is explicitly directed to a
textual correlate. The window looks out on a landscape but also doubles the
image's framing within the boundaries of the page and faces, verso to recto,
the opening lines of a written text describing the life of the saint. The image
is less an illustration of the text that accompanies it than each is a dialogic
extension of the other.

2.40 Medial hybridities of this kind would have troubled the early modern illu-
minator no more than authorial hybridities appear to have troubled Jerome.
Conceptual breaks between graphics and text have more to do with the
technologies of print and the institutions of publishing, in which graphics
and text are reduced to interchangeable but not equivalent units, than with
any basic trait of one or the other. An early modern writer or reader, before
this reduction was effected, would not have distinguished graphics from
text in this way (Olson 2003, Camille 2004). Similarly, the judgment that
textual poaching (writing and passing off as one's own what one has read)
is inappropriate or even avoidable requires internalizing certain late modern limits on automatisms of storage and retrieval. (Nelson anticipated this

problem in Xanadu's scheme of micropayments and transcopyright. Bush seems never to have considered it.) This makes the "reconfiguration" of authors and readers proposed by hypertext scholars such as Jay David Bolter (1991, 2001) and George Landow (1992, 1997, 2006) all the more interesting. The notion that readers of hypertext routinely appropriate agencies that have been reserved to authors for the last century or two of print culture seems not to derive from any special characteristic of the media operations involved, but from field effects of the textbase that hypertext shows us were there all along.

2.41 The recollection that sustains this extension can appear to function independently of media because it has been programmed into the form of hypertext. Again, this is not new. As Bolter and Ulmer observed as early as the mid-1980s, certain of the mnemonic regimes of the digital field appear to reinstate the memory techniques of the ancient Greek Sophists and later Latin and Renaissance authors familiar with the Greek traditions (Bolter 1984, 1991; Ulmer 1989, 1991).▸N2.21 The method of artificial memory (*hypomnesis*), explains Frances Yates (paraphrasing the *Ad Herennium*, the most complete of the surviving Latin memory texts), was to relate things (*res*) or words (*verba*) to visually striking images arranged in a particular place (in Greek, *topos*; in Latin, *locus*),

> easily grasped by the memory, such as a house, an intercolumnar space, a corner, an arch, or the like. Images are forms, marks or simulacra (*formae, notae, simulacra*) of what we wish to remember. For instance if we wish to recall the genus of a horse, of a lion, of an eagle, we must place their image on definite *loci*.
>
> The art of memory is like an inner writing. Those who know the letters of the alphabet can write down what is dictated to them and read out what they have written. Likewise, those who have learned mnemonics can set in places what they have heard and deliver it from memory. "For the places are very much like wax tablets or papyrus, the images like the letters, the arrangement and disposition of the images like the script, and the delivery is like the reading." (Yates 1974, 6–7)

2.42 The number of *loci* required by the method depends on the number of elements to be remembered. Remembering a series of things (*memoria rerum*: for example, legal points to be made when arguing a lawsuit) will require many fewer *loci* than remembering words of a speech or poem (*memoria verborum*). Whatever the number of *loci*, keeping track of their sequence will make or break the method, and the author of the *Ad Herennium* suggests marking *loci* at regular intervals with an impression that will serve as a counter: a golden hand for the fifth *locus*, the face of a friend named Decimus for the tenth, and so on (Yates 1974, 7). Later forms of the method propose similar indexing schemes. Writing in the sixteenth century, Cosmas Rossellius suggests ordering *loci* in alphabetical order. Early modern hermetic versions of the method mapped *loci* to alchemical or kabbalistic motifs (Eco 1988).

2.43 To apply the method, the mnemonist mentally retraces the *loci* in order—forward or backward—in the way that he might walk down a corridor; the counting-images or other index units serve as starting points and markers of his progress. As he passes by each *locus*, the image registered in it is conjured, and by association the thing or word for which it stands. The system is extensible: the mnemonist may construct as many *loci* as he requires, basing them upon real or imagined places; they need only be sized and oriented appropriately for the images they contain, and they may be reused so long as their sequence is not disturbed (Yates 1974, 8). When the memory of a thing or word is no longer required, its image can be mentally erased, and its *locus* readied for another (7).

2.44 To the modern mind, the method appears overcomplicated and excessively literal. The classical mnemonist would have stored up a vast archive of images, as many as one for every word he wished to remember, and would have somehow had to keep track of very many different programs for retracing multiple and possibly overlapping series. (How did the mnemonist distinguish them? Was a meta-memory palace needed in order to index the indexed *loci*?) The method's ingenuousness is more disconcerting to the modern mind. There can be no doubt, Yates observes with amazement, that movement through the *loci* was conceived of literally, no different from movement through an actual architectural space (Yates 1974, 4). (We need only consider the irreducibly figurative character of "desktops, folders, and windows" of the modern GUI ▶ 7.44 to grasp that the premodern mnemonists must have conceived of linguistic bases of memory's "spaces" very differently.) Also difficult to understand, she observes, is the extremity of prescriptions for forming the images: they should, proposes the author of the *Ad Herennium*, be of exceptional beauty or ugliness, or "stained with blood or soiled with mud or smeared with red paint" (10), so as to render them more memorable. The radicality of this estrangement seems counter-productive in a way since, according to the method, the mnemonist better remembers a thing or word in a form that, already at one remove, has been arbitrarily altered. Because there is no indication that the manner of altera-tion should be consistent for every locus in a series—the only constant is distortion—it is unclear how, in effect, the distorted image is to be decoded into an unmarked instance, or if this was even necessary. In later hermetic traditions (such as Giordano Bruno's *Ars reminiscendi*), this principle was pressed to extreme forms, involving systems of loci and images that appear to have had no *a priori* relation to words and things they recollected (War-ner 1989; Yates 1974, 246–65).

2.45 As Yates and other historians of classic mnemotechnique have observed, its strangeness to us is in part a consequence of changes in media between the times in which it was practiced and late modernity. We have, she pro-poses, so fully internalized systems of the printed archive that their artifice and inefficiencies have become naturalized. Equally capricious systems can be conceived only in wonder at their premodern alterity, their biological bases—the neuron has always been allowed to be more unruly than the letter—or their pathology. (It might be said of Freud that he developed a theory of memory that interleaved all of these formulae.)[N2.22] Late modern memory seems feeble by comparison to classic memory; we are astonished that the ancients appear to have been able to track so well and so unerr-ingly the contents of their archives, when we, in comparison, must fall back on elaborate devices so as to remember tomorrow's appointments. But this must be because, even as our methods of recollection have been changed, we have retained a nostalgia for the immediacy of reminiscence promised by the classic methods. The mediality of modern memory, for which recol-lection is primarily a set-theoretical operation of retrieval and recombina-tion based on automatisms of the signifier, fits imperfectly in that nostalgic model, because the latter depends on the fantasy of an interior, whereas the former must cross out of every such bounded space.

2.46 This difference, articulated strictly in terms of memory's medial bases, is where the characteristic mnemotechnique of the digital field—or what tech-nique we may conjecture it offers—departs from the classic method, even as it preserves some of the earlier method's formal logic in its reliance on arbitrary addresses, indexes, and positional techniques. This can be seen well before the advent of the digital archive in systems like Memex. Bush's device supports the researcher's memory of the images it preserves, "just as though" the originals were before him. But in this slight admission of an imperfect reproduction, Memex differs from the classical method, for which no such conditional was needed, no "just as though" to distinguish artificial from living memory. Bush's researcher works nearly two and a half millennia after this distinction was first proposed, and he will take it for granted even as he hopes to narrow it with prosthetics like the Cyclops camera. He is less confident of the immediacy of his recollection because of his dependence on media that he does not imagine reside in the mind, and he will perhaps be less willing to ensure a more forceful registration via manipulations of the record: blood, mud, or paint will gum up his memory machine in more than one way. Which is to say that he will be overconfi- dent of the need to preserve an inerrant record; anxiety elicited by the ever- possible infidelity of copies is close by here, the constant condition of the precision of modern laboratory practice.

2.47 But Bush's machine gives its operator a way out of this impasse that is in certain respects consonant with the classic method while also rejecting the fusion of the memorable and the image that appears unthinkable to a mod- ern consciousness, for which signifier and signified must be distinguishable. Memex preserves and recollects the memorable, not by marking it in a strik- ing way, but by recording relations to memorable things and words before and after, above and below, inside and outside. In short, it preserves the fluid extension of the classical method (the code word will properly situate the image of the page in a series, along the path of its recording and recol- lection), *without seeming to touch upon the image in any way.*

2.48 In several respects, this represents a more determinate ordering of the ar- chive. Despite the stated aim of Bush's device to preserve the integrity of page images (and thus, to implement a logic of reminiscence), in practice, Memex reinforces polyserial and extraserial relations of its units—a logic of rememoration or recollection, according to which their integrity is less significant than their positions in a system. This is a point of intersection between Memex and its successors' methods of recollection and a pathogra- phy of memory anticipated by Freud. Memory presents as structure, Freud discovered: its relational logic is more permanent than its objects. The most optimistic formulation of what the archive may accomplish must confront this subjection of its objects to its structure.

2.49 Even when the operator mistakes operations of structure for procedures of reproduction:

> By being able to reference anything with equal ease, the Web could also represent associations between things which might seem unrelated but for some reason did actually share a relationship. This is something the brain can do easily, spontaneously. If a visitor came to my office at CERN, and I had a fresh cutting of lilac in the corner exuding its wonderful, pungent scent, his brain would register a strong association between the office and the lilac. He might walk by a lilac bush a day later in a park and suddenly be reminded of my office. A single click: lilac . . . office. (Berners-Lee 1999, 38)

2.50 The "click" elicited by the scent of lilacs is less broad in its scope than the corresponding moment of Proust's novel of rememoration (which precursor, surprisingly, Berners-Lee does not acknowledge)—it recalls only the interior of an office and not the world of Combray.▸N2.23 But Berners-Lee's "associations between things which might seem unrelated but for some reason did actually share a relationship" is mythmaking with a comparable ardor. Buried within the allusion to neurology's contribution (the appeal to the "spontaneity" of the brain provides cover for what is essentially a semiotic) are, first, connections of spaces (the office, the park) and, second, the punctuality of a perception (the scent of lilacs, as undivided as a mouse click). Each is in its own way a foundation of the link asserted by this fable. But the technical specificity of the link—the finite, olfactible-audible-tactile moment of it (the UI gesture becomes more abstract but also more general) is, paradoxically, sustained by a diffuse network that seems idiopathic and unrepeatable. Berners-Lee's recollection machine depends on a parataxis that the practices of writing—of any form of writing, no matter how freed from the line and page it may seem to have become—cannot in fact capture. For Proust, in contrast, the textual presentation of sensations of taste and smell ("more fragile but more lively, more unsubstantial, more persistent, more faithful" [Proust 1999, 46]) represents an acknowledgment of their uncertain hold in the context of his writing. There, their provocation of memory is diffuse, structural; all of the textual and narrative elaboration from the memory of a cookie gives evidence of writing's limits, its inability to capture the kernel by which the memorable appears to have been evoked.

2.51 A system is required in order to backtrack to the kernel, or as nearly as possible: a textual sign re-presents the event or object; this generates new textual signs, sustained by an elaboration that pretends to record its point of origin but in practice can only prolong it in the defiles of language. A single click paired with an ellipsis that masquerades as a join between two terms marks the larger shape here, and the origin is so altered by this prolongation as to be—to have been, retrospectively—dispersed on its own terms. By which effect, paradoxically, it returns at the level of a system, its significance as the anchor of all that follows it sealed by the backward look of a future it anticipates.

2.52 Every ambiguity of memory's operations and location is entangled here with forms of oblivion. If, as Freud concluded as early as the unfinished *Project for a Scientific Psychology* (1895, Freud 1954, 1987), the medial bases of perception, memory, and consciousness must be exclusive of one another, then a materialist theory of their engagements cannot easily account for their localized functions (Freud 1955–66, vol. 1). This problem will remain critical for psychoanalysis for nearly thirty years, until the essay on the "Mystic Writing Pad" (Freud 1940–52, vol. 14, 1955–66, vol. 19; Derrida 1967, 1995; Kittler 1997). Only then—and only haltingly—is Freud able to rewrite the engram within a regime of *textual* structure, and extensive display surfaces in the verbal play of the dream, the joke, and the parapraxis. Even so, Kittler observes, he can go only so far as information technologies of his era: the Freudian engram cannot account for regimes of the signifier introduced by the intervention of the computer program (1997, 135). It will take Lacan, Kittler argues, to make the conceptual break that frees psychoanalysis from confusing psychic interiority with the magnetic charge of the signifier. ▸N2.24

> The enigmatic question of the Project concerning "an apparatus which would be capable of the complicated performance" of simultaneously transmitting and storing, of being both forgetting and memory, finds its answer at last. In circuit mechanisms, a third and universal function—the algorithm as the sum of logic and control—comprehends the other two media functions. Computers release the-

ory from an age-old constraint of having to conceive of storage as an engram—from cuneiform characters in sound through sound-grooves in vinyl. (Kittler 1997, 144)

2.53 A homologous development marks the trajectory from Memex to Xanadu: from the prejudicial interiority of the record, via apparatuses of storage and retrieval (reminiscence), to automatisms of extension and field effects supported by program methods (recollection, generativity). Distinctions between the textual record and its operations are, as we have seen, inconsistent in Memex from the beginning. The procedures of the device traverse their boundaries; surfaces are multiplied, interleaved; the trail—record of the record's form—points memory away from enclosure to structure, within which enclosure is at most a conceit of a system too complex to *imagine*. In Xanadu, programs of textual fragmentation and dispersion are further generalized; the expanding record, the ostensible rationale for the system, is quickly overtaken by effects of the maddeningly complex apparatus required to access every moment of its history, even those that have yet to arrive.

2.54 What is hardest of all to figure is the span of that history, given that it must be activated and sustained by media. "Everything," says Nelson, "is deeply intertwingled" (▶ Figure 2.04).

In an important sense, there are no "subjects" at all; there is only all knowledge, since the cross-connections among the myriad topics of

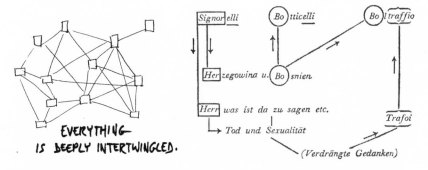

FIGURE 2.04. *Left:* The twingle. Illustration from Nelson's *Dream Machines* (1974). Image copyright 1974 Theodor Holm Nelson; reproduced by permission of Theodor Holm Nelson. *Right:* Freud's diagram of the Signorelli parapraxis, from chapter 1 of *The Psychopathology of Everyday Life* (1901).

this world simply cannot be divided neatly. Hypertext at last offers
the possibility of representing and exploring it all without carving it
up destructively. (Nelson 1974, DM 45)

2.55 The product of memory as a media technic is not, then, the docuverse as
it is now, but that which could be recollected of it in the future: the future anterior of what it will have been, given that which it is in the process
of becoming. The threads of the tangle cannot be divided neatly; they are
too many; you could not distinguish them all, or follow all their divaga-
tions—isolating them in this way would distort them. A diagram like those
shown in ▶ Figure 2.04 can only approximate the tangle. (As we will see
in later chapters, movements of analog devices—gears, spools, wheels—are
somewhat better at tracing its circuits.) "All structures must be treated as
totally arbitrary," Nelson insists, "and any hierarchies we find are interesting accidents" (1974, DM 45). So you need a program that tracks what matters—out of all of it, for all of it matters to what matters—and a suitable
container in which to put it, like an expanding desk or a unlimited store on
the back end. And: a procedure to recollect it all, in case something should
happen to the container. Thus is the text, in the broadest possible sense of
that term—the "text-archive-object," always-already a textbase (only a set-
theoretic mathematics seems applicable here)—pinned to the scene of historiation. The consistency and integrity of that operation can be established
only by a potential constellation of medial elements touched in a particular
way by its subject at a particular time. Such is the curious pact of the trail
and the permanent forms of the record that derive from it: it is repeatable at
a future date, even for a subject who may not be present then, and will one
day never again be present (Nelson 1974, DM 54).▶N2.25

2.56 But faith in the salvific potential of archivy must, at least provisionally,
repress the archive's basis in oblivion. A perfect memory, without a trace of
the originary fracture of the sign, would be a diseased memory, an infinite
and suffocating self-presence; not a memory at all (Derrida 1972). Remembering everything would be worse than intolerable; memory needs forgetting if recollection—and not something closer to hallucination—is to be
possible at all (Luria 1987, Eco 1988). A modern technic of memory could
be built on the fracture of the sign (one of the lessons of the reading machine
is that such a technic will, inevitably, be built on that basis), but it is hard to
have much faith in a future anterior when it rests on so unstable a founda-

tion. More typical is the specter of a crisis-event that sets the recollection machine in motion by threatening the erasure of its foundations. Bush's July and September 1945 Memex essays open with a statement of concern regarding new technologies of death created by the war effort, and the need to redirect the juggernaut of scientific innovation to the ends of preservation. The biologists, he observes, will return to familiar laboratory practices, as their "war work has hardly required them to leave the old paths" (1991a, 88).►N2.26 "It is the physicists," he proposes,

> who have been thrown most violently off stride, who have left academic pursuits for the making of strange new destructive gadgets, who have had to devise new methods for their unanticipated assignments. They have done their part on the devices that made it possible to turn back the enemy. They have worked in combined effort with the physicists of our allies. They have felt within themselves the stir of achievement. They have been part of a great team. Now, as peace approaches, one asks where they will find objectives worthy of their best. (Bush 1991a, 88)

2.57 "As peace approaches." This clause appears in the essay's first publication in *The Atlantic Monthly* in July 1945. It is omitted from the second in an issue of *Life* magazine of September of that year, by which time the war in the Pacific had come to a close and the peace forecast three months earlier had been achieved. But the technical context of Bush's argument also changed in a fundamental way that his readers in September could not have missed. Three weeks earlier, the August 20 *Life* had opened with a photo essay showing Hiroshima and Nagasaki "obliterated" and "disemboweled" by the Bomb, and included somber editorials announcing the dawn of "The Atomic Age" and warning of "'push-button' battles" and the need for new military and civil defense strategies in the postwar era ("The War Ends"; "The Atomic Age"). The issue closed with articles on nuclear fission, radar, and one of the first authorized accounts of the Manhattan Project and the Trinity test blast (Wickware 1945). The scale of the Bomb's destruction, the effects of radiation on survivors, and the weapon's transformation of political and moral landscapes of global conflict were as yet unappreciated by most Americans, who were grateful that the dropping of the Bomb had averted a projected Allied invasion of Japan. But we may assume that many readers of Bush's essay in *Life* came to his vision of a "possible new world

[of] man-made machines" with newfound anxieties. They had seen images of the Bomb's devastating power and knew of Bush's role, as head of the Office of Scientific Research and Development, in the Manhattan Project. They may have read S.J. Woolf's interview of Bush, published in the *New York Times* a week earlier, in which Woolf associates the development of the Bomb with Memex and other technologies of a postwar world.▸N2.27

2.58 The importance of the war's backdrop to the *Life* essay is borne out by the rest of the September 10 issue. Bush's essay is preceded by stories on "the fantastic secret weapons of Germany," the occupation of Japan, the wreckage of fire-bombed Tokyo—"only atom-bombed Nagasaki and Hiroshima (*Life*, August 20) had been more thoroughly destroyed" (*Life*, September 10, 34)—and the hardships of life in postwar Berlin. Softer news stories are marked by an awareness that the war's end brings new instabilities. The cover story on unionized automobile workers forecasts declining wages and increased conflict with management despite a projected postwar boom for the auto industry overall. Ads in the magazine lean heavily toward new generations of household and personal products spun off from wartime technologies or soon to be freed from rationing. Even so, scarcity and violence shadow the pleasant consumerist fantasies projected by the ads: readers are encouraged to get full value for their ration stamps by buying this brand of shoe, to wait a little longer for that brand of sofa as the maker is still working to cushion fighting men and instruments, and to keep asking for their favorite brand of hosiery, cigarettes, or instant coffee, as homeland production will soon resume. Advertisements for silverplate, engagement rings, and baby products are notably frequent.▸N2.28 In this context, Bush's *Life* essay seems both timely—Memex and its ilk are part of the nifty gadgetry of a coming postwar boom—and oddly belated, in that events between the two published versions of the essay have redefined the conditions of informational overload and loss. Bush's turn in the essay's introduction from the "lasting benefit . . . [of] man's use of science and of the new instruments which his research brought into existence" (Bush 1945b, 88) to the problem of the archive's usability ("the difficulty seems to be . . . that publication has been extended far beyond our present ability to make real use of the record" [89]) appears now to mask the short-circuiting of other pressing questions.

2.59 Nelson's concerns regarding the archive's efficiency are similarly focused on its susceptibility to catastrophic contractions. Simple redundancy of data, which would preserve copies from the destructive effects of a fixed ordering, is inelegant and inefficient ▶ 2.01. What is needed, he proposes, is a system that permits any ordering of the docuverse that does not permanently fix its units into any single order. The user of such a system would be free to pursue her or his wholly idiomatic clustering and threading of data without imposing those structures on other users, and the network structure of the docuverse would be ductile and reorderable, able to continue to function as a coherent whole despite local anomalies.

2.60 Consequently, losses of data must be handled in Xanadu in a particular way. The write-once universal address space includes addresses of content byte spans that have been removed from the system (for example, deleted by their owners or compromised by a system failure). These would continue to be valid, though they would point to data that no longer exists. Nelson has anticipated this problem: nothing prevents the redundant storage of byte spans on different devices; only the addresses of byte spans are fixed. Byte spans stored in only one physical location and then removed from the system would indeed be lost to it, but that outcome is not much different from what happens in other modern file systems: the front end would return an error message. Things get a little trickier in the case of byte spans which do not yet exist, as in principle they may also be addressable. But once again an error message can cover the inconsistency.

2.61 "Garbage collection" in such a space presents many problems. Most interpretations of Nelson's scheme assume that file deletion is not permitted, though how this can be guaranteed in a practical sense is unclear. Some mechanism for marking instances of a compound document as irretrievable must be supported; basic authorial privilege with regard to documents would seem to require this, as authors must be free to withdraw contributions to the docuverse if they so wish. Which means that some portions of the docuverse will exist in a condition that has no correlate in other systems for distributed file storage: byte spans may be stored in the system, but also be inaccessible to every user—materially present, formally demarcated, but walled off completely. The Xanalogical method anticipates that segments of its data space will become strange abysses of this kind ▶ 6.34.

2.62 Nelson ends *Computer Lib*, his 1974 manifesto on the transformative potential of popular computing, on a dismal note, drawing Bush's anxieties into the open. Club of Rome simulations of projected population growth and available food, he reports, indicate an inevitable world crisis of starvation and disease; ecological devastation and the proliferation of nuclear weaponry threaten humanity with more sudden ends (68). Computer technologies may offer a solution, he proposes, but only if they are more widely available and usable.

> We've got to get access to the Club of Rome models, and look for holes or strategies. If computer modeling systems doing this kind of work are made widely enough available, perhaps some precocious grade-schooler or owlish hobbyist will find some way out that the others haven't. . . . We've got to think hard about everything. (Nelson 1974, 68)

2.63 Nelson's *The Future of Information* (1997) ends on a similar note of warning—"the human race is approaching a terrible endgame, possibly the closure of history" (10.2)—and segues into an argument that improving storage methods, if it does not prevent oblivion, will at least record it more reliably.

> Every history has two stories about it. You either believe one or the other. Every massacre did or did not happen, every head of state was or was not an evil conspirator, every public event was or was not a coverup, everyone in prison says he was framed (and no doubt some are telling the truth).
>
> For the last five hundred years, since printing, we have lived under the paradigm of rational sharing of information, so that new evidence might come to light.
>
> What I fear is a world of tomorrow's information in which nothing is known any more, and everything is hoaxes and lies. (Nelson 1997, 10.6)

2.64 Here, lessons of the late twentieth century have been brought to bear on Bush's worry that the archive has become too extended for one reader to take it all in. This is one manner of figuring what it is that Memex might achieve: it incorporates as much of the archive's field effects as possible, making the archive seem containable and transmissible as an integral whole. Xanadu, in contrast, embraces field effects, not—at least not initially—so as to contain them but as the best option for grasping and preserving all the possible patterns they produce, in the hope that an accurate reading of some of them can be made in the future. "Past and future are always present," Nelson concludes,

> in everything around us and in everything we do. All of the human past that reaches the future must survive the present. And all ideas and knowledge must either join this new electronic literature, in a survivable form, or disappear.
>
> It is vital for the survival of humanity that we maintain our information base, even as it grows more complex. The power of hypertext and hypermedia is now partly understood. The power of full-power hypertext, and general open transmedia, awaits us. We need it badly. (Nelson 1997, 10.7)

2.65 The join of the text-archive-object *qua* object and the reading subject *qua* subject is marked by such forms of crisis. Paper moulders, libraries fall to dust; memory is as fragile and frangible as the record. Cicero recounts that the art of memory was founded on a scene of carnage.[N2.29] ARPANET, ancestor of the Internet and the grandest memory theater yet conceived, was conceived in a fantasy of general annihilation.[N2.30] Psychoanalysis began with Freud and Breuer's recognition that their hysterical patients "suffered from reminiscences," from which the concept of a talking cure emerged—in its essence, a technique for interpreting systems of loci whose significances are unknown to their most devoted users.

2.66 The last of this series is particularly relevant to the logic of the hypertext archive. The trajectory of psychoanalysis from interiority to structure mirrors the turn of hypertext from Memex's enclosure to Xanadu's hairiness. In the Freudian legacy, this trajectory did not signal the supersession of interiority, but its incorporation into textual functions (the alibis or guarantors of interiority) and a concurrent recognition of a deeper problem of memory's limits (Lacan 1966, 522).

2.67 *Hoaxes and lies.* In the abandoned 1895 *Project* Freud describes the process by which the mnemic image is recorded as an inscription of laterally fraying pathways ("facilitations," *Bahnungen*), along which quanta of perception are deflected so as not to overtax the psychic apparatus. (The condensation of a spatially diffuse mnemic scene into planes of an inscribed surface—in that respect, a scene of writing, as Derrida observes [1967]—is a foundational moment of this model. Even the multiplication of the layers or leaves of this inscription, as in Freud's "Mystic Writing Pad" essay [1925], does not alter this dependence on receptive surfaces—from which the mnemic image is *read back*—though it will introduce the figure of an absolute barrier beneath them all, a real limit of their medial logic ▶ 4.22.) From this process a pattern of discharge emerges, which is repeated by perceptions whose registrations follow existing pathways, becoming the "indication of reality" (*Realitätszeichen*) upon which judgment and recollection are founded (Freud 1955–66, 1:322–27; 1987, 416–22). The principal function of the pathways, then, is to integrate perceptions to the extent possible within a prior system of registrations, thus binding the dispersion of hostile mnemic images. The inhibitory structure that precipitates out of this binding is the kernel of the Freudian ego (324); Lacan's concept of the ego as fundamentally resistant to the effects of symbolization stems from this initial structuring of the mnemic image (Lacan 1978).

2.68 But the ego is fated to perform its work badly, since the system that produces it also exceeds it. (In Lacanian terms it might be said that the imaginary, of the three orders of constituting the subject, appears to her the most compelling—the most fascinating—but is actually the least determinate of her desire. The symbolic is the more insistent in its effects, the real the more implacable in its resistance.) The neurotic patient suffers from her memories; the repressed returns and from it spin off new connections and new symptoms. Each takes its place in a prospectively unlimited series of substitutions, retreating back to a beginning that is in turn revealed to be a false start (*proton pseudos*, the "first deception"), because it can be linked to another before it, and another before that, until the series drifts into abyssal recursion (Freud 1955–66, 1:352; 1987, 444).▶N2.31 Lacking a definite point of origin, capable of generating new meanings through new substitutions that extend its field of influence retrospectively and proleptically, the structure of the symptom-as-memory is in this respect "extimate" with the subject, says Lacan, crossing the interior and exterior of its operations without decisively fixing to either domain.

2.69 Only the concrete substance of signification (speech, writing, drawing, and so on), reiterated as the bases of media, can embody this crossing because only media can sustain the imprints of its effects while being able to be re-peated and transmitted, and thus to carry traces of its history and to serve as the basis of new responses to it. We may observe this dependence on media in the case of Freud's famous analysis of the "Signorelli" parapraxis, with which he opens his 1905 study of *The Psychopathology of Everyday Life* (1940–52, vol. 4; 1955–66, vol. 6). He expands on an 1898 essay, "The Psychical Mechanism of Forgetfulness," analyzing his inability to recollect the name of an admired painter while conversing with a fellow passenger during a day-trip by train to Trebinje, Herzegovina, while vacationing in nearby Bosnia in the summer of 1898. ▶N2.32 It is, we recall, the specimen parapraxis of Freud's book on mental slips, and its textual logic is therefore exemplary. In Freud's analysis, forgetting is less the misplacing of a signifier than its capture by the influence of other signifiers: *Signor-Herr, Bo-Bosnia-Boltraffo-Trafoi*; the sought-after name of Luca Signorelli, he stresses, was not merely forgotten, but falsely remembered, bound up with other names and pronouns in two languages, each of which has posed as a false double, an *Ersatzname*, for the painter of *The Four Last Things*. Freud's diagram of the parapraxis (▶ Figure 2.04) maps the "lateral binding" (*Verbindung*) of this process with typographemes that seem to pull the elements of the diagram in several directions at once. ▶N2.33

2.70 Lacan will advance the join of textual structure to systems of the signifier represented by this diagram to its logical conclusion. Simultaneously formal and concrete, meaning is effected and always parsed literally, in the way of a rebus, but also as though the signifiers were concrete things arranged and disarranged in space and subject to the peculiar physics—concussions, trac-ings, and trailings—of psychic reality. Read in this context, the 1905 depic-tion of displaced phonemes and syllables in Freud's errant memory is both a map of repression and, consequently, the signature of a dispersed signifier's generative potential amid the confusion that covers it. It is not hard to miss that the form has a certain arborescent structure as well. "What do we have before us?" Lacan asks—he seems to be referring to the 1905 diagram; he is certainly referring to the textual linkages that inform it:

> Nothing other than a pure and simple combination of signifiers. We are concerned here with the metonymic ruins of the object. The ob-ject is behind the different and particular elements that have come to play in the immediate past [*sont venu jouer là dans un passé immé-*

diat]. What is behind all this? The absolute *Herr*, death. The word passes elsewhere, effaces itself, backs up, is pushed away; it is, properly speaking, *unterdrückt*. (Lacan 1998, 39) ▶N2.34

2.71 *"Herr, was ist da zu sagen?"* (What is there to be said?). Freud recollects that just before the name "Signorelli" was lost, he had told his companion on the train an anecdote he had heard from another physician, concerning the stoicism of the Turks living in Bosnia and Herzegovina. "What is there to be said?" these Turks ask the doctor when a medical treatment is unsuccessful. "If he could be saved, I know you would have saved him." This phrase proves, says Freud, to be only a slip of one or two marks in his mind from a statement of resignation by a patient of yet another physician (doctors multiply here like the phonemes): *"Herr . . . wenn* das *nicht mehr geht . . . "* (if *that* comes to an end [lit. doesn't go any more])—that is, if a sexual disorder should prove incurable—*"dann hat das Leben keinen Wert"* (then life is of no value) (Freud 1940–52, 4:8; 1955–66, 6:3). Freud reports that the specter of "death and sexuality [*Tod und Sexualität*]"—he encloses these terms in scare quotes, as if they were a single concept—conjured by this second *Herr* (though a third and maybe a fourth are nearby) distracted him. He turned away from it as an inappropriate topic for discussion with a stranger, and for more personal reasons. "I was still under the influence of a piece of news which had reached me a few weeks before while I was making a brief stay at *Trafoi*," where he learned of a patient's suicide "on account of an incurable sexual disorder." The pull of the intersection of conversational probity with unhappy news on the fabric of his thinking—in the diagram, the "repressed thoughts [*Verdrängt Gedanken*]" are indicated at the lowest, presumably the deepest layer of the system—was sufficient to disorient his recollection of the (comparably inoffensive) painter's name. ▶N2.35 "My act of will missed its target and I forgot *the one thing against my will*, while I wanted to forget *the other thing intentionally*. The disinclination to remember was aimed against one content; the inability to remember emerged in another" (Freud 1940–52, 4:9; 1955–66, 6:4).

2.72 Freud's account of the background thoughts of the parapraxis plays, says Lacan, with all the ambiguities of suppression (*Unterdrückung*) and repression (*Verdrängung*) (1998, 39). *Signor* (the absolute *Herr*, that is, Death) is repressed, *verdrängt*; *Herr* is suppressed, *unterdrück* (42). Something has stopped: the metonymic shufflings of the signifier—its suppression—trace the wake of a traumatic passage, repressed and unspeakable except in the negative (*nicht mehr geht, keinen Wert*), imaginable only as relays between signifiers, indicated in the diagram as digraphs of inference and retro-action. ►N2.36

2.73 The simplicity of the diagram stands in this respect as either a condensation or, in light of the intimate history that appears to motivate and inform it, a screen for more complex scenes of influence. ►N2.37 Freud observes later in the book that Signorelli's self-portrait in a corner of one of the Orvieto frescoes (*The Rule of Antichrist*) was, so long as the painter's name remained out of reach, "ultra-clear" (*überdeutlich*) to him, "at any rate much more intense than visual memory-traces normally appear to me." That Freud should re-member Signorelli's face is unsurprising, since it is one of the most famous such insertions of a painter's image in a work not openly autobiographical. The painter stands with another figure, thought to be Fra Angelico, within the fresco but apart from the scenes representing the rule and fall of Anti-christ. (At least four episodes of Antichrist's career are shown, but the order in which they are meant to occur is unclear. As is common in religious art of the period, temporal and causal sequence are inconsistently translated onto fore and back registers of the image. Freud's diagram of the parapraxis repeats this mapping over its vertical and horizontal axes with a homology that seems not a coincidence: the diagram also recasts the fatal arc of a false *Signor*'s influence.) Whereas Fra Angelico seems to watch impassively the largest of the episodes in the foreground, Antichrist preaching to a crowd as Satan whispers in his ear, Signorelli looks directly out of the fresco at the spectator. His stern regard seems to admonish us to attend to the lessons of the painting and, perhaps, to acknowledge also the painter's role as the mediating figure between the present moment of our gaze and the last things it reveals.

2.74 But the extreme clarity of Freud's memory of the self-portrait is noteworthy. He observes that he was able to put it out of his mind only when, several days after the conversation on the train, a friend supplied him with the miss-ing word. Signorelli's face, as Richard Boothby observes, appears to have entered the network generated by the parapraxis less as a substitute for the master-signifier than as its correlate in the image.

> We can see the precise point at which the nexus of associations car-ried by the signifier "Herr" is abruptly shunted into the imaginary. The painter's portrait is the translation into imaginary terms of the

signifier "Herr." It is the "Signor" of the fresco itself. . . . It is only at this confused intersection of imaginary and symbolic, this point of crossed signals, that Freud's ability to remember is impeded. Other points of access into the same network of associations remain available to him, as is evidenced by the emergence of the "Bo" and the "traffio" fragments. (Boothby 2001, 85)

2.75 The crossing of signals, entangling visual imaginaries with textual structure, is in this regard another form of recollection, in that so misremembering the correlation of the visual field to its textual variant, the surplus that binds them is returned to our awareness. The broader significance of hypertext's vexed relations to technics of memory lies in the orientation of this problem within the situation of reading from the screen; the multiplicity and subtlety of textual operations may be best discerned where they contact the real matter of textual recollection. Much of hypertext design and theory has drawn on Memex's optimistic vision of an increasingly saturable enclosure—ignoring its traversals of the enclosure—and on Xanadu's assumption that those traversals may be made recoverable—ignoring the dependence of these systems on figures of crisis and absolute loss. New media's imagined triumph over material constraints of print depends on a repression of elements of the textual encounter for which there can be no encoding scheme in print or on the screen, and on a consequent impoverishment of textual operations as they are actually performed.

3.

Revenge of the Word
Grammatexts of the Screen

Hypertext is the revenge of the word on television. . . . With hypermedia, the image again takes its place within the system of text, the word again takes its place within the universe of the visible and the sensual.

—Michael Joyce, "La rivalsa della narrativa sulla televisione" (1993b)

The signs of writing, whether they be letters, blanks separating the words, auxiliary signs or typographic procedures of emphasis or demarcation, have a graphic substance: they are made of inked marks [*traits encrés*], of bars, of strokes, of loops, of periods. A first level of inscription is thus delimited, that of the letter or that of the trace, that one may call, though this denomination is not truly satisfying, the grammatic level [*niveau grammatique*].▸N3.01

—Jean-Gérard Lapacherie, "De la grammatextualité" (1984)

3.01 Text on the screen arrives and persists for the reader primarily as something seen. This aspect of the reading situation, which appears to be the fundamental common trait of reading from the screen and from the page, is so basic to reading operations that we may easily miss its particular valences in the GUI. The design philosophy of "direct manipulation" on which most modern user interfaces (UIs) are based takes as an axiom the equivalence of optical perception and visual knowledge: "what we see is what we get"; ideally, the interface shows us what we need to know to accomplish a given task, and in such a way that we will not mistake objects and operations it involves.▸N3.02 Significant reductions are at work in this equivalence. Neurological and cognitive aspects of vision are treated as factors of an engineering problem—how distinct must a screen object be, what are its differences from other objects, what shape, color, or texture should it have, if it is to be of visual interest? What aspects of its disposition may be hidden from the eye—or perhaps *must* be hidden from the eye—under these conditions? (Most of the apparatus of the screen performs its labors out of the user's sight or in spaces peripheral to it, whose outfitting she can only conjecture.) Cultural frameworks of visuality and visual knowledge are taken for granted; contested medial and epistemological bases of vision familiar to theorists and historians of still and moving images are rarely of concern to GUI developers, except where they touch on problems of software globalization. That these reductions appear not to pose any special problem for designers or users is one of the legacies of a post-photographic and -cinematic era, in which the optics of the camera and the projective screen have supplanted other relations of vision; and it must be an effect of a feedback loop instituted by direct manipulation: the more one thinks in its terms, the more one's thought adapts to them.

3.02   Yet, signs of the technical and medial complexity of the screen surface are never far from my consciousness. The staging of the surface is delicate trickery, the calculated effect of a mismatch between refresh rates of the display device and the human visual cortex. If I turn my head, change the ambient lighting, or adjust the settings of my monitor, the illusion of continuous and uniform surfaces is easily undone. ▶N3.03 I direct and respond to events shown to me through a keyboard or a pointing device such as a mouse or joystick. Between my gestures and the screen, several overlapping subsystems of hardware and software operate; what seems to hold them together is that communication between the input device and the operating system occurs rapidly enough to seem continuous and that I have become accustomed to moving my hand *here* while looking *there*, without thinking about the space between. ▶N3.04 Even so, a rapid typist can overload this scheme by striking keys faster than the corresponding characters can be drawn; a problem of early mouse-driven GUIs was "submarining," when the cursor seems to disappear if the pointing device is moved more quickly than the computer can recalculate its new position. In touchscreen-based systems and tablet computers, these mediations are only compressed and localized, and we can catch them if we wish: there is a small but perceptible gap between what is shown and the pressure of my digit or stylus: I press on the screen and something happens behind it, but only after something happens elsewhere. I may always become aware that reading from and engaging with the screen involves dispersions and elaborations of my actions and the objects to which they are directed.

3.03 Command line and graphical interfaces are in this respect not much different, as alphanumeric strings, control widgets, icons, glyphs, lines, and windows may all function as units of complex, overlapping ensembles in which
each unit stands apart and in relation to others.[N3.05] This is clearest in the
GUI, in which "text" easily slips into a mixed state—part-picture (those
glyphs stand for my keyboard strokes; even if I had written them on the
screen with a stylus, they would still stand for the trace of a gesture), part-
operator, part-operand (I can select any of them and perform actions with
and on them), part algorithm (to the computer, they are not letters at all, but
strings of binary code). But, as I will show in chapter 7, the visual segmentation
of the screen typical of command line interfaces also implies effects of structure that draw individual letters, sequences of letters, and lines into relations
that may be characterized as *textual* in a more general way than that term is
usually used in the language of human-computer interaction (HCI) ▶ 7.48.

3.04 A general model of textuality is the correct circumstance in which to interpret Michael Joyce's 1993 proposal, which I cited at the opening of this
chapter, that digital hypertext is "the revenge of the word on television." A
celebrated author of print and digital fictions, he could not have meant by
this a complete repossession of territory lost by the letter to the contours of
the screen; his own work demonstrates that its allures are too charged to be
likely to be abandoned. In any case, the screen is also a surface for writing,
and writing now takes place in a civilization of screens. Media "remediate"
other media (Bolter and Grusin 1999; Bolter 2001); they borrow from, inflect, and form changeable chimeras with one another ▶ 5.52. They do not
cleanly or completely trade off imaginaries that have coalesced around their
predecessors. This Joyce acknowledges in the second term of his proposal—
"the word again takes its place within the universe of the visible and the
sensual"—a universe that must also include the screen. Not repossession,
then; instead, a concurrency that may be the only possible path of return for
dispossessed media.

3.05 But Joyce's use of the term "word" in this context does not of itself evoke
media technics; despite the appeal to the visible and the sensual, there is
more of structure in it than substance. And that may be in the first consideration a path for a more forceful return of the dispossessed. The late
age of print is also the age of the world-picture (Heidegger 1977): of cunning conflations of letter and graphic in the service of simulation and refer-

ence, of windows and menus that domesticate the user's polyform relations to her archives, of handheld camera-phones and ubiquitous networks, of television screens that more and more resemble Web pages and a World Wide Web more like television than any of the digital agoras envisioned by Engelbart, Nelson, Berners-Lee, and others. Even as they are dispersed *procedurally*, visible forms of language in these systems tend toward forms of *operational* closure, in which they have been reduced to supporting roles of setting things before the eye. The well-worn critique of television's cultural and political impoverishment has been chiefly with regard to paradigms it installs and emphasizes. Joyce's complaint—I conclude this from a broader reading of his fiction and nonfiction prose—is directed more to syntagmatic effects of the idiot box and its siblings; in a sense to the absence or at least the suppression of syntagmas in those systems, and therefore the suppression of local disorientations of reference that may be realized only in traversing syntagmas. This structural dimension of the word's revenge might be realized along textual defiles that the "hairiness" of the back end embodies ▶ 2.32.

3.06 In the opening scene of an extended thread of *Victory Garden*, Stuart Moulthrop's 1991 hypertext fiction of the First Iraq War, Professor Thea Agnew of the University of Tara and Veronica Rainbird sit in Thea's living room {Resistance}. They are, respectively, a close friend and the sister of Emily Rainbird, who is at this moment stationed in the Persian Gulf and whose barracks will soon be struck by an Iraqi Scud missile. The impact of the missile will kill or spare her, depending on branches of the fiction the reader chooses, though the choice will have already been made before the reader can detect that there was a choice. (The contrast between the fragile, dreamlike artifice of a brightly lit reunion of Emily and her lover, and the chaos of his descent into madness in major threads of the fiction, will suggest the darker possibility. If the reader chooses the path to Emily's death, no hint of the happy ending is given. *Victory Garden* is unwavering in its course to a final state of narrativized crisis.) Thea and Veronica stare glumly at the light leaking from the edges of a TV set they have turned to face the wall,

> watching the auroras of living color that leaked from the edges of the tube and played across the wallpaper. [Thea] felt hollow, disconnected, almost viscerally shocked. She wanted another cigarette and she needed a drink. {Face the Wall}

3.07 Projective surfaces laid on projective surfaces: the auroras "play across the wallpaper," whose pattern is not described. They play thus not on a blank surface but one that is already structured, prepared in this way to reflect the crisis of meaning that the reversion of the television screen signifies. Though it is nearly blank, in the sense that the text reports nothing other than it is wall*paper* and not a wall, that slimmest of intervening surfaces within the ray leaking from the reversed screen suggests a more complicated relation of back to front ends.

3.08 Without the narrator's having drawn attention to this, Thea and Veronica are engaged in a version of a *Gedankenexperiment* suggested by Neil Postman. A television receiver, he observes, can also be used to light a room, as a display surface for printed text, to play music, or as a sturdy shelf for books: "I know one woman who has securely placed her entire collection of Dickens, Flaubert, and Turgenev on top of a 21-inch Westinghouse" (Postman 1986, 83). But such repurposings of the screen and its enclosure are, he concludes, unlikely: the image is too kinetic for the viewer's eye to long resist its attractions. Moulthrop lifts a fragment of this passage from *Amusing Ourselves to Death* and inserts it as an aside in the narrative series that passes through Thea's dimly lit living room. Television could be used for such non-televisual ends, the fragment proposes, "but it has never been so used and will not be so used, at least in America" (Moulthrop 1991b, {TV as Radio}; Postman 1986, 85). To get to this aside, we must pass through the serial structure of the thread, jumping out of Thea's living room into a mode in which feedback loops of this kind are not incongruous with the general mechanism of narration. (It is in turns such as this that hypertextual sequence demonstrates one of its influences on reading: in calling the Postman fragment an "aside," I mean to suggest that it is neither a digression nor a commentary, but a softer metalepsis than either of these forms. *Victory Garden* is laced with many such turns, and it is unexceptional in this regard.) Within the fictional space that this mechanism orients and borders, having turned the screen around (but not turning the set *off*) is less a rejection of the images it broadcasts than an open acknowledgment of their force within the fictional space demarcated by the room. Via the auroras (in "living color," a cliché of broadcast verisimilitude suggesting living autonomy), the images leak into that space. But because these imagined images are bordered and interrupted by a sequence of Moulthrop's text, they arrive before us in a form that is subdued, not only in that their description lacks detail and is no more precise than the pattern of the wallpaper, but also in that they are captive to the orienting effect of moving from node to node.

3.09 Back in Tara drunken frat boys *cum* cultural warriors gather in Thea's front yard to protest her leftist politics and to celebrate the onset of this, the latest Just War {Irresistible/Messages}. If the reader clicks on the wrong (the right?) word in the node, she is dropped into an endless loop that runs from Thea's living room to the "Just Say No Café" (geographically proximate, textually approximate), and back again to the living room. In the café, a crowd of graduate students channel surf the newscasts of the war. They sit in hypnotized silence, passing the remote control from person to person with the suggestion "Click when you feel like it, then pass it on" {Pass It On}. The scene and the suggestion are stagey, improbable, and more likely addressed to the reader than to anyone within the fiction. Yet they provide another orienting effect, because clicking to change images on a screen is also how one reads a work such as *Victory Garden*. If reading from the computer screen and channel surfing can be alike in this way, perhaps they are alike in most ways, and the numbing closure of the televisual imaginary may also draw into its penumbra new forms of reading.

3.10 Except for this out, Joyce's revenge of the word may bring about an effect of structure: these scenes of transfixed spectatorship and entrapped sameness are set in motion by *Victory Garden*'s sampling of and elaboration on its sources, and by discursive and narrative fractures between its nodes. Moulthrop's mixing of textual genres, tones, and narrative registers directs our attention to lures of the spectacle, and in the process signals a potential subjection of the televisual to other, *textual* programs: "We have television to demonstrate that connection is dead, dead and transfigured into something far less rare and strange, into the dross and chaff of Continuity. Stay with us as this war develops. And Now This" {Anonymous}. Connection—expressly in its difference from continuity—is a defining trait of hypertextual form: connection as provocation, connection as an algorithmic expression, connection as parataxis ▶ 6.07. The description of its death in television in this context must signal not only a mourning for that loss that Moulthrop shares with Postman and other critics of the culture of the idiot box; it must also signal a specific framing of that loss in and by operations of hypertext. In that medium—we have crossed over from a purely structural disorientation of image and word into disorientations that have a medial character, insofar as they must be realized on the screen—the hackneyed transition phrase "And Now This" may (or so it seemed in the golden age of hypertext fiction) name, not more-of-the-same but something-very-different: the promise of discontinuous series and complex surfaces. ▶N3.06

3.11 Certain aspects of Bush's reworked desk drawer and Nelson's evolutionary lists prefigured a join of textual structure to technics of media. Front-end forms of the trail keep Memex from devolving into a banal version of cinema and the Xanadu workstation from devolving into an "interactive" version of television. (We should not assume that because they were conceived first as systems for displaying words that Memex or Xanadu will directly escape such devolutions. The "television" that Joyce decries also might be rendered in words and letters; what troubles him is the flattening or narrowing of unruly signifiers.) An inconsistent intersection of inward-directed circuits with outward-directed field effects was a basic feature of Memex ▶ 1.44. Nelson's conception of the docuverse as an unbounded exteriority, a condition of reading more than its object, decentered Bush's archive but expressly did not surrender its clanking, clattering machinery; it only relegated most of this machinery to operations of the back end—which, it must be stressed, is located not inside the textual store but someplace else altogether. The tangled visual interdependencies of the Parallel Textface only hint at their complexity (▶ Figure 2.03).

3.12 In modern windowing UIs, such tangles as these are managed by dedicated window-server applications whose operations may be otherwise undetectable. Objects are "drawn" to buffers in computer and video memory, then composited by the window server before being rendered to the screen. As far as concerns programs that display results of any calculation—and the vast majority of calculations are not displayed—the buffers are the actual stage of representation; the screen functions as a site where the human agent may intervene, in the way of any other input device in this inconstant and varying ensemble, which is to say in some respect only by retroaction. Think of Thea and Veronica, or the patrons of the "Just Say No Café," in search of meaning on surfaces that are fundamentally delocalized from the spaces from which they are actually illuminated. Moreover, these complex surfaces must be repeatedly and continually refreshed and their disjunctions reopened, because periods of the screen and the program do not match those of the eye and hand. This the GUI represents to us in forms that have all but eliminated our awareness of a near-miss: opening or closing a window, scrolling its contents up and down or left to right. In their present forms, these are not reducible to panning, zooming, and related cinematic techniques for breaking the edge of the frame—though they clearly allude to those techniques—because in the window they may figure extensions of meaning that have no spatial character. Some of the procedural language of the GUI (we "scroll" and "zoom" windows) obscures this distinction.

3.13 The information corresponding to objects shown on the screen is most often recorded, retrieved, and processed differently in the archive; data that define the appearance and behavior of these objects may also be recorded there, and in intermediate locations and forms determined by requirements of storage, retrieval and display hardware, and the operating system and program. In the dispersed data-field that sustains the appearance of the screen's integrity, every trace is as substantial as every other; "blank" regions where nothing is shown (black or white, or another neutral hue) are no less the visible correlates of data than those where some *thing* appears to be shown. Additional registers of calculation and correlation—some imposed by the program, others imposed by the user—in which values of a pixel or arrangement of pixels are significant, may serve to distinguish blank from full regions of the screen, but they are nearly always of relevance to the user's requirements, not to those of the program or display hardware. The screen no more "shows" us a particular grapheme—for example, the configuration of pixels spelling out the word "screen"—than the printed page "shows" us corresponding aggregates of typographemes in its medium; in both cases, the arrangement of foreground traits (series of pixels, surface impressions, smears of ink) against a background (the field of the document window, the neutral regions of the desktop, the blank of the page) is a mere mark, which can function as a signifier only insofar as it is bound to one or more signifieds by the reader's conscious and unconscious recognition of its place in repertoires of signs.[▶N3.07] The reading machine does not concern itself with the meaning of the mark, only with its presentation on the reading surface. Even when that front-end function is linked to database-driven back-end functions, the manner in which the mark is presented to us—in that it is actively, dynamically, drawn on the screen in connection with some program operation that we cannot as easily discern—enforces a distinction between the mark's potential references and the substance of its presentation, which may in turn sustain or evoke other references.

3.14 I draw here on a terminology introduced by Jean-Gérard Lapacherie, who has stressed the need for a critical vocabulary for describing aspects of written and printed texts that are autonomous with regard to the reproduction of speech.[N3.08] In texts in which this autonomy is in evidence, he observes, the "graphic substance" of the letter, line, and page are foregrounded or are otherwise independent of the "phonic substance" and discursive structures they may also represent (1984, 283). "Grammatextual" (or "grammatic") aspects of such texts, Lapacherie proposes, are easily discerned in genres in which this aspect of textual elements is emphasized—the medieval *carmina figurata*, the calligramme, the concrete poem, extravagant or unusual applications of type, page layout, ink or paper color, or binding—but they are not limited to such genres. They must obtain in any text that takes advantage of "the varied resources of typography"—Lapacherie cites approvingly the opening line of Queneau's 1950 essay on "typographic delirium" (Lapacherie 1984, 284)—which is to say, in every text in which a disjunction of its representational and plastic aspects may be detected.[N3.09]

3.15 Lapacherie divides grammatextual genres into eight categories, factoring two levels of inscription (*letter* and *page*) with four degrees of figuration (*iconic*, *ideogrammatic*, *diagrammatic*, and *alphabetic*). "Letter" and "page" in this scheme constitute basic measures of the granularity of grammatextual effects. (They are defined exclusively by the model of the codex, which presents difficulties for extending the scheme to the screen. I will return to this problem.) In contrast, the four categories of figurative operations he proposes are more abstract, differing by degrees. Against these categories, works of literary art may be situated in relation to others according to the relative importance of the level of inscription and the predominance of figurative operations (1984, 292–93).

3.16 Iconic grammatexts are characterized by "the absence of the verbal text . . . in these texts, writing no longer represents a verbal message, and has total autonomy with respect to language" (Lapacherie 1984, 290). In visual and concrete poetry letters may be used as though they were brute graphemes, independent of their phonetic reference or their orthographic functions. Historiated initials of the illuminated manuscript represent similar extensions of the letter-as-grapheme, because of their ornamentation and independence from other alphanumeric elements (290) ▶ 2.26.

3.17 At the level of the page, the calligramme is the type of the ideogrammatic grammatext, to the degree that its contours are figurative (Lapacherie 1984, 290): Apollinaire's cascading lines on the subject of rain ("Il pleut"), Car-

roll's spiriform poem "The Mouse's Tale," Rabelais's eulogy to the delights
of the drink in the form of a bottle's silhouette ("Dive bouteille"), and so on.
In this case, mimographic effects are a consequence of, in Genette's words,
the "spatial disposition" of words or letters on the page, not of qualities the
reader may assign to individual graphemes (1976, 343). Letters or marks of
punctuation may also appear to mime (or embody) nonalphabetic objects or
events; and hermetic theories of writing's origins and occult significance are
often founded on this idea. Tory's *Champ fleury* (2003)—"the art and science of the proper and true proportion of the attic letters," based on analogies of the letters with proportions of the human body ▶ Figure 4.07—is the
type of this grammatext for the Latin alphabet.[▶N3.10]

3.18 Diagrammatic grammatexts are characterized by hierarchical relations encoded in spatial or serial aspects of the text.[▶N3.11] Though these aspects perhaps may also signify ideogrammatically, their diagrammatic meanings are
activated by how their parsing is oriented: for example, feelings of melan-
cholic isolation in E. E. Cummings's "a leaf falls on loneliness" are signaled
by breaks between and within words that fracture vertical and horizontal
axes of the text (Lapacherie 1984, 290). Though Lapacherie does not emphasize this, the conventional left-right, top-down seriality of the line and
page (for languages based on the Latin alphabet) is determinate of print
diagrams: to the extent that the reader's eye cannot take in, or neglects, the
whole of the pattern of the page, it must follow portions of that pattern in
sequence. This movement is implicitly translated into semiotic sequence,
which may also figure relations of priority or proximity (the distance between two elements on a page corresponds to other senses of "distance" or
"difference"). Conceptual determinisms of these patterns may be subtle but
compelling: Freud's reliance on nineteenth-century pictorial conventions for
depicting temporal and logical sequence (left to right: forward movement of
time or causality; top to bottom: successive layers or series of older or more
primitive elements) strongly influenced his verbal descriptions of psychic
causality (Davis 1995) ▶ 2.69. At the level of the letter, diagrammatic effects are most often figured, Lapacherie proposes, in alterations in the relative size of letters in a sequence, which may be used to figure motion away
from or toward the eye, or decrease or increase in the intensity of meaning
(Lapacherie 1984, 290).

3.19 Finally, alphabetic grammatexts are characterized by structures corresponding to the (ideally) nonfigurative traits of alphabetic glyphs (Lapa-

cherie 1984, 291). At the level of the page, the type of the alphabetic gramma-text, Lapacherie proposes, is Massin's celebrated book design for Raymond Queneau's *Cent mille milliards de poèmes* ▶ Figure 7.03. At the level of the letter, alphabetic effects are activated by programs that regulate syntagmas of the textbase (Inger Christensen's *Alfabet*, the length of which sections are based on Fibonacci's sequence), suppress letters or words (lipograms such as Georges Perec's *La Disparition*, liponyms such as Doug Nufer's *Never Again*), orient the text on the basis of letter positions (acrostics or mesostics), or substitute nonalphabetic glyphs for letters, as in a rebus. ▶N3.12 Lapacherie also includes in this class graphemic patterns generated by conventions of orthography: the capitalization of letters at the beginnings of poetic verses and the homography of poetic rhymes (1984, 291).

3.20 Grammatextual effects are not exclusive of one another, as no expressive text is characterized by only one level of inscription and one degree of figuration. A purely iconic grammatext would not be recognized as a text, since it could not demonstrate arbitrary structure of any sort. A purely alphabetic text, void of mimetic and semantic evocations, would be equivalent to a machine-generated sequence of symbols. Such objects might be of interest in their own right, but it is difficult to see that either would be capable of sustaining semiotic operations. Pure ideogrammatic and diagrammatic grammatexts appear by definition impossible: the analogy of the ideogram depends on spatial and serial hierarchy (diagrams) in addition to iconic and alphabetic support; unless defined exclusively in terms of sequence—an alphabetic trait—the diagram requires support by analogy.

3.21 Grammatexts are also determined by the performative situations in which they are encountered. An author may intend that grammatextual effects be foregrounded in her text; she may consider them unimportant or a nuisance. But the text must be *read* if they are to be activated. Reading's generative engagement with grammatexts (implicit in Lapacherie's descriptions, but never stressed as such) is, moreover, oriented by the manner in which they force departures from spatial and durative conventions of textual deciphering.

> The grammatic text no longer inscribes itself duratively; it also distributes its signs in the space of the page. It requires sometimes a tabular reading that takes into account nonverbal relations between the signs or groups of signs, copresent on the page. The "traditional"

page proposes an order of reading, from left to right, and from top to bottom, linearized and vectorized at the same time. The reading of a grammatic text can be made in all directions: there is no longer before, nor after, but contiguity of the copresent signs and simultaneous perceptions, outside of time and succession, outside of a final order. (Lapacherie 1984, 294)

3.22 *Revenge of the word.* Lapacherie's observations regarding contiguity and copresence are applicable also to reading surfaces of the digital field. As I showed in chapter 1, claims regarding the novelty of contiguity and copresence in new media are often made on the basis of caricatures of the actual operations of the printed page, line, and letter ▶ 1.07. A feedback loop is at work in such cases: a reductive model of textual signification emerges from a naïve model of medial development in which, for example, cinematic and televisual surfaces supplant print surfaces, and the serial pressures of the film and video narrative appear, retroactively, to compress and linearize print operations. (That these pressures are themselves effects of caricatures of film operations, which are never so strictly serial as is supposed, is ignored.) A truncated version of those operations then becomes a baseline for the backward glance that measures the progress achieved afterward.

3.23 A grammatextually sensitive reading of the screen frees us from the worst effects of this feedback loop. First, because it has the benefit of reminding us of the complexity of the printed surface and of operations of reading it invokes and sustains. A historical understanding of new media's relation to the old media requires that we appreciate this. Second, because it orients an approach to the screen that begins with formal analysis of its typographemes. On that basis we may more accurately correlate and distinguish some—not all—of the grammatexts of print and screen-based media, such that we may begin to account for what is common to both and specific to each.

3.24 Lapacherie's two levels of inscription, page and letter, pose an initial difficulty for a grammatextual model of the screen, in that these elements of written and printed surfaces have no precise correlates in the contemporary human-computer interface. It is not uncommon for computer applications to represent data on the screen in forms that implicitly or even openly evoke comparisons to the printed page—this is especially true of applications such as word processors that are used to create documents that will be printed—but this comparison is misleading in other, more telling regards. The modern GUI is a robustly multiwindowing environment, and it is not uncommon for a user to have many windows belonging to different applications open on the screen at the same time ▶ Figure 3.02. Some of these will be partly or entirely obscured; others will have been "minimized" to icons or other visually condensed forms. (The hybridity of these objects should not be neglected: they look like windows but are treated in other respects like folder, document, or program icons. In Mac OS X, for example, a playing QuickTime document window shrunk in this way continues to play in its thumbnail form.) As designers of modern GUIs develop increasingly sophisticated emulations of visual depth, more of the objects shown on the desktop are partially translucent, allowing others to show from beneath, or seem in other ways to allow visual and procedural traversals of layers.▶N3.13 The models for these visual forms, as Manovich has observed, are cinematic—montage and compositing (2001, 142–60)—with the important change that, while they aim at the creation of the illusion of consistent and permeable spaces behind the screen's surface, the user does not lose sight of the fact that elements shown thus concurrently derive from distinct sources.

3.25 In modern OSs, the majority of system processes are run in the background with no or very minimal UIs until some condition is encountered that requires user feedback. The principal function of these interruptions is to bring hidden processes to the user's attention in the semiotic registers in which she expects OS interactions, but they also have the effect of reminding her that basic aspects of the system are not under her control or in normal conditions even made available for her inspection. In extreme circumstances, when the system encounters an error condition from which no graceful exit is possible, the conceit of the windowing scheme is laid bare and the system drops out of the GUI and displays a textual diagnostic message without any of the usual window dressing. Confronted by one of these "screens of death," the user has no choice but to restart the computer and hope that the problem will be resolved when the OS is reloaded into memory ▶ 7.69.

3.26 The multiplicity, dynamism, and contingency of the screen's surfaces distinguish them in significant ways from surfaces of the printed page. It is possible within certain technical constraints (the relative opacity of paper stock, the

fineness and precision of printing techniques) to broaden and deepen visual
fields of the page, or, by methods of manufacture, overprinting, or binding
to augment apparent layers of printed forms. Various mechanical means
have been used to multiply concurrencies of printed forms ▶7.02. But the
dependence of such systems on analog foundations means that they cannot
match the richer concurrencies of the screen, where mutual influences and
crossings of visual fields are the rule rather than the exception. A grammatextual model of the screen that accounts for its difference from the page
must consider not only semiotic relays effected within formal units roughly
homologous with the page—the contents of windows and controls—but
also those relays that are effected in continuous and discrete fields that are
actively interleaved on the screen.

3.27 Similarly, the printed "letter" does not have a precise correlate on the screen.
There, letters (alphanumeric characters) and letter-like objects may always
be further subdivided into pixel-based patterns. These patterns may be recognizable to the reader as component shapes of the primitives from which
"letters" are constructed, but (especially in the modern GUI, where such
patterns abound) they may also operate as distinct and specifically grammatextual elements, signaling relative position, apparent depth, or more or less
expressive portions of a pattern. Crucially, these forms are dynamically activated on the screen, not only in the sense that they must be redrawn every
few hundredths of a second in order to appear continuously present—the
printed letter, in contrast, is rendered only once—but also in that their positions and appearance may be altered by the user or the system. Deformations of the screened letter are commonplace, as its size, color, and shape are
changed in relation to requirements of the UI, or to achieve aesthetic effects
that are impossible in printed forms.▶N3.14

3.28 Because they remain open to user- and program-driven change in the visual
context in which they are encountered, graphemes of the screen are in general more *polygraphic* than corresponding forms of the printed page.▶N3.15
They comprise plural, semiotically distinct, overlapping, and coincident signifying systems, most of which are not alphabetic or typographic in the narrow sense; this is true even of command line UIs. Elements of these systems
generate multiple synthetic and analytic crossings; it is not uncommon that
one will duplicate the meaning of another within one functional perspective and elaborate, qualify, or even depart from that system within another
functional perspective.

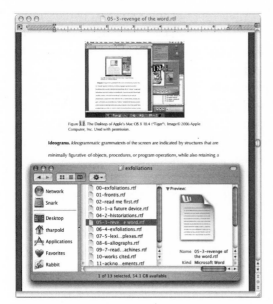

FIGURE 3.01. Multiple screen representations of an early draft of this chapter, in Microsoft Word 2004 and Mac OS X 10.4 (2007).

3.29 A simple example will illustrate the extent to which ongoing consideration of the functional significance of visual form—a hallmark of direct manipulation of UIs—may cause the semiotic registers of a screen object to proliferate. In a modern GUI, data constituting a "file" may be represented concurrently by several semiotically distinct and crossed signs (Figure ▶ 3.01).[N3.16] Its desktop icon may indicate the application used to create or edit it, and what kind of data—moving or still images, text, database, mixed formats—it comprises. The name assigned to the file typically appears adjacent to the icon, in a writing system that the OS supports. (Graphic traits of the icon may signify in one writing system—for example, the English-language name of the creator application—and the user-assigned "name," determined by the language to which the OS has been localized, in another.) The icon and name and other information about the file may be displayed in multiple formats, each of which may be shown concurrently if the user wishes. If the file is "open"—its contents displayed in one or more document windows—the user is confronted by additional dimensional semiotics, reinforced by enframing interface elements and their synchrony with other modes of displaying file information.

3.30 This brief description does not account for polygraphic or grammatextual effects of individual elements (pixels or patterns of pixels) from which the icon, list, or window are constructed—a more precise register of the screen's "letter" effects—nor does it take into account the activation of these elements and effects within a shared visual field that includes other such crossings of multiple signs of other files—a more precise register of the screen's "page" effects. Users of modern GUIs have become adept at parsing and navigating these plural fields without hesitation or deliberation. My description, moreover, does not account for performative aspects of the screen's polygraphy, how the significance of the visual forms it comprises may be determined by sequences in which they are encountered.

3.31 We confront in the last condition important questions introduced by the rich layering, framing, and segmenting of the screen in modern UIs. Should the window(s) and control object(s) that are the primary target of the user's input be considered the constitutive element(s) or present moment(s) of a conjectural unity? By what principles is that unity held together? Widespread UI terminology of "layers" and "tiers," "application windows" and "document windows," suggests that notional unities are managed as such by the OS and are present to the user in just this way—though modern GUIs also undercut these unities by littering the screen with docks, icons, palettes, and other controls that are specific to this or that GUI's idioms and whose positions among the layers of the screen and relations to the primary target may be unclear. The use of OS virtualization and emulation software ▶ 0.07 may populate the screen with elements belonging to more than one GUI, and require that the user traverse distinct and complexly interleaved UI regimes. Similarly, "cloud" computing services, in which users access applications and data stored on remote servers, usually via Web-based portals, may multiply these regimes. In theory, cloud applications like Google Docs are platform-neutral—they look and behave the same on any OS capable of accessing them—but, at least for the present, their interfaces are framed by the interfaces of the host Web browser and OS, which may differ dramatically from platform to platform.

3.32 If conjectural unities are discernible in these conditions, how are they *read* from the screen? Are they delimited by continuities and changes observed within defined regions of the screen—for example, within the boundaries of a document window or the layers controlled by a single program? In such a case, grammatextual effects would be activated principally within a given layer or tier of layers—those belonging to a Web browser, for example—and only secondarily within or across other layers and tiers. Or are conjectural

unities of so active and polyform a visual field defined by (at most) aggregates that are not visually or operationally bounded in that way, but may
comprise elements under the control of more than one program and OS,
reflecting at the level of the user's experience a version of the near or actual
parallel processing of the operating system? In that case, their significances
must be conceived of multiply and tabularly, simultaneously on several axes
and according to multiple, possibly inconsistent, semiotics—in other words,
something closer in its dynamic to collage than montage (Miles 2001).

3.33 But this may be a misleading opposition; the correct answer is: all of the
above. A rigorous grammatextuality of the screen would incur readings that
cross both localized operations specific to a program and general operations
that reach beyond it. To the extent that these crossings may be conceived
of as serially realized—one or more moments in the loop of the user's day
before the screen—it must also be understood to be closely joined to structures that parse and order the screen in multiple, extra-serial ways. Reading
from the screen shares this trait with reading from the surfaces of the illuminated page and the graphic novel: the reader's gaze "ricochets" over the
entire visual field—the term is Marion's (1993, 234), and is appropriate to
the physical dynamism and *friction* of this process. It is by this movement
over the surface of the screen—saccadic, halting, sometimes overshooting
its mark—that her reading will be cadenced and oriented. ▸N3.17

3.34 Applying Lapacherie's definitions to graphemes of the screen requires moving beyond exemplary traits he cites, since they are of exclusively serial in-
scriptions on opaque surfaces. Though it is more common than is widely
acknowledged, robust polygraphy is not a ubiquitous attribute of printed
grammatexts; more significantly, when they are copresent, multiple writing
systems in these media may have different meanings, but their operational
significances are usually commensurate. In contrast, polygraphy on the
screen often encodes different functional contexts and significances per-
taining to each writing system involved: textual and iconic representations
of a file, while ostensibly naming the same object, will offer very different
modalities of interaction with that object. Tabularity and polyseriality in
Lapacherie's examples are activated primarily in two dimensions, and constrained to visible facing surfaces of the codex. The pseudo-3D forms and
variable depths of the GUI add an additional dimension of reception and
ordering that is absent in the unadorned page and minimally present in the
illuminated page, the comic, and the graphic novel. As I have suggested, the

dynamism and programmed multiplicity of forms in this visual field extends the reach of tabularity and polyseriality in a manner that may not be describable as dimensional, if we hold to the geometric meaning of that term.

3.35 Therefore, the application of Lapacherie's four categories of print grammatexts to forms of the GUI must account for the distinctive medialities of the screen and page, and how on each of these surfaces grammatextual meaning may be activated and sustained in ways that have no clear correlates in the other. For surfaces of the GUI, this application is considerably complicated by the predominance of graphemes that are not textual, but which function as syntagmatic units in screen operations. Moreover, because a document displayed on the screen often resembles the printed page that might be produced from it, grammatextual traits of printed form may be carried over onto surfaces of the screen, even as they may be intruded upon by traits that appear to embody very different operations.

3.36 *Icons.* Iconic grammatexts of the screen are not equivalent to graphemes commonly termed "icons" in traditions of the GUI. They may include such graphemes, but only to the degree that they are conventional and have no necessary correlation to the program operations they encode.[N3.18] The most common of iconic grammatexts are in those aspects of the screen that support UI functionality but which are least involved in program execution: the eye candy (color schemes, some graphic textures and ornaments) that distinguishes one generation of a GUI from another, or one operating system from another. Screen grammatexts may be more radically articulated in those cases where a program's designer departs from the conventions of the UI or misuses interface elements in some way that subverts their usual meaning or application, as in the UIs of many video games and, more radically, in the work of typographer and multimedia artist Elliott Peter Earls ▶ 4.52.

3.37 *Ideograms.* The GUI window is a peculiar (and perhaps new) kind of window. In just the way that it doesn't quite resemble a window of the sort set into the wall of a building it may be said to be ideogrammatic in Lapacherie's sense of that term. The GUI window frames, encloses, sets apart—all of which are formal effects of an actual "window," unrelated to its purpose of admitting light and air or providing a view of the exterior. But the GUI window cannot perform those functions, nor can it open the gaze to the unrestrained depth of field that a real window discloses. The unconscious optics of the GUI window are of a very different sort than those presumed by the objectifying eye of Bush's Cyclops camera ▶1.28, or the divine vision figured indirectly in the perspectival precision of Antonello's painting of Jerome (▶ Figure 1.03). It is not that, despite its conceit of showing us the things "inside" our data stores, the GUI window looks inward rather than outward, but that, wherever it appears to be directed, it looks onto a surface that no amount of eye candy can cover. Magritte's paintings of overlapping canvases and windows represent something like this pure formalism abutting on a discernible limit, past which the UI, and not the viewer's optical system, is determinate. (The inconsistency or at least ambiguity of any effort to redirect the screen to ends away from this irreducible flatness is the context of Joyce's call for revenge on television and Thea and Veronica's dejected thought-experiment. ▶N3.19)

3.38 Similarly, the typical GUI desktop (▶ Figure 3.02) does not much resemble the surfaces of an actual desk ▶7.50. But it is an ideogram of a desk (more precisely, an aggregate of several such ideograms), signifying a well-defined procedural imaginary in which an ordering of the user's archive is executed and preserved. There, operations are possible (creating, moving, renaming, and deleting files) notionally associated with activities that occur on actual desktops (stacking documents or filing them in folders), even though the

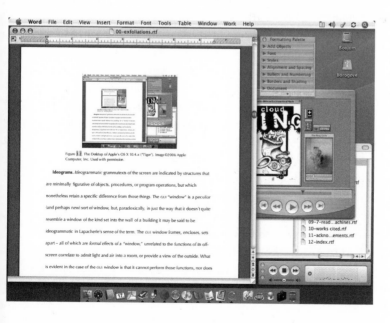

FIGURE 3.02.
Aqua, the desktop user interface of Apple's Mac OS X 10.4 (2007).

screen-based activities are very unlike their off-screen counterparts in both how they are executed and what they accomplish. The tension between the description of regions of the screen as windows or as a desktop, and the departures of what was shown on the screen from the meanings of those terms in other contexts was clearest in the early years of the GUI's rise to prominence. During that period, limited screen resolution and color depth, performance bottlenecks, and the primitive state of graphic design meant that users were confronted by images that bore at best cartoonish resemblances to windows, desktops, and folders. In the last decade, improved display technologies and the widespread use of photorealistic elements in GUI design have shifted the ideogram in these contexts toward increasingly finer visual reproductions of the concrete objects they represent.

3.39 A related ideogrammatic effect is marked by shared traits of interface elements of a GUI and the computer hardware used to run it. Icons resembling computer monitors, CPU enclosures, and peripherals such as mice, scanners, printers, and so on are commonplace in desktop GUIs. In that these screen objects stand for hardware components in the context of direct manipulation (the user selects a printer by selecting its icon on the screen), they function as iconic signs (in a Peircean sense of the term, but not in Lapacherie's grammatextual sense). But to the degree that they also evoke secondary traits of hardware, such as its shape, color, or texture, they carry ideogrammatic values that blend attributes of hardware and software with a common "look and feel." The paragon of this blending is the GUI of early NeXT computers, whose chiseled monochrome windows, icons, and widgets repeated aspects of the computers' distinctive black magnesium enclosures (NeXT Computer, Inc. 1992). A fainter blending is marked in the brushed metal windows of Mac OS X 10.4 ("Tiger"), introduced to the OS with a new generation of laptops with unpainted magnesium and aluminum enclosures (▶ Figures 3.01, 3.02). ▶[N3.20]

3.40 *Diagrams.* In the era of command line UIs, diagrammatic grammatexts of the screen were marked by the screen's division into command and editing regions, by hierarchical list structures, such as directory and file catalogs, by the syntax of commands executed on the OS prompt, and by in-text escape sequences, such as those specifying formatting that could not be shown on the screen but could be printed. ▶[N3.21] During the transition from predominantly command line to predominantly GUI-based OSs, rigidly orthogonal diagrams—somewhere between the wholly text-based rows and columns of the command line and the overlapping frames of windowing UIs—were common, as interface designers attempted to mark increasingly complex program operations using the limited graphic capabilities then available to them ▶ 7.49.[N3.22] These rigid, alphanumeric diagrams are present also in the modern GUI, and may be resurrected in something like their earlier forms via the UNIX terminal or the DOS command line. Most, however, are overlaid with and extended by new and nuanced characteristics enabled by modern display systems, or characteristic of the layered, multiple, and resizable window model of contemporary desktop interfaces.

3.41 The multiplication of windows and controls for managing them and the files they enframe foregrounds the greatly increased complexity of back-end data operations in the contemporary OS. Modern UIs serve as front ends to multitasking OSs capable of running concurrent applications, each of which may control many objects displayed on the screen (▶ Figure 3.02).[N3.23] An important characteristic of such interfaces is the manner in which they indicate which applications are running, which are the targets of the user's data entry (keyboard strokes or mouse movements), and which may require her attention. In most UIs, the implied hierarchy of concurrently running applications is marked by signs that also describe the applications' distinct and interrelated domains of control. For example, the way in which a word processor manages elements of its document windows is similar to the way in which the desktop UI manages directories containing files; the user moves from one to the other register of a screen presentation that combines these distinct domains with relative ease (▶ Figure 3.01). The common trope in these contexts resembles Russian nested dolls: an object "contained" by another object (synecdochically or metonymically) is shown to be "inside" it. To retrieve the object, the user opens its container, thereby revealing the object and making it the present focus of attention, which may also mean displaying signs of other objects that are contained with it (▶ Figure 6.06). Within the same level of containment, the arrangement of elements may communicate information about their similarity or difference. For example, GUIs often allow users to specify the visual arrangement of file icons within a directory folder, so that like files are more proximate than files unlike them (according to some metric that the user defines), or to arrange the positions of file icons so as to evoke a pattern that suggests the basis of their grouping. The copresence of such patterns with other representations of the units they gather—if, for example, the unit is opened to reveal that it contains text or images—will generate multitiered diagrams in which each level's values depend on levels above and below it.

3.42 We risk overemphasizing the importance of synchronically active diagrams while ignoring a trait that distinguishes screen diagrams from their print counterparts: the dynamism of the screen and the potential of diagrams to wink in and out of visibility and influence. Programmed time-based conditions of the text may in this regard assume diagrammatic significance, as is common in film, where what comes before and what comes after may indicate not only a causal or temporal sequence within the narrative, but also marked syntagmas determined by narrative or genre conventions (prelude, crisis, dénouement). The polychronicity typical of hypermedia narratives—"though I could list my past moments, they would remain discrete (and recombinant in potential if not in fact), hence without shape, without end, without story. Or with as many stories as I care to put together" ▶ 2.23—also typically polyserial in their interface presentation (▶ Figure 2.02), will often result in the expression of diagrams whose hierarchies are ambiguous or inconsistent ▶ 5.31.

3.43 Moreover, applications with substantial control over computing resources may be minimally indicated on the screen in a given moment; the visual complexity or prominence of an application at that time has no necessary relation to its operational importance. Some objects related to general interface tasks, such as application launching, general system preferences, and the like (functions controlled by the Mac OS X Dock, the Windows Taskbar, the Apple Menu, and Windows's Start Menu), are always displayed. The OS may always force some objects, such as error dialogs, to the foreground when the user's response is required. The proliferation of toolbars and palettes for changing application preferences, tool settings, style, color, document structure, and so on multiplies these effects within application layers. (Because their values may be toggled, or based on values of other controls, whether or not displayed data are selected, have been previously cut/copied/pasted, etc., diagrammatic dependencies in such applications can be maddeningly complex.) Moreover, applications' adherence to UI guidelines may be inconsistent and their designers are free to invent new uses of familiar elements, meaning that many diagrams may signify differently depending on the application with which they are associated, and the specific context in which they are activated.

3.44 Further ambiguities are engendered when meanings of screen diagrams are overdetermined by other structures or programs. This is common when diagrams are idiosyncratically or obscurely oriented, as is typical of poorly conceived or executed GUIs (Mullet and Sano 1995), and of works in which the subversion of GUI conventions plays an important role in their reception ▶ 4.51 ▶ 5.35. Since diagrams are the most elementary visual structures by which modern GUIs represent back-end database structures, it is to be expected that they will be activated even where the effects of other grammatextual forms are more significant.

3.45 The potential of such plural and even inconsistent effects for poetic or literary expression is particularly rich. Michael Joyce's hypertext fiction *Twelve Blue* (1996b), for example, combines subtly displaced diagrammatic conventions with a unique textual effect, itself obscurely diagrammatic, to mark structures of depth that Joyce has complained are difficult to sustain in Web-based fictions.[N3.24] The title screen and subsequent nodes of the fiction include an image of twelve colored threads crossing a blue-black field ▶ Figure 3.03. The "story threads" represent twelve months of a year, characters or pairings of characters—experiences of the same character may be traced by more than one thread—and their proximities represent narrative correlations. These are traversed by eight vertical cuts corresponding to the-

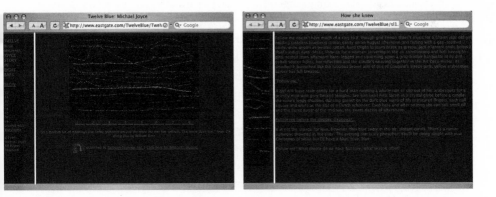

FIGURE 3.03. Michael Joyce's *Twelve Blue* (1996), viewed in Apple's Safari Web browser, Mac OS X 10.4 (2007). Shown are the title screen (*left*) and the first node ({now she knows}, *right*). Apart from the twelve colored threads crossing a blue-black field in the upper center of the title screen and in the left-hand frame of other nodes, and a few similarly abstract multicolored images nested deeply in the fiction, all visual elements are in shades of blue. Reproduced by permission of Eastgate Systems, Inc.

matic sections of the work. The parsing of the image thus into 96 implicit segments is applied by the HTML code to determine which nodes are displayed, such that the browser generates a request for the next page to display based on the coordinates of a mouse click in the image. This calculation of the next node is repeated within subsequent nodes in a restricted form based on the coordinates of the narrower version of the image.

3.46 The thread image, Joyce reports, "came first," apparently prior to his composition of the hypertext. He compares it to a score by experimental music composer John Cage (Joyce 1996b, 188), in reference perhaps to Cage's interest in precisely staged (scored) performances using "instruments"—radio receivers or pianos whose strings are jammed with screws, bits of metal, or rubber—whose sounds or pitch could not be predicted in advance of the performance. In *Twelve Blue* the local effects of the reading instrument are not so oriented by chance as in Cage's music (though they are also not entirely under the control of the reader-player); Joyce appears to have instituted them in the initial conditions of his composition. (The tabular arrangement of the threads and vertical cuts may also be an allusion to Cage's interest in the mesostic ▶ 3.19.) Such a constraining of the configuration of the textbase—in this case, an arbitrary diagramming of its permutations that forecasts, obscurely, serial and program bases of its presentation—is, as we will see, an operating principle of reading machines ▶ 7.22. It remains unclear how such a diagram could predict or track a narrative composed of verbal syntagmas—Joyce surely expects that we will recollect the Shandean precursor of all such diagrams—and so we are left with the fundamental ambiguity of a figure of something that is not amenable to being figured in that way, the assertion of a resemblance between ordered signs with not much else to sustain their putative homology ▶ 5.51.

3.47 This is, however, not the most arbitrary constraint of the work. Drawing inspiration from William Gass's meditation on meanings of the word "blue" (Gass 1991, 71), Joyce has composed his text so that each node contains the word *blue* and that all of the text is displayed in bright blue against a darker blue background. *Twelve Blue* is profoundly blue, but in a way that depends on our grasping that attribute, as Gass argues, as a version of the purest signifier. Which is to say that its significance in the foreground will dissolve into the background, the condition of blueness that has no immanent meaning, whenever we approach it too closely. The single link in each node of Joyce's hypertext—were they more frequent the effect would be, unexpectedly, less arresting—is programmed so that choosing it will change the color of its type to match the background. When these "sinking links" (Joyce 2000, 188) are activated, then, they disappear from the screen. ("Follow me—before the choices disappear," the narrator proposes in the opening node {How she knew} ▶ Figure 3.03.) Gregory L. Ulmer (1997) has compared the experience of the disappearing links to a species of drowning—a recurring theme in the narrative, in which two important characters perish that way—in that the effect seems to pull the reader into surfaces of the text, undoing her expectation that the browser interface will preserve the possibility of returning to its frame, because the "Back" function of the browser cannot (unless we empty the cache and start anew) recover fully a prior moment of our reading. One sort of blue does not direct the other (diagrammatically); each repeats the other (iconically and ideogrammatically) in its proper register; both seem to push the reading forward in the direction of a multiple blueness that is medially sensitive but means nothing on its own: "Twelve blue isn't anything. Think of lilacs when they're gone" {threads}. The diagram shifts here into alphabetic registers, and through them toward textual oblivion ▶ 2.50. ▶N3.25

3.48 *Alphabets.* In keeping with Lapacherie's use of the term to describe non-figurative traits of alphabetic glyphs and their syntagmatic arrangements, alphabetic grammatexts of the screen will be marked indirectly, in rhythms of program execution and the patterns of meaning they generate. The GUI's reliance on elements whose visual presentations appear to repeat off-screen counterparts (dog-eared pages, folders, trash cans, etc.) recenters our attention away from these liminal structures, onto objects manipulated on the screen. Constrained relations between those objects appear in this context to be incidental to the purposive character of the interface: we read, we act upon, we respond to, forms on the screen, often with minimal attention to the formal conditions of those activities. There is irony in this: the Turing machine is an alphabetic machine *par excellence*; grammatexts created and sustained by its computational methods will be activated by alphabetic operations of program code. In that regard, those operations are commonplace.

3.49 Alphabetic grammatexts that matter in the reader's reception of the text are those in which structures that are computationally produced or bound are discerned at registers of the text closer to the reader's interactions with it. For example, program operations and the underlying organization of the textbase may be recaptured by narrative and mimetic patterns, as when an arbitrary limit of the program is represented to the video game player as a natural limit of the game world, a boundary such as an impassable barrier, a door or a window that cannot be crossed. Rather than being alerted to the limit in terms of its computational significance—"You can't go past this point, because the data needed to represent what lies beyond it are unavailable"—she discovers, simply, that the door doesn't open or the forest has become impenetrable. Michael Joyce's reliance on the controlling logic of guard fields in *Afternoon, a Story* is a related form of recapture: the program's responses to the reader's choices are calculated according to an algorithm to which she has no access, which is never explicitly marked, and which can be construed only retroactively ▶ 6.11. Critics' characterizations of Joyce's hypertext as an uncompliant puzzle represent ex post facto motivations of algorithmic operations that they find perverse or capricious: traces of an alphabetic grammatext that short-circuits the basic pleasures of reading ▶ 6.17.

3.50 Alphabetic grammatexts may be more openly oriented with the procedural or spatial imaginaries of a fiction. Nick Montfort's *Ad Verbum* (2000) is structured in most respects like a classic Infocom text adventure game such as the *Zork* series ▶ 4.01: the player must navigate a series of connected rooms by typing in specific commands, collecting useful or valuable objects, avoiding hazards, and solving puzzles. But *Ad Verbum* adds to these conventional elements of interactive fiction (IF) an Oulipian twist. Behaviors of

the parser in four rooms of the house in which the adventure takes place are constrained by the initial letters of the compass points to which they correspond, N(orth), S(outh), E(ast), W(est). In each of these rooms, the parser understands and responds with only words beginning with that letter, requiring the player to dip into her thesaurus to find appropriate synonyms for typical IF verbs. Gameplay in the rooms is alphabetically determined both in the usual sense of that word and in Lapacherie's narrower application, in that the lipogrammatic constraint enforces a patterning of text generated by the game independent of its narrative or mimetic signification.

3.51 Programs of code may also be directly subject to alphabetic—and to other grammatextual—effects when they are expressed in the "graphic substance" of a text's reading surfaces. Here, narrative or mimetic recapture of the program is in a sense reversed: instead of providing an alibi for program limits, hiding or motivating them, graphemes of the text are openly constructed from elements of the program; they are built up from units of code, transposed from the back end to the front end of the system. Several electronic poets, notably John Cayley and Loss Pequeño Glazier, have produced works in which distinctions between code and text are collapsed in this manner ("codetext"). ▶N3.26

3.52 Giselle Beiguelman's *//**Code_UP* (2004), a Web-based re-envisioning of Michelangelo Antonioni's 1966 film *Blowup*, illustrates the potential of this technique to distinguish medial bases of cinematic and computational art forms ▶ Figure 3.04. In Antonioni's film, an unnamed protagonist (played by David Hemmings) is a successful fashion photographer in the swinging

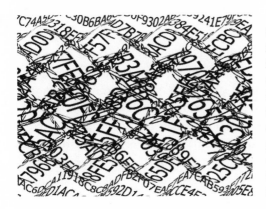

FIGURE 3.04. Versions of a scene from Michelangelo Antonioni's film *Blowup* (1966). *Far left:* one of the photographic stills featured in the film. *Center:* A portion of that image with its RGB values converted to a three-dimensional graph. *Right:* The hexadecimal values of the image converted to animated letterforms. Giselle Beiguelman, *//**Code_UP* (2004).

demimonde of 1960s London. One afternoon he chances on a pair of lovers in a secluded corner of a park and shoots some photographs of them from a distance. The woman in the couple (played by Vanessa Redgrave) breaks away and pursues the photographer, demanding that he turn over the photographs. He refuses. Intrigued by her desperation—she follows him to his apartment and offers him sex in exchange for the film—he develops the photographs, enlarges them, and seems to discover in them the basis of her concern: a man lurking in the bushes at the edge of the visual field, possibly holding a gun, and in the final shot the silhouette of a body, half-obscured by vegetation. Tacked to the walls in a series that wraps around his studio —surrounding him thus in the visual field constituted by the technical apparatus of his camera and developing equipment—the blowups seem to show Redgrave's having lured her lover to where another man waited to kill him.

3.53 //**Code_UP* is based on stills from Antonioni's film, including several in which the entire frame is filled with one of the mysterious photographs of Redgrave and her lover. Beiguelman converts the stills into digital formats, presumably by scanning them, and then manipulates textual and numeric representations of them to generate new, dynamic versions suited to operations of the computer screen. Some images are enlarged to such a degree that the browser window fills with uniform color, corresponding to individual pixels of the images, thus converted to a sequence of undifferentiated blots. The RGB values of other images are converted into three-dimensional graphs that may be rotated in the direction of the z-axis, thus appearing to reveal structures of depth in surfaces of the stills that cannot be detected on the cinematic screen. Presented with these objects, the viewer is as Antonioni's protagonist, fascinated by an artifact of the film's technical manipulation that seems to disclose hidden values.

3.54 Most compelling are the Flash animations that Beiguelman creates from hexadecimal and ASCII values of the digital images. She treats these code streams as a form of concrete poetry, setting them in motion, distorting their letterforms, treating them as surfaces as equally expressive and potentially generative of meaning as the original images. In a sense, these are examples of the purest of alphabetical grammatexts we may discern on the screen. They correspond to an image that we may situate among the narrative syntagmas of a defined text; aspects of the image mark its medium—a woman, anxious, is embraced by her lover; she turns to look at us; the image is a film still, enlarged so much that details are beginning to be lost—but in their actual form they are indecipherable because they are encoded in a scheme we cannot interpret. That they have been re-encoded as patterns of pixels in the shape of numbers and letters, moved and manipulated on the surface of the screen, means that a second-degree alphabetic operation has taken place. The original image has dropped away in this process—it cannot be reconstructed from the graphemes of the Flash animation—and any referent we may conjecture it to have represented has been dispersed by the insistence of the alphabetic grammatext.

3.55 Estrangements of screen grammatexts—when we remark some exceptional instance that hints at fundamental traits of textual operations—may be a basis for understanding not only alphabetic forms, but more generally conditions of grammatextuality as a medial basis for reading from any surface. This is the most active practice of reading, since it will not mistake imaginaries anchored in elements of the letter, page, and screen for the full extent of textual operations. I will propose in the next chapter that reading is a practice materially and procedurally bound to surfaces, the complexity of which is best grasped in boundary phenomena.

4.

Ex-foliations

When she was a child she used to especially like a certain series of illustrated books where every chapter or so was punctuated by an ink line illustration. She read these books as if they were tunnels where each illustration was a glimpse of light before you burrowed back under. It was like when you tarried too long underwater and had to pump your legs and pull the water down from overhead in long strokes behind you in order to surface. Breathless, the upper world seemed miraculous, a place of impossible beauty beyond the blue page of the water, too dazzling to look at for long. Tunnels in her own or any body likewise led to impossibly bright vistas.

In retrospect she realized that the illustrations in the children's classics were almost surely tied to some episode or chapter but she knew she never really saw them as such. Instead they seemed another story in each story, wordless and isolate, as secretive as icebergs . . .

—Michael Joyce, *Twelve Blue* (1996b, {waves})

4.01 Backward glances verging on nervous atavism are a trait of every medial shift, but appearances of the page and codex on-screen seem especially freighted with effects of nested and embedded textual surfaces. In video games, for example, written or printed pages are rarely created in the game world but they are often discovered there, usually in states of decay or incompleteness, to provide a partial backstory for the game or some piece of data that is needed to solve the game's puzzles. (Among the most telling evidence that the relation between narrative and play in games is more complex than it may seem is the number of games in which the player's avatar spends a great deal of time reading.) The found manuscript is among the oldest of pretexts for holding intra- and extradiegetic orders in productive tension, but in these cases that essentially narrative strategy is overdetermined by the incongruities of page and screen that the player either sees demonstrated before her or has internalized from other sources. A document must have come into being before it is shown to us; it has to be shown to us so that the game can start or continue; the method by which the document engages other mechanisms of the game program and game world signals, if not the subjection of the older to the newer medium, then a kind of succession between them that may imply subjection as an eventual outcome. When the player of *Zork* opens the mailbox placed before her in the first screen of the game and takes out the leaflet inside and reads it, she effects thereby a relay between textual and medial imaginaries in which the page gives way to and sustains its double.▶[N4.01] Only a few of the texts and fragments of texts scattered about the Great Underground Empire are advisory or instructive; most are tongue-in-cheek records of the game world's prehistory, which emerges only through the conceit of being read from a page that predates the screen.▶[N4.02]

4.02 Any bookshelf that appears in a computer game is sure to contain at least one volume that opens when retrieved, revealing a new point of egress, another passageway of the game world. The page as vestibule, embedded further in the vestibule of the screen, suggests, on the one hand, transmissibility: these images describe a point of entry for the eye—or, conversely, a way by which something in the machine breaks out to the surface of the screen and reaches out to the eye (▶ Figure 4.01).

4.03 On the other hand, the page as vestibule suggests blockage or recursion. In addition to the "linking books" that join the five ages of Rand and Robyn Miller's classic computer game *Myst* (Cyan, Inc. 1993, 2000), the player will

FIGURE 4.01. The final frame of the animated opening sequence of *Myst* (1993). To enter Myst Island and begin the game, the player clicks on the window on the right-hand page. The scene shown in the window zooms to fill the screen.

encounter three kinds of books on Myst Island: slightly or moderately damaged ones composed of fragments from Atrus's journals, containing partial
clues to the solution of the game; nearly destroyed ones, bearing mute wit-
ness to the apocalypse that preceded the opening of the game; and red, blue,
and green books that the player must assemble, page by page, in order to
hear the (untrustworthy) testimony of Atrus's sons Sirrus and Achenar, and
to free their father from his imprisonment. The first and last of these three
kinds of books are variants of the middle term in the series. Each is a *damaged* book: in that it deflects the reader-player's investigations; in that it is
presented as something stuck, rooted, and immovable (in *Myst*, the player's
avatar can carry only one page at a time, never whole books);[N4.03] in that it
is *unreadable*, except that it directs us to other avenues of discovery in the
game world. As the whole of the *Myst* game world is framed by the trope
of the linking book, the simultaneous luring and frustration of potential
readability marks an implicit commentary on the condition of playability-
as-readability (not the same as legibility) itself.

4.04 Nelson has proposed that hypertext design should take inspiration from
turn-of-the-century children's books that contained die-cut doors that
could be opened to reveal hidden texts or pictures (1990b, 241), or, more
generally, from practices of textual and narrative embedding that may have
their conceptual roots in such formal-mechanical examples. "Think of the
present document as a sheet of glass," he writes,

> It may have writing painted on it by the present author; it may have
> clear glass, windowing to something else; the next pane may be in
> turn made of more layers of painted glass, with more windows, and
> so indefinitely.
>
> Only when you step through the window—turning one glass page
> and going on in the next—do you reach the original that you wanted.
> But stepping through the window means you are now in another
> work. (Nelson 1990a, 2/34)

4.05 The metaphor of the window-in-a-page or -book and its variants are so
common a class of literary conceits that they constitute a convention of
imaginative writing. In children's literature (Lewis Carroll's Wonderland
mirror, Norton Juster's *Phantom Tollbooth*, C.S. Lewis's wardrobe) the
pedagogical significance of the conceit (the page is a "window" into another
world; reading inserts one into that world) is obvious. But a window of the

kind that opens into Myst Island can have no analogue in actual codices: you can't step through the page of a book, at least not one you could also read comfortably ▶ 7.01. Formal operations of the *mise en abyme* that Nelson proposes must in these cases remain imagined and/or bounded by physical limits, insofar as the book must conform to the body of the reader and the situation in which it is read. Material applications of the conceit—actual openings in the surface of the printed page—will always be confronted by this medial constraint and by its influence on the reader's conjecture of textual imaginaries.▶N4.04 For example, see the surfaces shown in ▶ Figure 4.02.

4.06 These are not representative of more common forms of the window-in-a-page, but they are clearer examples of an aporia that this structure must encode. These holes in the page cannot be closed individually (say, with a

 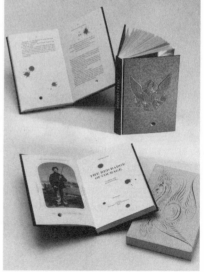

FIGURE 4.02. *Left:* "Seventeenth Flat," from Peter Newell's *The Rocket Book* (1912). The blank oval in the center of the typewriter corresponds to a hole in the interior pages of the book marking the passage of the eponymous bottle rocket through twenty floors of an apartment building. *Right:* The cover, typical pages, and slipcase of Westvaco's edition of Stephen Crane's *The Red Badge of Courage* (1968). Pages of the edition are spattered with drops of blood-colored ink, and a bullet hole perforates the front cover and most of the pages. Photograph courtesy of Karen Elder; reproduced with permission of MeadWestvaco Corporation.

small flap of heavy stock over each hole, as in "lift the flap" books). The only way to stop up the formal interruption they reveal is to close the entire book. In one case, even that strategy is not entirely effective.

4.07 Peter Newell's celebrated 1912 children's book in verse, *The Rocket Book*, recounts the misadventures of a bottle rocket launched in the basement of an apartment building by "Fritz, the Janitor's bad kid." The rocket travels upward through twenty floors of the building, bursting through the floor of each flat, interrupting some activity taking place there—through a dining table around which a family sits, a potted plant being watered, a children's dollhouse, a burglar pilfering the contents of a drawer, and so on—and then up through the ceiling to the flat above, where the process is repeated until the rocket is stopped inside a hand-cranked ice cream maker. ▶ Figure 4.02 shows the Seventeenth Flat, where

> A penny-liner, Abram Stout
> Was writing a description.
> "The flame shot up," he pounded out—
> Then threw a mild conniption.
>
> For through his Flemington there shied
> A rocket, hot and mystic.
> "I didn't mean to be," he cried,
> "So deuced realistic!" (Newell 2001b)

4.08 The "realism" of the episode extends across limits of the representational and the physical-mechanical aspects of the work. The rocket has burst from the typewriter carriage on its way to the next story of the building. Here, as in every scene of the book (including, incongruously, the one showing the rocket's launch), the center of the page is perforated by an oval that marks the missile's point of entry and exit from the scene. On facing pages, the perforation divides two four-line verses relating the alarmed responses of the inhabitants of each flat the rocket enters. Every page of the book, with the exceptions of the endpapers and title page, is perforated thus. The hole is the visual center of each page, and it is the functional center of the work as fiction and as medial object.▶N4.05

4.09 In 1968, the West Virginia Pulp and Paper Company (Westvaco) published a limited Christmas edition of Stephen Crane's novel of the American Civil

War, *The Red Badge of Courage* (▶ Figure 4.02).[N4.06] Designed by celebrated American typographer and graphic designer Bradbury Thompson,
the book was the eleventh in an annual series showcasing Westvaco's paper
and printing technologies and also represented a noteworthy—if finally self-
limiting—illustration of grammatextual and paratextual effects.[N4.07] Presented in the form of a soldier's battle kit, the book's black leather-grained
cover is embossed with a U.S. Army insignia fashioned from an actual Civil
War insignia. The front matter pages include a sepia-toned photograph of
an unknown soldier—"the designer's way of recognizing that soldiers carried sentimental mementos in their kits" ("Foreword," 15)—and a facsimile
reproduction of an instruction manual for the Springfield rifle issued by the
U.S. War Department for infantrymen. The typographic elements are based
on nineteenth-century designs or more recent designs modified to closely
resemble them.

4.10   The most striking visual elements of the Westvaco *Red Badge of Courage* are
the simulated bloodstains that appear on many pages—the endpapers are
marbled in hues of the same bright red—and the simulated bullet hole that
passes nearly through the book (▶ Figure 4.02). According to Jean A. Brad-
nick, the stains—there are hundreds of them and each is different—were
produced individually with an eyedropper of red ink, and then positioned
on galleys of the pages on which they appear ("Foreword," 14). The design
of the bullet hole was produced through a similar test-process: Thompson
and an expert on Civil War weapons "set up a makeshift firing range . . .
and methodically perforated discarded books with projectiles fired from a
.45 caliber revolver at various ranges" (14). Satisfied that a book of these
dimensions could stop a bullet, they decided on a less traumatic means of
incorporating the effect in the Westvaco book: the hole was created with a
specially designed drill bit patterned after a .45 caliber slug.[N4.08]

4.11   The bloodstains and the bullet hole are, each in its own way, openings into
the fictional imaginaries of the novel. The stains—scores of small, localized
red badges, framing the text but never entering it (they are always in the
margins, or at the base or top of a page, never overprinted), represent both
the marks of honor coveted by Crane's protagonist Henry Fleming and an
ironic commentary on their cost: blood flowing so freely must have come
from a mortal wound. The simulated bullet hole is overdetermined in this
way: a literal opening of the fictional imaginary, its point of contact with the
reader's experience of the page, it suggests that the join of these orders can

only be made traumatically, and must leave behind a permanent alteration of the reading surface. With regard to the novel's textbase, Thompson took the more cautious path: the bullet hole passes through the lower margin of the pages; it never enters the text. The conceit of the salvific page—a-book-stopped-a-bullet, the stuff of battlefield legends—is revealed and delimited by this small discretion: the hole perforates the substance of the page, but no word of Crane's novel is effaced.

4.12 Which is to say, the intervention of the hole is limited to the margins of what we may recognize, without irony, as the text's elementary body.[N4.09] As I have indicated above, it is a practical problem that perforations of the page are bounded by the physical limits of the work in which they occur. Even in the rare case when they extend through one or both covers of the book, they cannot go farther than that: the perforation in these cases may be said to open outward from the first or the last page, but its reach is ambiguous and, plainly, figurative or imaginative beyond that point. Crucially, however, this limit is unlikely to simply be present to the reader; it is recaptured by systems of the fictional worlds represented by the text. This recapture is oriented by imaginative intersections of the fiction with material traits of the page—in these cases, the perforations—but is not limited to them. All the operations of the page and its apparatus may be called upon to sustain this recapture so that it functions as a specific join of textual, narrative, and mimetic imaginaries. A reading of a copy of *The Red Badge of Courage* through which someone appears to have fired—accidentally—a .45 caliber bullet may be, it is true, understood to somehow encompass the bullet hole in the experience of the reading, but a *designed* opening of this kind must signal a strategic, prior linkage of mediality to that conjectural scene of reading. Equally as significant is the fact that the reader will always be aware of this linkage; her pleasure in the design depends upon her susceptibility to the allures of a calculated accident ▶ 4.58.

4.13 A third example illustrates the potential of the perforation to activate combinatorial narrative operations. Marc-Antoine Mathieu's *L'Origine* (1991) is the first of five graphic novels concerning the misadventures of Julius Corentin Acquefacques (Mathieu 2004). The novels are set in an absurdist dystopian world comprising strange interdimensional beings and forces and both futuristic and outdated technologies. A minor functionary of the Ministry of Humor, Acquefacques lives in a closet-sized room he shares at various times with other lodgers (overpopulation has forced exploitation of every available space). Each morning, he wakes from troubled dreams—like little Nemo, always falling out of bed (McCay 2005)—and wearily attempts to make his way through overcrowded city streets to his office. He is usually late or early arriving to work and often sidetracked by inexplicable mishaps. (It is not always clear that he has in fact awakened; several of the books take place in a dreamworld double of his waking life.) Acquefacques is resigned to his oppressive salaryman existence until he makes an astonishing discovery: his present and future are written in . . . a graphic novel; it is likely that the entire world is a graphic novel *about him.*

4.14   The six frames shown in ▶ Figure 4.03 are from chapter 5 of the novel, in which Acquefacques and Igor Ouffe, the Director of the Ministry of Research, discuss the significance of Acquefacques's discovery.[N4.10] Beyond their two-dimensional universe, Ouffe proposes, there is a three-dimensional universe in which their own is a part of a larger project. Moreover, there seem to be holes in the material structure of their world—"un trou de matière . . . ou une anti-case, si vous préferez" ("a hole in matter . . . or an anti-frame, if you prefer"). These are responsible for experiences of déjà vu and other temporal anomalies, because they permit moments of the past or future to be superimposed on the present.

4.15   Ouffe's argument is (brilliantly) demonstrated in the substance of Mathieu's text: the central frames of the two panel rows shown in ▶ Figure 4.03 are constituted by a single die-cut hole in the leaf comprising pages 41 (recto) and 42 (verso). In the row shown at the top (from page 41), the hole opens onto page 43 ("Un trou de matière?"), in the future of the reading in which we encounter it. In the row shown at the bottom (from page 42), the same hole opens onto page 40 ("Oui! À 2 dimensions!"), in the past of the reading. Thus, each of the printed frames occurs only once in the text, but is activated twice in the narrative. Conversely, the hole is not a part of the narrative sequence, but is activated twice in the text (Groensteen 2003, 26–27). It may not even be appropriate in this context to describe these surfaces as pages, since their intersection is formed by a strange extension by which the surface opens serially on its double. But this is not an infinitely deep opening, since a medial boundary in the three-dimensional world intervenes to mark its horizon.[N4.11]

4.16   *"I composed the holes."* I have used the term "perforation" to describe these forms in anticipation of an example that appears at first different from

FIGURE 4.03. "Un trou de matière?" The center panels of pages 41–42 of Marc-Antoine Mathieu's graphic novel *L'Origine* (1991). The middle frame of each row is framed by a die-cut hole in the leaf. The frame in the center of page 41 (top, shown here in gray) is printed on page 43. The frame in the center of page 42 (bottom, also shown in gray) is printed on page 40. In the original, all the frames are printed in black and white. Copyright 1990 Guy Delcourt Productions, *L'Origine*, by Marc-Antoine Mathieu. All rights reserved.

them—pages of the work in question include no physical openings—but that on closer examination represents an important limit-case of these phenomena.

4.17 Ronald Johnson's 1977 book-long poem *Radi Os* (▶ Figure 4.04) is based on an 1892 edition of John Milton's *Paradise Lost* that Johnson purchased in a Seattle bookshop. Events of the day before determined Johnson's responses to the text: he had heard a performance of Lukas Foss's "Baroque Variations," the first of which was based on Handel's Concerto Grosso, op. 6, no. 12. Johnson's opening note to *Radi Os* cites Foss's description of Variation I as a justification for his method:

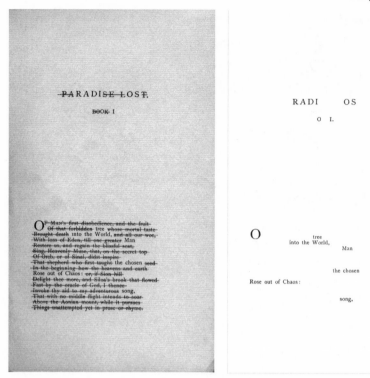

FIGURE 4.04. The inside cover and opening page of Ronald Johnson's *Radi Os* (1977). Beneath the scored lines in the image on the left, the original text of the 1892 edition of *Paradise Lost* from which Johnson produced his "perforated" text is visible. Images from *Radi Os* by Ronald Johnson (Sand Dollar Press, 1977; reprinted by Flood Editions, 2005); courtesy of the Literary Estate of Ronald Johnson.

> Groups of instruments play the Larghetto but keep submerging into inaudibility (rather than pausing). Handel's notes are always present but often inaudible. The inaudible moments leave holes in Handel's music (I composed the holes). The perforated Handel is played by different groups of the orchestra in three different keys at one point, in four different speeds at another. (Johnson 1977)

4.18 Johnson has introduced analogous "holes" into Milton's poem, erasing (his actual method is not described) portions of the 1892 page layouts so as to show only a few words, lines, or fragments of lines on each page. In this form, Milton's poem is "sifted" (Guy Davenport, in an afterword), "excised" and "x-rayed" (Selinger 1992), "corroded" (McCaffery 2002); the positions of the remaining words are unchanged, and those that have been erased are simply missing—only mock-ups of scored passages from the first and last pages of the text on the inside front and back covers indicate that the negative space of the page was once more populated.

4.19 Johnson's precursor in this project is William Blake, who used a relief etching technique to burn away "falsehoods" of *Paradise Lost* in his own epic *Milton*.[N4.12] As Steve McCaffery and Eric Selinger have observed, Johnson's text and method also echo more modern ancestors—Emerson, Stevens, and Pound. Neither McCaffery nor Selinger mentions Stéphane Mallarmé. The American's fundamental sympathy with the French Symbolist's privileging of linguistic and literary form over reference is implied in the system of *Radi Os*; any work of poetry after *Un Coup de dés jamais n'abolira le hasard* (*A Throw of the Dice Will Never Abolish Chance*, 1897) with as many blanks between its letters must evoke a reader's recollection of that poem.[N4.13] A decisive distinction between *Radi Os* and Mallarmé's poem is that Johnson's work is the more directly historiated ▶ 2.24: the perforations of the poem trace a specific intervention in an arc of literary influences and revisionings. That was also Mallarmé's purpose, only in his case the numerous intertexts of his poem are signaled by occult idioms of the Symbol; in Johnson's case, the occultation is more literal, more local, and undisguised: his primary intertext is, we recognize as we read, directly negated. Johnson's citation of Foss is perhaps misleading: the portions of Milton erased from *Radi Os* are not (barely) invisible—the textual correlate of Foss's "submerging" of Handel's notes—they are simply *not there*.[N4.14] We may be tempted to read from these pages a virtual, intertextually sustained form of depth, but the evidence of their opaque surfaces points in another direction: there, one text (poem) surfaces another, in a disarming transitive sense of the verb. That the first text is a fragment of the second is a problem of literary genealogy, but it is not a grammatextual consideration: in that context, "first" and "second" are placeholders for marking the limits of the eye's ricocheting paths.

4.20 Unlike Ted Nelson's Stretchtext concept—words and phrases dynamically expanding from within a line or paragraph or collapsing from those levels into more compact forms—Johnson's alterations of the Miltonic text are irreversible.[N4.15] The permanence of this effect in print suggests that we should exercise imaginative restraint whenever signs of textual interiority are presented in textual media. "Only when you step through the window—turning one glass page and going on in the next—do you reach the original that you wanted. But stepping through the window means you are now in another work" (Nelson 1990a, 2/34). Stepping through the window does not mean that the window frame will necessarily remain visible, so that we may retain at the periphery of our vision that small promise of a threshold. If we are now in another work, it may well appear to be the only textual world available to us, since the path from one to the other was lost during the unseen fraction of a second when the screen was refreshed. Johnson's pages are in this regard uncanny anticipations of the *superficiality* of the digital field—the manner in which the screen, regardless of the fictions of depth it appears to sustain, also *screens* in the way of an obstruction—and in this is able to sustain satisfactions that an actually limitless depth (if such a thing were possible) could not.

4.21 We may detect here the effects of a general principle of media: the infinity of every *mise en abyme* must terminate, materially, in the finest grain of the medium in which it is presented. Before that medial bedrock is reached, we are likely, moreover, to stumble against anticipations of it, because a minimal ensemble of medial elements (capable of supporting a specific grammar of their relations) will be required in order to sustain any illusion that something lies beyond the limit. The whole of a system of seemingly endless recursion is oriented by this structure; because it must be medially encoded, the system's potential for generating new depths must shift at some point to a different logic of representation. A fantasy of continuing recursion on the part of the reading or viewing subject remains possible, but it must be founded on a real limit that from another point of view appears to be the merest caprice. And that limit may be easily discerned from outside, as the obvious prop of the system's machinations.

4.22 Michelangelo Antonioni's *Blowup* (1966) demonstrates the operations of this limit in cinema ▶ 3.52. The film's critique of photographic "reality" is obvious; more ambiguous are the signs of a paranoid consciousness that this critique instills within the narrative's technical field, heightened by the narcissism and nihilism of its characters, who seem both stuck in a totalized field of vision and unable to care enough to do anything to change that. (The allure of the spectacle is satisfaction enough, as it keeps open the desire to watch and be watched.) The photographer's progressive enlargements of small portions of the images of the possible crime scene to the point of unreadability (it might be a gun, it might be a body, it might be anything) draw the audience into an optical regime that is, fundamentally, founded on the obscure image-object of *his* desire. Outside that regime, the object is the merest cluster of silver nitrate grains, a blot on a projection screen. The continuity of Antonioni's film traverses the disconnect that is anchored in the blot, thus evoking the audience's analogous traversal of image-objects (the scenes, the actors) projected on a surface that doubles the cryptic photographs, but is also distinct enough from them to stage their effects on the characters. ▸N4.16

4.23 In popular digital culture a similar enframing and arrested recursion is characteristic of virtual-reality scenarios such as those of *Star Trek*'s holodeck. In the television series and movies in which that epitome of postsymbolic communication is featured, every adventure in a virtual world remains, it should be noted, subject to the grammar of television or Hollywood. ▸N4.17 Visitors to the holodeck do not remain there indefinitely and they cannot travel just anywhere; they are aware or quickly discover that they move in a strictly confined landscape not much bigger than a large room, and that the simulated space is further limited by computational latencies and errors that often reveal its artifice. A wide range of "play within a play" scenarios are possible in this scenario, but these are always, they can only be, medially contingent on prior or pending enframings by which a real limit outside of the nested dramas is marked. These include the commercial break (the holodeck as a subtle machine for selling automobiles and dishwashing detergent); opening and closing credits; and the recapture of orders of the virtual world by narrative requirements of a "real" world, which is itself set apart from the spectator by surfaces of the small or large screen. Of course the viewer of the film or television episode is aware that she is watching actors playing at playing within a virtual space that appears real, and that will be revealed to be unreal before the credits roll. In this respect, *Star Trek* and the holodeck differ from other examples of embedded mimesis only in the fictional technology used to stage the interior drama. But that is in fact a basis for the holodeck's signification in this context: its spatial and computational limits are homologous with the crude backlighting and plaster-of-Paris boulders of the "classic" *Star Trek* soundstages; the viewer grasps on the evidence of each that a real limit of the representation is encountered within the obvious mediality of the television or theatrical presentation.

Her pleasure in the representation depends on this encounter; without it, she would be confronted by a true *mise en abyme*, more likely to induce anxiety than pleasure.▶N4.18

4.24 In works combining print and digital elements, boundaries of textual interiority will also mark incommensurabilities of these media. *Agrippa (A Book of the Dead)*, the 1992 collaboration between author William Gibson, artist Dennis Ashbaugh, and publisher Kevin Begos, Jr., framed a totem of the digital field within a perforated page, embedding a floppy disk in a cavity at the back of the book (▶ Figure 4.05).▶N4.19 Most of the printed pages of the book were taken up by uninterrupted sequences of DNA code ("C-A-T-G") from the genomic sequence of the fruit fly, set in forty-two-line double columns (also the layout of Gutenberg's Bible), interspersed with between six and eight copperplate aquatint etchings of DNA gel "motifs."▶N4.20

4.25 The famous innovation of *Agrippa*—"innovation" is perhaps too strong a word, as the concept of the disappearing book is older—was that principal elements of the work were designed to be consumed by a single reading.

FIGURE 4.05. *Agrippa (A Book of the Dead)*, pages 62–63 of the deluxe edition (Gibson, Ashbaugh, and Begos, 1992). Photograph copyright 1992 Kevin Begos, Jr.

Ashbaugh's etchings were overprinted with images from antique newspapers and photographic equipment catalogs in uncured toner ink, causing them to blur after exposure to light.[N4.21] The floppy disk contained a custom-designed computer program for displaying a 305-line poem by Gibson (author of *Neuromancer, Count Zero, Mona Lisa Overdrive,* and so on: founding texts of 1990s cyberpunk). Once run, the program began scrolling the text from the bottom to the top of the screen at a constant rate without allowing it to be reversed. After this initial viewing, another program on the disk encrypted the text of the poem permanently so that it could not be replayed.[N4.22] The aim, as Begos writes, was to divide the memory of reading from its archival setting—rendered by this split inoperable:

> I had this flash of an idea—do a "book" on computer disc that presents collectors and museums with an all-or-nothing choice: produce a text on computer disc that self-destructs after one reading. If collectors/museums want a pure 1st edition, that could only be the unread state. If they choose to read the text, it becomes only a memory, not a tangible physical object to be bought and sold.
>
> I was particularly happy about the quandary this would put museums and collectors in, because how could one even determine if the disc had been played, without playing it?[N4.23]

4.26 This barrier to rereading did not endure long after the work's release. Within twenty-four hours, copies of the text of the poem began to circulate via file transfer protocols (FTP) and by anonymous e-mail, and it quickly became a *samizdat* cult object of the early Internet. Only weeks later, excited repostings on public bulletin boards were being treated with scorn as old news.[N4.24]

4.27 *Historiation.* Every reading is, strictly speaking, unrepeatable; something in it, of it, will vary. Recollections of reading accumulate in relation to this iterable specificity; each takes its predecessors as its foundation, each inflects them with its backward-looking futurity. But we may speak rigorously about a sort of repetition, so long as we distinguish symbolic operations of our reading—our recollective patterning across specific iterations of the text—from imaginaries of reading—the phantoms of wholeness, of saturation, and of integrity—that would draw it to a close. *Agrippa* undertakes to encode this distinction in the matter of the work's presentation. The deluxe edition of the work wraps the codex in a cheesecloth "shroud," enclosed in a resin-impregnated paper and fiberglass case; the cover and most of the pages are scorched by blowtorch and lit match; the floppy disk is embedded in a cavity hollowed by hand from the final twenty pages of the codex, which have been glued together (and are therefore unreadable). The *floppy disk*: in order to activate Gibson's text, the reader must pry its container out of a book and insert it into the receiving slot of a Macintosh computer. The playback program is self-launching and self-terminating; once the disk is inserted, the reader is committed to one (and only one) reading. (And. Now. This. ▶ 3.10.) The requirement that she transport the unlabeled disk from the opening in the page to the opening of the disk drive underscores the incommensurability figured by the perforation, which is less an opening into imagined spaces of the book than a bordering within its pages of a surface beneath and beyond them. This incommensurability is confirmed by the self-encrypting sequence of the reading, by the remove of a gesture of the hand, by the refocusing of the eye, away from the printed surface. Paradoxically, it is the programmed oblivion of the work that is most responsible for its persistence in the medial and textual variants that continue to circulate on the Internet and in the urban mythology of 1990s new media (Kirschenbaum 2008, 240–42) ▶ 2.56. ▶N4.25

4.28 *Ode to Malevich.* In such cases, grammatextual and paratextual elements of the reading surface borrow from and subvert conventions specific to each. This crossing of forms is the material basis for a tension between the resistance of parts composing the object to being subsumed into an integral whole, and the situation of reading which by its continuity in time and space suggests that this is possible. John Maeda's 1995 work *The Reactive Square* captures several aspects of this imperfect crossing. The first of five "Reactive Books" ("digitalogues") produced by Maeda in the late 1990s, *The Reactive Square* is composed of a small codex printed on heavy stock bound with a mini CD-ROM. ▶N4.26 Apart from the prefatory material, postface, and colophon in English and Japanese, the paper portion of the work is composed of a series of ten tabbed pages numbered 0–9. On the recto of each, a black square stands at the center of a white field; the corresponding verso is solid black, with the word "tick" printed in reverse type near the upper third of the page. The mini-CD is held to the last page of the codex by folding tabs. It contains a single executable program, also named *The Reactive Square*.

4.29 When the program is launched, the computer screen fills with a black background, framing an image that resembles the book's "0" page, behind

FIGURE 4.06. John Maeda, *The Reactive Square* (1995). Images copyright 1995 John Maeda.

which tabs of the remaining nine pages are visible (▶ Figure 4.06). Unlike its printed versions, the black square on the screen is dynamic: it deforms— flickering, changing shape and/or color, fracturing into multiple animated sections—in response to sounds picked up by the computer's microphone and according to which of the tabs has been selected. The deformations are not unlimited—the restricted space of the visual field and the resolution of the screen constrain the square's possible responses—but they are unpredictable, contingent upon interactions of elements of which the reader has little or no control: the dynamic range of the microphone, the computer's conversion of analog sound to digital signals, the algorithms that generate the deformations. Within the bounded plane of the screen, the representation of the reader's speech, a musical passage played to the microphone, or ambient sounds it picks up are expressed thus as moving or changing forms drawn on the plane, returning always to the default shape of the black square; the preface to *Reactive Square* emphasizes the temporal qualities of the work's "reaction" to the user.▶N4.27

4.30 Maeda's original title for the work was *Ode to Malevich*, in honor of Kazimir Malevich's Suprematist icon *Quadrilateral* (1913–15).▶N4.28 Better known as *Black Square* or *Black Square on a White Field*, the painting is an unframed square canvas about 2½ feet in each dimension: a field of white dominated by a solid black square centered on the field and taking up about three-fourths of its area. The centerpiece of Malevich's assault on figurative art in the 1910s, it was not the first Suprematist image, but it and his 1918 canvas *White Square on a White Field* are considered the principal works of the Suprematist project and among the most celebrated

examples of nonobjective painting of the twentieth century. At the threshold
of a practice still recognizable as artistic, they remain resistant to aesthetici-
zation; their reduction of the chromatic language of painting is extreme and
unapologetic (Valliér 1975, 1979). For that reason—this is chiefly a matter
of optical perception but also of artistic program—they are notably resistant to strategies of interpretation based on visual depth (Jakovljevic 2004).

4.31 "[Malevich's] courage to abandon all decoration in pursuit of the simplest
of forms," Maeda observed in 2000, "such as a single square, inspired my
thinking about black squares that would exist only on the computer" (115).
But relations between Malevich's painted square and Maeda's printed and
digital objects are more complex, and possibly inconsistent, than Maeda
suggests. First, there is the dynamic character of *The Reactive Square*. Each
of the squares shown on the screen represents a multiplied (additive, magnified, disfigured) version of the pixel, the elementary unit from which their
initial and deformed states are constructed. Their deformations contrast
with both the pixel's binary logic and the series of unchanging squares
printed on the work's paper surfaces. We might consider these to represent zero-degree versions of the dynamic squares, were it not the case that
their obvious doubling of the pixel complicates a simple opposition between
static and dynamic images. At the limits of the screen's chromatic language,
the pixel can be switched "on" or "off" without ceasing to function as a
pixel. The difference between these alternatives is not one of absence versus
presence, but of opposed expressions of the same structure of possibility:
the memory registers corresponding to a pixel switched "off" are not empty;
they are set to the opposite of the value that corresponds to "on."

4.32 The compositional language of Malevich and his collaborators operates in
much the same way, in that colors assigned to regions of the canvas do not
function as figure and ground. *Black Square* is not meant to stand forth
from the visual space that surrounds it; their opposition is determined by
the shape of the square and not contrast in colors (Milner 1996). Similarly, *White Square* is not an empty canvas: the painted square is noticeably
cooler than the background and we can see that it has been painted on—but
even if this cue were not present, the white square would still be marked as
the most nearly pure expression of an elementary unit of the Suprematist
system and the form within the visual field of its fundamental geometry.
▸N4.29 *The Reactive Square* subtly revises this formal language, as a function of its hybridization of print (in which the application of a mark to a

blank surface always implies the opposition figure and ground) and digital media (in which such opposition is conventional, but not technically determined). The active pixel (black) is the base unit of positive expression, and the fundamental algorithmic structure of generative possibility is displaced into other registers: the program that controls the "reactions," the complex embodied relations of the disk, the page, and the requirement that the user redirect her attention between their surfaces. It is impossible for the user to take in the entire work (print and digital) within one homogenous space of reading, and this partitioning between the surfaces of reading the work, page and screen, is always active as its fundamental spatial rule.

4.33 Second, the structure of possibility that subtends Malevich's black and white squares was dictated by attributes of the surfaces on which he painted. He preferred square canvases. They were, moreover, never framed; there was no outside border of the image to split it off from its surroundings or to sustain a visual analogy between the shape of the square and the shape of the frame. [N4.30] As a consequence, the images tend toward conceptual non-differentiation. If figure and ground are discerned in them, this has more to do with cultural and historical predispositions to read the lighter color as the field and the darker as an object set against it. His paintings after *Black Square*, notably *Four Squares* (the canvas is sectioned into four black or white regions, as in a fragment of a chessboard, 1915) and *White Square*, resist the effort to read depth into their surfaces (Jakovljevic 2004, 20–24). In Maeda's work, this flattening of figure and ground is inconsistent. The stark, undifferentiated regions of the reactive square, the white "page" that surrounds it, and the black field that surrounds that may be read against the grain. If the viewer unfocuses her vision slightly, it is possible to resist any tendency to read these embedded fields as frames bordering on further, interior frames, and to see them as fully contiguous planes, all at the same level. But it is difficult to sustain this unfocused position for long: the cursor's movements "over" the image and most of the deformations of the square invite a reading that looks inward, to the center of the screen, and by this partitions its negative and positive fields in tropes of limited depth.

4.34 In this respect, operations of *The Reactive Book* more resemble *Black Square* than *White Square*, not just because Maeda's screen and page evoke the earlier painting, but also because the grammatextual vocabulary of the GUI dictates that the black pixel be the minimal expression of positive value, whereas Malevich's later painting explicitly rejects a reduction of achroma-

tism to positive or negative units (Valliér 1975, 1979). The conceptual genealogy of *The Reactive Square*—and thus its operational method—is complicated by the historical intervention of the GUI: ironically, its resemblance
to and dependence on regimes of print also evoke interface conventions that
had been well established for more than a decade. The work cannot easily depart from the founding tenets of WYSIWYG's semiotic, in which the
blank (white) field is marked by the (black) pixel.

4.35 We may, however, remark one aspect of *The Reactive Book* that is homologous with the nonobjective flatness of Malevich's paintings, and that points
to a basic and cunning legerdemain of WYSIWYG ▶ 5.31. The inward-
directed gaze of the viewer is stopped, blocked by the square each time
it returns to its default state, that is, each time it reproduces its printed
form. Whereas Malevich's frameless canvas signaled a collapse of figure and
ground and a structural grammar that embodies nonobjectivity by refusing
visual depth, Maeda's pixel-on-a-page-on-a-screen-in-a-program-on-a-CD-
in-a-book is oriented by an incommensurability of media that is returned
to our consciousness indirectly in the object that stops further speculation
about the interior of depth.

4.36 We encounter here a characteristic of visual media that appears to be a con-
tradiction, but is really a hallmark of their operation: they are composed of
aggregates of interleaved surfaces. In each, adjacent surfaces may be procedurally distinct in certain respects but will not sustain a firm distinction
between outside and inside—or will remind us periodically of the limits of
that distinction—even as they rely on visual conceits such as windows and
frames. These conceits, when they can be seen to open at all, open onto a
barrier that is, finally, immovable. Between surfaces—and *between* may be
too spatial a term; this liminality is not locational but procedural and temporal—there are divides that cannot be sutured.▶N4.31 The surfaces remain
distinct even though shuffled in a variety of ways, since they cannot merge:
like Marc Saporta's codex *cum* card deck of pages, they may be rearranged
and read off in new sequences, but they never conjoin in a continuous series
of strata.

4.37 From the desk at which I compose these lines, I can read the spine of a copy
of the first French edition of *Composition no. 1, roman*. Unaltered and
complete first editions of Saporta's 1962 novel are rare. Original copies of

Richard Howard's 1963 English translation of the text are easier to find in the used book market, but tend to be expensive. The rarity of both first editions is due in part to their mechanical attributes: the novel's pages are printed on one side only, unnumbered and unbound, and held together only by two flimsy cardboard covers (in the English edition, a cardboard cover and a paper band). As a consequence, individual pages are easily damaged or lost, and it is not unusual for "complete" copies of the novel to have been composed from the parts of several incomplete copies.

4.38 That its pages are unbound is the novel's famous medial trait. Brief instructions printed on the first leaf direct the reader to shuffle the remaining leaves like a game of cards ("Le lecteur est prié de battre ces pages comme un jeu de cartes . . .") and to read the units of the story in the order thereby produced. The sequence of paragraphs on each of the 150 leaves can form a coherent narrative sequence with those of any two of the other leaves, and so 10^{263} combinations of all the pages are possible (Grimm 1978, 282), many more than may be generated by Queneau's sonnet machine ▶ 7.25. The number of different variants of the story that may be generated is fewer. Though repeated shuffles (readings) will produce different sequences of events or make it appear that different characters are involved in them, Saporta's use of an exclusively present tense and minimal distinguishing between narration, thought, and speech push resequences of the textbase in the direction of a generalized series of snapshots of the lives of X, the novel's male protagonist, and his wife, mistress, and another woman (who may be an underage girl) whom he rapes or seduces.

4.39 This copy of the French edition appears to be complete. Regrettably, however, someone has bound it in a standard institutional cover—the cardboard wrappers are missing—probably in the order of the pages when the text arrived at my university's library some forty years ago. (I know that it must have been bound in the United States, since the title runs from top to bottom in the American direction, not bottom to top in the French direction.) This, I think, may account for the text's limited circulation. Only two readers borrowed it before I discovered it in 2006: once in 1967, shortly after the book was catalogued, and again in 1992. In both cases, they returned the book within a few days of checking it out, and I have always imagined that they brought it back in shocked disbelief that it had been bound. I am not sure why I have held on to it for longer than my predecessors. The obtuseness ▶ 5.24 of it, perhaps, fascinates me: mute testimony to the potentials of reading machines and the inertias of archival and bibliographic conventions.

4.40 The real barrier that enforces the separation of surfaces may also be evident in objects that are not strictly mixed (*Agrippa* and *The Reactive Square*), but that undertake to enclose one medium in another. ▶ Figure 4.07 shows pages of a digital edition published by Octavo, Inc. of Geofroy Tory's 1529 treatise on the relation of the Latin alphabet to the human form, *Champ fleury*.

4.41 Octavo's digital editions undertake to remain as faithful as possible to the visual appearance of the original objects. They are scanned in full color and at several resolutions, allowing multiple levels of zooming. The page images are heavily cross-linked with navigational aids and scholarly commentaries; the editions include extensive bibliographic information and notes concerning the provenance of each work. Some editions allow selection and bookmarking of passages and full-text searching. They are distributed in Adobe Systems' Portable Document Format (PDF), a robust and efficient

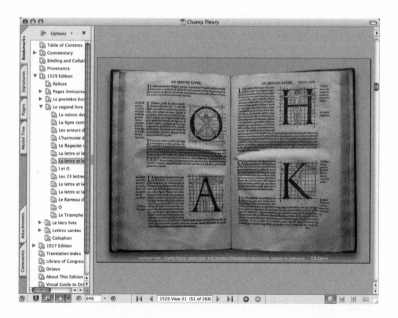

FIGURE 4.07. Octavo, Inc.'s digital edition of Geofroy Tory's *Champ fleury* (1529; 2003), viewed in Adobe Acrobat 7, Mac OS X 10.4 (2007).

file format that is device-independent and compatible with several operating systems. Titles in the series are well edited and uncommonly handsome. ▶N4.32

4.42   The high resolution of the images preserves some evidence of the material traits of the original works. Page surfaces are often wrinkled, foxed, and slightly translucent, and registration errors and imperfections in inking and printing are evident. What we see on the screen is very close to a high-quality photograph of the original book, embedded in the framework of Adobe's Acrobat software. In this regard, material specificities of the works are caught in a more tensive relation with elements of the GUI than is the case for the mixed print and digital works. The analog portion of the Octavo edition bears little resemblance to the codex pictured on the screen—in most cases, the user is unlikely to ever see the original text, and thus the medial dynamic of the work is almost entirely confined to the screen, between—again, that word should suggest a procedural liminality—the mechanism of the Acrobat application and the collection of pixels figuring the surface of the page. The disjunction of the original and its on-screen avatar is signaled by several aspects of the software—ironically, by some that are designed to improve readability: you "turn" pages by clicking on controls at the bottom of the window or by moving the thumbwheel in the scrollbar; you "jump" from section to section by selecting hypertext bookmarks.

4.43   In other words, polygraphic traits of the printed page are translated by or replaced by procedures and operations of the reading application's UI. These also are characterized by complex, inconsistent grammatextual effects, but some media-specific elements must intervene to sustain the reader's traversal of the two grammatextual fields, and one will always be in some way subservient to the other. The subjection of the page to the GUI would seem to be unavoidable in such cases, but the significance of this fact is more than pragmatic, because it touches on basic structures of intermedial semiotics. Our recognition of this permits us to see the objects within the window as, in this sense, informed or constrained by a real limit, beyond whose opaque surface nothing may be read. That each of these objects is marked by subsystems of perforation (the image of the supplicant in the *Book of Hours*, Tory's mappings of the human figure to loci of the Latin letter) does not change this. The global system of the reading software indicates that a homologous scheme of enframed surfaces is also characteristic of those openings of the page.

4.44 *Vicissitudes of the surface.* Such examples bring us close to thresholds of obscure regions. The perforation has, in effect, the form of a rim, a circuit around a site that its locus cannot touch upon: in this it resembles the bordering turn that Lacan associates with the source (Freud's *Quelle*) of the drive (Lacan 1973, 162–65). This fundamental structure suggests that we might include the page-as-object among the linguistic subclasses of Lacan's taxonomy of the delimited zones of the partial drives (along with the phoneme, the gaze, the voice, and the nothing [*rien*]). Those anatomical units of the book and the screen—its grammatextual organs and orthopedic systems, if you will—are paper or pixel variants of other zones catalogued by Lacan whose erotogenic functions are confirmed by bodily activities other than reading: the lips, the anus, the urethra, the vagina, the cone of the ear (Lacan 1966, 817).

4.45 Or the navel: Freud observes that there is always a spot in the dream that is "unplumbable," a *navel* (*"eine Stelle, an welcher er unergründlich ist, gleichsam einen Nabel..."*) (Freud 1940–52, 2–3:116; 1955–66, 4:111), where interpretation ceases to be productive. This is often taken to mean that the dreamwork is anchored in an absolute abyss, but Freud's metaphor is more precise than this: the bodily navel *folds back on its surfaces, just beyond its inner rim.* The homologous folding-back or -against itself of interpretation is contoured by the most archaic resistances that can be brought to bear on its medial presentation, and thus the genetic dimension of the fold is not hard to guess. Didier Anzieu observes that Freud runs into this inscrutable spot (*Stelle*) in the unraveling of the specimen dream of psychoanalysis, just as Oedipal undercurrents of the dream emerge. These are quickly tamped down, relegated to a footnote in Freud's text, literally moved to the margins (Anzieu 1988).▸N4.33

4.46 Rand and Robyn Miller cannily grasped the significance of this structure when they decided that the narrative method of the *Myst* video game series should depend on traversing umbilici in the form of "linking" books (these openings do not so much lead into another world as bring it forward by raising it to the surface of the page); and when they constructed the basic myth of the game world as a struggle between good and bad sons and good and bad fathers over possession of the mother; and when they illustrated the burned leaves of damaged linking books in the father's library with such extravagant labia that their anatomical analogy is unmistakable (▸ Figure

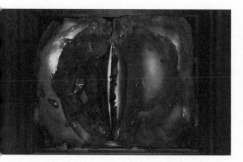

FIGURE 4.08. *Left:* One of the damaged books in the Library of Myst Island (Cyan, Inc., 1993). Books whose pages have been largely destroyed, such as this one, offer no response to the player's cursor. *Right:* A typical passageway in *Riven* (Cyan, Inc., 1997).

4.08). In *Riven*, the second game of the series, these forms are remapped to the landscape of islands of the Riven Age—entrances to caves, narrow crevices, doorways and portals—through which the player's avatar must pass as she unravels the problems of the game (▶ Figure 4.08). On the other side, she will soon be confronted by another such opening, and another, and so on; this series of invaginations, rather than depicting deeper revelations of the Age's mysteries, defines a closed loop, a threshold that leads back to itself. In other words, it is surface, folded or distorted in such a way as to open onto itself.[▶N4.34] These images are among the purest examples of the unreadable object in the age of the screen, and their evidence of a (sexual) crisis at the heart of the book and the archive must be understood as not only a motive of gameplay, but also of the game and its sequels' broader significance in the history of media.[▶N4.35]

4.47 The most common response to evidence of a real limit to reading is to ig-nore its effects ▶ 7.65. A manifestation of this strategy in digital simulacra of the page is that they all but discard evidence of its resistant materiality while retaining some of its formal traits. Thus, along with floating palettes and pop-up or pull-down menus, we encounter in digital editions running heads, margins, columns and gutters, page numbers; and devices for mark-ing one's place in the volume or on the page: Post-it Notes, paperclips, or dog-eared corners that may be turned up or down with a mouse click (▶ Fig-ure 5.01). Folded page corners on the left and right of the screen signal forward and backward movement, even though there is no visual analog of the gutter over which these facing "pages" might turn. Digital documents may resemble books some of the time (usually when "closed"), and then switch to another format when the conceit begins to fracture. Ostensibly, this repurposing of elements of the codex is motivated by their oft-cited familiarity to the user, who will more easily understand how to work the text if it resembles those whose methods she already understands.[N4.36] Names of the new reading machines, some made of software, some of hardware and software—most never released or discontinued—promise a compact resolution of medial difference: CyBook, eBook, Expanded Book, Dyna-Book, Glassbook, iBook, Living Book, PowerBook, Processed Book, Soft-Book, SuperBook, WebBook.

4.48 But "a book is not," as Ulises Carrión has observed, "a case of words, nor a bag of words, nor a bearer of words" (1993, 31). Nor is it merely—or even primarily—a "reading appliance" (Schilit et al. 1999). The page, the line, and the letter are more than (and also other than) the interface of the written and printed word. The appropriation in new media of conventions of the codex has occurred with little interrogation of the codex's substantive traits beyond their referential functions, or its periodicities and crises, the rich supports of effects beyond the mere making sense of words and images. (These are among the signal characteristics of the artist's book: folded, incised, deformed. The children's book usually deforms its medium with more caution, though examples of the field often represent substantive innovations in form and operation.[N4.37])

4.49 Projects in digital document design have attempted to figure analogs of paper-based reading by introducing mechanisms by which a digital document may be permanently altered each time it is read. Several projects have investigated this approach, layering the interface with maps of a document's use history, or by altering the appearance and behaviors of its navigation controls.[N4.38] Others have figured navigation history by evoking traces of material use: yellowing with age, deformation of the surface from handling, fingerprints, coffee stains, etc. While suggestive, these projects are hampered by the purposive character of "accidental" wear-and-tear: their designers conceive of the traces of use as metadata, describing not the potential resistance of the document's materiality, but rather the marks of its circulation among multiple users. These qualities are not, I would argue, equivalent to asemic attributes of the codex evident in its more adventurous forms. Grammatextualities and paratextualities of the page and the screen are not always intentional or even quantifiable in these ways.

4.50 *Reading is, before it can be anything else, surface-work.* Erasure (Ashbaugh, Blake, Johnson); folding (Massin's edition of Queneau ▶ 7.25, Roussel's *Nouvelles Impressions d'Afrique* ▶ 7.28); peeling (Barthes's onion layers, the Visible Woman's armorial plates ▶ 5.43); perforation (Newell, Thompson); plucking (*pflücken*: Freud's "Dream of the Botanical Monograph"); shuffling (Saporta, Michael Joyce, Shelley Jackson); and so on: ▶ N4.39 all are varieties of a crisis of surfaces that reading represses and memorializes, and that rereading, especially close, critical reading, must repeat. I propose the term *ex-foliation* for a loosely grouped set of procedures for provisionally separating the layers of the text's surfaces without resolving them into distinct strata or hierarchies, with the aim of understanding their expressive concurrencies. Since it must be bound to effects of historiation—that is, to the reader's (*this* reader's) recollections and anticipations of other significant surfaces ▶ 2.24—ex-foliation will be opportunistic, even capricious, in its address of surface-work. It implies no methodological responsibility, because it accepts a disjunction between the signifiers it isolates (they are immanent to the text or its performances) and the signifieds it derives from or articulates in response to those signifiers (the signifieds are a *historical* effect of historiation, specific to the reader). This it has in common with similar critical activities of textual decomposition and recomposition, such as Barthes's "starring" and "structuralist activity" ▶ 5.06.

4.51 It is my contention that the procedures of ex-foliation are well suited to the interpretation of the multiple and irregularly layered surfaces of objects in the digital field, especially those in which idioms of the GUI are of relevance to the expression and reception of meaning, or in which they are repurposed or subverted for aesthetic effect. The ancestry of human-computer interface design in human factors science and cybernetics has left that discipline unprepared to interrogate these operations; its emphasis is on diagnosing inefficiencies or ambiguities and reshaping user interfaces to defined, if evolving, conventions of program behavior. Literary-theoretical approaches to the digital field, while open in principle to aesthetic understanding, have been too often limited by their abstractions of program and interface and their emphases on narrative and mimetic operations. I will return to the second limit of our interpretation in later chapters and will end this chapter with an example of a text that challenges the first limit and illustrates a basic principle of my argument thus far: the material and grammatextual lessons of the codex, above all those of aberrant or eccentric codices, may be applied to objects of the digital field, in the expectation that *the specific*

mediality of the digital sign will be expressed most clearly in the outliers of
new media design practices.

4.52 For example, consider the images of printed pages interleaved in Elliott Peter
Earls's classic multimedia work *Throwing Apples at the Sun* (1996).▶N4.40
The overwritten pages shown in ▶ Figure 4.09 were scanned from Frank
P. Bachman's *Great Inventors and Their Inventions* (1918), an American
popular history of technology for children.▶N4.41 This portion of the original
text describes Alexander Graham Bell's experiments in the 1870s using a
dead man's ear as the receiver of a phonautograph, a device for capturing
sound as graphic information. The graphs shown on the right of the page
spread were copied from tracings on smoked glass made by the device.

4.53 The pages resemble other experiments in the "treatment" of found texts—
Johnson's *Radi Os*, but several of the overwritten pages also evoke Tom

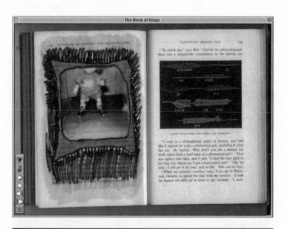

FIGURE 4.09. *Top:* "Pussy
cat pond," in Elliott Peter
Earls, *Throwing Apples
at the Sun* (1996). Image
copyright Elliott Peter Earls;
reproduced with permission.
Bottom: Frank P. Bachman,
*Great Inventors and Their
Inventions* (1918), pages
234–35. Collection of the
author.

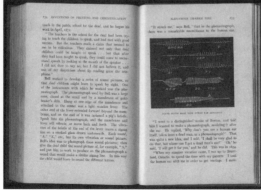

Phillips's *A Humument* (2005); the scorings of the text and hand-drawn illustrations and marginalia are typical of this genre. Retitled "The Book of Kings," Bachman's laudatory accounts of great inventors are in this context aggressively repossessed. The original copy appears to have been annotated by a previous owner, "William K——" (his name is scored out—rolling the mouse over it generates a sighing cry, "God bless you, William!"), who has inscribed the frontispiece with a fragment of doggerel: "I pity the river, I pity the brook, / I pity the guy who hooks this book."►N4.42 Rolling over these lines overlays the title page with the words "Great Inventors and Their Inventions by Elliott Earls," in one of Earls's original typefaces. (In addition to his typography and graphic design, Earls is renowned for his hyperkinetic stage shows, featuring simultaneous live and taped musical performance, madcap costumes, and multiscreen video, backed by a small factory of home-brewed electromechanical light and sound effects.) The repossession is further signaled by the selection of pages of Bachman's book shown in *Throwing Apples*. A note by Bachman reports that most of the chapter on Bell is based on the inventor's "own words," and that he "read and revised the description" (228). Earls's work thus rewrites a rewriting; he has taken over Bell's voice, textually marked in the narrative and materially marked in the graphs on page 235, and inscribed there a signature. This is the purest sign of historiation: a trace of a specific reading—specific to the reader and the condition of his reading, motivated by obscure and possibly indiscernible filiations of meaning—sharing the planes of the reading surface.

4.54 Linked to the pages of the Book of Kings are five examples of Earls's poster art, a catalogue of his typefaces, and numerous still images and snippets of video that may include some found material and home movies.►N4.43 The work's soundtrack is composed of drum machine loops, crashing cymbals, guitar riffs, whistles and applause of an audience, tape hiss, rattles, and chirps—"dark alt pop and suburban Hip-Hop," as Earls's Web site describes the songs.►N4.44 Lyrics and snippets of spoken word poetry are mostly in Earls's voice (usually reverbed or modulated in some way). A child speaks briefly; a woman sings tunelessly in the background. A poem, "Oranges of Hieronymus Bosch," about Henry Miller and 1980s pop sensation Sheila E. is read in the monotone of Apple's MacInTalk speech synthesizer: "I think he has stolen my life . . . those are my family roots—he devours them with gusto, with a verve and a nerve that excludes me. . . . Isn't she the tigress and the Euphrates?"

4.55 The elaboration of programmed responses ratchets up the force of this repossession. The text is an HCI nightmare, a farrago of GUI elements and
behaviors (▶ Figure 4.10).▶N4.45 Windows and controls open and close unpredictably; some controls seem not to behave the same way twice in a row.
Mouse targets (clicks and rollovers) are mapped irregularly: moving the cursor over or clicking on a shape in a window (a letter, a word, a contour)
sometimes opens another thread of action—another window, an animation,
a change in the soundtrack—but not always. Under other conditions, it may
open a different thread.▶N4.46 Some clicks deliver gnomic system messages
("Stiff poly legs . . . no rust ligaments," "Gilgamesh . . . I've fallen," "This
does nothing").

4.56 More than the other works I have discussed in this chapter, *Throwing Apples*
is a collection of surfaces bordered by the most frank fictions of disclosure,
which it openly and gleefully subverts. It remains, more than a decade after
its release, a bold example of a contrarian aesthetic: plainly the product
from the era of the GUI, it absorbs its conventions and redirects them—with
verve and dark wit—to other, unapologetically nonconformist, ends. Earls's
goals for the work are, first, self-promotion—it was and remains, as Kenneth Fitzgerald has observed, "the most baroque construction yet invented
to sell type" (1996, 42).▶N4.47 Second, the work as a whole—images, type,
sound, video, programming—is the product of a single individual working with off-the-shelf software and hardware and embodies an artistic program that Earls has, only half-ironically, described as "prosumptive" design
(Earls 1995). A fusion of consumption and production, *prosumption*—Earls
draws the term from the work of futurist Alvin Toffler—is characterized by
creative self-sufficiency and -reliance:

> MacWarehouse is the Rosetta stone. It is through this seemingly in-
> nocuous publication that we can gain a clear definition of the pro-
> sumptive designer, and better understand his or her role within so-
> ciety. Direct your own movies! Write your own music! Build your
> own recording studio! Desktop publish! Do your own accounting!
> I can bring home the bacon, fry it up in a pan—all on the Mac.
> *Elle* magazine for the infogentsia complete with implicit inferiority
> complex. Niki Taylor as Photoshop, smiles coyly from behind her
> Revlon patina and points to the "Real" supermodel in all of us. (Earls
> 1995)

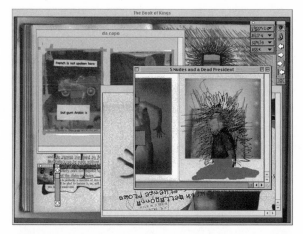

FIGURE 4.10. *Top:* "Hair pole (cat)," overlaid with multiple windows linked to it and menus and controls of the program, in Elliott Peter Earls, *Throwing Apples at the Sun* (1996). Image copyright Elliott Peter Earls; reproduced with permission. *Bottom:* Frank P. Bachman, *Great Inventors and Their Inventions* (1918), pages 74–75. Collection of the author.

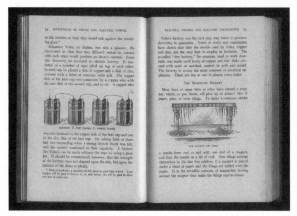

4.57 Fitzgerald rightly notes that the concept is not without political contradictions—"while everything Earls uses is off the shelf, those shelves aren't within everyone's reach" (1996, 42). The problem of access to tools is unchanged by even the most enthusiastic embrace of artistic pluralism. But a more materially relevant, medial, element is also encoded in the economy of prosumption: productive consumption is a mode of revision that leaves something of the subject behind in the matter of the archive that has enlarged by its operations. Bush's trails ▶ 1.39 and the products of Nelson's transclusions ▶ 2.03 and Barthes's structuralist activity ▶ 5.07 are not far from this.

4.58 Subscribing to a myth that inefficiencies of the book may be somehow corrected, many designers of new media appear to seek, in contrast to projects such as Earls's, to turn the digital artifact into a pure fetish-object, in what I would term a restricted economy of perversion: a phylactery, a reliable guarantee against the vicissitudes of reading, a meaning-making thing stripped of its ambiguity, contingency, and its fundamental, real insecurity. Rather than recognizing that the ramifying network exposes one to evidence of the farces of satisfaction, apologists of the new reading machines seem to hope that a well-designed *electronic* page or book will save us from the vicissitudes of the papered sign, on which the page's grammatextual registers *insist* in any reading. Earls's achievement reminds us that we should, instead, look at these surfaces, paper and screen, not through them. Designers and users in the digital field may need to be reminded of this, so that the late age of the book should not be accompanied by a forgetting of all that the word, line, and page can effect upon us.

4.59 During a lecture several years ago I introduced *Throwing Apples at the Sun* to a class of undergraduate students. One of them, a computer science major, came up after my lecture and complained that he found Earls's work disturbing, even repulsive. It violated, he said, every standard of human factors design upon which his computer science professors insisted. Moreover, he complained, it appeared not only to have no useful purpose but even to brandish that as a point of pride. In the course of our conversation, I observed that SuperCard, the software with which *Throwing Apples* was created, is a robust, object-oriented programming environment that requires strict adherence to program syntax, message hierarchies, and management of data and file types. The coding, original typography, and still image, video, and sound editing needed to produce *Throwing Apples*, I proposed, testified to Earls's extraordinary talents as a designer and programmer.

4.60 The student's opinion of Earls appeared changed by this. His objection to the work on principle was, he insisted, unwavering. But, he allowed, "it's pretty cool to think about how much work it must have taken to make it all look like a bad accident."

4.61 *Throwing Apples at the Sun* is the most typical work of digital media of the last twenty years. ▶N4.48

5.

Lexia Complexes

There is a kind of thinking without thinkers. Matter thinks. Language thinks. When we have business with language, we are possessed by its dreams and demons, we grow intimate with monsters. We become hybrids, chimeras, centaurs ourselves: steaming flanks and solid redoubtable hoofs galloping under a vaporous machinery.

—Shelley Jackson, *Patchwork Girl* {it thinks} (1995)

5.01 The term *lexia* was introduced to hypertext studies by George Landow in his 1992 book *Hypertext: The Convergence of Contemporary Critical Theory and Technology*:

> Hypertext, as the term will be used in the following pages, denotes text composed of blocks of text—what [Roland] Barthes terms a lexia—and the electronic links that join them. . . . Electronic links connect lexias "external" to a work—say, commentary on it by another author or parallel or contrasting texts—as well as within it and thereby create text that is experienced as nonlinear, or, more properly, as multilinear or multisequential. Although conventional reading habits apply within each lexia, once one leaves the shadowy bounds of any text unit, new rules and new experiences apply. (Landow 1992, 4; 1997, 3–4; 2006, 2–3) ▸N5.01

5.02 Landow's definition has been widely adopted by hypertext scholars writing from the vantage of literary and cultural studies, for whom it has become a critical commonplace. ▸N5.02 The circumstances of the term's derivation are rarely noted; they have also been misrepresented. ▸N5.03 Despite its success, however, Landow's version of the lexia is significantly different from Barthes's version, in that the former strips the latter of important functional attributes and neglects the specific linguistic and semiotic context in which the term was first applied. Barthes's lexia is a virtual structure of the reading situation. Landow's lexia is a concrete segment of the textbase. These forms may cross in a given reading of a given (hyper)text, but they are not equivalent; Landow's lexia is the more restricted and, I will argue in this chapter, the less effective as a critical concept. The term should be dropped from the vocabulary of new media studies or else redefined in keeping with Barthes's original use.▸N5.04

5.03 *The lexia as a "unit of reading."* Landow's stated source for the term is *S/Z*, Barthes's *tour de force* poststructuralist analysis of Honoré de Balzac's novella, *Sarrasine*. In that work, Barthes defines the lexia (*lexie*) as the primary "unit" in the reader's decoding of the novel's formal, literary, and cultural codes, and the basic segment of the critic's textual analysis (Barthes 1970, 20). This was not the first time Barthes had used the term in this way. Though he does not refer to them in *S/Z*, he had so used it in two important essays published in 1964, "Rhétorique de l'image" ("Rhetoric of the Image," 1964d) and "Éléments de sémiologie" ("The Elements of Semiology," 1964a).

5.04 In those texts, Barthes stresses the role of the reading subject in the lexia's operations. It is her engagement with a text, grounded in her conscious and unconscious knowledge of cultural systems that inform it, he proposes, that produces the specific parsings of signifiers that give the text meaning. These in turn sustain parsings of the text's signifieds and, more importantly, the evocation of signifieds that are not explicitly marked, but arrived at via the linguistic function of connotation.▸N5.05 For example, in his analysis of an advertisement for Panzani pasta, he notes that the three principal colors of the ad—yellow, green, and red—signal the pasta's "Italianity," eliciting, presumably, the reader's recollection of uses of the Italian tricolor in other contexts. Similarly, the studied casualness of the positions of the packages of pasta, tomatoes, onions, mushrooms, and grated Parmesan in the image evokes the pictorial tradition of the still life. Though that tradition is not explicitly signaled in the advertisement, the reader will grasp its relevance because she is familiar with other images in which the tradition is openly acknowledged (1964d, 41).

5.05 The lexia is the "large unit of reading" (*grande unité de lecture*) (1964a, 109) by which these literary-cultural connotations are sustained. On its basis, "each system of signifiers (lexicons [*lexiques*])" is made to correspond with a "body of practices and techniques" (109) known to the reader or viewer. These are formally and conceptually distinct from the text, but through connotation they come to function as signifieds of the text's lexicons. This mapping of signifiers to practices and techniques—even when anticipated by the text's or image's author—is specific to the reader; it is multiply oriented; it may even be internally inconsistent.

> Everything happens as if the image were read [*se donnait à lire*] by many persons and these persons could very well coexist in the same individual: the same lexia mobilizes different lexicons. . . . A plurality and a coexistence of lexicons exist in the same person; the number and identity of these lexicons form in a sense the idiolect of each of us. (1964c, 48)

5.06 As a "unit of reading," therefore, the lexia spans textual, cultural, and subjective dimensions of the reading encounter. As a critical concept, moreover, the term demarcates specific, even arbitrary, parsings of a text, whose significance depends on the reader's internalization of yet other texts and systems of meaning. These parsings are not—or not directly or principally—the consequence of an author's segmentations of the textbase, though she is responsible in most respects for the ordered material sequence of signifiers encountered by the reader. This is not to say that the reader's discernment of lexias and their significations are wholly original; they depend on her cultural and historical competencies, which may be shared with other readers, including the author. Other factors that may direct or limit the reader's recognition of a lexia's significance include institutional (ideological) and anthropological (experiential) structures; her degree of access to the archive anticipated or presumed by the author may compel her to mistake one reach for another. And, though Barthes does not observe this, it must also be the case that actualizations of lexias may vary for a given reader in relation to those that may have occurred in other encounters with the same text. In *S/Z* Barthes will stress that the lexia's connotations are not to be confused with mere association of ideas, because that is characteristic only of the "system of the subject," presumably a field that pertains only to her. Connotation "is a correlation immanent to the text or texts, or, if one prefers, it is an association operated by the text-subject [*texte-sujet*] within its own system" (1970, 15).

5.07 The context of these operations is spelled out in another Barthes essay of the early 1960s, "L'Activité structuraliste" ("The Structuralist Activity," 1964c).[N5.06] In that essay he contends that structuralism is not a school or a movement (its adherents are too diverse), and hardly a lexicon (its terminology is shared with a wide range of disciplines [213]). It is, he proposes, an *activity* characterized by an ordered series of certain "mental operations":

> The goal of all structuralist activity, whether reflexive or poetic, is to reconstitute an "object," in such a way as to make manifest in this reconstitution the rules of its functioning (the "functions" of the object). Structure is thus in effect a *simulacrum* of the object, but a directed and interested simulacrum, because the imitated object brings forward [*fait apparaître*] something that remained invisible, or if you prefer, unintelligible in the natural object. . . . Between these two objects, or the two times of the structuralist activity, *something new* is produced, and this novelty is nothing less than intelligibility in general. (1964c, 214–15)

5.08 "L'Activité structuraliste" is a kind of manifesto for practices of the lexia, which can be understood as both the support and the product of the cutting apart (*découpage*) and rearranging (*agencement*) typical of structuralist activity. Barthes's emphasis in the essay is on the activity's conceptual registers ("mental operations"), but his assertion that it produces something new implies that this must be materially sustained. The lexia would seem to fulfill this function in the manner in which it demarcates internal structures of the text or image and joins them to bodies of practices and techniques by which new meanings are attributed to those structures. Significantly, this attribution marks the discovered structures with something of its agent:

> The simulacrum is intellect added to the object, and this addition carries an anthropological value, in that it is [structural] man himself, his history, his situation, his liberty and even the resistance that nature raises in opposition to his spirit [*esprit*]. (1964c, 215)

5.09 To recast this argument in terms that I have used in earlier chapters, structuralist activity imprints its object with a signature ▶ 1.55 that is both original and faithful to a text's immanent structure. (This pairing of novelty and fidelity would be justified by Barthes's insistence that the generativity of connotation be something more than an association of ideas. However, associationism might also be incorporated into the model I propose here, insofar as it is activated by a textual semiotic.)▸N5.07 This effect is unique to the conditions in which the activity takes place and, we may presume, a history of prior reading that determines some of their aspects. In this context, the lexia can be understood to mark a point of contact between orders of the reader's archive—her cultural competencies, the prior trajectories of her textual competencies—and the object that is presented to her now. As she reads, she parses and reassembles, revises and recollects the archive and the object.

5.10 In brief, the lexia is activated—by this I mean something between the cognitive event of Barthes's "structuralist activity" and the linguistic-textual syncretism of Hjelmslevian catalysis—in relation to a specific situation involving a text and a reading subject.▸N5.08 Its partitioning of the text is above all opportunistic, as Barthes's definition of the term in *S/Z* emphasizes:

> The tutor signifier will be cut up into a series of short contiguous fragments, which we shall call lexias, since they are units of reading. This cutting up, it must be said, will be arbitrary in the extreme [*on ne peut plus arbitraire*]; it will imply no methodological responsibility, because it will be carried out only on the signifier, while the proposed analysis will be carried out only on the signified. The lexia will sometimes consist of a few words, sometimes several sentences; this will be a matter of convenience. It will suffice that the lexia be the best space possible in which one may observe meanings; its dimension, empirically determined, estimated, will depend on the density of connotations, which will vary according to the moments of the text. (1970, 20)

5.11 Barthes proposes only that the form of his interventions in *S/Z* is exemplary. His decomposition of Balzac's novella will not exhaust its significations; other segmentations of the tutor text might be effected under different conditions or with different aims, resulting in other spaces in which to observe the text's production of meanings. The critic's "starring" of the text (1970, 20) is arrived at empirically (one wonders what Barthes's drafts for *S/Z* looked like, what cuttings and rearrangements were discarded in the writing process), and it is pragmatic in the extreme. The critic's concern is foremost the "migrations of meaning" revealed by her interventions in seriatim presentations of the text.►N5.09 The extent to which meaning may be immanent to the units of which it is composed is not relevant to an analysis of its connotative system.►N5.10

5.12 Hjelmslev's influence on Barthes is clearest here. Glossematics' formalism is absolute; units of expression and content are defined purely in terms of a system of differences; their functions are activated in relation to the structures in which they are manifest. Planes of expression and content are divided and their divisions ordered and reordered without regard to their qualities. (This is Hjelmslev's most radical extension of Saussure: even the semantic register of speech is subdivided into atoms of meaning, semantemes, which combine in "concepts.") In the case of natural languages, these divisions are "non-conforming"—they are structured differently in each plane—though they are *isomorphic*: a segmenting of one is matched by a segmenting of the other, if not in a one-to-one relation of scale or function.►N5.11 Isomorphisms are detected by speakers of a language when they are confronted by new parsings of expression or content; this is the primary way in which they extend their grasp of the language and also how they may enlarge its potential significations. The linguist's and critic's method is similar, if more programmatic: working with a given corpus, she effects novel segments of the language-object—simulating thus an accidental encounter with a new phonemic or syntagmatic series. On their basis, she discerns functional segments and isomorphisms. Hjelmslev's version of this operation, "the commutation test," is notably more general than its correlate in phonology: he proposes that the test may be applied not only to units of the expression plane (phonemes), but to higher-level expressive units (words, syntagmas, perhaps constellations of syntagmas), and to units of content (Ducrot and Todorov 1972, 43; Siertsema 1965, chap. 9).

5.13 Barthes's procedures of cutting apart and rearranging, varying the terms of the fashion system, and starring the text resemble glossematics' commutation test, with three significant adaptations. First, he is willing to reduce or extend the scope of expressive segments as required to establish isomorphisms of content. The crucial factor in each case is "convenience": the segment's ability to evoke specific connotations in support of the critic's aesthetic or ideological purpose. Second, connotation is explicitly invoked as a factor in the commutation test: the validity of one or another expressive segment is measured by its evocation of signifieds *that are not a part of the corpus subjected to segmentation.* Third, this specific connotative application of the test is an indication of the global significance of the operation: the whole of the text's relational network is, Barthes proposes, accessible on the model of the individual cut:

> In this ideal text, the networks are many and interact, without any one of them being able to surpass the rest; this text is a galaxy of signifiers, not a structure of signifieds; it has no beginning; it is reversible; we gain access to it by several entrances, none of which can be authoritatively declared to be the main one; the codes it mobilizes extend as far as the eye can reach [*les codes qu'il mobilise se profilent à perte de vue*], they are indeterminable (meaning here is never subject to a principle of determination, unless by throwing dice [*sinon par coup de dés*]); the systems of meaning can take over this absolutely plural text, but their number is never closed, based as it is on the infinity of language [*ayant pour mesure l'infini du langage*]. (Barthes 1970, 12)

5.14 Landow cites this passage immediately before attributing to Barthes an anticipation of hypertext's segmentations, but he omits Barthes's parenthetical aside: "(meaning here is never subject to a principle of determination, unless by throwing dice [*sinon par coup de dés*])." The omission is significant. In its original form, the passage notes the arbitrary, performative character of the reader's attribution of meaning to the text. The structure of chance in this situation will always be inconsistently articulated: certain aspects of it cannot be known in advance, since they are effects of the reader's unique habits and history of prior reading and may depend on her anticipation of meaning across boundaries of textual units.[N5.12] (Joyce's "words that yield" depend on this anticipation, in that they pin node segmentation to larger lexial structures ▶ 6.10.) The deleted reference to throwing dice bears out multiple valences of these operations, anchored in the text's material presentation: Barthes can only mean by this to allude to Mallarmé's *Un Coup de dés jamais n'abolira le hasard* ▶ 4.19.[N5.13] Mallarmé's spatially dispersed, grammatextually nuanced text welcomes multiple and variable parsings of its surface beyond the conventional segments of line and page, inviting the historiated mobilizing of codes that Barthes associates with the cut.

5.15 All of Barthes's descriptions of the lexia, especially those of *S/Z*, are directed outward in this way, to contingent and connotative fields by means of which the "infinity of language"—a more Hjelmslevian than Saussurean concept—is sustained and programmatically extended (Barthes 1964a, 4.2–4.4). In support of this extension, the granularity of the lexia will vary, not according to principles of grammar or syntax or the constraints of the writing or display surface, but according to requirements of connotation. For the reader who is also a critic, these requirements are, above all, pragmatic ("all we require is that each lexia should have at most three or four meanings to be enumerated" [Barthes 1970, 20]); the principal difference between her method and those of a "mere" reader is that the critic's caprice in cutting and pasting the text will be undisguised.▸N5.14

5.16 *For the lexia, all the same.*▸N5.15 Landow's mapping of the lexia to a predefined syntagma (a "block") of the hyper-textbase cannot adequately account for complex and contingent operations evinced in Barthes's original definition. Landow's lexia is too much the measure of a prior segmentation by one subject, the hypertext's author. Barthes's lexia, in contrast, is founded on a more opportunistic, semiotically diffuse and multiple, subjective and situational, "unit of reading" that is both materially bound to the author's prior divisions of the text and the reader's resituating of it in relation to the prior history of her reading. If, however, we remap Barthes's original concept to defiles of the digital text, and if we retain the variable dimensionality and orientation of lexias indicated by the examples of *S/Z* and "Rhétorique de l'image," we may be rewarded with applications that Landow's restricted definition does not permit.▸N5.16 A single hypertext node might be parsed into multiple lexias, composed of parts of the words or images it contains.▸N5.17 A lexia might span multiple nodes; mnemonic labors of reading require this textual basis. It might be inductively joined to elements of another text, or to the text as a whole, *on the initiative of the reader*, without any indication of this relation having been explicitly marked in the text. In this third case, the lexia is activated as such by its engagement of other texts, according to the reader's linguistic and textual competence.▸N5.18 (The connotative extension I noted between the first line of Mallarmé's poem and a key phrase of *S/Z* represents an example of this.)

5.17 Such a model of the lexia provides a textual basis for contingent events of recollection and elaboration typical of hypertext reading. Because it is not a priori synonymous with a given syntagma (a node or series of nodes) and

may include textual patterns that do not signify sequentially, this version
of the lexia takes into account effects of structure that are bound to or activated by the reader's encounters with specific syntagmas, but do not correspond directly to their segmenting of the textbase. I have shown in previous chapters that such effects are central to operations of reading described
by Bush, Nelson, and other early theorists of hypertext. In later chapters I
will show that they are central also to operations of some analog reading
machines. In the remainder of this chapter I will argue that this model of
the lexia provides a useful basis for interpreting historiated reading in the
digital field.

5.18 *Lexia complexes.* In his 1995 book *Lexis Complexes*, Nelson Hilton proposes a series of close readings of works by modern British and American authors based on "lexis complexes" characteristic of their works. The
"lexis" portion of this term fits the Greek word it transliterates, meaning
"speech," "diction," or "style": the writerly vocabulary of an author, the
sum of her linguistic and formal vocabulary, habits, and tics (Hilton 1995,
1). The terms of a writer's lexis, he argues, are *complexes*—he cites both
the psychoanalytic sense of the term and its Empsonian use (some words
are *complex*). They are extensive, multivalenced; they spin out in networks
of meaning that exceed a writer's consciousness and intention. (The title
of Hilton's opening chapter is "Intentions in Tension": intentional aims of
a writer's language are drawn—the lexis is a ductile form—into networks
defined by signifying chains as general as a cultural lexicon and as specific
as the sum of her uses of a given word and her early experience of language
acquisition [15–16].) Nodal points (Freud's *Knotenpunkte*, 1940–52, vols.
1–2; 1955–66, vol. 5: chap. VII, E) of a writing, lexis complexes may also be
nodal points of a reading, in that the reader will bring to the text her recollection of associations and intentions and discover in the text its crossings
with that archive (Hilton 1995, 18). Hilton is intrigued by the possibility
that these points of intersection may indicate the more general structure
that binds the reader to the author's text. Leo Spitzer's "click" of recognition of the "one word, one line" that really matters and Michael Riffaterre's
concept of the hypogram represent models of such a structure (19). The
doubling and crossing of writers' and readers' lexes may, Hilton argues,
"image" archaisms of writers' literary language (21).

5.19 Lexias, in Barthes's version and the version I propose, may be a basis of
complexes in Hilton's use of that term. They are generated by (and genera-

tive of) multiple, virtual structures of meaning, variable in their reach and subtended by operations of the author's and the reader's archives, conceived both as enclosures (Bush's model) and extensions (Nelson's model). Thus the value of defining the lexia as an abstract and dynamic unit characteristic of a specific reading in a specific context; materially grounded but always in semiotic tension with orders beyond it. Sociolects and idiolects of reading are able to cross here: lexias may also—intuitively, Hilton's optimism seems justified—point to generalizable parsings and rearrangements of a textbase that indicate commonalities of reading or in some cases objective significations. For example, a trait that is common to different readers' scansions of a given hypertext, or one reader's multiple scansions of it over time, can be correlated, Douglas suggests, with a best-fit model for interpreting narrative ambiguities (Douglas 2000, 103–6). Distinct outcomes of these operations may be few in number, since the inductive and deductive procedures of reading will render some sequences unproductive and thus ill-favored (Ryan 2001b).

5.20   A convergence of technologies and critical theories of reading in the digital field—the premise of Landow's *Hypertext*—is marked in these operations, though the period of their convergence long predates hypertext. *Reading is one of the sciences of combinations*: Pascal's discovery of the mathematics of probability in 1654, Lacan observes, supplanted a science of things that are found always at the same place with another, of the combination of places themselves (Lacan 1978, 344). A distinctly modern practice of reading begins in that moment; a theory of the scene of reading as a product of stochastic phenomena and a fixed textbase is marked for the first time. Yet, certain elements of these combinatorics may be traced to even older practices, in the addressing schemes of artificial memory and their encoding of subjective history. The author of the *Ad Herennium* suggested that every fifth locus be marked by a golden hand and every tenth by the face of a friend named Decimus ▶ 2.42. Mixed variants of such schemes must, we can assume, be permitted—the face of a friend named Quinqus in place of the golden hand? Quinqus's hand? To be repeatable, a mnemonic must be contrived from the substance of a shared symbolic yet meaningful in a specific way to the one who applies it.

5.21   Why, for example, do I find this illustration from *Alice's Adventures in Wonderland*—*this* illustration, as it appeared in Voyager's 1991 "Expanded

Book" (▶ Figure 5.01)—more memorable than, say, John Tenniel's better-known depictions of Alice surrounded by a cyclone of cards, or seated with the Mad Hatter and his other guests at the Tea Party? Already, on the page—which this window is meant to emulate and expand—Alice's grasping hand and the White Rabbit's anxious withdrawal constitute a disturbing departure.▶N5.19 The image is one of the few of Tenniel's drawings for the Alice novels in which she poses a menace to the inhabitants of Wonderland, though it must also be said that the risk for the Rabbit seems more accidental than intentional. She does not mean him harm; it is only the difference of scales that poses a danger.

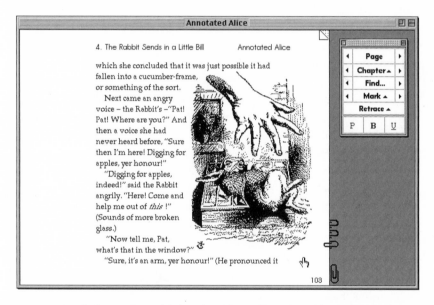

FIGURE 5.01. Quinqus shows his hand. " 'Now tell me Pat, what's that in the window?' 'Sure it's an arm, yer honour!' (He pronounced it 'arrum.') 'An arm, you goose! Who ever saw one that size? Why it fills the whole window!' 'Sure, it does, yer honour: but it's an arm for all that.' 'Well, it's got no business there, at any rate: go and take it away!' " From chapter 4 in Lewis Carroll's *Alice's Adventures in Wonderland* in the Voyager Expanded Book edition of Martin Gardner's *The Complete Annotated Alice* (1991), Mac OS 7.5 (1995). The illustration at the right edge of the page was drawn by John Tenniel for the 1866 publication of Carroll's novel. Note the simulated dog-eared page corner in the upper right, the paperclips inserted along the right edge of the page, and the HyperCard cursor (the pointing finger) in the lower right corner.

5.22 Yet the incongruity of the illustration in this context, within the Expanded Book and all that this entails in how the image is presented—"why it fills the whole window!"—seems to me increased by the machinery of the interface, the floating palette of control buttons, the ersatz paperclips to mark the pages, the simulated dog-ear, and so on. Here, contrasts of scale also appear to mark other, obscure interventions and associations, and in that respect to carry added, or perhaps different, significance than they might in an un-expanded book. Alice's great palm and fingers reaching into the page (the screen), echoed by the milder gesture of the cursor—HyperCard's seldom acknowledged legacy to the World Wide Web (▶ Figure 5.01)—signify in excess, on registers unrelated to her adventure or even to a tradition in print and film of clumsy giants and hapless dolls (Gulliver, *King Kong*, *Attack of the 50 Foot Woman*).

5.23 A difficulty in determining the nature of this excess, when and how it is pro-duced without being explicitly marked (mere analogy is not enough; there is no convention like the still life that we might cite here to wrap things up neatly) is a function of a formal limit of Barthes's concept of the lexia. I have stressed until now the lexia's connotative operations. While these may include suprasegmental traits, it is unclear how they may fully account for meanings that obtain only by indirection or suspension—in other words, as pure patterns of reading that may, without our really understanding this, orient our reception of a text's signs.

5.24 In a 1970 essay titled "Le Troisième sens" ("The Third Meaning")—it forms a triplet with the early essays on the semiotics of photography[N5.20]—Barthes proposes that some images evoke a level of meaning beyond communication (their "informational" values) and signification (their "symbolic" values), which he terms "signifying" (*signifiance*) (1982c, 45). This "third meaning [*sens*, also 'way']" of the image he characterizes as "obtuse" (*obtus*) (the others are "obvious"): something in the image's structure resists interpreta-tion, is fundamentally "aberrant" within it, but nonetheless orients our re-ception of the image without being drawn into well-tried conventions or idi-oms specific to a given artist. He cites examples in selected stills from Sergei Eisenstein's *Ivan the Terrible* (1944), in which details of the image vaguely refer beyond it without seeming to have anything expressly to do with the (obvious) meaning or symbolism of the scene from which they are captured: the curve of a kerchief on an old woman's brow, an actor's false beard jutting at an unnatural angle. These elements, he observes, "form a dialogism" with obvious meanings, but so obscurely, so "tenuously," that there is no guarantee that they are intended by the maker of the image (1982c, 49). They are accidental, even trivial or irrelevant from the perspective of interpretation. Yet they are, demonstrably, activated in or by attention to some quality of the image that evokes in an interrupted or fragmented way something beyond it, our response to which drifts on the relay of our having recognized this association:

> my reading remains suspended between the image and its description, between definition and approximation. If we cannot describe the obtuse meaning, this is because, unlike the obvious meaning, it copies nothing: how to describe what represents nothing? (1982c, 55)

5.25 Do I propose that some element of the image shown in ▶ Figure 5.01 is "obtuse"? My troubled response to Voyager's expansions of a page out of Carroll and Tenniel suggests something of this kind. Is it the content of the image—by which I mean Alice's monstrous hand *and* its correlate in the HyperCard cursor—that I find memorable, or its inconsistent hybridity, its naïve but culturally loaded "expansion" of Carroll's book? That the third meaning is an effect of media is implied in "Le Troisième sens." Barthes's concept relies on the still as the privileged site of the third meaning's mark on the filmic ("the still . . . is the fragment of a second text *whose existence never exceeds the fragment*; film and still meet in a palimpsest relation, without our being able to say that one is *above* the other or that one is *extracted* from the other" [1982c, 60]). The still, he asserts, supports "vertical" and "instantaneous" readings of the film that depart from its serial programs. The transposition of those programs to the snapshot of the still appears, in fact, to justify these readings and technical traits of moving and still photography to open the space of difference in which they are possible.

5.26 In the case of an expanded *Alice*, I am confronted by an object that openly simulates the printed page on the screen (with additional "features") and also signals deep incommensurabilities of these media. Thus the incongruity and obtuseness, of this reproduction of Tenniel's image in this particular framing, in which its darkly humorous dramatization of contrasting dimensions evokes a specific medial heteronomy—"so deuced realistic!" ▶ 4.09—

that neither the creator of the image nor, we may assume, the publishers of the expanded book anticipated.

5.27 *For example: Another way of breaking branches.*[N5.21] Midway through his decomposition of *Sarrasine*—by his own admission, it could have come at another segmentation of the novella, any (though he does not say this) but the first—Barthes compares concurrencies of narrative action to lacemaking. The grouping of codes effected by reading has, he says, the form of a braid; the work of reading, gathering and intertwining the inert threads, makes out of its voices something more than what each expresses individually. "We know the symbolism of the braid: Freud, considering the origins of weaving, saw in it the labor of woman braiding her pubic hairs to form the penis she lacks" (Barthes 1970, 166). A reader unfamiliar with Freud's 1932 lecture on "Femininity" may feel left behind in a rush (a braid?) of parataxes.[N5.22] But she should have been prepared for this. *Sarrasine* is a story of a naïve man's unrequited love for a castrato. Though at this point in the analysis La Zambinella's secret has not yet been revealed to Sarrasine—let us assume also that Barthes's reader has not read Balzac's novella before reading its decomposed version—Barthes has laid the groundwork for the relevance of Freud's myth of the braid, delimiting earlier spaces of castration's camp and the castrato's posterity (1970, 42–46). And in any case, the allusion to Freud is surely meant to seal the paratactic sequence narratives-lace-braid-phallus with a note of scandal. Even a careless reader of Freud "knows" of his notorious pansexualism, and his tendency to frame every relation in terms of one fundamental act. "Castration is contagious," Barthes writes, "it touches all that it approaches" (1970, 204).

5.28 (But: Freud does not in fact propose that women took up braiding to construct replacements for their missing penises. Shame, the feminine characteristic par excellence, he says, "has as its purpose, we believe, concealment of genital deficiency [*den Defekt des Genitales zu verdecken*]." Plaiting and weaving, he proposes, are technologies—women have invented few others, he adds [absurdly]—inspired by the growth of pubic hair during sexual maturity. "Nature herself would seem to have given the model which this achievement imitates. . . . The step that remained to be taken lay in making the threads adhere to one another, while on the body they stick into the skin and are only matted together" [Freud 1940–52, 15:142; 1955–66, 22:132]. Where Freud finds evidence of surface-work, Barthes reads labors of a pseudo-erection. The former might be seen to resemble the aporetic work of reading, and the latter a possibly defiant, probably quixotic, stand against the effects of such work.)

5.29 "We know [*on connaît*] the symbolism of the braid." Even the most original reading must at some point prop itself on a *doxa* particular to a given textual type. Or one that is overdetermined by a reading program, in search of prominences where an opening and a surface may be indicated, for example. *S/Z* is roughly contemporary with "Le Troisième sens"; the essay does not mention the lexia and the book does not mention a third meaning. But we may be justified in seeing a point of contact between the two concepts in this episode of the braid, the object of which (the Freudian phallus) would be the most obtuse and aberrant of all objects. If that is the case, then Barthes's reprisal of the term "lexia" from his earlier essays can be said to have been shifted by the pull of the third meaning, away from the field of connotative operations *stricto sensu*, to the field of expressive forms.

5.30 These will be indicated, not only by graphic, textual, and aural elements (iconic and ideogrammatic grammatexts) but also by sequential and algorithmic operations (diagrammatic and alphabetic grammatexts); by all the traits, then, of the "vertical" parsing of the segment, distinct from its serial presentations. Barthes's proposition that the fetish function of the braid illustrates reading's response to castration anxiety enters via the purest conceit of form, at the level of signifying (*signifiance*): the concurrency and entanglement of narrative actions in *Sarrasine* evokes, he writes, the image of Valenciennes "created before us under the lacemaker's fingers." This leads to the figure of the braid, and that to one of the more fantastic set pieces of Freudian anthropology: a scene of prehistoric women twisting their pubic hairs to obscure a primal cut. The sequence of these figures is itself a knotting or a braiding of incongruous elements and their combination in this way is the mechanism that makes the figure of the braid work. Which is to say: in the seriatim of the line and the page, between and across the units of Barthes's writing, interspersed with his segmentations of Balzac's text, the figure of the braid is held up, is motivated by programs of media, so as to provide a snapshot of a field state whose expressiveness exceeds the sum of the circuits that compose it. Likewise, we may remember, the Xanalogical braid achieves its archival usefulness by the manner in which it is sliced

▶ 2.01.

5.31 *For example: WYSIWYG.* Upon opening the Windows version of Shelley Jackson's 1995 hypertext fiction *Patchwork Girl; or, a Modern Monster,* the reader is confronted with the image shown in ▶ Figure 5.02.[N5.23]

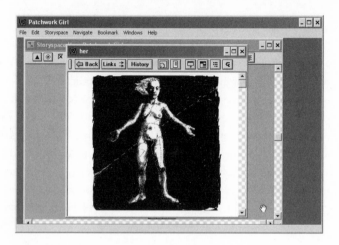

FIGURE 5.02. Shelley Jackson, *Patchwork Girl* {her}, 1st edition, Storyspace Reader 2.0 (2000), Windows XP (2001). Reproduced by permission of Eastgate Systems, Inc.

5.32 In its default configuration, the hypertext displays two windows on the screen concurrently: that belonging to the currently selected writing space (in this case, {her}), and that belonging to the Storyspace Map.[N5.24] The reader can switch the order in which the windows are stacked by selecting one or the other with the cursor. Thus, clicking on the titlebar of the window titled "Storyspace Map: Patchwork Girl," initially shown behind and just above the {her} space, brings the map view to the foreground and sends the {her} window to the background ▶ Figure 5.03.

5.33 The windows are visually distinct but procedurally integrated: activating a link in the currently selected writing space closes its window and opens the window of the space to which the link points; when a space's window is opened, the corresponding icon in the map is selected and, if necessary, the map zooms in or out and scrolls horizontally or vertically to reveal the icon more clearly. The map can also be used to change the sequence of spaces opened and closed: selecting an icon in the map replaces the currently selected writing space with that corresponding to the icon.

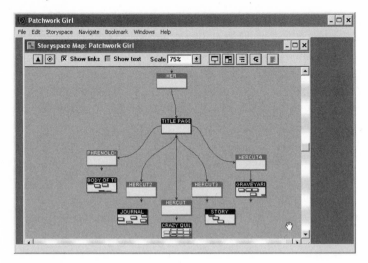

FIGURE 5.03. Shelley Jackson, *Patchwork Girl*'s Storyspace Map, 1st edition, Storyspace Reader 2.0 (2000), Windows XP (2001). Reproduced by permission of Eastgate Systems, Inc.

5.34 In their initial states, these document windows take up most of the visible space within the application window, though it is possible to reduce each to an arbitrary size and to expand the application window to the dimensions of the screen. In theory, this would permit the reader to see the whole of both windows (if perhaps not all of each window's contents) at the same time, assuming her monitor is sufficiently large to allow this. But that arrangement of the screen objects is an exceptional case; it does not fit either the typical or the default situations of reading Jackson's text, in which each window partly obscures the other.

5.35 The initial constraint on what may be seen at one time is *Patchwork Girl*'s first demonstration of a revision of the GUI's techniques of discovery ▶ 7.43: visually distinct, the windows are procedurally, semiotically, and grammatextually *entangled*; now one (complex) object, now two. The narrative effects of this semi-concurrency and semi-seriality are also multiplied, as the reader is free—and possibly encouraged—to interpret switching one or the other windows to the foreground as a sign of narrative sequence or simultaneity. The entanglement is sustained by further dimensions of this diptych (we must risk multiplying dimensions of the text in all senses; multiple ge-

ometries knot together in this way), which we may characterize as those of
depth (the procedural and visual interiority of the archive) and *extensibility*
(the archive's procedural and visual dispersal).

5.36 The dimension of depth is signaled by the formal similarity of visual fields
enclosed by the two windows. The map view (▶ Figure 5.03), which the user
will (correctly) assume on a first encounter describes the hypertext's deep
structure, schematically repeats the attitude of the Patchwork Girl's naked
limbs and torso (▶ Figure 5.02). Toggling between the windows—that is
how their similarity is syntactically activated—their anatomical correspondence is obvious: two series of spaces to the left, for her left arm and leg,
two series to the right, for her right arm and leg, one pair beneath, to mark
the downward vector of her stance and the visual insistence of her belly
and mons pubis. Already (I write here in terms of the logical thread of a
reading, not its temporal dimension, though it takes a quantity of time for
this logical relation to come into play), iconic values of the opening image of the Patchwork Girl and the map view are enjambed by the mere
event of moving from one window to the other. The feedback between them
is complex. Each, in effect, figures the other: the image as the embodied,
denser, version of the map; the map as the exploded, more limpid version of
the image. The map, *because its digraphs have been arranged in repetition*
of the Patchwork Girl's opening gesture, both represents a double of the
textual structure of the narrative (and, implicitly an example of the canon
of flowcharting, outlining, and graphemic visualization of narratives) and
signifies grammatextually, by way of its optical and procedural proximity
to the image. Because its parts repeat the map's arrangement, the image
is implicitly schematized as if composed of textual units: the Patchwork
Girl's gesture signifies, not only in relation to pictorial conventions for representing the female body, but also in relation to the map, which serves as
an intermediary to and elaboration of those conventions.▶N5.25 In the way
of the Panzani ad's allusion to the still-life tradition ▶ 5.04, the digraphic
text alludes to conventions of scientific and other textual genres in which
such objects are common; in the same way, the reader of *Patchwork Girl*
discerns the image's citations of those conventions, and thus activates a
lexia that joins them. In this case, however, the allusion's ironic or parodic
character—the distinction is hard to measure—is overdetermined by *Patch-*
work Girl's knowing reliance on idioms of the GUI. In the context of the
screen and in the presence of menus, window control widgets, and full-text

search features, we may reasonably expect that a flow chart–like diagram is a depiction of textual structure. But its collation here with the image of the Patchwork Girl illustrates a trait of diagrammatic grammatexts that is common in literary texts created for the screen: the orientation of hierarchies signaled by the diagram is ambiguously defined, overrun by ideogrammatic meanings. Which is determinate of the other is unclear, perhaps irresolvable.

5.37 In my reading of the hypertext, other visual-textual traditions are suggested by the Girl's initial stance. Facing us, her legs apart, arms open, palms turned upward, her position resembles a posture of prayer. In Christian art prior to the fifth century, the *orans* posture (from the Latin *orare*, to pray; in French and German, *orante*; in English, *orant* or *orans*) was chiefly associated with female figures in attitudes of ecstatic prayer or prophecy; thereafter, *orans* representations are almost exclusively of men in liturgical settings—though variants of the earlier, feminine imagery survive in minor artistic genres and in Marian iconography. ▶N5.26 In contemporary Christian practice, the *orans* is an element of the Catholic Mass (where it is assumed by the celebrating priest), and is common during prayer in charismatic Protestant traditions. In these contexts, the posture signals the supplicant's willingness to take on the wounds of faith (Christ is often depicted demonstrating the injuries of the cross in this posture).

5.38 The ironies of this system of intertexts are complex and multiple. The Patchwork Girl begins as a collection of body parts, resurrected from the grave by Victor Frankenstein to be a companion for his first monster. In Jackson's retelling, the Girl is saved from the second death recorded in Mary Shelley's novel by Mary herself, who hides the survival of her well-loved creation by writing it out of her text—and, indirectly, into *Shelley* Jackson's work. Each of these persons constitutes a *textual* subject of the fiction: the frame narrative is recounted by the female monster; a substantial thread of the fiction weaves passages from the novel with others purporting to be excerpted from Mary's secret journal. Some passages seem to slip from the female monster's voice to another voice that describes the conditions in which she writes a text that appears to be . . . *Patchwork Girl*. Crossings of fiction and metafiction multiply in this space; they are determined by structures of return, of revision—in short, of *resurrection*, in a complexly textual application of the term.

5.39 The Patchwork Girl's nudity is an obvious and ironic revision of the *orans*'s modern variants, especially of its Marian forms. The Girl does not demurely disguise her sex; she makes no pretence of purity or submissiveness; such concerns are irrelevant to her. Her openly sexualized position is profane in the strictest sense of that term; this invocatory stance embodies a relation to her maker from which immaterial myths of origin have been purged in every way except as ironic intertexts. They are replaced with textual myths, in which the signifiers *Mary* and *Shelley* are elements of an initial pact with the reader regarding the conditions of narration. The Girl's gesture in the image constitutes both an invitation to read and, in its dynamic pairing with the map that doubles that gesture, an invocation of strategies of reading, in which a potential narrative exhaustion is possible for the conjectural subject whose knowledge of the text the map appears to quantify and, in a precise and specifically grammatextual sense of the term, it also *graphs*.

5.40 *Dreams of the body jungle.* This heterogenous structural-narrative-anatomical complex is reiterated in the interposition of five spaces between the topmost pair of spaces ({her} and {title page}) and the array of nested and linked spaces at the bottom of the map, which compose the bulk of *Patchwork Girl*'s textbase and narrative sequences. The monumental textual forms of {title page} rest on as opaque a surface as any of the hypertext's several images—"PATCHWORK GIRL; | OR, A MODERN MONSTER | BY MARY/SHELLEY, & HERSELF | a graveyard, | a journal, | a quilt, | a story, | & broken accents | (sources)." The title's lines are linked to other units of the textbase, but its evocation of its print precursors (the title page of Mary's 1818 novel among them) blocks any readerly initiative to read the space as a mere index of other spaces. It stands instead as a wrapping of the text's interiors in a facsimile of an object whose function is degraded by the reversal of a print-based hierarchy of title and emblem, or title and half-title. The {her} image is the first thing we see when opening the text, and in the course of our reading, the title is revealed to us as an attribute of the image. {Title page} marks further scramblings of hierarchy: the two Shelleys (Mary and Jackson) are conjoined with something termed "Herself," who may be the unnamed female monster, some aggregate of the Shelleys, or of all three.

5.41 Four of the five spaces in the second tier of (▶ Figure 5.03) are variations on the opening image, its regions scrambled and dislocated (▶ Figure 5.04). Or *desutured*, as if moving through defiles of the map view must tear apart and

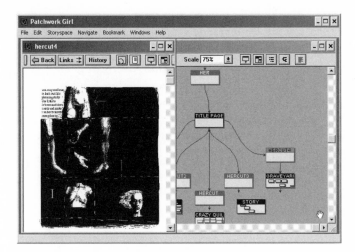

FIGURE 5.04. Shelley Jackson, *Patchwork Girl* {hercut4}, 1st
edition, Storyspace Reader 2.0 (2000), Windows XP (2001).
Reproduced by permission of Eastgate Systems, Inc.

disorder what had been stitched before, before the process of reading might
make it whole again. ▶N5.27

5.42 The fifth space in this tier, {phrenology}, shows a phrenological chart (presumably the head of the Patchwork Girl, her scalp shaven), its regions labeled so as to correspond to major threads of the space {body of text} to
which it is linked. But the labels are, the reader soon discovers, unreliable:
clicking on them takes you to nodes that at best fit the label approximately.
With this occult science of the pseudomap, the phrenological chart repeats
in simpler form the opening diptych's subversion of the map's utility. ▶N5.28
And it echoes in the quaint practice it celebrates, of divining meaning from
the irregularities of a surface, other practices of reading-as-palpating, as
lifting away or peeling back; as forms, then, of ex-foliation ▶ 4.50.

5.43 And in that peeling back, I find that other lexias are activated. These collations around and through the image of the Girl evoke a fetish-object of
American public-school education: the multileaf anatomical charts of the
household encyclopedia, or the life-sized idols (I use the word advisedly) of
junior high school biology courses: the "visible man" and "visible woman,"

transparent if unyielding flesh fitted over muscles, organs, and bone, their parts revealed and hidden by the lowering and raising of onionskin or the removing and replacing of an armorial plate. The introduction of the Patchwork Girl—naked and framed by a window enclosed by another that encloses others, hinting at windows, windows within windows, perhaps revealing other such bodies (▶ Figure 5.02)—invites the comparison to these memorable bodies of my adolescence. With one proviso: the ambiguous reality of the anatomized body, page, or idol must be accounted for, not swept away in the dilation of an imaginary invited by its portals: the opening reveal of Jackson's text cannot be construed as a mortification of the body's surface as the route of entry to an idealized interiority.▶N5.29

5.44 More important than the figure of the cut in *Patchwork Girl* is that of the scar that joins edges of a cut and inverts its section into a palpable and resistant barrier. Where the cut is dissective, the scar is aggregative, just as the organs that compose the Girl remain individual and whole, even after they have been transplanted into her. Her dream of an inner bodily world is nourishing rather than alarming:

> The hearts roost like pheasants on high bone branches. When I shinny up to examine one more closely I will discover the source of the sound I have been hearing since I first wandered into the jungle; the hearts are alive, they beat at a slow, nearly vegetable rate, with a deep cluck and boom. Intestines hang in swags from ribs and pelvic crests, or pile up like tires at the ankles of legs become trees, resting their thick links on the drenched mud. Ovaries hang like kumquats from delicate vines and through all this I will make my way, snapping the occasional vein as I pass so the cut ends dangle bleeding...
> {Dream of the Body Jungle}

5.45 More acrobatics in the treetops, though here the aim seems to be less to spin out possibilities of an arborescent trope than to intertwine its extremes in the shape of a peaceable space we also call an *arbor* ▶ 2.10. Its parts are segmented and integral, rather than breached. They can be climbed on and walked over and beneath—somatic correlates for wanderings of the eye and mind during the act of reading? They are *organized*, in the sense of having been made into something like organs, and they seem to function independently of the whole that is composed of them.▶N5.30

5.46 As for the perforated page, the surface persists as such beneath each of these windows ▶ 4.36. The figure of the "visible woman" would function in this context as an emblem, not of realized or potential discovery, but of the return of an object's opaque resistance, its libidinal charge, after the shock of the revelation. What is left over, what remains, when her gesture appears as forthright and demystified? The frank display of her potential interiority does not exhaust that scene of its biological or textual generativity—once more, the map misleads, encourages us to assume that this conceit of the GUI holds true without ambiguity. Her arms and legs are held open (this is what we see first, when we *open* the hypertext), as if to say, *WYSIWYG* ("What You See Is What You Get," the rallying cry for defenders of the GUI in the early period of its ascendancy ▶ 7.43); all is phenomena here, no noumena.

5.47 But the procedure of discovery in this case also subverts its aims; the return of the noumenal object seems to be unavoidable after a period of reflection, as if it were there all along, hiding from me in plain sight. This visible woman is anatomically accurate in a way that her encyclopedic and plastic sisters were not. Nude but not depilated, her pubic triangle is positioned at the window's center. It diffuses into shadows encroaching on her limbs and torso, and is doubled—twice—by the suture passing from lower left to upper right. Against this backdrop, the Patchwork Girl's stance seems candid but also abstract: this is a 1-bit image: black or white, 1 or 0, leaving no room for nuances below the dimensions of the pixel.[N5.31] That the image is in reverse (white on black, as in a negative) emphasizes the constraint: without the intercession of a third term, every depiction of structure must be restricted to a juxtaposition of discrete alternatives.[N5.32] Which is to say, it is restricted to a positive instance of the negativity that this juxtaposition embodies: the dynamic syncretism of the initial diptych is thus repeated at the screen's smallest unit. We may remember Barthes's description of the G-string as the real terminus of the striptease, though all the Patchwork Girl's garments have been stripped away. (How? By the wind that also lifts the hair on her head? Doesn't this signal the influence of an agent beyond the borders of the window?) The sequined undergarment, Barthes observed, marks the limit of a mineral world that halts the disclosure of biology—"the (precious) stone being here the irrefutable symbol of the total and useless object" (Barthes 1970, 148); that structure of stoppage is effected in this image by the indivisibility of the pixel. Once more, as in the inner surface of the perforated page, reading is stopped at a surface that embodies (the image of the Girl's exposed pubis does just this: *embodies*) a barrier beyond which reading can no longer be generative. (Except that in this case, a turn is effected medially, permitting an exit from this terminus.)

5.48   Here is, as the Rat-Man said, something . . . singular. ▸N5.33 Except that, unlike the genetic scene of Freud's obsessional patient, and the torn, burned, and split surfaces of *Myst* ▸ 4.46, *nothing is missing*. Those sites are punctuated by crises of unreadability figured as crises of loss; on the contrary, the opening stance of the Patchwork Girl seems to carry no qualities of dispossession. Which is not to say that a durably unreadable object is not marked here; only that its unreadability is not meant to be experienced as traumatic. A thread of the deep structure of the *orans* posture emerges here in the fullest ambiguity: such concerns—characteristic of a sexualized primal scene of interpretation—are, as I have noted, irrelevant to her. Yet she is made of disjoint parts, unfinished, unstable, destined to disperse. ("I am the Queen of dispersal. I am most myself in the gaps between my parts" {dispersed}.) Presented to us in this form, she is a thoroughly modern Girl: in a nod perhaps to Jackson's love of children's fiction, this monster is also L. Frank Baum's accidental, raggedy girl, the one who dances constantly and dislikes good behavior, but reimagined as a figure of melancholy humors and brave desire. ▸N5.34

5.49   *Piecework.* There *is* an act of flaying in the text apart from my efforts to peel away its carapaces and it constitutes one of the most important events of the narrative. Before she departs from Mary, the monster and she engage in a private ritual to seal—to suture—their union. Mary cuts a small circle of flesh from her calf, and the Girl cuts another the same size from a knotty scar on her thigh. ("We decided that as my skin did not, strictly speaking, belong to me, the nearest thing to a bit of flesh would be this scar, a place where disparate things joined in a way that was my own" {join}.) The fragments of flesh are swapped and stitched into place by Mary ("She was pale but her hands were steady as she joined us" {join}).

> We wrapped the bloody rags in a towel with a large stone and sank them into the lake. We were cool as we bade each other farewell there on the muddy shore in a light rain. I do not know what came of that off-shoot of me, if it dried and fell off or lived in its ring of scars. But

I am a strong vine. The graft took, the bit of skin is still a living pink, and so I remember when I was Mary, and how I loved a monster, and became one. I bring you my story, which is ours. {us}

5.50 In this version of the Frankenstein myth, Mary, not Victor, sinks the remainders of her procreative work in dark waters, away from Percy's watchful gaze. ("For her part, she chose a Piece of skin Percy would likely never miss, in a place where bandages could be easily explained if they should be discovered" {join}.) Literary influence and legacy—reading and rewriting—as piecework, surgery, varietal joined to rootstock and vice versa. Crucially, this is not a cutting and suturing that uncovers and synthesizes; it merely displaces units from one local system to another.

5.51 This imbrication of textual subjects is marked by the object suspended from the central axis of the Patchwork Girl's stance. Titled {crazy quilt}, when opened it reveals the arrangement of nodes shown in ▶ Figure 5.05.

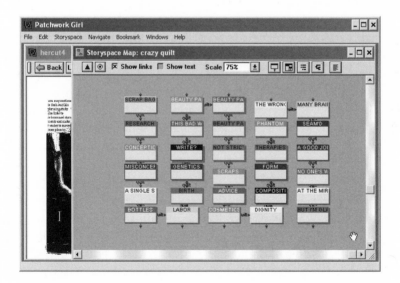

FIGURE 5.05. Shelley Jackson, *Patchwork Girl* {crazy quilt}, 1st edition, Storyspace Reader 2.0 (2000), Windows XP (2001). The icons corresponding to nodes gathered in the writing space are gaudily colored, evoking the quilting tradition for which the space is named. Reproduced by permission of Eastgate Systems, Inc.

5.52 The icons corresponding to nodes gathered in the space are gaudily colored and stacked in irregular columns and rows.[N5.35] This disorder and motley evokes the tradition for which the space is named—"crazy quilts" are stitched from scraps and remnants; little effort is made by the quilter to arrange them according to color or pattern—and compactly figures the space's textual and narrative structure.[N5.36] Each node in the space is an aggregate of fragments lifted from multiple fiction and nonfiction sources (L. Frank Baum's *The Patchwork Girl of Oz*, Mary Shelley's *Frankenstein*, Barbara Maria Stafford's *Body Criticism*, Klaus Theweleit's *Male Fantasies*, the Storyspace user's manual, texts by Cixous, Derrida, etc.). These have been interleaved with short passages from Baum's and Mary Shelley's novels so as to form mostly coherent sentences and paragraphs of a parallel narrative that at least some of the time appears to concern the Patchwork Girl. The sutures between the fragments are obvious—the grammar turns slightly, the tone of the language changes, a digressive phrase is abruptly opened or closed—but also restrained enough to suggest a plausible chimera formed from the whole. And to induce—Jackson's reader is soon aware of this operation throughout her text—a response.[N5.37]

5.53 An experienced hypertext reader will click at any juncture of two linguistically or semiotically incongruous sequences in search of the gloss that relates them. (Hypertext meets intertext: the link will often serve as the locus of such an agrammaticality, by which is signaled an encoded precursor text. Isn't this also the lexia's syntagmatic basis? "Meaning *insists*," Lacan says, "but none of the chain's elements *consists* in the signification it can provide."[N5.38]) But the structure of the nodes in {crazy quilt} is more subtle than this convention: each chimera contains only two links, and neither points to a true gloss. One link enframes a series of dashes below the chimera: clicking on any of the dashes opens the next space in the {crazy quilt} sequence. Gloss, then, as (a literal) parataxis: the sequence turns across the pattern (▶ Figure 5.05) from the top of one column, down to its bottom, and then from the bottom of the column to its right, up to its top, like stitching a quilt. Or more abstractly, the looping turns of a suture. "The dotted line is the best line—more innocent than the solid line, fiercer than the pacifist fold—even what is discontinuous and in pieces can blaze a trail" (Jackson, *Patchwork Girl* {dotted line}). It is more roundabout than the shortest line, but the shortest line was always a sham figure, imposed on a topography that turns and contorts many ways at once.[N5.39]

5.54

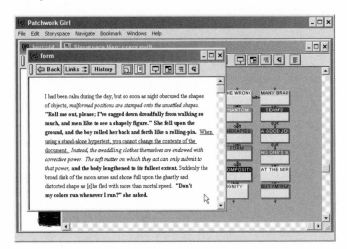

FIGURE 5.06. Shelley Jackson, *Patchwork Girl* {form}, 1st
edition, Storyspace Reader 2.0 (2000), Windows XP (2001).
Reproduced by permission of Eastgate Systems, Inc.

5.55 The other link in each chimera leads to its double in a space titled {notes},
contained within {scrap bag}, the first space of the {crazy quilt} sequence.
Each such second has the same name as its first, but the boundaries of the
fragments from which it is constructed are marked by changes in typestyle
(italics, bold, underscores). These styles are also applied to entries of a
short bibliography at the end of the second space, indicating the fragment's
source. Gloss, then, performs as set-theoretic recursion, with a turn outward to the intertext that sustains this movement. (And as an example of
connotation sustained by the appeal to another reader's authority? How else
would we know where the fragments come from?) For example, the space
titled {form}—

> I had been calm during the day, but so soon as night obscured the
> shapes of objects, malformed positions are stamped onto the unset-
> tled shapes. "Roll me out, please; I've sagged down dreadfully from
> walking so much, and men like to see a shapely figure." She fell upon
> the ground, and the boy rolled her back and forth like a rolling-pin.
> When using a stand-alone hypertext, you cannot change the contents
> of the document. Instead, the swaddling clothes themselves are en-

dowed with corrective power. The soft matter on which they act can only submit to that power, and the body lengthened to its fullest extent. Suddenly the broad disk of the moon arose and shone full upon the ghastly and distorted shape as she fled with more than mortal speed. "Don't my colors run whenever I run?" she asked.

— —

5.56 —is doubled by a space in {notes} also titled {form} (▶ Figure 5.06):

I had been calm during the day, but so soon as night obscured the shapes of objects, *malformed positions are stamped onto the unsettled shapes.* **"Roll me out, please; I've sagged down dreadfully from walking so much, and men like to see a shapely figure." She fell upon the ground, and the boy rolled her back and forth like a rolling-pin.** <u>When using a stand-alone hypertext, you cannot change the contents of the document.</u> *Instead, the swaddling clothes themselves are endowed with corrective power. The soft matter on which they act can only submit to that power,* **and the body lengthened to its fullest extent.** Suddenly the broad disk of the moon arose and shone full upon the ghastly and distorted shape as [s]he fled with more than mortal speed. **"Don't my colors run whenever I run?" she asked.**

Mary Shelley, *Frankenstein, or, The Modern Prometheus*, first published in 1818 (mine is the Penguin edition, edited by Maurice Hindle, 1985), p. ?; p. 242.

Barbara Maria Stafford, *Body Criticism: Imaging the Unseen in Enlightenment Art and Medicine*, by Barbara Maria Stafford (MIT 1991), p. ?

L. Frank Baum, *The Patchwork Girl of Oz*, first published in 1913. Mine is the Ballantine edition, p. 164, p. 60.

Jay David Bolter, Michael Joyce, John B. Smith, and Mark Bernstein, *Getting Started with Storyspace* (Eastgate Systems, 1990–1993), p. ?

5.57 The expanded/doubled chimera contains only one link; clicking anywhere within the body of its text returns the reader to the unexpanded chimera. Nelson's Stretchtext ▶ 4.20 seems close at hand.

5.58 Two aspects of this scheme deserve emphasis. First, in the map the visual layout of spaces in {notes} closely resembles that of {crazy quilt}, though the distributions of subnodes in the spaces do not match exactly. The most obvious difference between them is that, whereas the nodes of {crazy quilt} are brightly colored—the only use of color in the hypertext—those of {notes} are in black and white. Thus, a *multiplying* of grammatextually significant attributes within {notes}—the changes in typeface and style, by which diagrammatic relations are signaled—is matched by a corresponding *reduction* of grammatextually significant attributes of the maps—many colors to only two colors (or only one, if we take into account the constraint of a 1-bit palette). This inverse pairing of multiplied and reduced attributes indicates, subtly, the rhetoric of this pseudo-gloss. Something more is given, but something is also taken away. What appears to be an expansion of the first text is in another sense a contraction of its signifying potential in the second text.

5.59 Second, the annotations of the expanded chimeras are incomplete or infelicitously constructed: as in the double {form}, above, portions of the citation apparatus are missing ("p. ?") or redundant ("Barbara Maria Stafford . . . by Barbara Maria Stafford"). The extent to which these irregularities and redundancies were programmatically constructed by Jackson is unclear. It seems most likely that most are the signs of authorial haste and, above all, of a subjective reading history. Thus: "mine is the Penguin edition," or more subtly: "[s]he fled with more than mortal speed," the text of the 1818 original lightly emended to match linguistic self-consciousness and gendered economies of its 1913 (Baum) and 1995 (Jackson) variants. But not *silently* emended. An unremarked repair of this kind—changing a pronoun to reflect the gender of the creature to which it is now applied—may be generally an author's prerogative, but Jackson has been careful throughout *Patchwork Girl* to mark her writerly interventions. Narratively, this scruple is fitted to the Girl's rejection of the account of her interrupted creation and dispersal and her explanations for Mary's having hidden the truth of her (the monster's) creation and fate. The earlier, the authoritative, account must be, on its surface, a falsehood, or the Patchwork Girl wouldn't be here to demonstrate that it is. Textually, the scruple marks other slippages and promotes other circuits. A Girl who is puzzled by her mannish qualities and who lives a part of her history in male drag—which in this case must be a metatextual as well as gendered state. An author who is at some level uncertain of her limits. The first-person possessives scattered throughout the {notes} spaces ("Mine is the . . . edition" and so on) are, exceptionally, signatures of one who has read from her archive, and in writing, writes between the pasts of multiple reading and the futures of others. When Mary or her monster writes in the first person, we are aware, obscurely, of (at least) a third who is also present. ▸N5.40

5.60 *Chimeras.* I emphasize this circuit of writing and reading subjects because I wish to propose that it is a higher-order relation of a subjective encounter with textual structures. Apart from interpretations we may characterize as idiopathic, only isomorphisms of local textual structure with structures of a shared symbolic (a common history of reading) will persistently activate these circuits. (This is the operating principle of "archaisms" of Hilton's lexis complex. It is also the cultural basis of Barthes's early definition of the lexia.) We may expect such multiples to be activated in every text insofar as it touches upon other texts and so is at least in part captive to their grammars and relay structures. Only the reader's conscious or unconscious grasp of them is required to bring them to bear on the text at hand.

5.61 *Historiation.* But what of isomorphisms that may be marked only in the expression of an idiopathic reading? Can I be confident that lexias spanning the Patchwork Girl's opening gesture, the *orans* posture, and the visible woman are not merely effects of my "system of the subject" ▸ 5.06, and therefore may not have significance for other readers of the hypertext?

5.62 On the one hand, the question is made moot by a definition of the lexia closer to Barthes's than to Landow's. Reorienting the concept of the lexia away from a purely node-based segmentation of the text to parsings that are more variable and opportunistic, and including within the lexia's purview grammatextually activated expressions that may have no direct relation to the text's on-screen chunking, means that objective characteristics of the text will necessarily be bound to elements of a subjective reading encounter. My specific cutting up of a few exemplary lexia of *Patchwork Girl* implies no methodological responsibility; it is motived only by the density of connotations elicited by these arbitrarily selected units of the text ▸ 5.10. My lexial articulation of the hypertext is defensible if it engages a particular history and system of reading, recording thus an emergent structure—a trail—that is manipulable and transmissible ▸ 1.58.

5.63 On the other hand, the possibility that my reading of *Patchwork Girl* must be, whatever else may be said of it, *my* reading goes to the fundamental problem of historiation's role in the articulation of lexias, most of all in texts such as Jackson's in which graphic traits of the object presented to the reader plainly determine its meaning and reception. The effects of historiation are aggregative and noncommutative ▶ 2.30; their products will be inconsistent and hostage to the hazards of reading and the contingencies of my memory of reading. Those points of departure for my (re)imaginings of the texts' expressive surfaces are necessarily multiple and open to future revisions, some of which may become part of a sociolect of reading, while others will persist only in the trails within a more local and intimate store. The exemplarity of *Patchwork Girl*'s is in that its mixing of the two Shelleys, Mary and Jackson, their monstrous amanuenses, their reader and her archival multiples, will be sustained, shaped, and reshaped over the course of a reading (or between multiple readings) directly in relation to the fiction's polybiographic codes. Its themes of doubles and monsters, its evocations of things that cannot be held firmly in one place for more than a moment, are brought into effect as a consequence of its joining of schemes of discovery to other modes of textual projection. Can the chimera, bombinating in the void, consume its second intentions? Rabelais's question, Eco notes, refers to an impossible creature, impossible actions, and an impossible place, but its very positing as a question brings them into subtle being. ▶N5.41

5.64 I will show in the next chapter that multiplications of textual voices may also be subtended by multiplications of scenes of writing and reading deriving from hardware and software variants introduced along the upgrade path. Until recently, the challenges that such variants pose to the analysis of digital fictions have not been widely appreciated.

6.

Allographs

Windows of *Afternoon*

It's understandable, I suppose, to think of this all as some sort of techno-literary game, a cryptogram, or garden of the forking etc., the minotaur at its end.

I, for instance, think of Djuna Barnes.

For years I told a fraudulent anecdote about when I helped the executrix of the cummings estate clear out Estlin and Marian's Patchin Place house. There was a mysterious woman, dressed all in black, a veil over her face, a black-thorn walking stick. One afternoon, Gerry introduced me to her, saying "This is Michael Joyce, he is a writer." It was the first she ever said this. Usually she would introduce me to people saying, "He wants to be a writer."

The woman in black said, "Joyce? I knew Jimmy in Paris, you know. He was a wonderful man."

I forgot who she was but in later years told the story, claiming she was Djuna Barnes, who I knew also lived on Patchin Place. It made a good ending, a rite de passage. After a number of years, guilt and curiosity caught up with me and I wrote to Gerry to ask her who the woman really was.

She wrote back and said Djuna Barnes.

—Michael Joyce, *Afternoon, a Story* {V Woolf} (1987)

6.01 Michael Joyce's *Afternoon, a Story* (1987) is an artifact of literary hypertext's first wave to which one seems compelled to return. As early as 1992, Robert Coover described *Afternoon* in an essay for *The New York Review of Books* as a "landmark," and the "granddaddy of hypertext fiction." Though it is unclear which fictions Coover meant to be *Afternoon*'s prospective grandchildren, one must take seriously the family romance anticipated by this now-famous designation. Its effects are evident everywhere in the theory, criticism, and pedagogy of hypertext, in which the work serves as a privileged model and counter-model: included in every course reading list, alluded to in every critical discussion, ranged among digital media's most serious challenges to regimes of print, or offered (more recently) as the limit-case that illustrates how the first wave is something we have left behind.[N6.01] With the possible exception of Jackson's *Patchwork Girl* ▶ 5.31, no other literary hypertext can claim as secure a place in the genre's small canon of acknowledged masterworks.

6.02 The historical bookend to Coover's early celebration of *Afternoon* is his complaint, less than a decade later, that we have—already, too soon—left the golden age forecast by Joyce's fiction. The unrelenting hyperkinesis and graphic monomania of the World Wide Web, Coover lamented in a 1999 lecture, have "sucked the substance" out of the digital field's lettered arts, reducing its signs to "surface spectacle."

> Literature is meditative and the Net is riven by ceaseless hype and chatter. Literature has a shape, and the Net is shapeless. The discrete object is gone, there's only this vast disorderly sprawl, about as appealing as a scatter of old magazines on a table in the dentist's lounge. Literature is traditionally slow and low-tech and thoughtful, the Net is fast and high-tech and actional. As for hyperfiction, the old golden age webworks of text have largely vanished, hypertext now used more to access hypermedia as enhancements for more or less linear narratives, when it's not launching the reader out into the mazy outer space of the World Wide Web, never to be seen again. Notions of architecture, mapping, design: mostly gone. Genuine interactivity, too: the reader is commonly obliged now to enter the media-rich but ineluctable flow as directed by the author or authors: in a sense, it's back to the movies again, that most passive and imperious of forms. (Coover 2000)

6.03 *Writing Machines*, N. Katherine Hayles's 2002 study of new media and print fiction, repeats elements of Coover's eulogy for procedures of early literary hypertext, but reverses his sentiment. She argues that the transition remarked by Coover, away from limited polyseriality (node replaces node, the reader moves along obscure but determinate paths: narrative operations typified, she observes, by *Afternoon*) to more structurally "nervous" performances (Talan Memmott's Web-based *Lexia to Perplexia* is her example), represents a salutary engagement of digital media with new compositional methods.[N6.02] Freed from the technical limitations of early authoring tools and computer operating systems, literary authors of the second wave, Hayles observes, work in more complex and graphically rich development environments, such as Flash, Shockwave, HTML, VRML, and repurposed software originally developed for video games. They may also assume that their texts will be read on more capable computers, outfitted with faster processors, more memory and more storage space, larger color screens, and full-time network access. Moreover, she proposes, the shift to these more technically sophisticated conditions for writing and reading in the digital field also marks a more authentic break from traditions of print than the examples lauded by enthusiasts of earlier texts. "These first-generation works," she writes,

> were more like books than they were like second-generation electronic literature, because they operated by replacing one screen of text with another; much as a book goes from one page to another. Despite the hoopla, first-generation works left mostly untouched the unconscious assumptions that readers of books had absorbed through centuries of print. They were a brave beginning, but only a beginning. Not unlike the dumb terminals . . . now thought of as quaint antiques, these works opened up pathways of change that would, when more fully exploited, make them seem obsolete. (Hayles 2002, 37)

6.04 Though her readings of individual first- and second-generation texts are historically nuanced, Hayles's characterization of the earlier texts as a "brave beginning" evokes a critical commonplace of cinema studies, that the earliest cinema more closely resembled works composed for the nineteenth-century stage than the more distinctly filmic works of the mid-twentieth century. Yet it is the case in all such medial transitions that a general arc of technical evolution will obscure local inconsistencies and contradictions. As Lev Manovich has demonstrated in the example of Dziga Vertov's 1918 film *Man with Movie Camera*—from which he derives the "language" of new media—the details of such generational shifts are exceedingly complex (Manovich 2001).

6.05 Coover's complaint that the digital letter was in an earlier age less enmeshed in graphic and kinetic imaginaries than it is now is perhaps justifiable on quantitative grounds. (Hayles's formulation of this technical and conceptual regression-progression is more problematic. I will return to it shortly.)

Hypertexts of the 1980s and 1990s were less oriented by the eye candy typical of the Web, but they were no less subject in their basic operations to graphic regimes and programs of the screen, as these were fundamental to user interfaces used to write and read those texts. Crucial to the commercial and artistic breakthrough of Storyspace, the authoring system most closely associated with early literary hypertext (and the application with which *Afternoon* and most of the golden-age texts Coover cites were composed), was its reliance on and incorporation of the Macintosh GUI.[N6.03] As I noted in chapter 3, when it is read within a GUI's visual and procedural planes, the most unadorned text will be subjected to the illocutionary influences of icons, buttons, menus, windows, and other interface widgets. It will be caught up in paratextual and grammatextual structures on its periphery: borders and control of document windows, the overlapping or intersection of these elements with others on the screen, like and different from them, audio and visual feedback. In short, all the visual, aural, and procedural resources of the "desktop" apply to the situation of reading in this way. Perhaps more important than that graphic signifiers have been jammed against textual ones—writing has always been so crowded, programs of the image and the text have always knotted in this way—is the problem of what their interleavings and disjunctions represent in the present moment of reading.

6.06 This historical, in some cases genetic, problem remains a fundamental concern for interpretation of the first wave and its legacies. Coover's eulogy for the literary excellence of early hypertexts and, with different emphasis, Hayles's assertion that the second wave surpassed the first by doing what it aimed to do with greater effect, displace our attention from how we read these objects in the situation of the screen that stands before us. The criteria Hayles proposes to mark the second from the first wave simplify relations of technical change to literary change, and obscure intractable but basic problems of the historical currency of much about the new media that is not-quite-new.[N6.04] Nostalgic and counter-nostalgic responses to 1990s literary hypertexts alike stress their historical importance, but without accounting fully for their critical-theoretical *persistence*. The most obvious risk in this is that these texts will thus appear to be of interest only to the literary historian, or, worse, relics of the digiterati's *Wunderkammer*, belonging there with other *disjecta membra* of an era before Flash and the iPhone set us free. Canonicity travels hand-in-hand with belatedness. But *historiation* in the sense I have used that term involves the experience of a specific reading subject insofar as her reading is tied to determinate, primarily visual, traits of the text, and these will also include residual forms of older medial forms. What is missing from a simple model of belatedness is a more complex historical *presence*, in which traces of these texts' development are marked in the responses and uses made of them now.

6.07 This is Ted Nelson, writing in 1992:

> The purpose of computers is human freedom, and so the purpose of hypertext is overview and understanding; and this, by the way, is why I disapprove of any hypertext (like Michael Joyce's *afternoon* . . .) that does not show you the interconnective structure. (56) [N6.05]

6.08 Nelson refers here to one of the first three editions of *Afternoon*. Let us assume that it is the third edition (▶ Figure 6.01), the first published commercially, released on floppy disk for the Macintosh in 1990. [N6.06] In this edition, each node of the hypertext (called a "writing space" in the technical vocabulary of Storyspace) is displayed in a single, fixed-size window. Text, window borders, menus, and other widgets of the UI are drawn in black on a white field (1-bit color). [N6.07] With the exception of the title page, which includes a blurry image of a man standing apart on a crowded sidewalk (is this Peter, the principal narrator of *Afternoon*? his identity remains unresolved), and two more compact images, deeply buried in the textbase (to which I will return), the text includes no graphics. All is sequence: each node seems to displace its predecessor, filling the window's frame and erasing that which has come before. The window's resemblance to the visual field of the printed page is unmistakable, though also folded back on itself, recto and verso as the same field, the purest abstraction of a blank surface.

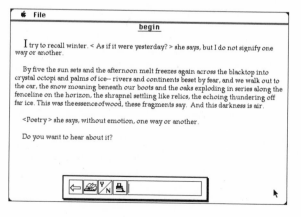

FIGURE 6.01. Michael Joyce, *Afternoon, a Story* {begin}, 3rd edition, Storyspace Readingspace 1.0 (ca. 1990), Mac OS 6 (1990). Reproduced by permission of Eastgate Systems, Inc.

6.09 Early editions of *Afternoon* lack alternative representations of textual structure ("map" and "outline" views) that are possible in other Storyspace Reader formats. The reader is thus unable to determine the position of a node in a series, how many nodes have been read, and how many remain to be read (except, of course, in her anticipation or recollection of this or another reading; this is essential to her construction of meaning while reading). Joyce's disabling of those views has often been cited as the most important limit imposed on any reading of *Afternoon*, though few critics have observed that this restriction was not imposed as a matter of course by the Storyspace application; it was deliberately chosen by Joyce. As a result, much of the criticism tends to mistake Joyce's design decision for a general trait of hypertext literary practice or of its first-wave avatars. ▶N6.08

6.10 A further restriction of readers' comprehension of *Afternoon*'s structure is effected at each juncture of a reading. Words or clusters of words in a node that are linked to other nodes—Joyce calls them "words that yield"—are distributed throughout the text without any indication of their potential activation of new reading sequences.

> I haven't indicated what words yield, but they are usually ones which have texture, as well as character names and pronouns.
>
> There are more such words early on in the story, but there are almost always options in any sequence of texts.
>
> The lack of clear signals isn't an attempt to vex you, rather an invitation to read either inquisitively or playfully and also at depth. Click on words that interest or invite you. (Joyce, *Afternoon* {read at depth})

6.11 The reader must advance through node sequences without fully understanding the scope or narrative logic of yield words. ▶N6.09 There may be more than one such word or cluster within a node; different yield words may point to the same target. Often, where a yield word leads depends upon the prior history of a reading; some nodes cannot be viewed until another node or a sequence of nodes—a "path"—has been viewed. This restriction or direction of movement is accomplished through the use of "guard fields," invisible boolean expressions attached to links that determine their targets. For example, the node shown in ▶ Figure 6.01, typically the first the reader of *Afternoon* encounters after the opening screen, leads to twenty possible destinations. Which may be arrived at depends on values of the guard fields, and whether the reader is viewing the node for the first time or returning to it from other nodes, and which of those nodes she has visited. Of the best-known literary hypertexts written with Storyspace, *Afternoon* appears to have made the most extensive use of this feature.

6.12 Nelson's objections to *Afternoon* are not surprising. Though he has long eschewed many of the idioms of the modern GUI, he has promoted a model of hypertext reading that touches on the GUI's primary epistemological conceits: semiotic disambiguation, reader-directed control, potential saturation of data relations ▶ 7.50. For Nelson hypertext is distinguished from plain old text expressly in that link structures reveal, and make accessible and recoverable, the textbase's possible networks of meaning ▶ 2.54. Joyce's heavy use of guard fields and his decision to disable access to global representations of *Afternoon*'s structure must then run afoul of Nelson's insistence on the absolute priority of readerly comprehension.

6.13 Other critics have also complained of the hypertext's resistance to readerly control. In an influential 1997 book on new media culture, Steven Johnson writes that reading *Afternoon*

> was a bit like watching a Godard film with a projectionist who insists on randomly swapping reels. The links between different pages seemed more anarchic than free-associative; and what you were left with resembled a collection of aphorisms more than anything else. You couldn't help wondering how a John Grisham novel would fare in the medium, where a strong narrative might make your reading "choices" more consequential. (S. Johnson 1997, 125)

6.14 He compares the then-current crop of hypertext fiction writers to "Parisian *philosophes* of '68" whose fascination with the author's demise he considers evidence of a "self-interested *ressentiment*" (S. Johnson 1997, 124). Demands imposed on the reader by *Afternoon*'s narrative operations—which Johnson assumes are representative of hypertext in general, such is the legacy of Coover's "granddaddy" label—are only increased, he complains, by perverse ministrations of its projectionist, who insists on showing us its already disordered parts even more out of sequence. In contrast to more robust American models of fiction (exemplified by the dependably cinematic Grisham), the narrative of *Afternoon* is weak, unassertive, unable to sustain a good read: sick with a solipsizing case of French flu.

6.15 The comparison is facile, pop-cultural shorthand for more complex literary filiations—and, one must assume, evidence of Johnson's preference for fictions more generous in their direction of the reader. Nonetheless, his complaints may signal an important problem of initial critical responses, pro and con, to Joyce's hypertext. Analyses of *Afternoon* in the first decade after its publication tended to treat its fracturing of narrative—as much the effect of the guard fields as of the supposed freedoms of the links, though this was rarely noted—as the model of the new medium's subversions of the line and the page. Broad claims were made about the significance and originality of hypertext on the basis of this one, most accomplished, example of the form. Early enthusiasts of *Afternoon* often compared its supposed revisions of writing, reading, and the institutions of publishing and pedagogy to general theories of textual and intertextual meaning associated with the *philosophes* that Johnson appears to disdain: Barthes, Derrida, Genette, and Lacan.▸N6.10

6.16 *Afternoon*, the enthusiasts proposed, demonstrates hermeneutic indeterminacies that are mostly hidden by systems of print and conventions of reading that these systems and their institutionalizations have engendered. Joyce's fiction, moreover, thematized these indeterminacies in such a way as to make their contributions to the reader's role in narrative production self-evident: the method for resolving the text's aporias forced on her by its structure doubles the protagonist's circumambulations. (What did Peter see on the way to work? How was he involved in the accident that may have taken the life of his son? What must he do—what is he unable to do—to determine the extent of his complicity in the tragedy he may have witnessed? How does the reader decide which of these questions may be answered, and which is the correct answer?)

6.17 Critics with more sympathy for literary theory than Johnson also adopted this scheme of formal and procedural doubling. In *Cybertext*, his pathbreaking 1997 study of ergodic literature, Espen Aarseth terms *Afternoon* a "reluctant narrative" or a "game of narration" (1997, 94) in which the text's secretive logic short-circuits narrative closure and saturation.▸N6.11 Also assuming *Afternoon*'s procedures to be typical of all hypertext fiction, he unfavorably compares its misdirections to tmesis, the practice of skipping and skimming celebrated by Barthes in *Le Plaisir du texte* (*The Pleasure of the Text*) (1973):

Hypertext reading is in fact quite the opposite: as the reader explores the labyrinth, she cannot afford to tread lightly through the text but must scrutinize the links and venues in order to avoid meeting the same text fragments over and over. . . . Hypertext punishes tmesis by controlling the text's fragmentation and pathways and by forcing the reader to pay attention to the strategic links. The disoriented movements of a reader looking for fresh links in a hypertext . . . might be confused with tmesis. This is not, however, Barthes's "textual bliss" but, rather, the reader's textual claustrophobia as she skims the *déjà-lu* nodes. (Aarseth 1997, 78–79)

6.18 Hypertext fiction forces the reader to skip where *she would not choose to skip*. It punishes a practice freely available in other textual forms and forces her to abide by interests of unknown or obscure parties.▸N6.12 "To make sense of the text," Aarseth continues, "the reader must produce a narrative version of it, but the ergodic experience"—that is, her work against the text's fracturing of narrative continuity—"marks this version with the reader's signature, the proof that *afternoon* does not contain a narrative of its own." Joyce's text is, he concludes, an "important limit text, on the border between narrative and ergodics" (95)—damning thus with faint praise, given the strength of his other complaints. His objections have since been taken up with more fervor by the circle of game studies scholars loosely centered around his contributions to that field. They have argued that the narratological emphases of new media studies in its first two decades—which were based largely on the example of *Afternoon*—have been grossly misleading as to the innovations of new media, especially in non-hypertext genres like video games.▸N6.13

6.19 Even if one rejects these arguments as extreme, it is clear that the narratological prejudices of theory and criticism of the 1990s limited our understanding of hypertext in other ways. The schemes of narrative encoding and decoding on which most of the early critical literature was founded for the most part treated too lightly or neglected outright crucial elements of *Afternoon*'s medial situations, or relied on overly abstract models of their operations. This abstraction, moreover, contributed to critics' complaints of *Afternoon*'s excessive narrative contingency (for Johnson, an evidence of its debility) and its dispossession of the reader (Aarseth's objection: the text reserves too much of its programs to itself). Lost in the mix, pro and con, were significant problems raised by the hypertext's varied visual and procedural attributes.

6.20 *Second intentions.*[N6.14] For there are several *Afternoons*. Nelson's 1992 complaint is directed against what may be described as the "classic" instance of Joyce's text. Initially available only for the Macintosh, its features and appearance remained largely unchanged on that platform until 2007 (▶ Figure 6.01).[N6.15] Readers of Windows versions have encountered an object that is different in many respects.

6.21 Application and document windows of the Windows Storyspace Reader (▶ Figure 6.02) may be resized, and their elements are drawn in colors of the Windows system palette. The Reader is outfitted with new buttons and menus. The application palette of the Mac OS Readingspace does not appear here, because its functions have been moved to menus at the top of the window and to the toolbar near the bottom. Several window, menu, and toolbar controls and the features they represent are unique to the Windows version: the Mac OS version has no History or Bookmark feature; the Links function is represented there by an uncaptioned icon resembling an open book. In the Windows version, each of these is documented by a tool tip bar at the bottom of the document window, which is also absent from Mac OS versions.[N6.16]

6.22 In the Mac OS editions, the contents of every node fit within the limits of the document window. This has been set to boundaries of the original Macin-

FIGURE 6.02. *Left:* Michael Joyce, *Afternoon, a Story* {begin}, 4th edition, Storyspace Reader 1.3 (1992), Windows XP (2001). *Right: Afternoon, a Story* {begin}, 7th edition, Storyspace Reader 2.5 (2007), Mac OS X 10.4 (2007). Reproduced by permission of Eastgate Systems, Inc.

Allographs

tosh's 9-inch monitor, less the menubar at the top of the screen. The dimensions of this window and the typeface cannot be changed and no scrolling is required (or possible). The image on the screen is fixed, flattened in some respects: the classic versions are pagiform not only in sequence (each node replaces a prior node completely, and only one node is visible at any time) but also in the appearance of their surface: all that the reader sees in the present moment is what has been put before her; the interface suggests in only minimal terms that the text may have any dimensionality beyond this.

6.23 In contrast to the Mac OS editions, the Windows editions are quarto or folio to octavo or duodecimo; the relation of the lines of the text to the negative space of the visual field is alterable and thus altered. Clicking on the "Minimize" icon in the upper right corner of document windows will shrink them to a stub containing only the node's title and the window's control widgets. Clicking on the "Maximize/Restore" icon returns windows to their previous dimensions. Resized to reveal its lower right corner, the window can be arbitrarily resized again by dragging the corner in- or outward. As its boundaries are changed, its contents will rewrap if necessary, and scrollbars will appear along the right edge if the text does not fit in the window. The window can also be dragged by its titlebar within the application window, which may also be resized and moved on the monitor by the same methods.

6.24 By default, successive nodes viewed in the Windows Reader are displayed in a single document window, as in the Mac OS Reader. But the Windows user may also elect to keep document windows open within the frame of the application window until they are explicitly closed (▶ Figure 6.03).

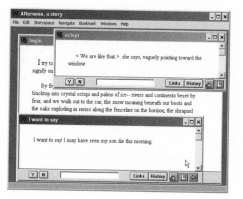

FIGURE 6.03. Michael Joyce, *Afternoon, a Story* {begin}, 4th edition, Storyspace Reader 1.3 (1992), Windows XP (2001). The "Keep windows open" preference setting has been enabled. Reproduced by permission of Eastgate Systems, Inc.

6.25   With this setting enabled, newly opened document windows are displayed on top of those previously viewed. The frontmost window is the active node, but any document window can be brought to the foreground by selecting it with the cursor. The rigorously pagiform and punctiform sequences of the classic (Mac OS) version are dramatically altered by this multiplying and layering of text windows in the Windows Reader, in which emergent narrative series may be effectively recast as stacked structures. Reading slips into tropes of simultaneity and depth; nodes seem less to replace or revise each other than to vie for the reader's attention. The resemblance of screens of the classic version to the printed page—though it is a page with only one side, a topological oddity except in the realms of the GUI—is changed when successive surfaces seem to be stacked or shuffled. (Here, once more, conceits of the GUI overpower efforts to read these nested frames in other ways. Recall how Maeda's citation of Malevich's nonobjective canvases was so directed by the GUI toward a tropology of depth ▶4.32.) Moreover, the reader's freedom to reorder document windows without activating any link between them substantively changes the visual encounter of reading *Afternoon*. In the classic version, the narrative sequence has no discernible spatial orientation (each node replaces its predecessor, without appearing to arrive from any direction); here, it may be expressed in terms of the z-axis of the UI. The Mac OS version requires practices of surface-work of the kind I described in chapter 4. The Windows version opens up the surface of the screen, and introduces to it semes of perforation and interiority. Perforation is not unlimited in this case (it must be limited, as I have argued ▶4.12): its limit is marked by the surface of the application window, which appears to stand as the lowest layer of the stacked windows.

6.26   Intimations of depth and ways of traversing it are evident in other navigational features unique to the Windows Reader. Its reader may open a "roadmap" of nodes linked to any selected node. (In this context, selection carries a valence it cannot have in Mac OS editions, where only one text window is visible, and so must always be the "selected" node.) The reader may open a History dialog, showing already-visited nodes in a scrolling list sorted in the order in which they were encountered, an explicit remapping of paths of the reading to an orderly vertical structure. She may search for keywords, alphanumeric strings, and writing spaces anywhere in the hypertext (▶Figure 6.04).[N6.17]

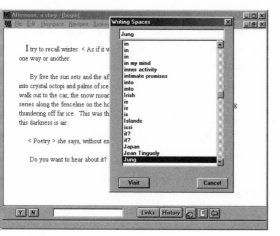

FIGURE 6.04. Michael Joyce, *Afternoon, a Story* {begin}, 4th edition, Storyspace Reader 1.3 (1992), Windows XP (2001). Most of the nodes shown in the "Writing Spaces" window are not linked to {begin}. By choosing to visit any of these spaces, the reader is able to circumvent the linking structure imposed by the current node's guard fields. Reproduced by permission of Eastgate Systems, Inc.

6.27 Setting aside for the moment their effects on the reader's representation of its textual structure, these alternative tools for reading *Afternoon* in its Windows editions are a boon to the critic and student. Jumping directly to a node located in this way allows one to skip over intermediate nodes in a sequence and avoid detours forced by the guard fields. This makes it easier to refind a node or to discover nodes or sequences that one has not read before, since in the classic editions these can be found only by trial and error, and some may never be located. The comprehensive list of nodes shown in ▶ Figure 6.04 reorients that process to a simple alphabetical sort.

6.28 When I have introduced *Afternoon* to readers without prior experience of hypertext fiction, the Macintosh users among them often complain that Windows users are free to ignore ambiguities and aporia that must be, they suppose, essential to an authentic encounter with the text. Reading a hypertext, they propose, should be as procedurally as it is narratively challenging—the critical literature, pro and con, of the literary first wave appears to justify this proposition—and the interface of the Windows Reader makes it easy to get around the text's programmed resistance to comprehension. Textual fidelity is never so simple as this complaint presumes, of course; the relations of variant to variant across the history of a work that has persisted as long as *Afternoon* are complex; the pressures of the upgrade path and the evolution of program features are numerous and inconsistent; they easily front for other sympathies and understandings of interfaces to the digital field. But the temptation to locate in procedural difficulties of *Afternoon* the kernel of what the text is or does demonstrates important traits of its historical reception. These include the expectation that its mysteries must be pried from it with care and determination and—the other side of the same coin—that the prying could be made easier with the right tool. ▸N6.18

6.29 The apparent disconnect between much of the published criticism of the 1990s, which was based on the classic version and stressed *Afternoon*'s resistance to comprehension, and the features of the Windows Reader, which reduces or eliminates some of that resistance, has elicited perplexed responses from my Windows-using students. They worry that they have missed something. The "story" of *Afternoon* remains difficult to work out, but the working of it, the parsing of its textual parts, is not very challenging if one takes full advantage of features of the Windows Reader. More than once a Windows-using student has suggested that the complaints of Macintosh users indicate their envy of her comparative freedom to investigate and master Joyce's text. Even a text that stipulates its difference from conventions of seriality, she has proposed, may be further deserialized, its procedures turned against its prescribed subversion. The "Table of Instructions" for Cortázar's *Hopscotch* (*Rayuela*), for example, prescribes two sequences for reading its 155 chapters (Cortázar 1963, 1966). If the reader has accepted the premise that she may read the novel's chapters in a different order than that in which they are bound, what is to stop her from scrambling Cortázar's prescriptions? Enhanced navigation features of the Windows version of *Afternoon* permit readers to generate new textual sequences—to read outside paths programmed, albeit complexly and contingently, by Joyce; many of these new sequences cannot be generated in any other way, because the guard fields would block them. Their potential to also produce new understandings of the work seems certain.

6.30 Yet, there must also be an accounting here for what I would term *literary* operations of sequence and structure, in relation to which a more thorough decoding of the text may not be the highest priority of reading. In a 1995 essay reflecting on the early development of the Storyspace authoring system, Joyce writes,

> What I really wanted to do, I discovered, was not merely to move a paragraph from page 265 to page 7 but to do so almost endlessly. I wanted, quite simply, to write a novel that would change in successive

readings and to make those changing versions according to the connections that I had for some time naturally discovered in the process
of writing and that I wanted my readers to share. In my eyes, paragraphs on many different pages could just as well go with paragraphs
on many other pages, although with different effects and for different
purposes. All that kept me from doing so was the fact that, in print
at least, one paragraph inevitably follows another. It seemed to me
that if I, as author, could use a computer to move paragraphs about,
it wouldn't take much to let readers do so according to some scheme
I had predetermined. (Joyce 1995, 31)

6.31 Joyce's language in this passage emphasizes formal multiplicity—"paragraphs on many other pages, although with different effects and for different purposes." Narrative investigation, in the sense of decrypting or resolving a story (*histoire* or *fabula*), is not mentioned; it would seem in any
case to be implicitly subject to the authorial fiat emphasized by the passage
("according to some scheme I had predetermined"). The program Joyce describes here would leave his reader less free to derive meaning from node
sequences than she might assume on the basis of her ability to choose which
link to follow at a given juncture of her reading. In contrast, if she were able
to circumvent the determinacies of that program, she must also be freed
from other algorithmic operations it may impose. In that case some procedures of reading will be decoupled from textual systems, bringing those
procedures—and indirectly, those systems—more under the control of the
reader's initiative and interests. The result need not be a less compelling or
even, in its way, a less faithful rendering of the story, but it must be different
from a reading that accepts all constraints imposed upon it.▸N6.19

6.32 Programmatic parsings of the textbase against or outside of prescribed procedures are methods of reading: tmesis at its most directed and most productive, the lexia's reach at its most circuit-like ▸ 5.16. (In grammatextual
▸ 3.14 terms, these practices are most likely to mark out ideogrammatic or
diagrammatic signs; iconic and alphabetic signs are less susceptible to these
methods because they are more difficult to encode as commingled commands and parameters.) This is nowhere more clearly demonstrated than
in the case of full-text searching and the ways in which it opens the digital
text's surfaces to strategies of discovery. Paper indexes and tables of contents
are materially bound to the pages they reference; the hand and eye remind
us that we are still within a common operational space when we move from

one to the other. More discontinuous dependencies of paper and type, the catalog and the concordance, may approach the Find function's interruptive quality, but they cannot reproduce its punctuating quality. Finding in the textbase of a work such as *Afternoon* may more nearly resemble the flipping of pages in a book to locate the word or the line in our visual memory of a page, in the sense that the search's target stands apart, its position and its isolation more significant than its context. This decontextualization is initially marked in the Windows version of *Afternoon* in that only the name of a found node is shown in Find dialogs. The user must select a node in the hits list to jump directly to it. But that characteristic of the search, analogous to the reader's mental isolation of a mark or a pattern of the printed page—"the passage I'm looking for is near the upper third of the verso, just after a paragraph stop"—is overdetermined by the purposive quality of the Find command and by elements of the UI. These suggest that the target node is retrieved from *within* the textbase, and not from structures that might be better characterized as nonorientable—in a topological sense—prior to the execution of the search.[▸N6.20] Finding in this context appears to uncover the text's mysteries, to reveal its buried treasures. Other, more discontinuous and errant modes of textual relation are obscured.[▸N6.21]

6.33 For example: in Windows versions of *Afternoon*, the reader can easily locate a space titled {Jung} (▸ Figure 6.05):

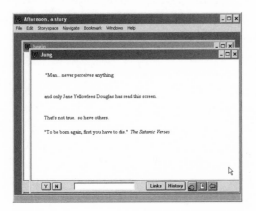

FIGURE 6.05. Michael Joyce, *Afternoon, a Story* {Jung}, 4th edition, Storyspace Reader 1.3 (1992), Windows XP (2001). Reproduced by permission of Eastgate Systems, Inc.

6.34 Unique among the 539 nodes of *Afternoon*, {Jung} comprises no inbound links; it is thus inaccessible from any other node. Known to a small circle of early critics as *Afternoon*'s "Janespace"—a term coined by Stuart Moulthrop after Jane Yellowlees Douglas discovered it—{Jung} provoked substantial debate about what its presence and disconnection from the rest of *Afternoon* might represent.▸N6.22 Joyce has professed ignorance of its provenance and most of its contents, and guesses that it may have begun as a forgotten erratum.▸N6.23

> It would have been quite unusual (given how I had to work with Storyspace in that early version, where there were fewer navigational mnemonics in the interface) to leave a space without text and move on thinking to come back later. In any case, I did. It simply sat there (filling with irony and association, I guess, a Jungian space). Then when Jane (excitedly) called to ask about it (I'm not sure when this was but at least a year after the first edition which was distributed at [H]ypertext '87). I took the first opportunity I could to write a little note there (with a quote from J[ung]) as a homage. The note said "Man . . . never perceives anything
> and only Jane Yellowlees Douglas has read this screen."
>
> Time, as they say, passed and *Afternoon* went through other editions (with largely cosmetic/interfacial changes) and in the course of preparing one of those editions I checked the space again and found the following addition: "That's not true. so have others."
>
> Since the reader text of *Afternoon* is constructed from my Storyspace "manuscript" and uses a special reader-builder, not the release version (in order to get the icons and dialogs, otherwise it's functionally the same), I knew that the reader who had inscribed this note had to have been privy to my version of the text. I rounded up the usual suspects: my wife Martha said she hadn't written in it, Mark Bernstein [of Eastgate Systems] wasn't even aware there was an unlinked node; no one else claimed to know how the note got there. I assume that either someone is purposely spinning a mystery here or that some time when I was elsewhere a reader looked through the "manuscript" *afty* and made that addition. I swear I did not. (Personal correspondence with Joyce, February 8, 1994)▸N6.24

6.35 The citation of Salman Rushdie's *Satanic Verses* appears to have been added by another party before the release of third edition. No further changes or additions were made to the node in later editions. No one who had access to the textbase of *Afternoon* during the production of the first three editions has owned up to responsibility for the interpolations unclaimed by Joyce.

6.36 Though {Jung} is the best-known such object, Janespaces appear to be not uncommon in node-link hypertexts. A 2002 survey of twenty-eight commercially published Storyspace texts found Janespaces in all but twelve (Bernstein 2002, 176); it seems likely that they will also be found in texts authored with other hypertext tools. There are several reasons for assuming this to be true. An author may, as Joyce proposes he did, forget that a node was created in an early draft without having been linked to any other nodes. If it remains unnoticed during later revisions, it might persist through to the final draft. Nodes may also be left unlinked intentionally, when they function as temporary placeholders or containers for an unfinished thread or the author's notes to herself or others in anticipation of future revisions to the text. Such a node is comparable to comments inserted by a programmer to document data structures and operations of her program. Ignored during program execution and usually invisible to users, comments are primarily employed as mnemonic and heuristic devices to support program debugging and revision.

6.37 In these cases, a Janespace would constitute an avant-texte or peritext valued by the genetic critic: the trace of material, historical conditions of composition, preserved in a form that may, potentially, be read backward, so as to deduce those conditions. Whereas for printed texts such traces are usually limited to objects preliminary to the published version—the coffee stains on Balzac's manuscripts or Joyce's corrections to printer's proofs of *Ulysses*—for digital texts the author's more direct control of intermediate states of the manuscript may mean that avant-textes and text are merged in a single polyform (but undifferentiated) object. The concept and formal boundaries of the "draft" in these cases will be more uncertain than they are for comparable works in analog media. And discerning them will be made more complex by the heterogenous uses of media typical of digital practice in the present era and for much of the foreseeable future. Included among Michael Joyce's *fonds* in the Harry Ransom Center are, Kirschenbaum has discovered, one of three surviving manuscript pages for *Afternoon*. It is marked with a coffee stain (2008, 183) ▶ 4.49.

6.38 The literary and genetic significance of a third cause for an unlinked node is more complex. The author may choose, under some conditions, to incorporate an element that is undocumented and inaccessible to normal reading methods. Two forms of this practice are common in the production of digital media. For purposes of copyright enforcement, programmers or designers may embed "software watermarks" in their code or data; some graphic design and page layout applications can add these watermarks to files they create. Though imperceptible to users and generally irrelevant to program execution, watermarks are easily discovered with forensic tools and may be a legal basis for prosecution for software piracy.

6.39 The more playful variant of this technique is known as an "Easter egg." Here, a hidden feature is inserted in program code, accessible only when the user executes a command with a specific parameter, or only when uncommon operations are performed. Famously the product of programmers' boredom and late-night, hypercaffeinated whimsy, Easter eggs are often robustly intertextual, half miniature *romans à clef* (documenting insider knowledge of the program's development or some bit of computer lore), half encrypted messages (whose significance may be as obscure as the method for revealing it). They often embed forms or variants that include them—for example, a compact version of a video game or of one of its precursors may be played on a device inside the game world. Their performative character is, uniquely, homologous with procedures for the normal use of the program or text, and in this regard they represent a reflexive and often parodic application of those procedures.

6.40 The history of *Afternoon*'s {Jung} node appears to combine several of these scenarios. The unlinked space began, according to Joyce, as an authorial slip, unremarked in later revisions. Once discovered by Douglas, reported to and annotated by Joyce, the space took on a function resembling the Easter egg: an inside joke and an ironic commentary on the significance of its production and discovery. An extension of Joyce's elliptic citation from *Man and His Symbols* invites this comparison:

> Man, as we realize if we reflect for a moment, never perceives anything fully or comprehends anything completely. He can see, hear, touch, and taste; but how far he sees, how well he hears, what his touch tells him, and what he tastes depend upon the number and quality of his senses. These limit his perception of the world around him. By using scientific instruments he can partly compensate for the deficiencies of his senses. For example, he can extend the range of his vision by binoculars or of his hearing by electrical amplification. But

the most elaborate apparatus cannot do more than bring distant or small objects within range of his eyes, or make faint sounds more audible. No matter what instruments he uses, at some point he reaches the edge of certainty beyond which conscious knowledge cannot pass. (Jung 1968, 4)

6.41 Joyce's fragmentary citation of Jung's description of technical boundaries of conscious knowledge seems a wry commentary on two aspects of his (Joyce's) project. First, his imperfect command of textual orders that his fiction might aim to incorporate: Lolly, a main character of *Afternoon*, is a Jungian analyst; Joyce speculates that he created the {Jung} space as a holder for text related to her, but he does not remember having done so. In any case, he is sure that he did not originally intend the space for a quotation from Jung.▸N6.25 Second, in relation to Joyce's *rediscovery* of the node within the Storyspace editor—in which its presence is easily discerned (▸ Figure 6.06)—

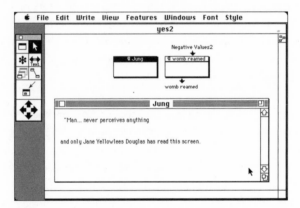

FIGURE 6.06. Michael Joyce, *Afternoon, a Story* {Jung}, 3rd edition, in the "structure" editor of Storyspace 1.5, Mac OS 6 (1990). The text space of {Jung} is shown opened in the lower half of the screen. Its writing space is shown in the upper half, to the left of the space {womb reamed}. Both spaces are contained by the space {yes2}. In this view, hierarchically ordered writing spaces are displayed as nested windows. Reproduced by permission of Eastgate Systems, Inc.

6.42 —the limit of knowledge that the original passage describes also marks the author's subjection to his writing and reading tools, and the fantasies of textual mastery they may sustain.▸N6.26

6.43 The later annotation of {Jung} by a third party shifts it into more complex genetic and metanarrative conditions, broadening its ironies to include Joyce's imperfect control of his text's circulation, the dispossessions of the editorial cycle, and the accidents of its medial conditions. As with the fragmentary quote from *Man and His Symbols*, the citation of the first line of Salman Rushdie's novel (▶ Figure 6.05) opens an intertext that appears to reflect back on conditions of knowledge subtending Joyce's fiction. "To be born again, first you have to die"—Gibreel Farishta sings this line as he falls to earth from an exploding jetliner, thus beginning his metamorphosis from Bollywood film star to angelic counter-philosopher. The line's mock *sang-froid* is notably textually aware: Farishta and his companion Saladin Chamcha must perish in one narrative order before they may be (miraculously) reborn in another. Their deaths are a precondition for the story that is to follow, and that text's opening announcement of this prepares the way for recursions of its first chapter (which ends with the explosion immediately preceding their freefall) and the magical realism of subsequent chapters. The opening question of *Afternoon*—"Do you want to hear about it?"— operates also in this way, both opening the narrative's initial conditions— the reader is invited to hear a story, which seems mostly to be about Peter's unfinished attempts to discover something he may already know—and opening the initial conditions of the reader's engagement. She is called to answer, to choose; *Afternoon* begins with the formal crisis that the choice embodies, and the question must be understood to refer also to the potential performance of the work on all registers of its textual program. ▶N6.27

6.44 The anonymous interpolator of {Jung} marks here also the complex authority of her intervention. Akin to the apocryphal "Satanic Verses" for which Rushdie's novel is named—lines said to have been inserted by Muhammad in the text of the Koran dictated to him by the angel Gabriel, but later repudiated by him when he was scolded for this interpolation—these additions to {Jung} are unauthorized; they belong to another text. By their insertion in this space—by which I mean, the fact that they have been inserted, and what it is that was inserted—they draw attention to the boundaries of authorial control of *Afternoon*'s textual program. Moreover, they do this expressly as an effect of its medial condition. They could have been inserted only by someone with access to a preproduction version and with no compunctions about altering it in this way without Joyce's permission. The instability of the authorized/unauthorized opposition thus marked by the intervention would remain hidden, visible only to Joyce, to whom it was directed.

6.45   The typographic attributes of the nodes are also altered between the first
five Mac OS editions, the sixth Mac OS edition, and Windows editions of
Afternoon. The typeface, letterspacing, and leading (interline spacing) in
editions of both platforms cannot be altered by the reader. Because Windows and Mac OS assume different baseline resolutions for the display of
type (96 versus 72 dpi), characters in the same point size will appear optically smaller on the Windows screen than on the Mac. In the Windows
editions, this difference appears to have been compensated for by using a
larger point size for the body text. That document windows of Windows
editions and the sixth Mac OS edition may be freely resized, however, produces more complex and inconsistent effects. Body text in most of the nodes
is soft-wrapped, that is, aligned to margins defined by the boundaries of the
window. If the window is resized, paragraphs are reflowed to the new margins. In most nodes, such changes are unlikely to be of significance, since
line and paragraph breaks in them have no effect other than to mark turns
in dialogue or units of narration.

6.46   In other nodes these breaks are ideogrammatically or diagrammatically
charged. Here, Joyce has introduced irregular spacing between words or
word fragments, or a line break in the middle of a phrase; rewrapping can
mask or exaggerate these irregularities. In some series of nodes, word spacing is used to effect a rudimentary form of cel animation in which words
appear to step across the screen as the user flips through the series. Resizing the window below a certain threshold destroys the effect. In other series, changes in margin widths, paragraph justification, or type size mark
shifts in narrative focus or the insertion of citations from other authors'
works.►N6.28 Reflowing text is less destructive of these traits, but may still
lessen their distinctiveness if the window is made very large.►N6.29 These
examples cue us to a more general basis of these effects: even in those cases
where breaks in the text appear to have no specific significance, resizing
the document window will change the distributions within and ratios of its
textual and graphic elements to its negative (white) space. A paragraph that
fills the screen of the classic version will seem less substantial when reduced
to a few wrapped lines in a larger window; a node that comprises only a
few words will seem less abrupt or concentrated when the negative field surrounding it is reduced.

6.47   Regimes of grammatextuality are absolute; changes in the visual or material
presentation of a text will influence the reader's reception of it. The canons

of typography and page design in scribal and print traditions take this as an axiom; conventions of the screen incorporate this axiom as the basis of effective interface design, and, inversely, as the basis of the user's privilege to alter visual forms according to her needs. The difficulty is in deciding which changes are inconsequential and which are significant—and even then, it may be possible to distinguish between degrees of significance. Differences in typeface or type size do not matter much if basic attributes of the face are more or less consistent across versions. Alterations to word-wrapping and line breaks caused by window resizing are more significant, but they are also avoidable. The Windows OS reader may choose to preserve the document window in its default state—to which it is returned when the application is closed—or she may understand that the default state is preferable for reading certain kinds of nodes.

6.48 Of greater significance are changes that alter sequence or segmentation during reading. The augmented search and navigation functions of the Windows Reader are a clear example of this. As I have observed, they offer the reader opportunities for direct engagements with *Afternoon*'s narrative logic, but only by setting apart constraints of that logic that are obviously of importance in the classic version. A reader of the Windows version may traverse segments with such freedom that Aarseth's complaint of *Afternoon*'s reluctance will seem a criticism of its obscure story, and not of its form.

6.49 A more subtle instance of change to the text's segmentation is marked in the manner of its framing on the screen. The textbase of classic versions of *Afternoon* is not only chunked in the ways that link-node hypertexts are always chunked; but the extent of its chunks also appears to have been dictated by attributes of the display device on which the text was composed, the 9-inch, 72-dpi monitor of the Macintosh 512K.[N6.30] None of the nodes of the classic versions includes a scrollbar or other of the GUI widgets used to display text hidden beyond the edges of a field, because none is required: the whole of every node fits within the 512K's screen (▶ Figure 6.01).[N6.31] *No other aspect of* Afternoon's *textual structure is as arbitrarily or as directly mapped to medial conditions of its reading*; few others can have been as determinate of Joyce's syntactical and lexical choices, while also nearly independent of their reference. I can only say "nearly" here; the complexity of this relation of textual programs to visible space is difficult if not impossible to measure; its effects can only be guessed and only in general terms. Some patterns of text and narrative must have been eliminated and others emphasized in the course of *Afternoon*'s writing, and some textual strings emended, segmented, or rejected when they threatened to exceed the limits of Joyce's canvas. It is likely that he assumed there would be a close correspondence between the surfaces on which the text was composed and on which its finished form would be displayed: in each of these conditions of viewing, the canvas defines its boundaries; only a very minimal border sets off the background and foreground of the reading surface.[N6.32] (The subtlety of the avant-texte has eliminated all traces of Joyce's decisions in these matters, which can only be inferred retrospectively from the absolute limit of the framework that forced them.[N6.33]) Because it preserves the screen's original ratio, the classic Mac OS Reader also preserves traces of this visual constraint of the text's composition.

6.50 In contrast, the Windows Reader, because it offers the possibility of resizing the window, frees the reader from this medial patterning: the scrollbar and the draggable window edge propose always to dissolve a frame that the classic edition reasserts with every change of nodes: *Je rime à dait . . .*[N2.11] The sixth Mac OS edition, based on a new version of the Storyspace Reader (2.5.1) for Mac OS X, also permits resizing of the windows, and reflows body text and adds scrollbars as needed if the window is too small to show all the text of the node. As a consequence, a basic trait of earlier Mac OS editions, signaling (if only indirectly) a determinate condition of Joyce's composition of the work, is easily obscured in this and we may assume all subsequent editions of the text.[N6.34]

6.51 We touch here on the toughest knot of a text's historical-medial situation to its expressive potential and reception. We may be confident that the material traits of *Afternoon*'s writing and reading are determinate of its meaning, but we cannot be sure of the precise nature of this relation. Its influences on Joyce's compositional practice can only be conjectured in the most general way (he meant to parse the textbase into screen-sized portions; a not insignificant detail, but what does this mean with regard to lexial structures derived in the course of a reading? ▶ 5.14). Its influences on his readers are clearer—they may be detected in the surviving evidence of the classic editions of his text—but this also requires accounting for an intervening twenty-year history of medial evolution. The eye candy of the Web, the habits of reading that it has engendered, and the pleasures it affords must inflect readers' responses to the comparably plainer surfaces and more obscure apparatus of *Afternoon*.[N6.35]

6.52 In such conditions, the effects of material-graphemic markings of specific situations and historical arcs of reading run up against the paratexts of the digital field. Separating para- from -text in printed forms can only be, as Genette has noted (1987), a capricious undertaking, since their difference tends to diffuse the more closely one attends to the effects of one on the other.▶N6.36 But this caprice is also the necessary outcome of a prior inmixing of mediality and liminality that is particularly relevant to this case. The screen-based segmentation of *Afternoon* is important—and the need to account for it is important for the critic—because it marks a lexia complex, in the sense of a conjunction of terms that I have drawn from Barthes and Hilton ▶ 5.18: it presents concrete evidence of parsings of textual structure by the author that coincide with those effected by the reader. One version of the text preserves the evidence of this coincidence; another does not.

6.53 *Allographs.* Features of the text-as-technical-apparatus ("features" in the idiom of popular computing), features of the text-as-imaginary ("features" in the topographic sense of the word): confronted by its frontispiece (▶ Figure 6.07), the reader may pass to either of two circuits. One we might term the fiction proper, the node that opens the narrative with its famous question, "Do you want to hear about it?" (▶ Figure 6.01). The second describes a brief epicycle of a kind that is less common in printed forms than in hypertexts, a series of instructions in the use of *Afternoon* and recommendations for reading strategies. (Less common, but not unheard of: some print texts require such aids for the uninitiated: Cortázar, Queneau, Saporta. Mallarmé's preface to *Un Coup de dés* is as much a "Read Me" file as a statement of poetic principles.▶N6.37) As in a bramble, there are tangles and recursions in these instructions. The narrative voice in them is inconstant and moves

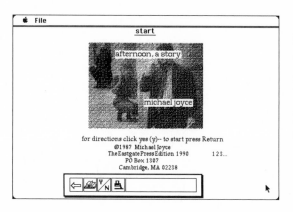

FIGURE 6.07. Michael Joyce, *Afternoon, a Story* {start}, 3rd edition, Storyspace Readingspace 1.0 (ca. 1990), Mac OS 6 (1990). Reproduced by permission of Eastgate Systems, Inc.

quickly from technical matters to more literary and meditative observations on the methods of the text and their significance—shifting, that is, from something like an impersonal *voice of the program* to a more personal *voice of the author*. The nodes mix . . .

- Unambiguously descriptive and catechrestic forms. For example: "This story is created with STORYSPACE, a hypertext program which is both an author's tool and a reader's medium"; "You move through the text by pressing the Return key to go from one section to another (i.e., 'turn pages'); and you click the Back arrow (on the bar below) to go back ('page back')"; "Respond to questions using the Yes/No buttons." The self-consciousness of even these simple descriptions is indicated by the scare quotes ("turn pages") and the typologically-marked slippage from sign to referent (Yes/No).
- Ambiguously figurative assertions. For example: "I haven't indicated what words yield, but they are usually ones which have texture . . ."; "The lack of clear signals isn't an attempt to vex you, rather an invitation to read either inquisitively or playfully and also at depth . . ."; "Closure is, as in any fiction, a suspect quality, although here it is made manifest . . ."
- Outright metaphor and intertextual citation. For example: "These are not versions, but the story itself in long lines. Otherwise, however, the center is all—Thoreau or Brer Rabbit, each preferred the bramble . . ."; "the real interaction, if that is possible, is in the pursuit of texture . . ."; "sometimes what seems a loop, like memory, heads off again in another direction . . ."; "There is no simple way to say this."

6.54 Portions of the sequence are reproduced verbatim in Eastgate's instructions on the CD-ROM; a diligent consumer of *Afternoon*'s paratexts may feel that she is reading doubles.

6.55 And she is. Instructions for how to read, if they are as in this case also a statement of literary method, represent a special subset of the paratext, procedurally similar to the blurb (*prière d'insérer*), with its invocation of the ideal situation of reception, promoted by the publisher but often written by the author (see Genette 1987). The nodes were clearly composed for early Mac OS editions, since they mention traits of the text that are not present in the Windows edition, and do not mention features specific to the latter edition. Perhaps the voice of the author must trump that of the program in such contexts—at least that privilege of authorship remains intact: correcting these inaccuracies in the textbase would have meant rewriting prose that commingles technical and literary matters. ("You move through the text by pressing the Return key . . ." "They are usually ones which have texture . . .") But separating these discourses (assuming for the moment that a discourse is something that belongs decisively to one or another voice—in reality, such a distinction will falter) would strike at the very center of the conceit that holds the allographic whole of *Afternoon* together, and that demands of us that we pay particular attention to the inmixing of forms and matter, of disorder and improbable order applied to the concrete objects it proposes for our pleasures.

6.56 My observations in this chapter are generally in keeping with those of theorists and practitioners who have complained that the strong narratological emphasis of new media criticism in the 1980s and 1990s neglected other qualities of the digital sign and the conditions of its reception.▸N6.38 At the risk of over-generalizing the important work of the first decade of criticism, I think it fair to acknowledge that much of the response to hypertext fiction's first wave—the works of Coover's golden age—focused chiefly on what the reader was expected to look for—not at—in these texts, not at the level of the pixel, its aggregates, or at operations of the program, but beneath and beyond these things: what she aimed to see within material registers of the text. There is nothing new about such a characterization of reading; Carrión's objection that a book is not a bag of words targeted just this (mis)understanding of printed reading surfaces ▸ 4.48. A similar model of reading-as-seeing-through may explain critics' misgivings concerning *Afternoon*, as well as enthusiasts' celebration of it as a ritual of disclosure. Both responses are sustained by a fixation on an object-to-be-disclosed, and not an attention to the surface-work of reading, especially of reading grammatextually rich texts, as I stressed in chapters 3 and 4. Or to-not-be-disclosed: I will argue in chapter 7 that these formulae are a pair, recto and verso of the same structure, by which more programmatic engagements with the matter of the text are evaded. I will also argue that these models of reading the screen are closely, if complexly, aligned with optical and procedural conceits of the GUI.

6.57 In some respects, *Afternoon* is a work primed to elicit readings for depth. Early criticism of the text insisted (correctly) on the importance of its nar-

rative misdirections. Thematically, the text is oriented by multiple forms
of deferral, postponement, and circumlocution (Douglas 2000, Harpold
1994). These forms are coterminous with—that is, they touch upon and
are doubled by—some of its visible traits and with the obscurity of its programmed responses to readers' actions. It seems probable that this homology of theme, presentation, and procedure prompted subsequent negative
assessments of *Afternoon* (those of Nelson and Johnson) and milder, skeptical reports of their limits. (Hayles's ranking of it among the "brave beginnings" of the first wave is typical of the latter response.) Aarseth's complaint
that *Afternoon* sabotages readers' efforts appears, ironically, to have been
addressed by changes to the Windows releases that opened alternative relays
for reading, some of which might be said to return control of the reading
situation to the reader. The "Locate writing space" and "Find text" dialogs,
for example, offer her paths of reading that open it to more assertive and
direct engagements, at the cost of fundamentally realigning her contacts
with its surfaces. The addition of these features to the Windows releases
encodes what I am tempted to describe as Nelsonian objectives for reading *Afternoon*. They introduce, where they were minimally present before,
clear signs of "overview and understanding" ▶ 6.07, in opposition to the
classic releases' enforcement of other kinds and relations of meaning.

6.58 This is not to suggest that narratological analyses of *Afternoon* or other hypertext fictions will not continue to be productive, even when such analyses
stick to structuralist models of narrative operations. I have taught *Afternoon*
as a model text under just such conditions and have found that students effectively work within them and also appreciate the challenges that the text
presents to a restrained narratology. But "narrative" and "narratology"
in this context must also be defined in ways that address nonnarrative or
extra-narrative traits of the text, which may be mistaken for narrative traits,
or which may, *au paratexte*, influence narrative reception (Harpold 2005,
2008; Ryan 2001a, 2006). Codes of narration are not exclusively hermeneu-
tically oriented; the situation of reading is not dedicated solely to the work
of deduction (Barthes 1970). Naïvely reductive or absurdly expansive models of narrative form, meaning, and pleasure will misrepresent this—not the
only or even the primary—modality of the reading encounter.

6.59 Technical difficulties for critical reading of narrative structures are much
the same as for nonnarrative structures. Parsimony is usually the best guide,
but it is also necessary to widen the definition of what is taken to be mean-

ingful in the matter of the text and to include in this traits of texts and their operations heretofore neglected because of critics' predisposition to look first beneath the surfaces of texts. This requires, broadly speaking, two closely related kinds of tasks.

6.60 *To take as an axiom for criticism that the software variants of digital texts and the hardware and software conditions under which they are read are necessary subjects for literary-historical and literary-critical investigation.* That is, to move beyond the ahistorical, narrative-obsessed decodings of texts' meanings that have dominated new media criticism for most of the last two decades, toward other approaches that attend more to texts' concrete and historical expressions. We must carefully document all the relevant traits of the texts we describe, and provide images and other representations or descriptions of their operations. [N6.39] Medially conscious critical practice must incorporate histories of the development and dissemination of texts: not just local variants (this or that version or release) but also the particulars of computer hardware and software—including those used by the critic in her work—that may shape the reception of text. [N0.14] The need for this level of detail is heightened by the phantasmic dimensions of the computer. One feels one knows more or less, as Derrida remarks, how a pen works (2001, 155). Few critics and artists are as sure of the operations of the hardware and software they use with increasing devotion in their professional and private lives. This has shaped imaginaries of composition and reception in the digital field, binding them to fantasies of knowledge and agency that are in several respects the rationales of modern operating system and program design. As the GUI is for the moment the most visible evidence of how these imaginaries are structured, that seems a good place to begin.

6.61 We must also consider effects of historiation within these visual-textual domains ▶ 2.24. The graphemic traits and operations of texts determine how we read them in relation to and as a consequence of our memories of reading like texts. Expressions of these traits in variants of the "same" work(s) read on a different version of the operating system or ported to a different operating system, or read from hardware that is faster, more responsive, with a larger display surface, and so on, may elicit distinctly different responses to those traits. Or they may foreground or obscure aspects of the text that are more or less discernible in one or another circumstance. (For example, the screen-sized chunking of syntagmas of classic versions of *Afternoon* is unmarked in Windows versions of the text and is easily erased in the sixth Mac

OS edition.) These differences will be at least partly initiated and sustained by specific visible-textual and operational attributes of media, and the paratexts and intertexts it evokes in the memory of reading like surfaces. The reader's prior experience of different software and hardware configurations is determinate of her understanding of the present moment of her reading. So too the author's prior experience of software and hardware will shape the affordances she encodes in her work and the conventions of procedure and meaning she embraces or attempts to subvert. We may find useful models for these investigations in genetic-critical studies (Ferrer 1998; Lebrave 1994; Deppman, Ferrer, and Groden 2004) and the emerging field of software cultural studies (Fuller 2008).

6.62 For the present, we lack a general method for making sense of the contribution of applications and operating systems to writing for the screen. Writing machines for the page, say, the pen or the typewriter, define in very basic ways what kinds of marks may be recorded and, within certain conventions of syntax and sequence, how they may be ordered and segmented. These tools may also be easily turned, such that their limits are weakened or embraced in a calculated way. The tools of digital writing may also be turned, but generally less radically, since the complexity of computer software and hardware renders them especially liable to malfunctions if they are pushed too far away from their normal operations. Reading from the screen is even more constrained in this respect, because the reader usually has minimal knowledge and even less control of the programmed logic of the text. Criticism of the print paratext will provide few leads in these matters, since direct analogies between functional forms of the interface and formal divisions of the page or grammatical structure are officious at best. Jerome McGann has demonstrated the need for a critical poetics of the page's "visible resources," even as he has shown that such a discipline is, at best, still in its infancy (McGann 1993, 2001). It remains difficult to think through the relation of page space and letterform to signifier, signified, and referent in the printed artifact. The complexity of their transpositions to the computer screen, invoking thereby more than a century of cinematic and televisual resources, can only increase this difficulty ▶ 3.06. ▶N6.40 The emerging disciplines of platform studies (Montfort and Bogost 2008) and literary-digital forensics (Kirschenbaum 2002, 2008) show great promise in the analysis of these and other material correlatives of digital literature and art.

6.63 *How do we account for the multiplication of allographic registers of the digital text?* Authorial autonomy is a convenient fiction well suited to ideologemes of the best-seller list and the critic's need for simple forms of address. But a basic fact of literary production is that it is always an allographic system. Without the collaborative labor of page and book design and typesetting—to set aside the small armies involved in tasks related to the procurement, editing, proofreading, and disseminating of a printed work—it cannot make the transition from "manuscript" to "text" (White 2005, 25). Digital texts are no different in this respect; their authors may be more dependent on hidden collaborative labor, since their tools are, by the nature of how they are produced and by virtue of technical and market forces that shape them, enmeshed in complex dependencies of production and distribution. Most of these dependencies have only the slightest (if any) correlation with artistic concerns, having mostly to do with organizational behaviors: what can be done, what must be done, what must be abandoned or postponed in order to hit the release date, increase market share, or overrun the competition.

6.64 At the level of the desktop, authors of digital literary texts for most of the past two decades have been notably constrained in how and to what extent they may control the presentation of their texts. Accomplished visual artists who can master complex textual programs are no more common among authors for the screen than among authors for print, though this may be changing as graphics applications have become capable of automating or at least streamlining the creation of sophisticated effects. (Complex animations and video are still relatively rare in extended digital literary texts, perhaps because authoring tools for those media are still targeted primarily to professional users.) Collaboration between visual artists and literary authors is not uncommon, but the general rule is still one-person production: the same individual composes the textbase, determines its articulations, and creates what non-alphanumeric elements it contains. The marketplace for digital literary works, such as it is, nearly demands this model; no one seems to be making a living from these works. In historical terms, this meant that digital works of the first and second wave were typically not so elegant or subtle in their typographemic forms as many printed texts with equally small readerships, because the institutional bases for the divisions of labor this would require are immature.

6.65   Relevant to this problem is the emphasis of many authoring systems on defining and managing document structure rather than controlling the graphemic attributes of the reading surface. Little of the fine control required
for a digital *Un Coup de dés* or *Radi Os* ▶ 4.17 is available in an otherwise
powerful authoring tool such as Storyspace, and it is difficult to assess the
effect of visible resources when little care has been paid to them in the tools
for building them up (McGann 2001, 175, 185). This limitation has been
considerably reduced on the Web, where support for still and moving images and script-driven interactivity has increased the variety and allure of
attributes of the reading surface and their responsiveness to the reader. Yet,
as Alan Liu has observed, the underlying logic of HTML, the markup language that drives most of the visible Web, is oriented by a Modernist privileging of form over content—which is to say, logical form, well-behaved
structure (2004, 222). Fractious, inconsistent relays of grammatextual fields
will be marked in such an environment, but they are hard to program into
it ▶ 7.07.

6.66   Historically, the absence of control of grammatextual nuances has signified in its own right. Rather than marking a liberation from a constellation
of physical traits in the paper docuverse (page and margin sizes, typeface,
character and line counts, justification, and so on), the fluidity of corresponding traits on the screen can be said for the most part to have figured
a pretense that they do not matter, or do not matter much. Perhaps with
good reason: variability in the text's visual presentation poses difficulties
not only for critical interpretation, but also for theorizing contributions of
grammatextual elements to texts received in these conditions. This remains
a particular problem in the analysis of texts displayed in Web browsers,
where such traits—if any are specified—may be suppressed or ignored.
Where none is specified, the qualities of the text are determined by default
application settings, whose selection depends more on the habits of programmers and the vagaries of the layout engine and operating system than
concerns of aesthetic or operational nuance.

6.67   Effects of a lack of fine typographemic control in first-wave authoring tools
may be more generalized in the form of a frequent disconnect between what
authors and readers require and what designers of hardware and software
conclude is appropriate. For example, I think it safe to assume that the two
computer applications most used by creative writers and digital fine art-

ists today are, respectively, Microsoft Word and Adobe Photoshop. Both are all-purpose applications with numerous and diverse features, many of which are rarely called upon by even the most adept user. Even so, each application is oriented to specific frameworks of use. Photoshop includes many functions suited to "creative" ends, but it is marketed to and designed primarily for commercial graphic artists and photographers. Microsoft Word is described by its publisher as the anchor of a suite of "office" applications, which means (one may presume) that it is designed primarily for writing business letters and reports. The question then must be asked: How are the products of artistic or poetic labor created with such tools constrained by the ways in which those tools encode affordances characteristic of more pragmatic contexts of use? To suggest that they are constrained in this way does not mean that they are impoverished—obviously, an artist may repurpose even the narrowest constraint to new and productive ends; aesthetic effects may be derived from the inconsistency of the object's logic with conditions of its production or presentation. Fictions of the first wave did not surrender aesthetic operations of the grammatext to functions of the GUI; they worked those functions and the conventions they defined to subtle effect. Designers of new tools for digital writing and reading can hardly be faulted for wanting to expand the affordances of those tools as hardware and software platforms mature. Artists will once again rework the tools to new, possibly unforeseen ends. The historiographic problem lies in how we have applied the new tools to the old texts, or in how we have reimagined the old texts in terms of the new tools.

6.68 Perhaps the limitations of the early authoring programs for the incorporation and control of graphics, typeface control, and screen layout helped to perpetuate Coover's myth of a golden age of hypertext. To what extent was software's lack of support for grammatextual nuance a signal of and a justification for a prior expectation that hypertext's literary effects are realized at levels of the syntagma, the line, and the letter? Another effect of the upgrade path and the new capabilities it brings: if works of the silver and bronze ages shifted the preponderance of effects toward graphic registers, this has been accompanied by a decreasing emphasis on qualities of narrative and mimesis (and their peripheral phenomena) that may be achieved only by the play of alphabetic glyphs arranged in long sequences ▶ 2.19. "Back to the movies," then ▶ 6.02—with the proviso that the medial conventions this implies may not be so clear as Coover proposes ▶ 3.22.

6.69 The purchase of the visible on meanings of the digital text is inextricably yoked to the present situation of the screen, and by this to messy inconstancies of software publishing and the upgrade path. It may be possible to read from a position that stands apart from the most naïve forms of the backward glance and the impulse to reduce the matter of the text to its semiotic and thematic depths, but this can be done only if we apply ourselves to set apart interiority as only one of the allures of texts in the era of the GUI. The reductive impulse looks through the screen in search of the satisfactions of another scene; in this, it misses too many of the wheels and pinions of its stagecraft.▸[N6.41] Conceiving of digital reading solely or even chiefly as a practice of excavating meaning from the machine's secret registers means mistaking for signs of depth objects that may be best thought of as stuck to the surface of the text: jammed, with the reading subject, someplace among the clattering apparatus of the reading scene.

7.

Reading Machines

The machine is the structure detached from the activity of the subject.
—Jacques Lacan (1954)

Because it can produce a few notes, tho' they are *very* flat,
and it is nevar [*sic*] put with the wrong end in front!
—Lewis Carroll (1896)▶N7.01

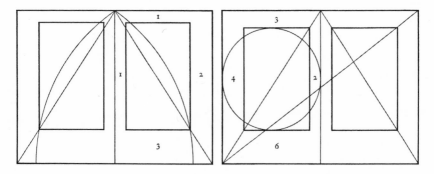

FIGURE 7.01. *Left:* "Framework of ideal proportions in a medieval manuscript without multiple columns. Determined by Jan Tschichold, 1953. Page proportion 2:3, Margin proportion 1:1:2:3. Text area proportioned in the Golden Section!" *Right:* "The secret canon, upon which many late medieval manuscripts and incunabula are based. Determined by Jan Tschichold, 1953. Page proportion 2:3. Text area and page shown the same proportions. Height of text area equals page width. Margin proportions 2:3:4:6" (Tschichold 1975, 1991). Reproduced by permission of Birkhäuser Verlag, Basel.

7.01 Jan Tschichold, in his 1975 treatise on book design, *Ausgewählte Aufsätze über Fragen der Gestalt des Buches und der Typographie* (published in English as *The Form of the Book*):

> Two constants reign over the proportions of a well-made book: the hand and the eye. A healthy eye is always about two spans away from the book page, and all people hold the book in the same manner.

The format of the book is determined by its purpose. It relates to the average size and the hands of an adult. Children's books should not be produced in folio size because for a child this format is not handy. A high degree or at least a sufficient degree of handiness has to be expected: a book the size of a table is an absurdity, books the size of postage stamps are trivialities. Likewise, books that are very heavy are not welcome; older people may not be able to move them around without help. Giants should have books and newspapers that are larger; many of our books would be too large for dwarfs. (Tschichold 1991, 36)

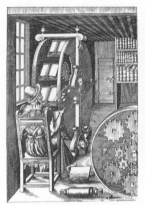  

FIGURE 7.02. *Left:* Agostino Ramelli's reading wheel (1588). From *The Various and Ingenious Machines of Agostino Ramelli* (1976), plate 188. *Center and right:* Daniel Libeskind's wheel, based on similar principles, constructed using sixteenth-century tools and methods. Daniel Libeskind, *Reading Machine,* Installation at Venice Biennale, 1985.

7.02 Agostino Ramelli, writing nearly three centuries earlier, describes his design for a mechanical reading wheel (▶ Figure 7.02):

This is a beautiful and ingenious [*artificieuse*] machine, very useful and convenient for anyone who takes pleasure in study, especially those who are indisposed and tormented by gout. For with this machine a man can see and turn through a large number of books [*vn homme peut voir & lire vne grãde qvãtité de liures*] without moving from one spot. Moreover, it has another fine convenience in that it occupies very little space in the place where it is set, as anyone of intelligence can clearly see from the drawing. (Ramelli 1976, 508)

7.03 The image on the left in ▶ Figure 7.02 shows Ramelli's engraving of the device; the photographs in the center and on the right are of a wheel based on similar principles created in 1985 by architect Daniel Libeskind.▶N7.02

7.04 Each of these excerpts represents a prescription for the comfortable use of the codex, the form of the book most familiar to the modern reader: folded sheets stitched in quires and bound between two covers, turned right to left or left to right, converse to the direction of the script in which it is printed. Tschichold, with characteristic plainness, describes an ideal type of this object, well fitted to its user's hands and eyes. Ramelli, with characteristic immodesty, describes a device that repairs the codex's deficiencies: it may take up much of the surface on which it rests; its use may occupy both hands of the reader; it is difficult to operate more than one at a time.

7.05 To hold even a small book in one's hands for an extended period of time can be uncomfortable; larger books are more unwieldy; some oversized volumes, such as single-volume dictionaries, are impossible to handle thus for all but the most vigorous readers. The reader must find a place for the book, close enough to the hand and eye that it is easy to turn and read the pages, but far enough away that other activities of the body are not too much restricted. Reading in a reclining position, on a sofa or in bed, can mean having to use one's torso as a bookrest. Reading at the dinner table crowds the service and demands one-handed gymnastics of cutlery and drinking glass. Reading in a crowded subway or train, we have to hold our arms at length or right up against our breast. For all the pleasures it affords us, the book also gives us minor discomforts and requires a surprising amount of open space for a thing that seems eminently compact and portable.

7.06 For those who take delight in study these problems are multiplied, since many books are many times more cumbersome. (The scholar's fate, as Bush lamented: to be surrounded by ever-mounting, ever more disordered piles of books and papers. Wondering where to store them all also means wondering how to find a perch from which to read them all.) Ramelli's ingenious wheel can retrieve any of several volumes quickly, and maintain each at an unchanging angle to the eye—"indeed," he adds, "they will always remain in the same position and will be displayed to the reader in the same way as they were laid on their small lecterns, without the need to tie or hold them with anything" (Ramelli 1976, 508). Finding the best angle at which to turn and view the page is also a concern for Tschichold: in the paragraph following the lines cited above, he deplores the decline of reading and writing on the steep surface of a lectern, "a healthy and reasonable position," he notes, "that has, alas, become rare" (Tschichold 1991, 37).

7.07 Tschichold and Ramelli's prescriptions are specific to relations with what might be termed *usable* codices. Tschichold excludes very large and very small books as innately clumsy or trivial. A book the size of a table may be better used . . . as a table.▸N7.03 One of still greater dimensions can only monumentalize the book as such (at its extreme, Dominique Perrault's controversial design for the Bibliothèque Nationale François Mitterrand), or, inversely, emphasize in comic or tragic terms disjunctions of the hand and the page, as in cartoons in which a diminutive person wrestles with the pages of a normal-sized book.▸N7.04 Infelicities of the very small book extend these disjunctions to an intimate level: there, the hand and eye over-master the page, so that the page disappears under the fingertip and the eye strains to decipher the text. In all measures, then, the page's ratios should be matched by corresponding ratios of the reading situation—not too big or small, too close or far ("the Golden Section!"), too regular (banal and limiting) or too irregular (lopsided and awkward).▸N7.05 The actual values of mass and distance may vary in relation to the sizes of the text and the reader's body, but their relative proportions—as those of the page itself—should not vary much.▸N7.06 Other conditions of usability in this vein may be imagined: a book must, for example, be able to fit on a shelf and the spine should hold the book block in place.▸N7.07

7.08 Considerations such as these will have pragmatic significance, but their basis is more fundamental, in a formal correspondence between the human relation to an expressive object (the codex) and the relations of the units of that object. Each register, Tschichold presumes, should be rational; each should be oriented toward the most complete coincidence of procedure and form. Efficient reading will be determined by definite procedures, fitted to syntagmas of expression (words and lines on a page or the spread of two pages).

7.09 Tschichold's claim to have rediscovered the canon of the medieval page directs us also to earlier crossings of these elements in the *ordinatio* of medieval and early modern scribes. These systems of the illuminated page—in modern terms, they could be characterized as design guidelines—prescribed the kinds and positions of its elements: the roles of margins, illustrations, and historiated initials ▶ 2.26; the use of multiple columns of text, spaces between words, markings of major and minor subdivisions, and so on. The *ordinatio* encoded general principles of textual order, building into structures of the page the visual grammars of scholastic reasoning that have persisted with only minor changes into the modern era. By defining how knowledge should be represented on writing surfaces, they defined what was considered to be rigorous argument and reason in an intellectual order in which written marks were the principal relays of thought (Camille 2004, 20; Stoicheff and Taylor 2004b, 11–12).

7.10 Tschichold recovered these systems, he claims, by meticulous empirical investigation:

> The old law has been lost, and it was not to be found again with *feeling* alone. This is where I have succeeded by measuring countless medieval manuscripts. The rediscovered canon, shared here, is free from all arbitrariness and ends all laborious groping. In all its many variations it will inevitably lead to books where page format and text block agree with one another and become a harmonious unit. (1991, 61–62)

7.11 Rational form begets rational form, now and in the future. Tschichold has refitted harmonies of the "old law" to the modern reading surface in only two respects, concessions perhaps to an intervening history in which situations of reading have multiplied. First, by his observation of the reader's varieties and the need to adapt the page to them, rather than the reverse (big books for giants, little books for dwarfs). Second—though this is not strongly marked in the passages I have cited—by his emphasis on the suppleness of the page and book. The "morality of good design" (the subtitle of the English translation of the 1975 treatise) is, above all, a measure of care for the places of the hand and eye and the units of expression they manipulate. This is also a primary concern of Ramelli's wheel.

7.12 Like most of the objects depicted in his theater of machines, the reading wheel is a conjectural device meant to demonstrate its creator's technical virtuosity. It was probably never constructed within Ramelli's lifetime. But reading wheels of a different design, turning horizontally in the manner of the modern-day lazy Susan, are known to have been common in Europe by the early fifteenth century; John Willis Clark (1977) and Bert Hall (1970) propose that they may have been introduced there as much as two hundred years before.►N7.08 Sometime between the sixteenth and nineteenth centuries, they appear to have morphed into two kinds. One resembles the earlier wheels: a rotating lectern capable of holding a small number of books that can be consulted seriatim. The revolving lectern designed by Thomas Jefferson on display at his home in Monticello is an example of this kind. The second was a common fitting of Victorian libraries: a revolving bookcase, on which many books are arranged on parallel shelves, with spines facing out or stacked at a slight upward angle, covers facing out. This version of the wheel probably inspired the wire-frame display cases still found in American drugstores and airport newsstands, and usually reserved for light reading or bestsellers. Here, rotation is primarily a method for saving space and supporting a kinetic form of browsing, rather than the serial, multicursal modes of access facilitated by the earlier designs.

7.13 L. Carrington Goodrich (1942) and Joseph Needham and Ling Wang (1965) have shown that the earliest known descriptions of the horizontal form date from mid-sixth-century China. Known as *lun tsang* ("revolving repositories"), the Chinese wheels differed from the European designs in several respects. They were much larger—sometimes requiring teams of operators —and held many more texts. Often, these were scrolls stored lengthwise in individual recesses in the outside face of the wheel. *Lun tsang* were most common in Buddhist temples, where they were used in the collation of scripture and, later, in ritual functions that did not involve removing the texts or reading them (Needham and Wang 1965). Whether or how the Chinese wheels may have influenced the design of the European wheels is unknown.►N7.09

7.14 Ramelli's chief innovation is to have turned the reading wheel's axis 90 degrees to the vertical, so that its user sits before a surface that moves up or down, toward or away from her in a cycle that closes on itself, like a waterwheel or a modern-day Ferris wheel. In the context of his other designs, this change is not surprising, since Ramelli's book is full of images of waterwheels, water pumps, fountains, and lifting and moving machinery, many of which are driven by gearing on a horizontal axis. The section of the book that includes the reading wheel is preceded by a long series of images of assault machines and weaponry, ending with several plates showing machines that would allow an individual to move heavy objects without assistance.▸N7.10 Here, however, something interesting is marked. The three plates just before the one showing the reading wheel are of complex fountains and an ornate vase, and each of these designs uses water or air pressure to drive movements and songs of mechanical birds. The wheel may be introduced, in other words, in an epicycle within the larger argument—given the wheel's method, can this be a mere coincidence?—and as one of several conjectural machines whose purpose is simulation.

7.15 *The wheel simulates a textual field.* Ramelli's wheel has assumed a totemic role in new media criticism, where it has been cited as an example of hypertext *avant la lettre*. This is demonstrably true, but not—or not in the most important way—because the wheel permits more efficient seriatim reading of multiple texts. It is instead the topology of reading realized by the wheel's rotations that marks it as an authentic precursor of the digital field. This aspect of the wheel has been neglected by historians, who have focused on Ramelli's stated aim of easeful study ("especially for those who are indisposed and tormented by gout"), and his use of epicyclic gearing to keep the lecterns at the same angle as the wheel turns (Ramelli 1976, 578n55). The wheel is a "revolving bookcase," but in that respect it is more than an efficient means of fetching a book or a passage from a book, in the way that the machinery of Bush's "intimate supplement" ▸ 1.14 is more than a handy device for sorting and retrieving page images. Retrieval is only one of the reading machine's modes of textual labor; more fundamentally, it aims to provide access to defiles of a textual field that a mere series of pages or books cannot.

7.16 Memex engages this logic in registering an idiosyncratic (signature) archiving, Xanadu by containing the effects of any one arrangement of the archive so that it does not preclude others. Ramelli's wheel resituates problems of circuits and fields ▸ 1.44 by figuring their relation as a system of concentric and intersecting cycles. It brings any one text quickly to the hand and eye and it describes a locus within which expressive units are moved in multiple directions. That is, it moves the units—letters, words, pages— in a circuit that is orthogonal to movements of the hand and eye while turning from recto to verso or verso to recto, projecting the surface of each page into a third dimension. The multiple rotations of the combined wheel/ book/page apparatus project a shape less like a circle than a series of nested toruses, or doughnuts, and represents thus a richer and more general description of textual structure than any of the device's parts is able to figure on its own.

7.17 Libeskind's version of the device (▶ Figure 7.02), constructed three centuries later, was the first of three "lessons on architecture" he devised around problems of reading, memory, and writing. "When I read Vitruvius and Alberti," he writes, "and they said every good architect must first make a machine to do architecture, I thought that if I'm going to be a good architect I must follow the tradition to its end. So I tried to do it in a particular way" (Libeskind 1991, 39). The wheel was created entirely using sixteenth-century tools and methods and without any modern sources of power (Libeskind and his team worked by candlelight after sunset). It was roughly hewn (no sandpaper), big and heavy; Libeskind observes that it creaked as it moved and required substantial effort to turn (39). The wheel's recreation of a particular reading of architectural history—an "almost forgotten process of building" and "a monastic faith in the craft of making" (39)—would have seemed embodied not only in its mechanism, but also in its materials. Remember the crossing of real and textual time in Xanadu's slicing of braided versions ▶ 2.01, which Nelson compared to a species of time travel, in that the braid and the slice substantiate—literally, give substance to—the archival past (1974, DM 54). Even before the user of Libeskind's wheel begins to turn the lecterns, she understands that the gesture invokes a form of rememoration out of the chaos of her personal store. ▶N7.11

7.18 The other lessons on architecture that Libeskind created around the time he made the reading wheel bear out this mnemonic structure. The second lesson, on remembering architecture, also created using early modern tools and techniques, fancifully recreated the lost mnemonic theater of Giulio Camillo out of gears, spools, ropes, weights, and printed texts glued to boards, blocks, and the machine's supports (Libeskind 1991, 51). ▶N7.12 It is unclear that operating the device did anything other than move its parts: a ramshackle, mechanistic rummaging through the attic of architectural memory, foregrounding one or another of eighteen "subordinate spectacles," local parts of a whole that refuses synthesis and obtains what meaning it can from the caprices of Libeskind's prior reading. (He cites as inspiration Miguel de Cervantes, Giordano Bruno, James Joyce, and Constructivist architect Vladimir Tatlin, an early colleague of Kazimir Malevich ▶4.41.▶N7.13) The third lesson, on writing architecture, was a modern, industrial machine comprising more than 2600 wood, graphite, and metal parts. Modeled after the writing loom Gulliver is shown at the Academy of Lagado (Swift 1957–69), it was composed of forty-nine revolving cubes. The faces of the cubes were marked with text and abstract designs—the names of saints, abstract plans of cityscapes from Europe and Africa, divinatory symbols—and rotated at different speeds when cranks along the side were turned, so as to present different composite sets of cube faces to the top surface, in the manner of a platen press. Given the complexity of the rotations, Libeskind observes, the initial combination of the cube faces may never be repeated if a crank has been turned. The ghosts of Swift and Roussel may be summoned here, and rotations of the *lun tsang* seem also nearby:

> Once in motion, the stockpiling and accounting of places, cities, types of buildings, gods, signs, saints, imaginary beings, forgotten realities, will present almost insurmountable difficulties for the operator, yet these are difficulties which can be eliminated through the revolutionary discipline of this turn towards a Buddhism of Action. (Libeskind 1991, 56)

7.19 Circuits and fields: each of Libeskind's lessons embodies an extensive semiotic by means of an apparatus that moves texts in multiple directions and with irregular rhythms. These are subdued brambles, and limited arborescences, but they succeed in working their extensions while adhering fairly strictly to the constraint of the printed page, whereas Joyce's yield words ▶6.10 and Lacan's arbors ▶2.10 seemed to draw operations of language away from that surface.

7.20 Libeskind, however, eased this constraint with the books with which he stocked the reading wheel. There were eight in all, each handmade and of different lengths. The pages of each were printed with sequences of letters formed from eight words or short phrases—"I sought words which are no longer readable in the text of architecture" (Libeskind 1991, 39–40)—fractured by irregular character spacing and punctuation▶N7.14—so as to appear to be nonsense, unless they were read across interruptions of the spacing and punctuation marks. The reader seated at the wheel, turning its lecterns (backward or forward), then turning pages (forward or backward), and then parsing the texts over and against the structure that the printing has imposed on them, must describe by these movements of the hand, eye, and text a Ptolemaic circuitry of vast complexity.

7.21 We are returned by this image to the system of textual loci characteristic also of Vannevar Bush's design for the Memex: the cumulative paths of each reader, concretely realized by movements of the reading machine. In the case of the Memex, these were marked out by rotations of the spools of film and exchanges of film between users, and their formal logic condensed in the trail. In Ramelli's and Libeskind's designs, the vertiginous circuitry of such a system is encoded in the intricate gearings of the wheel and the books' more subtle operations. As significant as these are circumstances not shown in images of the wheel as it is being used: the user has to decide which texts to place on its lecterns. She has, in fact, to determine the relative addresses of the elements that the wheel will turn before it is put into movement.

7.22 Ramelli has already thought of this, though it may be hard for us to see the evidence for it. Henry Petroski observes that the books on the shelf at the fore of the room in Ramelli's engraving are arranged vertically with their spines facing out. "Ramelli was as forward-looking," he writes,

> as he was inventive. There appear to be few if any other contemporary depictions of books on shelves that have the same rigid arrangement that Ramelli shows. In the sixteenth century it was still much more common for books to be displayed on a sloping shelf with the decorated front exposed, as they were on lecterns in monasteries, to be leaned against the wall behind a shelf, or to be placed flat on a horizontal shelf with their top, bottom or fore-edge out. When books were shelved in a vertical position, it was the fore-edge and not the spine that was faced out. (Petroski 1999, 118–19)

7.23 The practice of labeling books' spines was, Petroski notes, not common in Ramelli's time. For a casual visitor to the study shown in his engraving of the wheel, the shelved books would have seemed as indistinguishable from one another as they appear in that image. Only the books' owner—that is, only someone for whom they might be classified according to textual and

haptic schemes that their arrangement on the shelf might not capture—
would be able to tell them apart easily. Because private libraries were not
large by modern standards, "the scholar could be expected to know each of
his books by size and thickness, by color and texture of binding" (Petroski
1999, 119). The mundanity of this practice obscures its formal basis and its
absolutely determinate role in programs of reading. What modern reader
has not scanned a row of books on a shelf, her eyes just enough unfocused
so as to pass over their titles and pick up only their size and thickness, color
and binding? What we do in this situation is to interleave the shelf's prior or-
derings with other—paratextual, intertextual, wholly subjective—schemes
of organization and rememoration. Before she sits down at Ramelli's or
Libeskind's wheel, the user has already performed a similar operation or
has allowed another to do it in her place; the books have been initially
ordered by having been placed on this or that lectern. Or she will soon
do this: after spinning the wheel a while she must stop its movement, rise
from her seat, and swap texts from the lectern to the stationary shelves and
back, and start again. Her mobility is limited—like the Memex user ▶ 1.49,
she cannot travel very far from the machine if she wishes to make use of it
(is this not one implication of Ramelli's mention of gout—that the reader
will be hobbled in some way by a dependence on the wheel?), but she has
a limited freedom, to draw its circuits into other systems of ordering and
collating texts.▶N7.15

7.24 In the context of automatisms of a reading machine, this initialization of
the textbase and a partial freedom from its circuits are of the highest consequence. (The collector's passion: her archive comprises disciplined and
undisciplined events of reading alike: from their chaos, a specific order
emerges; even from the most automated reorderings, it pertains only to her
▶ 1.54.)▶N7.16 In that light, the wheel describes a more complete figure of
textual practice than may appear to be the case, since it will encompass
the past and present of any reading encounter that makes use of such a
supplementary mechanism. This is the beauty, ingenuity, and convenience
of the device: like Bush's archive-as-office-furniture, its concrete operations
describe paths of a reading habit that is both generative and retrospective.
Which is to say that the wheel's generative potential is, in part, determined
by its encoding of a reading history, in that the sequences it produces are
founded in part on an initial order that the wheel then elaborates. Or discovers: virtual orders, collations, and intersections that would not other-

wise become evident. But these, too, may be presumed to have been there all along, *in potentio*, waiting for the wheel to make it possible to recollect them.▸N7.17

7.25 The wheel's ability to figure these patterns is, however, limited. The principal reason for this is clear: the units it can reorder and recombine are too few and too large. (Until the trail began to drift toward pure structure, the Memex was similarly limited, to recombinations of its page images.) Libeskind's wheel was designed to hold eight books, Ramelli's as many as twelve. A larger wheel with more lecterns can be imagined, but practical matters—the difficulty of turning a larger circle, the boundaries of the room's floor and ceiling—will soon preclude further expansion. The user is able to swap texts on the lecterns for others from her shelves, but again a pragmatic boundary must intervene in the time required to move books on and off the lecterns. There is no way to subdivide the books and so mix their parts without respect to their bindings.

7.26 In this regard, Ramelli's invention is comparable to other stagings of the codex that multiply paths of reading without disturbing basic operations of the page or line. Saporta's *Composition no. 1* (1962, 1963) permits recombinations of its textbase that are more complex and contingent than if it were segmented in the usual way, but the smallest units of these operations is the page.▸N7.18 Massin's celebrated edition of Raymond Queneau's *Cent mille milliards de poèmes* (1961) lowers the unit threshold another step. In that work, individual lines of the ten sonnets that compose the textbase are printed on the recto of strips of heavy paper stock (▸ Figure 7.03). Each line of each sonnet is interchangeable with the corresponding line of the other sonnets: any of the ten first lines can be slotted into the first position; each first line is compatible with any of the ten second lines, which may be slotted into the second position—and so on, up to the fourteen positions of the sonnet form.▸N7.19 Interleaving the lines in every possible way by folding the paper strips back or forward will generate all 10^{14} permutations of the textbase, or 100 million million poems.

7.27 Queneau estimates that a person working at the text 24 hours a day would take more than 190 million years to review all the poems it is capable of producing. But even that dizzying prospect is bounded by the work's reliance on a hinge mechanism: the chunking of the textbase at the level of the

FIGURE 7.03. Massin's book design for Raymond Queneau's *Cent mille milliards de poèmes* (1961). The lines of the ten sonnets that compose the textbase are printed on strips of heavy stock, which the reader can fold individually to produce 100,000,000,000,000 unique poems. Collection of the author.

line prevents its shuffling method from figuring many more subtle circuits that so dedicated a reader might locate.▶N7.20

7.28 Like these noteworthy reformulations of the codex, the wheel is designed for texts whose parts follow one another in the usual way: in Latin alphabets, from top to bottom and left to right; in other alphabets, in other directions but no less determinate or lineal at the level of the page. It projects the space of reading along axes more complex than the basic hinge of the codex, but it cannot describe textual patterns whose operations are more dispersed. It presumes the relative integrity of the page and the line; it cannot account for field effects of the letter or the grapheme. Extraserial semiotics typical of iconic or ideogrammatic grammatexts would, as Roland Greene has observed, stop it short (1992). Implicit diagrams of color or dimension, and alphabetic operations beyond volume and page sequences (such as anagrammatic or algorithmic schemes) will not be answerable to its rotations. More elaborate seria keyed by textual patterns but not written in them—Barthes's lexia ▶ 5.03, Hilton's complex ▶ 5.18—may be conceived of as somehow anchored to the lectern or the wheel, but they must also extend beyond its mechanical elements into fields that touch on them only in the most figurative way. The wheel efficiently dislocates the page from simple forms of seriality, but it cannot encompass more general systems of reading, because it cannot account for effects below and beyond the thresholds of the units it circulates.

7.29 What will be the effect on this circuitry if its textbase starts off by being more complex, in that its parts do not follow one another in the usual way? Among the direct descendants of Ramelli's wheel is another device, constructed in the 1950s by Juan-Esteban Fassio to assist in the reading of Raymond Roussel's *Nouvelles Impressions d'Afrique* (*New Impressions of Africa*).[N7.21]

7.30 Roussel's 1932 poem in four cantos is the most formally complex work by the most formalist writer of the early twentieth century. In its published forms, Roussel's notoriously baroque methods have been mapped onto material traits of the line and page, engaging their grammatextual characteristics—particularly in the format in which Roussel intended the poem to be read—to a degree perhaps unmatched by any other work of that era.[N7.22] Each canto begins with a brief "impression" of Africa, interrupted by a parenthetical aside, which is interrupted by another, and so on, until up to five levels of parentheses are reached, at which point the levels begin to close again. Matching sections of each level may be separated by hundreds of lines, and may be further interrupted by footnotes, some containing their own parentheses. The footnotes often run over into several successive pages. Because they must be read where they are encountered and in their entirety in order to preserve the poem's rhyme scheme, the reader frequently has to turn back and forth across multiple pages to follow a footnote to its end and then to resume her reading where the note began.[N7.23]

7.31 (Rather than parentheses to set off these embedded series, Roussel had originally planned to use a different color of type for each level of the body text and footnotes. But printing the work in this format proved too costly, and so the typographic scheme of nested parentheses was chosen. Most modern editions of the poem have kept to this scheme, possibly for the same reasons of economy, although a 2004 edition has recast the poem with color type. (Which colors Roussel planned to use are unknown. The editor of this edition justifies its color scheme—green, white, blue, red, yellow, and black, printed on gray paper—by appealing to the canons of heraldry and evocations of each of these colors in other works by Roussel (*sans l'image historiant l'armorial . . .* ▶2.25). Even in a casual reading, the difference between the two schemes is striking. Whereas the diagrammatic significance of changes in the color of type seems to register primarily in terms of a visual layering of the text—the brighter colors especially appear to hover over the gray background—the levels marked by parentheses seem more to merge with the poem's textual sequences, standing out mostly when a series of opening or closing parentheses occurs at the beginning or end of a line.[N7.24])

7.32 Then there are the illustrations, fifty-nine in all, by Henri-Achille Zo. Roussel commissioned them in a famously roundabout manner, contacting Zo anonymously through the intermediary of a private detective agency. Given only a list of cryptic "indications" for each image ("An empty street. In the foreground, a lamp-post"), Zo was never shown the text of the poem until after its publication. Though some images seem to directly represent characters or events of the poem, most do not, and are related to its themes and patterns by way of the schemes of successive and symmetrical pairs they mark in relation to the units of the textbase they enclose, and, more radically, by virtue of their material and semiotic interruptions of the verse form.[N7.25]

7.33 These operations are activated by the work's unique engagement of its imposition.[N7.26] In its first edition, *Nouvelles Impressions* was published in a sextodecimo (16mo) format, meaning that the printer's sheets were folded into 16 leaves, or 32 pages per signature (Caradec 1964). Uniquely, the text and images were imposed so that lines of the poem were printed only on the outside recto of each folded leaf, and the next image on the inside recto of that leaf. Because the book was published untrimmed—up until the mid twentieth century, it was common for books to be published uncut in this way—the reader was forced either to cut the pages in order to see the image hidden in the folded leaf, or to pry open the leaf and view the image within the fold. A more dimensional relation of reading from a codex may not be possible if it is to remain in its binding.[N7.27]

7.34 Fassio's machine to assist in the reading of Roussel's poem must embrace as many of the systems of its printed form as possible, while ostensibly offering some enhancement of their operations. To the degree that this is possible, it happens on three fronts.

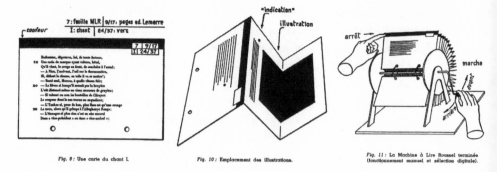

FIGURE 7.04. Juan-Esteban Fassio's reading wheel for Roussel's *Nouvelles Impressions d'Afrique* (Fassio and Caradec 1964). Shown are the formats of the cards and the method of operating the crank.

7.35 *The circuit.* Fassio's device resembles a Rolodex (▶ Figure 7.04). Affixed to each card is, in most cases, a section of the text set off discretely by a level of parentheses. (The unit of segmentation is therefore the digression, rather than the line, page, verse, or canto. We are already in a different mode of parsing the textbase than those supported by Ramelli's and Libeskind's wheels.) These sections appear to be arranged in the order in which they are encountered in the poem's normal sequence. Though this is not clear in the illustrations shown above, the size of each card varies according to its parenthetical level: the more deeply one moves into the parenthetical structure, the shorter the card, so that the levels are indicated by the extension of higher-level cards beyond those at lower levels. Each is marked with a series of codes identifying the portion of the poem it contains, a cross-reference to its occurrence in the novel's first edition, and a color code identifying its level of parenthetical embedding.

7.36 To work the device, the user turns its crank:

> The *visual aid* of the 6 colors and the *manual aid* of the different "radii" allow [her] to stop the machine at a given page with a finger, or to turn the crank either forward or backward to relocate passages interrupted by the parentheses. (Fassio and Caradec 1964, 66)

7.37 This "manual operation and digital selection" (66) is easily visualized; harder to imagine are the polycircuits these procedures can produce from the textbase. Fassio and Caradec's article describing the device includes four extremely complex diagrams of the cantos, figured as "a series of spheres of different radii, concentric and eccentric" (▶ Figure 7.05).

7.38 If the operating wheel coincides with the contours of these diagrams, it can do so only in a space constituted by the latter, to which the movements of the former are fitted by the simple path of rotation. The user's method of reading from the machine does not resemble these diagrams in any other respect; even their forbidding traceries are more rational and regular than the spinning, halting, and doubling back (and their mirror forms in the other direction) that the cranking hand and the arresting finger enable. "Arresting finger": the pataphysical manicule,▶N7.28 it recollects gestures of Jerome and Memex's user (▶ Figure 1.02), and anticipates a baseline form of the GUI's representation of user agency (▶ Figure 7.06). Via Fassio's crank, the operating hand and the textual field are inmixed—the digit's ex-foliative effect could not be more concretely figured ▶ 4.50.

7.39 *The fold.* Roussel's indications to Zo and the resulting illustrations are affixed to the upper portion of the card containing the "verse to which it corresponds" (Fassio and Caradec 1964, 66), which is then folded over (▶ Figure 7.04), probably to replicate the hiding of the images in the uncut leaves of the first edition and to make it easier to turn the wheel. An important departure from the original format of the images is marked here in two respects. First, Fassio must decide to which parenthetical segment of the text the image corresponds: a kind of cut must be made, because in the original, the segments often span the folded leaves, meaning that a single image is

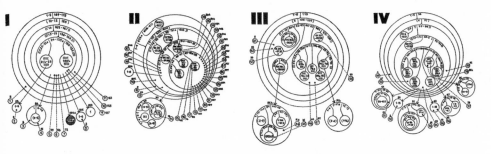

FIGURE 7.05. Juan-Esteban Fassio's reading wheel for Roussel's *Nouvelles Impressions d'Afrique* (Fassio and Caradec 1964). Shown are Fassio's diagrams of the poem's four cantos.

attached by the fold to more than one segment, and a segment may be attached to more than one image in the same way. How Fassio has resolved
this problem is unclear; this is perhaps the most radical departure of his
reading machine from the poem's first presentation, in which the continuity
of the poetic line and the fold are subverted by the parenthetical scheme and
the interruptions of the images. Second, the image is exposed on the wheel
by unfolding a continuous surface on which are imprinted both the text
and image. This is again different from the system of the first edition: while
that surface was materially continuous (the leaves were uncut), its attach-
ment to the binding meant that it could not be fully extended. The reading
wheel shows us more of the relation of these units, and thereby suppresses a
discontinuity that is basic in the original. ▶N7.29

7.40 *The machine.* Fassio's reading machine undertakes to minimize two "in-
conveniences" of the original format of the poem:

> The *physical effort* of continually turning the pages forward and
> backward; *the entropy of reading*, arising from the digressions be-
> tween parentheses, leading to a partial forgetting (or even a complete
> forgetting in the most serious cases), of the "so-called" principal
> texts [of the poem]. (Fassio and Caradec 1964, 63)

7.41 In this respect, Fassio and Caradec propose, the machine for reading Roussel is similar to Ramelli's wheel (the Italian's depiction of the wheel is figured prominently at the beginning of their essay).

7.42 Textual inconvenience ▶ 1.06 and the risk of forgetting what matters when
a textbase projects its operations in ever-greater complexity—these are recurring concerns of the reading machine. But they are also signs of the machine's potential to generate new and unforeseen field effects. Somewhere
between the wish to harness that potential—that is, to keep it managed
productively—and the vertiginous disturbance of surrendering to it is the
true axis of the machine's rotations. This Fassio and Caradec seem to suggest even as they propose a further improvement in its efficiency:

> The handyman [*bricoleur*] could naturally replace the [arresting] fin-
> ger with an electronic system; one could also replace the crank with
> an electric motor controlled by a pedal situated under the foot of the
> seated reader. (Fassio and Caradec 1964, 66)

7.43 We may also imagine what would happen if an electrical finger should fail or the pedal jam: the cards would whir around in a blur; the hidden images, pulled out from their folds by the centrifugal force of rotation, would slap noisily against the device's housing. The specter of a cinematic discontinuity would return, in the way that it was liable to do for the Memex ▶ 1.19.

7.44 *The first deception.*▸N7.30 Once again, it is a problem of inside and outside: of the interior and the extension of the reading machine and the archive; of how the former encircles the latter; of how these circles are traced and also brought to an end in accord with the operator's gesture.▸N7.31 In a 1982 article for the journal *Byte*, the designers of the XEROX Star, the first commercial implementation of the GUI, described the achievement of the "desktop" interface (▶ Figure 7.06) in this way:

> A subtle thing happens when everything is visible: the display becomes reality. The user model becomes identical with what is on the screen. Objects can be understood purely in terms of their visible characteristics. Actions can be understood in terms of their effects on the screen. This lets users conduct experiments to test, verify, and expand their understanding—the essence of experimental science. (Smith et al. 1982, 260)▸N7.32

7.45 The history of GUI design since 1982 is peppered with similar formulae, correlating events of the screen's surfaces with a reality presumed to exist independently. (Complicating this correlation is the fact that the division between the screen and that other space is becoming more diffuse as the real is more mediatized. This is one implication of Manovich's proposal [2001] that the human-computer interface is a "cultural interface" and has become a primary method by which humans now understand their lifeworld.)

7.46 Advertising campaigns are often the plainest demonstrations of fantasy structures of popular computing, and we may detect a shifting emphasis in the ways in which GUIs were marketed to users as computing technologies matured.▸N7.33 The Lisa OS (1983), the first commercially available GUI-based system, was "so advanced that you already know how to use it," a theme echoed in early advertisements of Lisa's successor, the Macintosh (▶ Figure 7.06). "Suddenly and without warning," proposes an ad for Visi On (1984), an early competitor with Microsoft Windows, "your personal computer becomes everything you actually bought it to be." "OS/2:

A funny thing happens when you design a computer everyone can use.

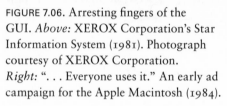

FIGURE 7.06. Arresting fingers of the
GUI. *Above:* XEROX Corporation's Star
Information System (1981). Photograph
courtesy of XEROX Corporation.
Right: ". . . Everyone uses it." An early ad
campaign for the Apple Macintosh (1984).

It's not about fixing old windows, it's about opening new doors" (1992).
Mac OS 7.6 (1997): "Now, wherever your mind goes, your computer will
follow even faster." Windows 98 is "the part of the machine that is human." "Mac OS X. Suddenly, other operating systems seem so 20th century" (2001). "Come on in," ads of Windows XP (2001) assured users, "the
digital world's fine." Windows Vista (2006) offered to "bring clarity to your
world." The older systems promised to be perfectly matched to already-
existing methods—that was always the general conceit of the screen: we
recognize ourselves in it ("if you can point, you can use Macintosh, too").
Two decades later, the user seems to have fallen behind or is maybe not
ready for the world that has arrived; she needs an update. "Vista," a name
more suggestive than "Windows" of limitless vision, will clarify her world:
a reversal of the older formula (though this turn is not new in itself)—now,
the screen will be the basis of our self-recognition ▶ 7.67. In cinematic culture, our dream life is often staged as a movie; when will we—or do we
already—dream in a language of windows, icons, menus, and pointers?

7.47 The GUI has achieved such a dominance in contemporary computing culture that few users are aware of the rancor of early responses to it. The
moral panic of professional and popular presses of the 1980s and early

1990s, in which the new interfaces were decried as gimmicks and omens of declining computing literacy, now appear out of proportion to the actual effects of the turn from the command line. [N7.34] Equally forceful assertions by the enthusiasts of graphical interfaces—that they are easier for novices to learn and experts to master, that they better support a biologically based predisposition to visual understanding—seem proved by the overwhelming commercial success of graphic interfaces (Gentner and Nielsen 1996).

7.48 Even so, the GUI's victory has not been absolute, and the progressive narrative promoted by its supporters mistakes certain facts. The command line remains the most efficient way of executing many procedures in modern operating systems, and "power users" of these systems pride themselves on knowing how to manipulate files efficiently from the terminal window. [N7.35] While text-centered interfaces are in general the older mode, interfaces with GUI-like behaviors were developed in advance of the best-known command line systems. [N7.36] Text-centered interfaces have always been supported by visual parsings anticipating (and later, emulating) techniques central to graphical interfaces.

7.49 In the earliest text-centered interfaces, methods of the page and the typewriter linked syntagmas of the command line to the geometry of the screen. The user types to the right of the C prompt; the return character closes an inquiry and opens a new point of entry; the cursor parses this line, the next, and the whole of the screen as it moves, segmenting their blankness into regions of potential meaning. This segmentation of the two-dimensional field was the central conceit of the earliest line editors and word processors; their ordering of the screen imaginary was made plain in the columns and rows of spreadsheet applications. The assertion by the command line's devotees, that it penetrates more deeply into the stack of mediations between the user and the hardware (Stephenson 1999, 18), has the ring of truth only because the command line arrived earlier, when the stack seemed more shallow, before it became clear that the screen's permeability was always a trick of wishful thinking.

7.50 These anticipatory plagiarisms and modern hybrids indicate that something happened in the transition from command line to window, widget, and menu, other than a turn from manipulating letters to manipulating pictures. In point of fact, the blank region to the right of the C prompt was not so empty as the GUI's evangelists have proposed. Or, rather: the blank regions of the screen have always been—they remain—empty in a particular way, such that they seem prepared for us to discover something in them. The reader in this condition is enmeshed in a prior relation of veiling and unveiling; knowledge is disclosed out of a void primed for that disclosure; the screen frames its object as something ready-to-be-filled.[N7.37] (This was never more evident than when the spreadsheet UI morphed in the late 1980s from a grid of numbers generated by arithmetical formulae to rows and columns of multitiered "scores" and "tracks" in media editing applications like Director and Final Cut Pro.[N7.38]) Whether we begin with knowledge in our heads or before us—a distinction favored by Donald Norman, one of the earliest supporters of the GUI—the methods of direct manipulation presume the possibility of locating knowledge from the position of a supposed subject for whom the whole of the digital field is meaningful. If some things "make us smart" (Norman 1993), it must first be that knowledge is marked in or by them. The problem that remains for the subject-as-user is to position herself in relation to the other on whom she depends—author, designer, programmer, corporate body responsible for publishing the framework of her reading activity: a conjectured figure in an allographic series that is a basic condition of the screen ▶ 6.53.

7.51 As Nelson has many times observed, the modern GUI *insists*, specifically and idiopathically, on particular orders of knowledge by virtue of its capacity to name them:

> Why is this curious clutter called a desktop? It doesn't *look* like a desktop; we have to tell the beginner *how* it looks like a desktop, because it doesn't (it might as easily properly be called the Tablecloth or the Graffiti Wall). . . . We are told to believe that this is a "metaphor" for a "desktop." But I have never personally seen a desktop where pointing at a lower piece of paper makes it jump to the top, or where placing a sheet of paper on top of a file folder causes the folder to gobble it up. I do not believe such desks exist; and I do not think I would want one if it did. (Nelson 1990b, 237)

7.52 This form has more and more become the characteristic *ordinatio* of the informational era, its "cultural interface" (Manovich 2001). That is one regrettable effect of its grammatextual operations: by design, the GUI-as-reading-machine is encircled, enframed, despite—or more precisely, in negation of—the evidence that it also gives of textual field effects. In contrast, the analog reading machine (Bush's Memex, or Ramelli's wheel, for example) describes in more open terms the limited circuitry of the page, line, and letter. It hints at negativities that its turnings are able to transmit *because* of their material inefficiencies.

7.53 The abstraction of textual relations often attributed to digital media is incomplete; the fantasies of dematerialization (decorporealization, imaginarization, derealization) that sustain it are among the oldest and most pervasive of the digital field (Hayles 1999; Stallabrass 1995; Bolter and Gromala 2003). With regard to the textual conditions of reading, they play a confidence game of positive forms: there, plainly reductive representations of reading's circuitry and negativity are presented as models of normal reading practice. The new media, it is argued, widen the scope of those models or exceed their limitations; in point of fact, transformations of the reading scene celebrated by new media advocates often begin from a functional model for which obscure and inconsistent determinisms of textual operations may be eliminated by more careful engineering. (The digital text, so this line of argument goes, will make away with the letter's troublesome materiality and liberate the information it holds prisoner.) The aspiration to merely simplify and clarify requires a willful mistaking of real conditions of reading from the screen.

7.54 Somewhere in the early to mid-1990s, the crossing of positions I mean to mark here was at its most concrete. During this period, UI design was fascinated by naïve illusionisms, and screen interfaces were crafted to resemble real-world analogs. Programs for taking notes displayed pages in spiral-bound paper notebooks. Programs for playing digital video imitated TV remotes. User files were stored in and retrieved from file cabinets and desk drawers. (The decisive distinction here: Memex was a desk outfitted with screens, not a screen ornamented with a desk ▶ 1.16.) In their earliest instances, GUIs had incorporated iconic and ideogrammatic elements such as these—the file folder, in and out trays, the trash can—but the newer designs attempted to unify this approach across the UI, dispensing as far as possible with forms specific to the screen and replacing them with objects thought to be more artless. This was the period of "cyber" and "virtual" at their heights—cyberspaces, virtual worlds, virtual realities; the popular and critical literature are stuffed with fantasies of demedialized information practices promoted under one form or another of potted philosophical realism.

7.55 *Calling a spade . . . a spade.* The most interesting of these efforts were modest GUI designs that aimed far short of the immersive splendors of the holodeck but whose ethos may be traceable to *Star Trek*'s fetish for embedded mimesis ▶ 4.23. The best known of these were Bob, Microsoft's much-maligned foray into these fields,[N7.39] and Magic Cap, an OS developed by General Magic, Inc., for portable computers ("communicators"). About the size of a mass-market paperback novel, first-generation Magic Cap devices incorporated a 4-bit grayscale touchscreen, landline or wireless data and voice capabilities, and ports for add-on devices such as full-sized keyboards and telephone handsets.[N7.40] In 1996, an 8-bit color version of the OS was developed as a stand-alone application for Windows 95, though this was never commercially released.[N7.41]

7.56 The default workspace of the OS, called a *scene* in Magic Cap, is the Desk (▶ Figure 7.07).

> The Desk is the heart of your communicator. From the Desk you can begin virtually any communicator activity. On the Desk are the objects that you'll use most frequently—a Telephone, a Name card file, a blank postcard for creating electronic messages called *Telecards*, a Notebook and a Datebook. The In box on the wall contains new Telecards you have received and the Out box contains new outgoing Telecards waiting to be sent. Also on the wall is the Clock, and behind the Desk is the File cabinet, in which you can file your Telecards, notebook pages, and other items. (General Magic, Inc. 1995, 5)[N7.42]

7.57 Other scenes depict adjacent rooms, including a Game Room, a Storeroom for managing archives, and a Library for storing digital "books" for the device (▶ Figure 7.07).[N7.43] Rooms are connected by hallways and, via doors, to a street by which the user can enter other buildings, hallways, and rooms, to access services associated with them.[N7.44] In each scene, the objects on the screen appear visually and, to some degree, operationally synonymous with corresponding places and things in the off-screen world. This partial synonymy is the fundamental conceit of the UI, though it is not adhered to slavishly: there is no restroom on the hall, no wait for an elevator, no monotonous subway or car commute ▶ 7.72. The *magic* of the UI's objects is in their frank embrace of the ambiguity of the conceit, in that they do, and do not, look to be what they emulate. Thus, for example, the cartoonish Telephone icon conveys two meanings to the user: this region of the screen

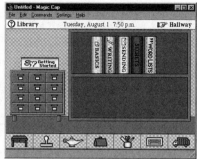

FIGURE 7.07. *Left:* The Desk of General Magic, Inc.'s Magic Cap OS. Tapping
on icons on the desktop or in the bar at the bottom of the screen opens
a corresponding application. *Right:* The shelves of Magic Cap's Library.
Tapping on the card catalogue opens a list of books installed—without,
incongruously, opening a drawer in the catalogue. Note the pointing hand
at the top right of the screen, used to navigate between "scenes" of the OS.
Shown is Magic Cap for Windows 1995 (1996). Reproduced by permission of
Intellectual Ventures, LLC.

activates an aggregate of functions that *are* a telephone (which is to say,
they operate mostly as one might expect a telephone to); they are also *not*
a telephone, but a semiotically contracted figure of that device, adapted to
and oriented by other affordances of the communicator.

7.58 Seen from the vantage of a dozen years after, Magic Cap's nostalgia for then
already-lapsed modes of work and play, and adherence to them is perhaps
clearest in this cartoon Telephone. The Desk is in several respects a strangely
retro scene. The user's calendar is a clasped date*book*; she enters notes on
a spiral-bound *pad of paper*; she reviews her address file with a Rolodex of
cards; and the greatest anachrony of all: in 1995, her desktop *includes no
computer keyboard or screen*. The communicator was supposed to replace
those, of course, but—as we have already seen—such crossings of the inside
and outside introduce persistent formal inconsistencies ▶ 7.72. Why should
a telephone appear to reside inside a communication device, except as a way
of calling out some of the device's voice and data functions in a more compact, transmissible sign? (In a wireless era, Apple's iPhone has switched such
artifices with new ones, by bringing the desktop inside the telephone.) Despite the frequency with which the term is applied to them in the language
of HCI, such mimographisms[N3.10] as these are not, or not only, *metaphors*.
If we consider only their mimetic functions they are closer to catachreses,

"dead" metaphors that lost their dynamic qualities when they became our everyday words for things for which we have no other words, like the "leg" of a table or the "arm" of a chair. (Except when describing the etymology of the term, does anyone really associate the GUI's "desktop" with an actual desktop anymore?▸N1.18)

7.59 Their deeper significance is in the manner in which they *name* operations of the screen: the collection of pixels on the screen that designates a telephone is a *Telephone*, and the user's manuals and online help will remind us of this fact if we lose sight of it. It is really as simple as that. There is, as Lacan observes in Seminar IX (1961–62), something idiotic (*idiotique*) about the proper name that makes it an efficacious mark (*marque*). As Saul Kripke argued, the name designates but does not describe; it is always empty in a way, in the manner of the catachresis ("think of lilacs when they're gone" ▸ 3.47). Nonetheless, Lacan says, the proper name shows us something fundamental about the sign, in that despite its emptiness the name transmits *something*, a surplus (*reste*) that is carried along as the guarantor of its designation.▸N7.45

7.60 Slavoj Žižek has argued that descriptivist and antidescriptivist theories of naming cross in this real surplus that sustains the name. The surplus, he proposes, lacks positive consistency but induces effects as though it were consistent. The antidescriptivists, he concludes, mistake this anchor of the "rigid designator" for its relation to the chain. Conversely, the descriptivists foreclose the contingency of the chain's pinning to this anchor (the nominal "baptism" of antidescriptivist theory). "The radical contingency of naming implies an irreducible gap between the real and modes of its symbolization: a certain historical constellation can be symbolized in different ways; the real itself contains no necessary mode of its symbolization" (Žižek 1989, 97). Thus for Lacan the proper name is the purest form of the signifier (Grigg 1998): there is more associated with it that is nonsignifying (nonrepresentational and not capable of being represented) than is the case for other signifiers. Some glue holds together the spatial-textual patterns of the specimen parapraxis; twingles must be attached to one another by *something* (▸ Figure 2.04).

7.61 *Traveling shot.*▸N7.46 The relevance of this formula to names of objects on the desktop is this: the anchor of the proper name (Telephone, Notebook, Clock) constitutes a point of contact between the screen's visible and medial attributes, the back end's abstraction of real operations into manipulable symbols, and the persistent real operations that subtend its potential expressiveness. Consider the wheel's groaning, frictive machinery, the (probable) sound of the trailing end of a spool slapping against the Memex lens housing ▶ 1.21, or the gearing of an ammunition feed ▶ 1.33. Ramelli's and Libeskind's inventions pointed to a real basis beyond their rotations, but could not encompass that basis. Bush's device might have produced such an excess from its circuits, but it could not have fully represented it within a system of page images. The GUI is equally incapable of figuring its real limits. But it may be more effective in appearing to join the circuit's ends around those limits than its precursors because, on its way to becoming a "cultural interface" (Manovich 2001 ▶ 3.01), the GUI has more naïvely than cinema and television absorbed their illusions of continuous and commutative sequence ▶ 3.10. The wheel's operations resemble cinema in a basic way, but there is no way to turn it fast enough to create the illusion of a continuous textual field, and its basic units are probably incompatible with that illusion. Because Memex's operations are photographically recorded, we might expect it to push that version of the reading machine toward continuity. But spools of countless page images do not reduce to a kind of cel animation of *the* page; Memex is a combinatorial device, not a compositing tool ▶ 3.24. In any case, the trail fractures any possibility of continuity. Far more effectively than these, the screens of the GUI in the present cultural moment sustain an imaginary of unbroken reference and saturated connectivity, and have bound them in popular consciousness to seeming analog correlates, stripped of their mechanical and operational complexities.

7.62 The desktop *icon* is thus revealed to have been misnamed: it is an *ideogram* founded on a linguistic intervention that a purely iconic form would be less able to support, because it must have "total autonomy with respect to language" ▶ 3.17. This intervention, this forced baptism of obscure system attributes, sutures the "user model" to "what is on the screen," so long as she is prepared to look upon its surfaces in a particular way. The key to understanding the GUI in its specific role as a reading machine is to grasp the full effect of this suturing, which is clearest in the desktop's most ingenuous forms, like Magic Cap. It sidesteps inconsistencies at the heart of the correspondence it proposes, between that which is real in the object beyond the screen, and the imaginary objects that stand in for the real on the screen's surface.

7.63 Yet the names of the screen, *qua* names, will also transmit residues along with their designations. Operations of the reading machine reach a limit where the real object is discovered to have escaped these circuits: where the unreadable surface *surfaces*; when the machine's operations fall short of the textual procedures it enables. In neither case can this disclosure of a limit be said to constitute a failure of the machine. (Though failures, strictly speaking—error conditions of software or hardware—may also reveal this real limit, in that they bring the unreadability that characterizes it forward.) They are, instead, evidence of its surest mechanism. *The unreadable surface is the final substrate on which readability is cast, precisely to the extent that it is neither flat nor deep, but resistant to both conceptions of its presence* ▶ 4.16 ▶ 4.44. The machine's inability to match the complexity of the textual field follows from the apparent fact that, if it is to operate at all, it can do so only within the symbolic, where chainings of signifiers will always exceed any attempt to rationalize their combinations, even if this were in the interest of freeing their potential for new combinations. (This accounts for a basic paradox of Nelson's Xanadu: the refusal to "carve up" knowledge is promoted always as a way of guaranteeing understanding. There seems not to be room in this scheme for the misunderstanding characteristic of the unconscious—though perhaps it has been relegated to the "hairy" interior ▶ 2.35.)

7.64 In another respect, however, such a contextualization of the reading machine is misleading. The symbolic's most radical characteristic is not that it is open to new combinations, but that its openness is founded on its disconnect from orders of the imaginary and the real. Whatever traces of this disconnect the machine may figure, however incompletely, are, perversely, the hallmarks of its most fundamental productivity.[N7.47] The circuit is, in the final analysis, a fantasy structure: of the textual enclosure (an image as old as Jerome's cell ▶ Figure 1.03); of the archive's wholeness, equivalent to the wholeness of the subject whose memory is constituted by it (an image as old as Aristophanes). The Freudian revolution decentered these myths of textual enclosure and wholeness (Fink 2002, 171; Lacan 1966, 797), even though the effects of this have yet to fully register for designers of the modern reading machines. Yet the decentering leaves the reading subject off-kilter with regard to herself, and the system of her archive entangled with bits of the resistant stuff of which it is composed.

7.65 *The (reading) machine is the structure detached from the activity of the subject.*[N7.48] It can keep on going without a consciousness to direct it, because what passes for consciousness is more machinic than it seems (Lacan 1978, 62). But that is not enough for a true reading machine, only for the seriatim linking of letters, words, pages, windows, or screens. To make a machine that engages the complexity of textual fields, you need something even hairier ▶ 2.35. If, as Bush proposed, an archive can be automatically constituted—by the Cyclops camera with a minimal intervention by the operator ▶ 1.29, by Memex II without any intervention, and by Memex III from her thoughts alone ▶ 1.50—it is still the case that the signature of the order will be subjective. The subject returns to the reading machine when, in effect, something jams the mechanism, turns it in an unanticipated way, pushed by a pressure of the real that the machine is not designed to anticipate. This is why, ultimately, the modern reading machine should clatter, clank, and rattletrap its way along: contrary to the fantasy of transparency and efficiency that is often its justification, its material inefficiencies are the generative matrix of its operation. If its operator were actually presented with a perfectly tuned, predictable, and traversible system, she would risk losing her grasp on that which most provokes her.[N7.49]

7.66 The early modern *ordinatio* as a proto-canon of informational fetishism: in the traditions of HCI, the tangled, rattletrap conditions of something so fundamental, but so complex as the "use" of an object are schematized and simplified; their phenomenal structure is flattened, their negativities made positive. This is no surprise; no more than linguistics ▶ 2.21 (less so), these disciplines have no theory of desirous use—no theory of the subject's division by the symbols she manipulates in search of a limited satisfaction. Yet this division has since Freud and, moreover, since Lacan moved the Freudian model of rememoration from the immanence of the interior to the extensivity of fields, to be the very condition of any practice we might characterize as "use" (Lacan 1991b, 238–46, 269–70). A truly direct manipulation of a display that has become reality aims also to have pushed away all evidence of the negativity that constitutes it.

7.67 The consistency of an Other beyond this spectacle (codified, we may imagine, in human interface guidelines and prescriptions for sound usability) who will guarantee such an operation—"the ideal interface is no interface— 'I think, therefore the computer gives me what I thought about (and what

I should think about)'" (Van Dam 1997, 64)—is the dearest of the fictions the subject draws from this structure (Lacan 1998, 394). The "usability" that would be the measure of the display's correspondence with the real is in this sense rigorously useless, because it must be impetuous and precipitate in its claims, founded as they are on the assurance of the Other's good will (Harpold 1994). *That* is their use. Which is not to say that the language of usability is deluded or cynical; only that it reproduces, necessarily, fantasies of the circuit and the field, and imaginarizes the disjunction between language and the real that is the basis of the circuit and the field ▶ 1.44 (Lacan 1994, 155).▶N7.50 Satisfaction, in the absolute form that the fantasy appears to forecast, also has to be set aside in this operation because that is the only engine that can effectively drive another turn of the system.

7.68   As a reading surface, the primary function of the screen as it is presently constituted—that is, of all the widgets, menus, buttons, icons, and so forth that compose the avatars of "knowledge on the screen"—is to protect the user from qualities of the screen that are unreadable. Here, historiation—in all of its medial and subjective specificity—crosses the barest alibi of the interface.▶N7.51 The screen *screens* us from something that the page also obscures, but seems to do so less effectively, less consistently. In the opaque substance of the page and its avatars, we are reminded again and again of a real limit of reading that the reading machine is propped upon. The screen, in contrast, presents its surface as the thinnest of coverings of a navigable space that remains open to our entry and departure. ("You are standing in an open field west of a white house, with a boarded front door. There is a small mailbox here . . ." ▶ 4.01) It presents us with an *imaginarized symbolic* that appears immune to perturbations introduced by media's real attributes.

7.69   This protective effect of a positive screen-object—a fetish object, in the strictest sense of the term—was encoded in the screen's early forms (the rows and columns of the first spreadsheets) but its clearest instances are marked in the mature contours of the modern GUI. Of these, the best example may be the "Bliss Screen," the default desktop that appears when Windows XP is launched for the first time (▶ Figure 7.08).

7.70   *Traveling shot.* Bliss (*jouissance*) is possible here, pure freedom in the form of a cunning disavowal of desire. For, practically speaking—though this is

FIGURE 7.08. The "Bliss Screen," the default Windows XP Desktop (2001).

also its impractical, its *useless* function—the Bliss Screen is figured in so gratifying a form to take the place of, to cover over, the sign of a deeper technical crisis: the reviled "Blue Screen of Death" (BSOD), a spray of gobbledygook, white text on a blue background, that Windows throws before its user when an unrecoverable error is encountered. (The satisfactions of the Bliss Screen are made all the more clear by a popular enhancement to Windows that allows the user to "save" her screen by replacing its image during periods of disuse with a double of the Bliss image, emptied of all icons, menus, and other sigla of the UI: a topography of pure departure.[N7.52]) The blue screen does not reveal a real limit—by definition, that is outside the OS's powers of demonstration—but it shows us that the system cannot contain or mediate the trace of a missed encounter that drifts away as our gaze is turned from it.

7.71 It can be no accident that the pacifying expanse of the Bliss Screen resembles the Alpine meadow that Freud describes in his 1899 essay on "Screen Memories" (*Deckerinnerungen*, literally "cover memories").[N7.53] Fondly recalled by a patient whom we may be certain was Freud (Bernfeld 1946), the landscape frames in that remarkable essay (the first truly psychoanalytic meditation on memory) a complex space of uncertain nostalgia, anchored regret, and hope: a *field* of desires whose significance passes unrecognized for the one whose pleasure is in their staging.[N7.54] Microsoft's October 2001 advertisement for introducing Windows XP supports this comparison, nearly to the point of crudely repeating most of the elements of the Freudian original. You may remember the television ads: to the pulsing beat of

Madonna's techno dance hit "Ray of Light," ecstatic users of the new operating system rise and soar over the astonished, upturned faces of friends and coworkers. They fly arms outstretched toward a horizon of absolute satisfaction, captured in this image as in the happiest vacation portrait. Their movements are repeated on the computer screens of entranced spectators as the ad's captions explain, "you can / you talk / you mix / you edit / you share / you connect / you soar." These seem less descriptions of what the prospective user may do with the new software than of what she will become: you = can, you = talk, you = mix . . . "And I feel like I just got home—and I feel—quicker than a ray of light," Madonna sings. "Yes, you can," the ad promises in triumph.

7.72 The Microsoft commercial superficially resembles but also seems undermined by the celebrated music video for Madonna's song, directed by Jonas Åkerlund and released three years before the XP launch ("Ray of Light" 1998). In the music video, Madonna sings and dances, her image partially merged with a backdrop of time-lapse photography of mostly urban and suburban highway scenes: workers driving, riding the subway to and from their jobs, rushing in and out of office buildings, riding escalators up and down, hurrying through lunch, and so on, interspersed with images of a clock, its hands spinning through the hours. That the workers are engaged in a mostly pointless pursuit is reinforced by a sequence about a minute into the video that crosscuts between a sonogram of a fetus *in utero* and a hamster running frantically on a wheel. (The video's obvious stylistic citation of Godfrey Reggio and Philip Glass's 1982 film *Koyaanisqatsi: Life out of Balance*, one of the most famous film statements of the derealizing and dehumanizing effects of modern life, seems a curious intertext for software that is supposed to make office work more fulfilling.) The accelerated workday does wind down—workers drive or ride home, stop at the grocery store, do their laundry, go to the gym—before the song slows briefly during sunset and then picks up pace again as people rush back to the city to play in amusement parks, bowling alleys, pool bars, and, most of all, to dance in clubs. But this recreational postscript to the workday is missing from the Microsoft commercial, because it means to sell the idea that labor is play.

7.73 The slogan for the XP advertising campaign was to have been "Prepare to fly" (Elkin 2001). But the release came only six weeks after September 11, 2001, and that cruel spectacle of an Other's monstrous pleasure could not

be ignored in marketing the new OS.▸N7.55 Microsoft's advertising department decided that showing the user already in flight (yes, you *can*) rather
than promising that she would fly (*prepare* . . .) was the more discreet option. It was believed less likely to remind would-be consumers of something
they would just as soon forget.

Acknowledgments

I have stored up in my mind what I learned from others, and then written out sometimes what was borrowed, sometimes what was my own, without distinctly remembering which belonged to each ▶ 2.35.

This book has benefited from many exchanges with colleagues and students at the Georgia Institute of Technology and the University of Florida. Those who read and commented on early drafts or helped me in other ways to understand what I was trying to say include Luis Alvarez-Castro, Jay David Bolter, Richard Burt, Matthew Causey, LeAnn Fields, Paul Fishwick, N. Katherine Hayles, George P. Landow, Nick Montfort, Stuart Moulthrop, James Paxson, Kavita Philip, Arkady Plotnitsky, Gerald Prince, Jean-Michel Rabaté, Peter Rudnytsky, Gregory L. Ulmer, Edward White, and Julian Wolfreys. Marie-Laure Ryan, a most discerning reader for the University of Minnesota Press, made valuable suggestions for revisions. Nancy Evans, the scrupulous copy editor at Wilsted & Taylor Publishing Services, resolved many difficulties of an unusually complex manuscript.

Kevin Begos, Jr., Elliott Peter Earls, Shelley Jackson, Michael Joyce, and Ted Nelson responded with uncommon generosity to inquiries regarding their creative work and scholarship. Mark Bernstein provided invaluable answers to my questions about the early publishing history of Michael Joyce's *Afternoon* and Storyspace, the hypertext authoring system used to create it. My conversations with Catherine Stollar Peters regarding The Michael Joyce Papers archived in the Harry Ransom Center increased both my understanding of Joyce's methods and my appreciation for the challenges of digital archivy. Karen Elder spoke at length with me about the career of graphic designer Bradbury Thompson and helped me acquire a splendid photograph of Thompson's Westvaco edition of Stephen Crane's *The Red*

Badge of Courage. Russ Taylor of Brigham Young University's L. Tom Perry Special Collections, Harold B. Lee Library, kindly offered to scan a new image from *La Vie, mors et miracles du glorieux Saint Jherome* for my use. Randall Renner of the University of Florida's Digital Library Center solved the problem of how to photograph Raymond Queneau's *Cent mille milliards de poèmes* in an open position. Bob Crimi was most helpful in my securing permission to reproduce drawings by Alfred D. Crimi and directed me to other materials regarding Crimi's career as an artist and illustrator.

In this project as in all the rest, my greatest debt is to my closest reader, Jeanne Ewert, whose discernment, forbearance, and love sustain me.

Notes

Read Me First

N0.01. "First wave": I draw here on N. Katherine Hayles's distinction between first- and second-generation electronic literature (2002, 37). She situates this division sometime between the first edition of Michael Joyce's *Afternoon* (1987) ▶ 6.01 and Shelley Jackson's *Patchwork Girl* (1995a, 1995b) ▶ 5.31. More recently, Hayles has recast this periodization in terms of "classical" versus "contemporary" or "postmodern" phases, *Patchwork Girl* being the major culminating work of the classical period (2007; 2008, 7). The postmodern phase, she proposes, is a consequence of the expansion in the mid-1990s of the Web and an associated shift in new media art toward more graphically rich interactive works.

N0.02. "Late age of print": an evocative phrase introduced by Jay David Bolter (1991).

N0.03. To speak of *the* GUI as I will often in this book simplifies the present situation of popular computing. Despite the dominance of one and to a lesser degree two families of graphical interfaces (Windows OS and Mac OS, published by Microsoft and Apple, respectively), there are many demonstrably different GUIs and variants of GUIs in use today. Legacy or minority user interfaces, which often differ in their visual idioms, procedures, and operations from those that are better known, are used by enthusiasts of older or unusual hardware and operating systems. Non-monolithic interfaces—so-called because their user interface is more clearly separable from the underlying operating system—in use in the Linux community resemble the better-known interfaces but tend also to differ from them in how command-line functions are integrated into the GUI. Moreover, a given operating system may support multiple distinct variants of a primary GUI, each permitting considerable customization such that only structural and procedural aspects of the interface are constant, while the visual appearance of nearly all of its elements is changed. If one takes into account the historical arc of human-computer interface development, including interfaces

246

for now-abandoned operating systems and hardware, traits of *the* GUI splinter into variants and one-off cases. However, just as we may (with some obvious reservations) speak of "painting" as a set of practices that is mostly consistent in its optical methods from the period of the Quattrocento to the twentieth century (as, for example, Lacan's discussion of visual art assumes [1973, 97–113]), it is possible to characterize *the* GUI as a general condition of the expression of meaning in the contemporary digital field, and to assume that, *mutatis mutandis*, individual GUIs have in common basic models of knowledge, agency, and visual-textual representation.

N0.04. Cf. the essays collected in Liestøl, Morrison, and Rasmussen 2003; Montfort 2003; Montfort and Bogost 2008; Kirschenbaum 2008; and Whalen 2008. Forthcoming titles in the MIT Press's Platform Studies series, edited by Bogost and Montfort (2008), represent a major initiative in this direction.

N0.05. An *operating system* (OS) manages basic tasks of a computer's hardware and software, including the allocation of memory and data storage, the priority of processes under the control of running programs, the control of input and output devices, and network communications with other computers. Users of modern computers rarely interact with the OS; the *user interface* (UI) is their front-end point of contact with the back-end functions it controls.

N0.06. Kendall 1998 quotes J.B. Holm, who converted a series of kinetic works by Canadian poet bpNichol from Apple II BASIC to HyperCard, complaining that the conversion was "like translating a verb tense from a foreign language with no equivalent verb tense." Montfort and Wardrip-Fruin 2004 offer recommendations to authors of electronic literature for creating texts more likely to survive changes in hardware and software systems, and documenting texts' behaviors to preserve a record of their operations. The ambitious X-Lit Initiative, which calls for the development of standards for metadata description, migration, and emulation of digital literature, is based on their recommendations (Liu et al. 2005). (*Metadata* are data "about" data—the term is often used in no more specific sense—structured, encoded information that describes characteristics of data.)

N0.07. The digital technologies that have dramatically increased the portability of archival materials—think of an iPod in place of a room full of phonograph records—and enabled random access to the most elementary units of an archive's textbase also permit publishers' control of access at the same level of granularity. As digital rights management (DRM) software is embedded in more of the playback devices we use, it will become more difficult to read, view, or listen to our archives in ways that we may once have done.

N0.08. Mini vMac 3.0.4 (© 2008 Paul C. Pratt) is the Mac OS port of the vMac project, distributed under the terms of the GNU General Public License, version 2. Other vMac ports are available for Microsoft Windows and X-Windows systems (see http://minivmac.sourceforge.net).

N0.09. Nelson 1987b. On Guide, see Brown 1986 and 1987. Guide for UNIX, released in 1986, was the first commercially available hypertext system. Guide for Mac OS and Guide for Windows, released in 1986 and 1988, respectively, were the first commercially available hypertext systems for those platforms.

N0.10. In June 2008 the entry level iMac, Apple's baseline desktop system, runs on a dual 2.4 GHz Intel Core 2 Duo processor and supports a maximum of 1 GB of RAM. It houses a 20-inch, variable resolution LCD color monitor, a 250 GB hard drive, an integral read/write CD/DVD drive (Apple discontinued support for floppy disks in 1999), multiple high-speed ports for peripherals, and built-in Gigabit Ethernet and wireless network capabilities. It runs the tenth generation of the Mac OS, OS X 10.5 ("Leopard"), which has no code in common with the 1987 System 6 and cannot run any program created for pre–OS X systems.

N0.11. In Guide, linked text "unfolds" and "folds" at the site of the link, expanding or contracting levels of textual detail, as in a dynamic outline (Brown 1987, 36). (Though Guide's designers do not mention it, this scheme strongly resembles Nelson's Stretchtext ▶ 4.20.) *Typed* links (also known as link classes) are differentiated according to the nature of the relation they establish between linked texts—citation, specification, comment, refutation, and so on. Few modern hypertext systems have used link types; those that have usually indicate types with a distinctive mark or label at the site of the link. Distinctively, Guide embeds link typing in behaviors of the cursor: as the cursor passes over a link, it changes to reveal the link's presence and type. Links are otherwise invisible, and the user may be "unaware that the document he sees on the screen is made up of a lot of interlinked substructures" (Brown 1987, 35). This approach was criticized for forcing users to drag the cursor over the screen in order to discover the presence of links, in effect, reading with an extended digit. But counterarguments are possible: Michael Joyce's "words that yield" ▶ 6.10 and Juan-Esteban Fassio's "arresting finger" ▶ 7.37 demonstrate that reading textual surfaces in this way may also increase the reader's awareness of complex textual structure.

N0.12. Personal correspondence, June 2005.

N0.13. See esp. Rothenberg 1999 and Rothenberg and Bikson 1999. For critical views, see Bearman 1999 and Granger 2000; the latter is more sympathetic to Rothenberg's proposal for the development of generalizable emulators that will run on future computing platforms.

N0.14. Except where noted otherwise, I used the following hardware and software to read and capture images from the digital texts discussed in this book. CPUs: Power Mac dual 867 MHz PowerPC G4 and iMac 2.16 GHz Intel Core 2 Duo. Host OSs: Mac OS 9.2.2, OS X 10.0–10.5. Guest OSs: Windows 95, Windows 98, Windows XP, and Windows Vista. Emulation and virtualization tools: Apple Computer, Inc.'s Classic emulator for Mac OS 9; Mini vMac 3.0.4; Microsoft Virtual PC for Mac OS, versions 6 and 7; Parallels Desktop for Mac OS, versions 2 and 3.

N0.15. Whalen 2008 observes that few emulators attempt to reproduce characteristics of the display devices contemporary with the older software, which were often of lower resolution and color depth ►N5.31 than those of more recent systems. Consequently, graphic elements and especially typography of older software, which may have been modified (distorted) so as to be more legible on older screens, appear differently on the modern screen.

N0.16. The Electronic Frontier Foundation's Web site includes a growing archive of case law related to this problem, at http://www.eff.org/issues/dmca. Abandonware sites are easily found on the Internet, but the legality of downloading files from them is usually suspect. Individual programs distributed on the sites or whole sites themselves often disappear and reappear, under threat of legal sanctions by copyright owners. The Internet Archive's Classic Software Preservation Project (CLASP, http://www.archive.org/details/clasp) is the largest abandonware archive to have secured an exemption to the Digital Millennium Copyright Act from the U.S. Copyright Office (the exemption is set to expire in 2009). However, many of the files in the CLASP archive cannot be downloaded, even for purposes of research, because the copyright owners have forbidden this.

N0.17. Between the first draft of this sentence in 2005 and the last in 2008, prospects for this kind of digital archivy have improved considerably. Several new initiatives have been formed to address the preservation of literary and artistic works in obsolete software formats. (See Liu et al. 2005, Manoff 2006, Hayles 2007, and Tabbi 2007 for analyses of the taxonomic and technical issues involved.) The Electronic Literature Organization's release in October 2006 of Volume 1 of the *Electronic Literature Collection* (Hayles et al. 2006, also included in Hayles 2008), a Web- and CD-ROM–based collection of classic electronic art and fiction, is a model for future endeavors of its kind. (The *ELC* includes several works I discuss in this book.) In 2007, The University of Texas at Austin's Center for American History (available at: http://www.cah.utexas .edu) and Stanford University's Stanford Humanities Laboratory (available at: http://shl.stanford.edu) announced major efforts to establish repositories of classic video game software.

The acquisition in 2005 by the Harry Ransom Center of the University of Texas at Austin of the *fonds* of hypertext author Michael Joyce represents a significant test case for the preservation of digital manuscripts. The Michael Joyce Papers (available at: https://pacer.ischool.utexas.edu/handle/2081/289) include 371 3.5-inch Macintosh floppy disks, 8.38 GB of data stored on hard drives, and 60 manuscript boxes (Stollar 2006; Stollar and Kiehne 2006; Kirschenbaum 2008). The variety of storage media, their age and varying reliability, and the diversity of data types and formats they contain have posed numerous challenges to the Papers' archivists, who have demonstrated the value of a multitiered approach that combines the use of legacy hardware and software and modern data migration techniques (Stollar 2006; Stollar and Kiehne 2006).

N0.18. Two more cases in point. Most of the illustrations of GUI elements and behaviors of modern OSs in this book are of software running on Windows XP or Mac OS X 10.4 ("Tiger"). As the book was being written, each of these OSs was replaced by a substantially new and changed version: Windows Vista (in late 2006) and Mac OS X 10.5 ("Leopard," in early 2007). I address traits of the newer OSs several times in the book, but I have stuck with the older ones for practical reasons: so as not to get too bogged down in the details of specific OS transitions, and because many of the tools I needed to complete my research were not available for Leopard or Vista. A few general observations about each may be of value here.

"Leopard" involved a substantial rewrite of underlying OS code but, apart from its dropping of support for the Classic Mac OS ▶0.11, the significance of its changes for new media historical research have been mostly minor. With one exception looking forward: changes to the graphics subsystems of the OS have dramatically altered appearances and behaviors of some elements of the GUI. Core Animation, a real-time layer-based animation engine built into the OS, enables application interfaces to control thousands of layers of different media types on the screen at the same time, with full support for variable transparency and other visual effects. In the first year of Leopard, few applications have embraced these new capabilities, but it is probable that Core Animation will push interface idioms more in the direction of cinematic techniques such as rotation, panning, and zooming ▶3.12.

More significant, many of Leopard's underlying changes pave the way for its successor, OS X 10.6 ("Snow Leopard," due for release in 2008). Among the rumored features of Snow Leopard is one of the Holy Grails of the modern GUI: support for resolution-independent interface elements. (Earlier versions of OS X included limited support for resolution independence, but not in user-level features.) In a resolution-independent UI, objects on the screen are drawn as collections of vectors (shaded geometric forms), rather than as raster images (patterns composed of individual pixels). Whereas raster-based art is prone to muddiness or "jaggies" when scaled (made larger or smaller), vector-based art is theoretically scalable to any size without loss of clarity or precision, limited only by the resolution thresholds of the display device. The move to a largely or wholly vector-based UI will pose significant challenges for designers, as some shading and texture effects are difficult to render optimally using only geometric forms, but the broader significance of the move may be the changes it effects in basic idioms of the interface. Many of the aesthetic conventions of the modern GUI have depended on assimilating or masking pixel-level irregularities of screen objects. The elimination of these irregularities will alter basic traits of these objects and may well change operations associated with them.

Despite its Windows name, Vista is completely different from XP. In addition to new and updated features and applications, the dramatically changed look and feel of the Vista GUI includes redesigned icons, widgets, and controls, variable transparency, and sophisticated compositing effects. (To support the new effects, Vista requires far more powerful hardware than previous releases of Windows. Problems of hardware obsolescence have been acutely felt by those upgrading to the new OS.) Menus of Microsoft's Office applications, upgraded to new versions about the same time as Vista's release, have been replaced with a scheme of tabbed "ribbons" and "galleries" that emphasizes graphic exemplars over textual labels. Complicating matters further, Vista ships in two "experiences" ("Basic" and "Aero," differentiated by their support of features of the new GUI) and six "editions" targeted at different hardware configurations and user markets.

Vista's changes to the UI's visual registers will doubtless be followed by mutations of Windows idioms (and possibly those of other OSs) for encoding knowledge and representing user agency. Its influence on the conventions of the desktop will become clear only as the OS is more widely used and its operations spill over into other cultural fields.

N0.19. On the title page of each of its electronic releases, Joyce's text is titled *afternoon, a story*, but the capitalization and punctuation of the title are more varied in Joyce's published writings and unpublished correspondence and papers (Kirschenbaum 2008, xvii). In keeping with the style sheet of Minnesota University Press, except when quoting from those sources I have elected to capitalize the first and third words of the title and use the comma, thus: *Afternoon, a Story*.

1. "A Future Device for Individual Use"

N1.01. Nelson had used the term "hypertext" in lectures and unpublished papers as early as 1963 (Nelson 1999b).

N1.02. As in Borges's famous fragment (1972, 131).

N1.03. A comprehensive history of modern hypertext has yet to be written. The essays collected in Nyce and Kahn 1991a, Zachary 1997, and Mindell 2002 provide valuable background on Bush's pre– and post–World War II careers and his work on Memex and related technologies. Subsequent developments in hypertext are more unevenly documented. Bardini 2000 and Barnes 1997 summarize the contributions of Douglas Engelbart's oNLine System (NLS) (1968), while Oinas-Kukkonen 2007 untangles the complex history of Bush's influence on Engelbart. Nelson's (1990a, 1/22–38; 1992) and John Walker's (1994) autobiographical sketches describe the early years of Xanadu ▶ 2.01. Gary Wolf's skeptical account of the project (1995) provides information not found anywhere else, but must be read with Nelson's and other Xanadu team members' responses (Nelson 1995). Jeff Conklin's classic survey (1987) remains a good source on systems of the 1970s and 1980s. Nielsen 1995 offers a short history of the major systems, ending in the early 1990s. Akscyn, McCracken, and Yoder 1988 describe ZOG and KMS, its commercial successor, one of the earliest multiuser, distributed systems (development on ZOG began in the early 1970s). Halasz 1988 describes NoteCards, an influential early single-user system developed at the Xerox Palo Alto Research Center in the 1980s, and compares its features to other systems. Yankelovich et al. 1988 and the first book in Landow's *Hypertext* series (1992) describe Intermedia, a multiuser hypertext environment developed at Brown University, no longer in use. Brown 1987 describes OWL Guide, an early commercial single-user system, also no longer in use ▶ 0.08. Bolter 1991 discusses early versions of Storyspace, the desktop hypertext system used by authors of most of the first wave of literary hypertext ▶ 6.08. Bernstein 2002 and Kirschenbaum 2008 (164–78) review the development of Storyspace. Berners-Lee 1999 recounts his role in the development of the World Wide Web and acknowledges his debts to Bush, Engelbart, and Nelson.

N1.04. The reader is equally free to take so liberal an approach to the order of this book ▶ 6.53. It is not necessary to read its chapters (and in many cases, the paragraphs) in the order of their numbering or according to the direction of their titles—the imperative "Read Me First" ▶ 0.01 notwithstanding.

N1.05. Genette 1987 is the classic literary-theoretical statement of this problem.

N1.06. In citing thus his observation that these attributes are "marked" in our readings, I slightly displace McGann's use of that term in this context (for example, 2001, 198), which, as N. Katherine Hayles notes (2005, 99), is closer in some respects to text markup (HTML, SGML, and the like) than to a material trace recorded in the matter of the page. I will return to the problem of material anchors of the reader's perception of textual structure, particularly in relation to surfaces of the screen, in chapters 2 and 3.

N1.07. See, for example, the examples and critical observations collected in Adler and Ernst 1990; Bright 2005; Drucker 1998; Higgins 1987; Jackson, Vos, and Drucker 1996; Mœglin-Delcroix 1997; Rasula and McCaffery 1998; Rothenberg and Clay 2000; K.A. Smith 2000, 2003, and 2004; Weiss 1984; and White 2005. White makes the important observation that dominant strands of twentieth-century literary criticism have assumed (incorrectly) that texts featuring unconventional graphic devices must be self-reflexive (that is, the devices are invariably *about* textuality, rather than in possible service of the text's meaning) and, a corollary of this idea, texts without such devices evoke no metatextual engagement of the text's graphic surfaces.

N1.08. Whereas I did endorse McGann's proposal in Harpold 2003. McGann actually says that the powers of the book "far outstrip the available resources of digital instruments." I agree with Hayles that this is an overstatement, though perhaps not with the same emphasis as she: "one looks in vain in [McGann's] *Radiant Textuality* for similar deep insights into the multiple causalities, complex feedback loops, and emergent processes through which electronic texts are made, stored, and disseminated" (Hayles 2005, 38). McGann's writings show his deep interest in generative structures bound to surfaces of the material page and activated by the reader's encounters with those surfaces, but he does not seem as interested in noting the specific ways in which they may also be activated by attributes of the screen, perhaps because, focusing his arguments on challenges of encoding of printed texts in digital forms, the reduction and abstraction of the former seems to strip away the bases of the "hypermedia powers" of the latter. Yet, as Hayles rightly insists (2005, 97), bases specific to the digital field, independent of and also transformative of the print original, may be activated in ways that have no correlation with those of the page. Hence, assessments of greater or lesser hypermedia potential must always be considered with respect to the media ecology of the surface. This entanglement of homology and difference will be a dividing point between Bush's archive of page images and Nelson's docuverse composed of byte spans ▶ 2.04.

N1.09. After I first offered this comparison in print (Harpold 2003), I discovered that Nelson had used it earlier (1974, DM 44), in a passage that I must have read years before and then forgotten.

N1.10. "Inner structure . . . package of information." An assertion that prioritizes textual structure covers a trope that means something else: text as a container; all the manipulations of structure aim at getting more deeply and reliably into its interiors. This inconsistency drives Nelson's and Bush's writings away from a purely formal regime of signification. The entire history of hypertext theory and criticism cannot escape the pull of this prejudicial turn toward an imagined interior.

N1.11. "As We May Think" was first published in July 1945, in *The Atlantic* (Bush 1945a). In September of that year, a condensed version of the essay, with illustrations and different subheads, appeared in *Life* magazine (Bush 1945b). (The passages I cite include material from both versions, as reprinted in Nyce and Kahn 1991a, 85–110.) A short summary of the *Atlantic* text also appeared, without byline, in the July 23, 1945, issue of *Time* magazine, under the title "A Machine That Thinks." In Bush's earliest writings on Memex, he does not capitalize the first letter of the device's name. In later writings, he uses the capitalized form, "Memex," without the definite article, and most of those writing on Bush and Memex have followed this example. I have retained the lowercase form only when Bush used it.

N1.12. See, for example, Conklin 1987; Landow 1997; and Nielsen 1995. See Nelson 1974, 1990a, 1999b, and 2002 for descriptions of Xanadu's data structures and system operations. Nelson has often cited Bush's essay as an inspiration for the design of Xanadu; lengthy citations of "As We May Think" are included in Nelson 1974 and Nelson 1990a.

N1.13. "The Xanadu stations, or SilverStands, will be the local outposts of the network, parlors with a homey futuristic atmosphere, staffed by an attentive crew in perky uniforms. Besides being an actual storage and transmission depot, the SilverStand will serve as an induction and training office, a 'drop-in center,' a place for advertising, promotion, public relations, goodwill . . ." "Quieter carrels," away from the hustle and bustle of the foyer of the Xanadu franchise ("where the true Xanies hang out"), will be available in the back of the building, for those of a more scholastic temperament (Nelson 1990a, 5/6).

N1.14. "Dry photography": earlier in the essay, Bush speculates that forms of instant photography requiring no liquid chemistry may be developed (1991a, 91–92).

N1.15. On Jacques de Vaucanson's duck (1739), see Cottom 1999 and Riskin 2003. On Wolfgang von Kempelen's Turk (1770–1854), see Jay 2001 and Standage 2002. Jay's essay includes several reproductions of eighteenth- and nineteenth-century cut-away views of the Turk that resemble Crimi's illustration (▶ Figure 1.01). A happy coincidence of this comparison: Bush's example of Memex's usefulness in research is an investigation of "why the short Turkish bow was apparently superior to the English long bow" (1991a). Crimi's depiction of the bows in use (▶ Figure 1.02), however, more resembles "Iroquois warriors than English or Turkish soldiers," as his drew them from documents on Native Americans he discovered at the New York Historical Society (Nyce and Kahn 1991b, 59). An accomplished fine artist who had painted celebrated frescos for public art projects in and around New York City, Crimi worked during World War II as a technical illustrator for the Sperry Gyroscope Company. His drawings of Sperry bombsights and gunsights (▶ Figure 1.04), used as illustrations for a January 1944 story in *Life* on wartime aviation, appear to have led to the contract for "As We May Think" (Crimi 1987, 150–55; Nyce and Kahn 1991b, 59) ▶ 1.34.

N1.16. Crimi's abstraction of the technologies Bush describes is clearest in his illustrations of "the super secretary of the coming age" ("the machine would take dictation, type it automatically, and even talk back") and "thinking machines [that] would solve not only the most difficult mathematical problems but even problems of logical thought" (Bush 1945b, 114, 118). The drawing of the "thinking machine" for example, shows little more than unlabeled panels of dials, switches, and vacuum tubes.

N1.17. The scientific record, Bush complains earlier in the essay, is growing too fast for the researcher to take in even the small portion that is directly relevant to his research. "The summation of human experience is being expanded at a prodigious rate, and the means we use for threading through the consequent maze to the immediately important item is the same as was used in the day of square-rigged ships" (1991a, 89). Nearly half a century later, Tim Berners-Lee will cite the accelerating growth of the record and the need for new protocols for document storage, annotation, and transmission as a justification for the World Wide Web (1989, 1999).

N1.18. A complete spatial genealogy of Memex would place the interior of Bush's desk in relation to domestic interiorities celebrated by other archivists of enclosure than Bachelard (Perec's essays on the "infra-ordinary" [1989] would be foremost in that genre); and to the "glossary" of objects, actions, and events that Derrida links to the coffin, the cartouche, the tomb, *tire, tirer, tiroir,* and so on—all of which creep conceptually from an interior to its frame and the supplemental effects that the frame induces (Derrida 1978).

N1.19. Mindell's excellent history of pre– and post–World War II analog computing (2002) shows that these developments were more complex and inconsistent than I propose in this brief summary. Bush's contributions to analog computing are central to Mindell's account. In a chapter on the Sperry Gyroscope Company, he signals the importance of Crimi's illustrations of Sperry's fire control servomechanisms (▶ Figure 1.04, ▶ 1.34), but does not associate the illustrations with Crimi's drawings for the 1945 *Life* essay.

N1.20. Prototypes of the Rapid Selector and the Bush Comparator, high-speed microfilm coding and retrieval devices constructed by Bush's research team at MIT, were plagued by similar difficulties. A 1940 report prepared for Bush by John Howard, a graduate student working on the Rapid Selector, found that the machine's 12-character keycodes would perform poorly in relation to conventional search methods. In a trial search of 52,000,000 Social Security records, the Selector took fourteen hours to locate a requested record; a simple alphabetical lookup scheme could complete the search in one minute (Burke 1991). Veith (2006, 1234) notes that Memex improved on the sorting method of the Rapid Selector by recording an additional hard link between page images associated by a user keycode, in the form of the index number of the second page image ▶ 1.39. This would have permitted Memex to jump more efficiently between linked page images, but it could not have compensated for the inefficiencies of keycode searches or the mechanical limitations of the spooling mechanism.

N1.21. If Memex is to operate in a hybrid medial environment that includes documents created with different, sometime incompatible technologies ("today we make the record conventionally by writing and photography, followed by printing; but we also record on film, on wax disks, and on magnetic wires"), then labors and inefficiencies of document conversion seem inescapable. The backstory of this problem reveals an unsurprising gendered division of labor: "The advanced arithmetical machines of the future will be electrical in nature, and they will perform at 100 times present speeds, or more," Bush predicts. "Such machines will have enormous appetites. One of them will take instructions and data from a whole roomful of girls armed with simple keyboard punches, and will deliver sheets of computed results every few minutes. There will always be plenty of things to compute in the detailed affairs of millions of people doing complicated things" (1991a, 96–97).

N1.22. See Virilio 1984.

N1.23. See http://www.columbia.edu/cu/iraas/wpa/murals/surgery.html. The fresco is reproduced in Crimi 1987, 131.

N1.24. The entangled semiotic of interior and extension that I describe here presupposes a subject for whom this semiotic is perceptible—a subject that, in fact, is expressed as such at the point of bijection. This subjectivation of the point of bijection is absolutely crucial to the orders of imagination that are built up around it; the reading machine cannot operate without this, and its contemporary instances in the page and screen require this absolutely. In contrast, Hayles's proposal that Saussure's model of the sign may be remapped to operations of the binary base of computing appears to mistake the location of these operations. "Voltages at the machine level function as signifiers for a higher level that interprets them, and these interpretations in turn become signifiers for a still higher level interfacing with them. Hence the different levels of code consist of interlocking chains of signifiers and signifieds, with signified on one level becoming signifiers on another" (2005, 45). Saussure's model requires a subject of language, for whom and through whose practices signifier and signified are articulated. In Jacques Lacan's revision of Saussure, which Hayles's description of cascading registers of signifiers and signifieds resembles (cf. esp. "L'Instance de la lettre," in Lacan 1966, 515ff), this subject is inextricable from their articulation ("the signifier is that which represents the subject to another signifier," etc.). Changes in voltage in and of themselves do not signify, because they cannot be directly registered by a subject, for whom they might express a value. It is only through the intermediation of semiotic systems (the "code" of machine instructions to which Hayles refers, and layers of higher-level programming "languages" by which these instructions are interpreted) that they may be generative of potential meaning. (Hayles's model is already front-loaded in this regard: "voltage" and "change" are terms of a semiotic in which physical phenomena are measured and oriented toward expressive ends.) The enigma, as Kittler has observed, is just where the subject enters this system of strata and dispersals, as real phenomena of the machine will be accessible as such only through the retroaction of language (1997, 50).

N1.25. "*he* or another user of Memex": Here and in some passages below, I depart from my usual practice of referring to the user or reader with a feminine pronoun. Reviewing an early version of this chapter, Nick Montfort correctly observed that Bush seems not to have envisaged a female Memex operator.►N1.21

N1.26. I was alerted to this passage in Bush 1929 by Mindell's discussion of Bush's early work on power system transients (2002, 146).

N1.27. On July 10, 1945, in the same month that the *Atlantic* Memex essay was published, Bush was awarded a U.S. patent for a justifying typewriter (Bush 1945c). (He had filed the patent in 1942.) The device used a series of key-activated switches and relays—adaptable to a regular, nonjustifying typewriter just as Memex might be adapted to a regular desk enclosure—to feed a line of keyed text into a temporary memory unit, calculate the escapements required to justify the line in printed form, and then type the composed results as an integral character sequence. The patent suggests that Bush was thinking about electromechanical store and forward schemes while he was working on drafts of the Memex essay between 1939 and 1945 that could conceivably have been generalized to units above and below the page. Perhaps the allure of the page image, joining as it did familiar syntagmas of film and the codex, was too great for Bush to have considered a solution involving more variable-sized textual aggregates ▶ 2.02.

N1.28. Bush had described prototypes of these systems, the Voder and Vocoder, in the opening pages of "As We May Think," but they were not integrated into Memex (Bush 1991a, 94).

N1.29. Bush does not differentiate between the user-invoked trails and the machine-generated trails of trails, though these are obviously different kinds of data and would, presumably, have to be stored and accessed in different ways. Intriguingly, he proposes that the device's attention to the user's reading history might be used to weight its future attentions if Memex were instructed to replay a trail repeatedly. Because the mechanism "remembers what it has been caused to do," this would reinforce the trail's significance and prime Memex's attention to similar patterns in subsequent readings (1991a, 176).

N1.30. This supplemental screen introduces an interesting problem: how heavy must Memex be, with all those cogs, wires, spools, and the growing mass of its store? You could not easily move it, so you need to be free to move around it. Ramelli's wheel would be difficult to move about the scholar's study, so the scholar—hampered by infirmity though he may be—must be free to roam ▶ 7.22. Nelson's solution to the portability problem will take two forms. First, in the docuverse, which residing everywhere resides nowhere in particular. Second, in the Silver-Stand: a fixed location visited by the mobile user; because its commercial model is the drive-in, mobility is encoded in every span of its architecture.

N1.31. In 1966, Bush drafted an essay on extrasensory perception in which he proposed that ESP might be used as the ideal interface for machine control. Originally planned for the essay collection *Science Is Not Enough*, the essay was never finished (Kahn and Nyce 1991, 140–41).

N1.32. Bush's proposal that trails be color-coded to indicate their age (1991a, 171) may be the first description of typed hypertext links. ▶[N0.11]

N1.33. See, for example, Bernstein 2002 and 2004a, and Bernstein, Millard, and Weal 2002.

N1.34. Cf. H. J. Jackson 2001, on the "great divide" between the "A[nnotator]s" (those who fill in the blanks) and the "B[ibliophile]s" (those who do not). Jackson stresses the political character of their difference: "Those opposed regularly describe notes in books as rape, addiction, sacrilege, 'crap,' noise, invasion, parasitism. In this sort of intemperate language we hear undercurrents of fear comparable to the alarm expressed by the authorities at the possible consequences of 'the private reading of particular readers' at the Reformation and of the rapid expansion of the reading market at the end of the eighteenth century, especially in wake of the American and French Revolutions. The great divide between As and Bs is no doubt also at some level political, the conservative force of the

Bs seeking to restrain dissent, the As to incite it. (The unregulated growth of the Internet today prompts similar reactions)" (240). Jackson is on the side of the Annotators, with a few, mostly pragmatic, reservations.

A comparable faith in generative, progressive effects of collaborative annotation—reading and writing outside of institutional inertias—is encoded in Bush's device, especially in the later designs. Engelbart's program for "collaboration support" will emphasize these qualities of the emergent archive (Engelbart and English 1968, Engelbart 1986); by the time of Berners-Lee's design for the World Wide Web, they will be shifted in the direction of user "freedom" and "empowerment" (Berners-Lee 1989, 1999). In Landow's description of the "reconfiguration" of authors and readers, institutional revolution is a condition and consequence of the hypertext archive: the Annotators have become authors in their own right (Landow 1992, 1997, 2006; ▶ 5.01).

2. Historiations

N2.01. In the discussions of Xanadu that follow, I generally do not distinguish between capabilities of different versions of the system (xu60, xu65, xu67, etc.—they have proliferated as Nelson has unpacked the history of the project). I take these to represent landmarks of implementation of Xanadu's basic operations, rather than re-imaginings or extensions of them. (In contrast, differences between Memex I, II, and III mark certain aspects of their design as fundamentally different ▶ 1.45.) See Nelson 1999b.

N2.02. Nelson defines the *docuverse* as "a swirling complex of equi-accessible unity, a single great universal text and data grid" (1990a, 2/53).

N2.03. A "byte" is a measurement of data storage, typically consisting of eight binary digits or "bits." In general, it is also the smallest contiguous sequence of bits that represent a discrete object in memory (a number or alphabetic character, for example), on which basis computation is possible. The retrieval and display of byte spans in Xanadu are controlled by protocols called "FEBE" ("Front-End-Back-End") and "BEBE" ("Back-End-Back-End"). None of the instructions and data exchanges they require are shown to the user, to whom the end result might be piped via any number of front-end systems. ("How many Xanadu people does it take to change a light bulb? None: that's a front-end function." See Nelson 1990a, 4/61–78.) In this model, back-end and front-end do not demarcate precise divisions of the operational space of the system so much as different domains of agency, whose bijection is the only constant ▶ 1.29.

N2.04. Transclusion was originally called "quote-windows" (Nelson 1975, 24).

N2.05. Two versions of Internet Protocol are currently in use. The most common, IPv4, uses a 32-bit (4-byte) numeric string to represent approximately 4.3 billion (2^{32}) unique host addresses. (As some portions of the IPv4 address space are reserved, the actual number of available addresses is fewer. However, the addresses of networked devices that are not publicly visible to the global Internet—for example, those behind a router that serves as a gateway to the global Internet—need only be unique within their local network.) The most common notation for IPv4 addresses is "dot-decimal," composed of four numbers ranging from 0 to 255, separated by decimal points (for example, "128.207.202.195"), each part of which identifies different entities within networks and the hosts connected to them. IPv6 is a newer standard based on 128-bit addresses with an upward limit of approximately 3.4×10^{38} unique addresses, or ten billion billion billion times greater than the IPv4 address space. This is thought to be sufficiently large to give a unique permanent address to every device that might be conceivably connected to a universal Internet. Xanadu's humber/tumbler scheme aims at an analogous level of precision, but differs from IPv4 and IPv6 in that it maps document states, not device locations, and in that its "accordion-like" notation (1990a, 4/13) extends from an "ur-digit" (1990a, 4/27) corresponding to the initial node of the system, out to addresses of any length required to identify every unique byte span (1990a, 4/15–60). Xanadu's scheme is not incompatible with IPv4 or IPv6, because the tumbler scheme could function as a software layer over an IP network layer.

N2.06. The algorithm appears to have been published for the first time in the third number of the journal *La Psychanalyse* (Lacan 1957). Similar equations were developed in the course of Lacan's fourth seminar, on *La Relation d'objet* (1994 [1956]), a *compte-rendu* of which was published in 1957, but these did not include the big-S/little-s form.

N2.07. The mathematical equations, graphs, and illustrations appearing in Lacan's published works are a frequent subject of Lacanian criticism. The intemperate and uninformed chapter on Lacan in Sokal and Bricmont 1998 is the best-known attack on Lacan's "mathemes." Charraud 1997, Plotnitsky 2002, Labbie 2006, and the essays collected in Glynos and Stavrakakis 2002 are among the best recent serious discussions of the mathemes and their significance in Lacanian and post-classical thought. Van Haute's book-length study (2003) is an exemplary analysis of the 1960 "graphs of desire" (Lacan 1966, 793–827; 2006, 671–702), possibly the most difficult and important of Lacan's diagrams.

However, I am aware of no extended treatment of the typographic provenance, history, and legacies of these images. That they are among the most often transmitted elements of his teaching is evidence of their importance, and why I have chosen the example of the images of "L'Instance de la lettre" as a testbed for the concept of historiation ▶ 2.24. The stylistic evolution of the images over the half-century of publication of official versions of Lacan's texts, beginning with the essays collected in *Écrits* (1966), through the Seminars of the 1950s–1970s published under the direction of Jacques-Alain Miller, is striking. The spareness and simplicity of the early black-and-white equations and graphs contrasts, for example, with the four-color, finely rendered diagrams of knots in Seminar XXIII (2005). Formal homologies and auto-citations abound between the early and late writings, and represent an internal tracery of Lacan's thought: the bar of the "algorithm" of "L'Instance de la lettre" is multiplied in the "four discourses" of Seminar XVII (1969–70); the loop-de-loops of the supplement to the Seminar on "The Purloined Letter" (1954–55; 1966, 48) are echoed in the graphs of desire (1960), the circuits of the partial drive in Seminar XI (1964), the knots of Seminar XXIII, and so on. A properly *typographic* history of Lacan's texts would also have to consider the role of the unofficial transcripts of the Seminars. Most of these documents, which often differ substantively from the published versions, are typescripts photocopied to the point of illegibility (now circulated via the Web), and are illustrated with hand-drawn diagrams and equations presumably copied from Lacan's writing on a blackboard as he lectured. Their crudeness evokes a feeling of proximity to the act of inscription (Lacan's scribbles as master signifiers) that the authorized versions do not. The legacies of Lacan's typographemes are traced on these two opposed and intersecting paths, between the immediacy of the unauthorized image, usually read only by the completist and the devotee of an archival counter-history, and the fineness and precision of the official image, firmly lodged in the store of the canon.

N2.08. Since the late 1950s—about the time "L'Instance de la lettre" was written—it has been known that substantial portions of Saussure's *Cours* are the work of the editors, who interpolated materials that are not in the manuscripts and lecture notes. (See Engler 2004 and de Mauro's addenda and notes to the 1982 Payot edition of the *Cours*.) Among their additions is the diagram of the tree (Saussure 1982, 441n132). That the most recognizable emblem of semiology was not the work of its founder is of greater significance than that Lacan neglects to observe this misattribution. Even so, the genealogy that "L'Instance" presupposes (without, cannily, spelling it out) is by this fact the more significant for the model of reading I am developing: the first diagram, by which I mean the original of Lacan's "faulty illustration" of the sign, was itself an elaboration, the product of prior, vigorous, and extensive readings of Saussure's texts, which were themselves constructed by a backward glance with no determinate point of departure.

N2.09. See, for example, in *The Interpretation of Dreams*, Freud's dream of looking out a railway-carriage window at the passing Tiber River (1940–52, vols. 1–2; 1955–66, vol. 4: chap. V, B); and his patients' dreams of "the platform moving toward the train" (1940–52, vols. 1–2; 1955–66, vol. 5: chap. VI, F) and of a father's mortal injury in a railway accident (1955–66, vol. 5: chap. VI, G). In *Jokes and Their Relation to the Unconscious* (1940–52, vol. 6; 1955–66, vol. 8), several of the jokes are set in train stations and railway cars, most notably, the joke about the two Jews meeting on a train platform at Galicia (chap. III, 4), to which Lacan refers in the "Séminaire sur 'La Lettre volée'" ("Seminar on 'The Purloined Letter,'" Lacan 1966, 20). The text of the Seminar had been published a year before "L'Instance de la lettre," in the second number of *La Psychanalyse* (1956).

N2.10. With evident satisfaction, Lacan notes that his introduction of the anagram preceded the publication of Saussure's notebooks, which recorded three years of obsessive decoding of anagrammatic messages he thought were hidden in classical Latin poetry (1966, 503n2). On Saussure's notebooks, cf. Starobinski 1971.

N2.11. Lacan quotes the final stanza of Valéry's 1952 poem: "—No, says the tree, it says No! in the scintillating [*étincellement*] / Of its superb head, / Which the storm treats universally / As it does a blade of grass" (Valéry 1957, 1:115). The fragment anticipates a passage later in the essay—or perhaps the later passage retroactivates the fragment—when Lacan proposes a line from Victor Hugo's 1871 poem "Booz endormi," "His sheaf was neither miserly nor hateful," as an example of metaphor. "Metaphor's creative spark [*l'étincelle*] does not spring forth from the juxtaposition of two images, that is, of two equally actualized signifiers. It flashes between two signifiers, one of which has replaced the other by taking the other's place in the signifying chain, the occulted signifier remaining present by virtue of its (metonymic) connection to the rest of the chain" (1966, 507). In 1957, Lacan's French-speaking readers would have recognized that "Booz endormi"—a text memorized by every French schoolchild of the period—includes one of the most famous rhyming tricks of modern French poetry, "Tout reposait dans Ur et dans *Jérimadeth*" ("All was at rest in Ur and Jérimadeth"). No place in the Bible was called "Jérimadeth," but this forged name at the end of a line rhymes with its pair in the stanza ". . . et Ruth se demandait . . ." (". . . and Ruth asked herself . . ."). Pronounced as it is written, *Jérimadeth = Je rime à dait*, "I rhyme with 'dait.'" Hugo's joke is emblematic of systems of wordplay that Lacan draws on in his elaborations on *arbre*.

N2.12. *Through the Looking-Glass*, Carroll 1991, chap. 6.

N2.13. See Nancy and Lacoue-Labarthe's (1973) and Fink's (2004) analyses.

N2.14. There are no common bibliographic standards for citing individual nodes of hypertexts. I will identify them by embedding the node's title in curly brackets.

N2.15. See Fink's discussion of this passage (Lacan 2006, 808n504), which he translates also with "historiate." A cognate of the term, *s'historier* (literally, to make one's history, to tell one's story), appears in an important passage of Lacan's seminar on the psychoses (Lacan 1981). Discussing the Wolf-Man's memory of the primal scene, Lacan proposes that the "primitive impression" of the scene remained in the Wolf-Man's store of signifiers, meaning nothing to him because it had failed to "enter into his story (*histoire*)." Subsequent events, says Lacan, bound signifiers of the scene to the Wolf-Man's nascent sexual awareness and gave the fragmentary memory of his parents' embrace its traumatic significance. "In effect, sexual desire is that which allows man to historiate himself (*qui sert à l'homme à s'historier*), to the extent that it is at this level that the law [of desire] is introduced for the first time" (1981, 177; 2002, 45).

N2.16. *Recollects*: in his early writings, Lacan distinguishes between two kinds of memory, *remémoration* and *réminiscence* (1966, 519; Evans 1996, 162). The latter—in English, *reminiscence*—is an imaginary phenomenon; Lacan associates it with the (to him, absurd) notion that past experiences and affects associated with them may be resurrected in memory *qua* recurrences of something actual and unmediated by the signifiers bound to them. Freud's understanding of how memory operates—throughout his work, but especially in his 1895 *Project*, and the books on dreams and bungled actions, and the cases of the Rat-Man and Wolf-Man—is, Lacan argues, a theory of *remémoration*, which I translate (following Evans) as *recollection*. Recollection is a symbolic phenomenon—remembering as a suspensive scansion and a parsing of the subject's characteristic signifiers, marking its patterns in the form of symptoms, bungled actions, the products of dreamwork, and so forth.

N2.17. Nelson introduced these concepts in 1965 in the same paper in which the term "hypertext" was used for the first time. Mentions of "ELF" are rare in Nelson's later writings, where this initial distinction between file and information structures is collapsed and the term "zippered list" is used to describe both.

N2.18. Cf. Nelson's essays on ZigZag (1998, 1999a), a multidimensional data editing and browsing protocol based on principles of the zippered list.

N2.19. In this movement (recollection in place of reminiscence), the consistency or completeness of the speaking subject is surrendered to imperatives of structure: "I identify myself in language, but only by losing myself in it as an object. What is realized in my history [*histoire*] is neither the past definite as what was, since it is no more, nor even the perfect as what has been in what I am, but the future anterior as what I will have been, given what I am in the process of becoming" (Lacan 1966, 300).

N2.20. Schaff 1956, Letter lxxv, 334.

N2.21. See also Storkerson and Wong 1997 and Rossi 2000.

N2.22. "premodern alterity": see Yates 1974 and Spence 1994. On "biological bases," see G. Johnson 1992 ("even as you read these words, a tiny portion of your brain is physically changing. New connections are being sprouted—a circuit that will create a jab of recognition if you encounter the words again"). On "pathology," see Luria 1987, whose remarkable patient S—— appears to have independently discovered the classic mnemotechnique, complexly fused with idioms of his synaesthesia.

N2.23. Or a childhood Montana: ▶N3.26.

N2.24. See Freud's letter to Wilhelm Fliess, October 15, 1897 (Freud 1954, 221–25); and *The Interpretation of Dreams* (1940–52, vols. 1–2; 1955–66, vol. 4: chap. 4).

N2.25. Cf. the conclusion of the unfinished "Memex II" essay, where Bush figures this entanglement of the subject's mortality and the record's fragility explicitly as a problem of patrimony: "Can a son inherit the memex of the father, or the disciple of his master, refined and polished over the years, and go on from there?

In this way can we avoid some of the loss which comes when oxygen is no longer furnished to the brain of the great thinker, when all the pattern of neurons so painstakingly refined becomes merely a mass of protein and nucleic acid?" (1991b, 183).

N2.26. The significance of the new disciplines of information theory and cybernetics for concepts of biological and embodied subjectivity seems not to have occurred to Bush, who was not a participant in the early development of those fields. See Hayles 1999, esp. 50–75.

N2.27. Zachary (1997, 285) observes that the Woolf interview (1945) and similar stories in the popular press of the period exaggerated the importance of Bush's role in the Manhattan Project. Readers of the *Life* essay would have thought him more central to the development of the Bomb than he actually was.

N2.28. Advertisements for consumer goods play a less significant role in the July 1945 *Atlantic* version of the essay because of the magazine's then practice of publishing "serious" essays in a section apart from more populist fare, where the advertisements were also placed. The ads appearing in the July *Atlantic* are, however, similar overall to those in the September *Life*, with fewer promises of ramped-up production of goods and a greater emphasis on heavy industry. An ad for General Motors ("Victory Is Our Business") is uncannily apt to the context of Memex. It shows a young boy staring off into space, one hand bracing his chin, another holding a book open: "Something has clicked in that young head. Some word or phrase has struck a spark and he's off on a lonely tangent of thought all his own. . . . Ask the engineers where the good, new things come from and you may be surprised to learn that most of the big problems are solved first in people's heads" (110).

N2.29. Cicero *De Oratore* 2.86.352–55. Simonides of Ceos is credited by Cicero with discovering the art of memory after a banquet at the house of a miserly nobleman named Scopas. Simonides chanted a lyric poem in honor of his host, concluding with a long passage referring to Castor and Pollux, but Scopas refused to pay him the agreed-upon fee for the panegyric. Soon thereafter, Simonides received a message that he should go outside, as two young men wished to see him. As soon as he left, the roof of the banquet hall collapsed, crushing Scopas and his family such that none of the bodies could be identified. "The story goes that Simonides was enabled by his recollection of the place in which each of them had been reclining at table to identify them for separate interment; and that this circumstance suggested to him the discovery of the truth that the best aid to clearness of memory consists in orderly arrangement." The two men who called him away from the banquet were, unsurprisingly, Castor and Pollux.

N2.30. See Baran 1962, the first discussion of a "Distributed Adaptive Message Block Network," and the basis of methods of the modern Internet. Baran proposes the system as the model with the best chance of surviving a surprise Soviet nuclear attack.

N2.31. Interpretation is exhausted by this recursion but that does not prevent it from being figured by signifiers that, in effect, pin the recursion to a manipulable object. The "navel" of the dream is one such object ► 4.45. The Signorelli diagram ► Figure 2.04 functions similarly, in that it holds the dispersion of the system it represents in check so that it may be manipulated by Freud.

N2.32. "The name that I tried without success to recall . . . was that of the artist who painted the magnificent frescoes of the *Four Last Things* in Orvieto cathedral. Instead of the name I was looking for—Signorelli—the names of two other painters—Botticelli and Boltraffo—thrust themselves on me, though they were immediately and decisively rejected by my judgement as incorrect." Freud does not mention his destination by name, but Peter J. Swales's deduction that it must be Trebinje appears conclusive (2003, 48).

N2.33. Solms observes that the diagram is typical of Freud's later graphic depictions of mental processes. His early illustrations of these processes, expressly neurological in their idioms, were gradually supplanted by graphemes with similar connective and branching traits, but in which language fragments and functions now occupy the nodes (Gamwell and Solms 2006). In those images, the direction of movement in the circuit is often ambiguous; it may be multiple; in any case, the circuit is never understood to exhaust connections between the nodes, but only to indicate the most significant of their relations. Everything is deeply intertwingled ► 2.54.

N2.34. It is likely that Lacan's remarks here refer also to his "Graph of Desire," which was developed over the course of Seminar V (Lacan 1998). See also Lacan 1966, 793–828.

N2.35. Swales observes that the diagram as reproduced in the 1898 essay differs from the 1905 diagram, chiefly in that the earlier image includes no arrows indicating the influences between its elements, and the phrase *Thema von Tod und Sexualität*, shortened in the later essay to *Tod und Sexualität*, is nearer the center of the diagram (2003, 29–31). Unaccountably, he notes, the reprinted 1898 essays in both the *Gesammelte Werke* and *Standard Edition* reprise the 1905 version of the diagram.

N2.36. Lacan's language in this passage is ambiguous. I read his reference to "the word" (*le mot*) as referring to the unspeakable *Signor* (i.e., Death as the absolute master), and not the variants of *Herr*, which Lacan consistently refers to as "signifiers."

N2.37. Lacan suggests that the background of Freud's decoding of the parapraxis is Freud's anxieties about his sexual potency (1998, 39). The close relation of the Signorelli parapraxis to the much-storied "Aliquis" fragment—the specimen example of the second chapter of *The Psychopathology of Everyday Life*, but more bound up with the Signorelli example than by mere sequence, as Freud admits (though he doesn't say much more than that)—marks an important situating in the book of a system of signifiers that represent Freud's mnemic signature in the work. They are marked concretely in the typographemes of the Signorelli diagram. The only such image included in a catalog of linguistic slips that should lend themselves to many such representations, the diagram has the feel of a foregrounded landscape, calculated to be as exemplary for what it covers as for what it shows.

What it covers is in several respects unclear and may be unknowable. But it is clear that Freud's role in the presentation of these accounts is more careful—and, in another sense, less controlled—than was thought for much of the hundred years since their publication. A growing body of scholarship has documented and decrypted the best-known of the specimen parapraxes and demonstrated that some of their elements have been disingenuously reworked by Freud so as to better fit his theory; others are far more autobiographical, usually in an unflattering manner, than he lets on; others may have been fabricated outright. The clumsiest digging in these strata by anti-Freudians is easily dismissed. But there are several critics of Freud who have done their work very carefully and whose conclusions cannot be ignored. First among these is Peter J. Swales, whose 1982 decryption of the "Aliquis" fragment—he concludes that the friend worried that his mistress has missed her period was in fact Freud, and that his mistress was Minna Bernays, Freud's sister-in-law—is probably the best-known (the most derided and the most praised) of these projects. His 2003 unpacking of the Signorelli episode, in several respects the sequel of that essay, is a model of deeply learned historical and textual detective work, discovering numerous inconsistencies and improbabilities in Freud's account of events, and substantial evidence that he conflated entirely separate misadventures of memory and language into a single, terribly convenient package, while suppressing data that would render it less convenient. Though I find most of Swales's argument convincing—no one before who has written on the Signorelli parapraxis has so thoroughly traced its context in and incorporation of Freud's private life—I am reluctant to find in this evidence of Freud's "mendacity" and "imposture" (Swales's terms, and he uses stronger) a reason to toss out the baby with the bathwater. "*Ceterum censeo*: There is no more Unconscious" (63). This seems to me an extreme conclusion.

Moreover—though I will admit straightaway that this distinction is less serviceable in other contexts—the truth or falsehood of Freud's narrative is not determinate of its function on the surface of the page, for a reader (Lacan, me, you), and is irrelevant to its evocation of a tradition of arborescent typographemes that long predates it (Davis 1995, Warner 1989), and that continues to exert its influence on the visualization and traversal of textual orders.

3. Revenge of the Word

N3.01. Lapacherie 1984, 288.

N3.02. The classic papers on direct manipulation are Shneiderman 1987 (first published in 1983) and Hutchins, Hollan, and Norman 1986.

N3.03. Peripheral vision is more sensitive to screen "flicker," noticed when the refresh rate of the image approaches from above the eye's threshold for distinguishing individual film or video frames in a sequence. As ambient lighting is increased, sensitivity to flicker also increases. This is why cinema (usually shown in a darkened room) generally may have a lower refresh rate (24 Hz) than desktop video monitors (66 Hz or higher), which are often viewed under brighter lights.

N3.04. Engelbart and English 1968. This dual requirement of synchronization and familiarity applies to other input devices. I cite the mouse and keyboard as only the most common of such devices.

N3.05. In the terminology of GUI design, a "widget" is a discrete element with a specified function, for example, a button or toggle used to change the appearance of a window.

N3.06. Some characters of *Victory Garden* never watch TV, though its spectacle also encompasses them. Brian Urquhart openly eschews television, though he does closely observe a bank of video monitors while leading a demonstration of the NVACS ("Neuro-Verbal Analog Conversion System"), a virtual reality–based "dream processor" that displays video output from its subject's dreams {Envax Scamdee}. This passage opens into a long Tara-in-Nighttown free-for-all paralleling Urquhart's breakdown. Tate, the Tara University Provost whom Urquhart believes to possess the "answer to everything," spends most of the fiction in the University Planetarium, wondering how it is that the Earth has managed to be missed by a comet that should have wiped out the planet {Perigee}. With his eye on the heavens, Tate attends to the big picture; perhaps this is why he functions as the persecuting agent of Urquhart's increasingly delusional worldview.

N3.07. One of the legacies of the GUI is that certain colors or arrangements of pixels shown as the background to icons and windows are partly drained of meanings that might be otherwise attributed to them (the checkerboard black-and-white pattern of the early Mac OS, simulating gray; the Kelly green of Windows 95) or complex graphics displayed as the default background (the rolling meadow of Windows XP's "Bliss Screen" [▶ Figure 7.08], the "Aqua" swirls of Mac OS X "Tiger," the abstract horizon of Windows Vista, the aurorae and star field of Mac OS X "Leopard"). They become under these circumstances the zero-degree graphic state of the desktop, the signifier of general conditions of its use ▶ 7.68. This effect is notable in early GUIs such as NeXTSTEP 1.0, in which the desktop is a purely interstitial construct: the user cannot place objects on it or otherwise modify its appearance (NeXT Computer, Inc. 1992). The effect was also a characteristic of command line interfaces in which continuous black or white backgrounds were used to indicate a neutral state of the screen, though this may not have been noticeable before GUIs demonstrated that any color pattern or image could play this role.

N3.08. Lapacherie 1984. See also Lapacherie 1982, 1990, 1994. Lapacherie's use of the adjective "grammatic" refers to spatially inscribed and demarcated aspects of the trace, rather than to conventions of correct usage: *grammar* in the more usual sense of that term. However, the operational field of the *gramme* must also cross into those conventions, and in that crossing, the implicit phonocentrism of Lapacherie's characterization of grammatextually unmarked forms of writing might also be nuanced. These unmarked forms of writing Lapacherie calls simply "text," reserving the adjective "grammatextual" for marked forms. Baetens substitutes the pair *scriptotexte/grammatexte* for Lapacherie's terminology (2001, 13), which may more clearly situate the opposition between forms of text, and not between text and something like it, more or less. (An ambiguity that we have already seen in definitions of *hyper*text ▶ 1.13.) But Baetens's terminology, I find, overemphasizes practices of inscription—once-and-for-all registrations of text on a surface—neglecting media in which the spatial logic of the *gramme* may be variable and dynamic.

N3.09. Queneau 1950, 191–96. The essay is devoted primarily to Nicolas-Louis-Marie-Dominique Cirier (1792–1869), whose typographic experiments anticipated those of the early twentieth century. On Cirier, see also Blavier 2000, 595–604.

N3.10. Genette (1976, 71–83) surveys several eighteenth-century natural histories of the alphabet based on conjectural mimographisms of individual letters, dividing them into *ideomimographisms* (the grapheme resembles an object) and *phonomimographisms* (the grapheme resembles in some way the sound to which it corresponds). Rasula and McCaffery 1998 include other examples of such systems.

N3.11. Lapacherie draws this use of the term *diagram*—"an icon of relation"—from Peirce and Jakobson. Cf. Jakobson 1971.

N3.12. All but the rebus example are my own. In Fibonacci's sequence, each number is the sum of the two previous numbers (0, 1, 1, 2, 3, 5, 8 . . .). Christensen's poem sequence (1981) was composed in Danish. Susanna Nied's 2001 English translation preserves the sequence's mathematical scheme. Mesostics, a poetic form made famous by composer John Cage, is a text written or printed such that a word or phrase is spelled out by a column or columns of letters in the middle of words or phrases in horizontal rows.

A lipogram is a text that programmatically excludes or otherwise constrains the use of a letter or letters. Perec's *La Disparition* (1986, originally published in 1969) includes no words containing the letter "e," the most common letter in French orthography. The remarkable skill with which Perec exerts control of his text's grammar and vocabulary is justly famous, as it is possible to read the text without noticing the constraint. Several initial published reviews of the book seem to have done just this.

A liponym is a text that programmatically excludes a word or words. Simple forms of the practice, of more narrative than textual significance, are common: the reader never learns the name of Dashiell Hammett's Continental Op, the narrator of Alain Robbe-Grillet's *La Jalousie* never uses the first person pronoun. The more interesting form of the practice, from a grammatextual point of view, is one in which the program is carried to such an extreme that it determines the whole of the textbase. Doug Nufer's *Never Again* (2004, originally published in 2002) is a progressive liponym, a two-hundred-page novel in which no word is used twice.

Perec's novel has been translated into English (by Gilbert Adair, 1994) and Spanish (by a team of five translators, 1997a). Both translations preserve Perec's basic constraint: as in the original, the English text includes no "e"s; the Spanish text includes no "a"s—because, the translators reasoned, "a" is the most common letter in Spanish orthography (Paraye 1998). That translation is possible for texts such as these suggests that the alphabetic grammatext is expressed formally: more significant than that a given glyph is the vehicle or support of meaning is that it should be (as is clearest in the Spanish translation of Perec's novel) subjected to an algorithm whose meaning is of an entirely different order. However, the glyph's activation of meaning apart from effects of the algorithm cannot be entirely excluded from consideration of the overall signification of the text: a precise translation of Nufer's novel that preserves its constraint seems impossible.

N3.13. This layering of objects on-screen is an illusion in one important respect: the values of individual pixels are determined by contents of the current screen buffer; obscured portions of any object on the screen may be stored in video memory so as to be recalled quickly when the object is brought "forward," but they are not in any sense "underneath" the current value of pixels of the object that appears to be on top of them.

N3.14. For example, electronic poet John Cayley has produced several works in which morphological transformations of character and letterforms—notably, between Chinese and English-language texts—are generated by programming systems. The meaning of literary "translation" in such an environment comprises not only semantic but geometrical and topological dimensions. See Cayley 2003 and the texts available online at http://www.shadoof.net/in.

N3.15. "[A polygraphic text] is one in which are used simultaneously, either distinct writing systems—the Latin alphabet and Chinese ideograms, for example—or different 'styles' of the same writing system—for example, Roman characters and Gothic letters on the first page of the newspaper *Le Monde*, or hieroglyphics and hieratic signs in Egyptian funerary manuscripts" (Lapacherie 1990, 396).

N3.16. "Data constituting a 'file'": I use this awkward phrase to mark an important fiction of the UI: groupings of information treated integrally as a single unit, a "file," are often composed of multiple elements managed by different subsystems of the OS and application program. It is common, for example, for attributes of the file that determine its visual presentation and manipulability on the desktop to be controlled by file management subsystems of the OS that are distinct from subsystems of the application (word processor, image editor, etc.) that create the data represented in this way. Moreover, some OSs represent as a single file to the user a collection of smaller files "packaged" in this way to simplify the manipulation of the collection in the UI.

N3.17. In this regard, robustly grammatextual forms (especially those in which iconic elements are explicitly present along with textual graphemes) emphasize medial bases for tabular reading practices familiar to any reader of still images. Images are rarely taken in by the eye in one instant. They are "scanned" by the viewer according to complex tracing patterns that determine the viewer's perception of the structure and meaning of the image (Gandelman 1991). We may presume that similar scanning patterns inform the reading of moving images, such as those typical of cinema and computer-based multimedia. In these cases the viewer's saccadic tracing of the framed image is simultaneously directed and limited—vectorized—by the implicit forward momentum of the image's presentation.

N3.18. The metric of iconicity of the print grammatext is its degree of departure from instrumental, alphabetic signification. Similarly, the metric of iconicity in the screen grammatext is its departure from signification of instrumental meaning within the interface.

N3.19. This begs the question of what, exactly, a *window* is in the contemporary cultural moment, in which the term is widely applied to framing structures that seem to serve chiefly as points of entry to *medial* imaginaries, which may or may not have determined spatial qualities. On this subject, see Virilio's prescient 1981 discussion of "the third window" of timeshifted video. Friedberg 2006 shows that aspects of this problem date back at least to Alberti and the early Renaissance. She cites Antonello's painting of Jerome in his cell as an example of then debates on the functions of windows (35).

N3.20. Such mappings of hardware to elements of the UI are often short-lived. Since the release of Mac OS X 10.5 ("Leopard"), more of Apple's desktop and laptop computers are encased in brushed metal enclosures, but the brushed metal look has been dropped from the UI's window styles in favor of a uniform gray shade.

N3.21. Because in most cases these commands must specify directory paths of the files to which they apply, they are by definition diagrammatic. For example, the MS-DOS command

C:\ copy a:\file.txt c:\file.txt

copies the file "file.txt," currently on the "A" drive, to the "C" drive. The "C:\" string at the beginning of the line is the "prompt," and indicates that the default file path for commands is the root level of the C drive. The "copy" command cannot be executed without an indication of the storage hierarchy of the computer.

An *escape sequence* is a series of characters that triggers a command state in a computer or peripheral device. In early non-WYSIWYG word processors, nonprinting codes of this kind were used to turn on and off character formatting (italic, superscript, etc.).

N3.22. A related and more general diagrammatic marking of textual structure, possible in both command line and GUI environments, is effected by constraining displayed text to definite regions of the screen, limiting text that can be displayed and possibly orienting its syntactic structure. See my discussion of these effects in Mac OS and Windows editions of Michael Joyce's *Afternoon* ▶ 6.45.

N3.23. A *cooperative multitasking* environment is one in which each program has access to the processor only when it is surrendered by other programs; each must periodically give up control of the processor to allow others to run. When one program in this environment crashes, other active programs (including the operating system) may lose access to data stored in memory that they need to run or terminate cleanly. To prevent this, memory assigned to a program may be protected, that is, isolated from memory assigned to other programs. A *preemptive multitasking* environment is one in which the operating system allocates processing time based on priorities it assigns to the tasks being run by active programs: the OS preempts a task's access to resources if more important tasks need them. The memory assigned to each task is protected, preventing an unexpected termination of one task from also bringing down others.

On single-processor systems multiple program tasks are not actually executed at the same time; each is accorded a *slice* of the processor's time. (In a preemptive system, the task is unaware of others that are running.) To the user, all the active programs should seem to be executing simultaneously, though this illusion may be betrayed when programs are given too little processing time to complete their tasks, or the operating system has trouble juggling the queue of pending tasks. To increase the efficiency of multitasking, an operating system may support *multithreading*, in which different parts of a program, called threads, are executed (more nearly) concurrently. Multithreading is typically used to spread computing tasks across multiple processors and to separate interface-related tasks (updating the screen, reacting to user input) from background computational tasks, so that each runs more responsively.

N3.24. "It seems to me that the web is all edges and without much depth and for a writer that is trouble. You want to induce depth, to have the surface give way to reverie and a sense of shared shaping of the experience of reading and writing. Instead everything turns to branches" (M. Joyce 2000, 187).

N3.25. Cf. Ulmer's 1997 response to *Twelve Blue*, which emphasizes the function of the "choral word" in Gass's meditation and its joins with Joyce's text: "the *inventio* and *dispositio* are governed by the principle of *blue* (every possible usage) rather than by a thesis statement or a story (although the text both argues and narrates)." His essay includes a biographical turn that compactly illustrates the effects of historiation (more medially bound, but not otherwise different in its generative aspects from Ulmer's concept of the *mystory*): "It so happens that

I have never stopped thinking of the lilacs that grew in the backyard of my child-hood home, the very scarcity of flowering bushes in Montana making their brief but fragrant appearance all the more impressive. I am hooked."

N3.26. See Cayley 2004 and Glazier 2001 and 2004. John McDaid's HyperCard fiction *Uncle Buddy's Phantom Funhouse* (1993) is an early example of this technique (Moulthrop 1991a).

4. Ex-foliations

N4.01. "You are standing in an open field west of a white house, with a boarded front door. There is a small mailbox here . . ." (Infocom, Inc. 1983). The letter in the mailbox reads, "WELCOME TO ZORK! / ZORK is a game of adven-ture, danger, and low cunning. In it you will explore some of the most amazing territory ever seen by mortals. No computer should be without one!"

N4.02. For example, the Guidebook in the Lobby of Flood Control Dam #3, which communicates nothing about how to work the Dam's controls (or even that this is desirable in order to advance the game), only the circumstances of its construction: "FCD#3 was constructed in year 783 of the Great Underground Empire to harness the mighty Frigid River. This work was supported by a grant of 37 million zorkmids from your omnipotent local tyrant Lord Dimwit Flat-head the Excessive . . ."

N4.03. The restriction of carrying one page at a time is lifted in *Riven*, Cyan's 1997 sequel to *Myst*.

N4.04. See Drucker 1995 (esp. chap. 6) and G. Smith 2003 for invaluable historical and descriptive analyses of this formal structure.

N4.05. Newell had previously explored applications of this device in *The Hole Book* (2001a [1908]). In that work a character named Tom Potts, fooling with a gun, fires the bullet through a clock on his mantel. The bullet proceeds through the wall and then numerous surfaces *perpendicular* to the earth—that is, orthogo-nal to the trajectory of the rocket in *The Hole Book*. It circles the globe and returns back to Potts's apartment, where it is stopped by the stout icing of a cake frosted by his new bride. Potts is thus saved by the immature cooking skills of a newlywed woman and, we are given to understand, incomplete rituals of hymen.

N4.06. I am indebted to Lisa Hager for bringing this text to my attention through the generous gift of a copy of the book.

N4.07. Thompson directed Westvaco's annual American Classic Book series (*The Red Badge of Courage* is the 1968 release in the series) and, from 1938 to 1962, *Westvaco Inspirations for Printers*, an industry journal noted for its adventur-ous use of color and type. See Callihan 1982 and Thompson 1988 for examples of other titles in the Classic Book series.

N4.08. Thompson had experimented with the use of die-cut holes in covers, revealing portions of frontis pages, in several issues of *Westvaco Inspirations*. These were pamphlet-length works, and thus did not permit a hole more than a few pages in depth (Thompson 1988).

N4.09. A restricted variant of this structure is a common feature of contemporary mass-market paperbacks, in which a die-cut opening in the front jacket of the book opens onto a false jacket page, whose design (usually an image) shows through the opening. I've made no programmatic study of this subject, but my impression is that in the United States this jacket design is most common among books in popular genres: detective and spy fiction, science fiction, romance fiction, and westerns. Its primary function seems to be to increase the visual appeal of the book jacket; only rarely does it mark complex interiorities of the book as such. It may be the case, however, that the semiotic of disclosure that this design marks *in principle* has proven particularly appropriate to these genres, in which narrative tensions are typically sustained by crises of discovery. Thomas Allen's *Uncovered* (2007), a series of photographs of pulp paperbacks whose cover elements have been incised and folded to create three-dimensional dioramas—gangsters, molls, and cowboys rising out of the formerly flat covers—demonstrates this to humorous effect. The relation of such design elements to attributes or conventions of fictional genres, and the consequent role of those elements in the marketing of fictions, seems a ripe field for investigation.

N4.10. My use of gray to highlight the "anti-frames" of the comic follows Groensteen 2003, 26.

N4.11. The *Acquefacques* novels are marvels of paratextual and grammatextual play. The remaining four novels in the series include irruptions of color into the black-and-white panels (Acquefacques opens a lens in a lighthouse at the edge of the world, letting in colored light); die-cut spirals attached to multiple pages (he stumbles into a dream vortex that opens into a realm of photographs that includes abandoned drafts of the novels and of Mathieu working at his desk); reversible bindings (two versions of Acquefacques approach one other from opposite ends of the book and meet in a mirror in the center); 3D images (he falls into another vortex and enters a stereoscopic universe; the book includes a set of 3D glasses, held out to the reader by the custodian of the warehouse of "outdated comic scenery"); and so on.

N4.12. "It is the book Blake gave me (as Milton entered Blake's left foot—the first foot, that is, to exit Eden) his eyes wide open through my hand. *To etch* is 'to cut away,' and each page, as in Blake's concept of a book, is a single picture" (R. Johnson 1977, "Note").

N4.13. Marcel Broodthaers marks this spatial legacy of Mallarmé's poem in his 1969 recasting of *Un Coup de dés* as an "image" (Broodthaers's subtitle, in place of Mallarmé's "Poëme"). The book is a near-facsimile of the 1914 Gallimard edition in which the original text has been replaced by horizontal black bars. These have the same dimensions and page positions of Mallarmé's famous cascading lines. The later work preserves as its foreground the spatial logic that is probably the basis of most readers' memories of the text, at the expense of its legibility as text (Mœglin-Delcroix 1997, 20–24).

N4.14. In this regard, Johnson's compositional method differs from Blake's, who is known to have reused copper plates from earlier illuminated works in some later works, and to have purchased used plates from platemakers. In both cases, Blake re-etched the plates with new designs, erasing only those portions of the plate needed for lettering or new relief lines. Traces of this procedure are clearly visible in several illuminated works (Viscomi 1997). In contrast, the published edition of *Radi Os* carries no trace of the portions of the 1892 text that were erased. This is, above all, a consequence of the medial environments in which the two poets have exercised their respective practices of revisionary composition. Blake is working in the stratigraphic field of relief etching, in which palimpsest structures are a natural by-product of the writing process. Johnson is unable to reproduce these structures in the comparably shallower/flatter field of the printed page, where erasure is more absolute.

N4.15. "There are a screen and two throttles. The first throttle moves the text forward and backward, up and down on the screen. The second throttle causes changes in the writing itself: throttling toward you causes the text to become *longer* by minute degrees. Gaps appear between phrases; new words and phrases pop into the gaps, an item at a time. Push back on the throttle and the writing becomes shorter and less detailed" (Nelson 1974, DM 19; see also Landow 2006, 93–98). Though Stretchtext is arguably as expressive a model for dynamic text operations as link-node structures, few hypertext authoring systems support it. (OWL Guide ▶ 0.08 was a notable exception.) Some literary hypertexts have made use of variants of Stretchtext, most often in association with combinatorial methods and appropriated texts. For example, *Regime Change*, a "textual instrument" created by Noah Wardrip-Fruin, David G. Durand, Brion Moss, and Elaine Froehlich (2004), interleaves text and images of a (quickly discredited) 2003 news report of Saddam Hussein's death at the beginning of the Second Iraq War, with passages from the report of the Warren Commission on the assassination of John Fitzgerald Kennedy. Clicking on highlighted terms of the news report opens "bridges"—word-for-word identical syntagmas—into the Warren report, which are then reinserted into the news report, merging the two narratives in an apparent expansion of the report (Wardrip-Fruin 2005).

As the Web has come to dominate popular and research discourses of the digital field, syntagmatic patterns of links and nodes have become fixed in the minds of most users as the defining attributes of hypertext and the more continuous or performative paradigm of Stretchtext has been further displaced. A significant part of hypertext's history is lost in this (Wardrip-Fruin 2004), but it may be too late to reverse course by insisting that Stretchtext is a species of hypertext, as Nelson proposed. Instead, we might argue that Stretchtext and hypertext (by which I mean primarily its link-node form) are forms of "multiple text" (M. Joyce 1991) oriented by different topologies of and operations on the textbase. In this vein, Fassio's reading wheel would represent an analog device that embraces, in its segments, its folds, and their circulations, aspects of both models ▶ 7.28.

N4.16. Cf. Jameson's contrasting of "modernist" *Blowup* with Brian De Palma's "postmodernist" *Blow Out* (Jameson 1992, 37). Jameson associates the former with "motive energies" of an earlier moment of modernization that reached their pinnacle in futurism's exhilaration in mechanical forms (36). The latter film, he proposes, is characteristic of a new order of "reproductive processes": "the aesthetic embodiment of such processes often tends to slip back more comfortably into a mere thematic representation of content—into narratives which are *about* the processes of reproduction and include movie cameras, video, tape recorders, the whole technology of the production and reproduction of the simulacrum" (37). The films may also be contrasted in that each sustains medially bound fantasies of recursion central to their plots. In Antonioni's film, the real basis of (arrested) recursion and the fantasy of endless *mise en abyme* are represented primarily in a visual medium (cinema) that is congruent with its narratively privileged double (photographic enlargement). In De Palma's 1981 film, this isomorphism is weakened by the remapping of the recursion system onto sound technologies (evidence of a political assassination accidentally captured by audio technician Jack Terry, played by actor John Travolta). Despite the film's accomplished score and sound editing, it remains a primarily visual text, requiring of viewers that they resituate the object of Terry's investigations (the sound of a gunshot captured on audio tape) to a visual correlate: initially, a flashback showing Terry's conjectured version of the car crash, and, eventually, a film of the crash that Terry synchronizes with his tape recording to prove his conjecture.

N4.17. "Post-symbolic communication": a nonsense phrase introduced by virtual reality pioneer Jaron Lanier. In the era of such exchanges, Benedikt explains, "language-bound descriptions and semantic games will no longer be required to communicate personal viewpoints, historical events, or technical information. Rather, direct—if 'virtual'—demonstration and interactive experience of the 'original' material will prevail, or at least be a universal possibility" (1991, 12–13).

N4.18. The error of critics who promote the holodeck as a model for narration or mimesis in the digital field (e.g., Murray's *Hamlet on the Holodeck*, 1997) is that they have mistaken a literary conceit for a general model of literature. They neglect in this the reader's understanding of the conceit's genre and medial determinisms. We might want to play Hamlet for a while, but no one in her right mind wants to *be* Hamlet, since there is no possibility of not being him: of going to school somewhere other than Wittenberg, of having one's widowed mother marrying someone other than one's father's murderer, of not seeing a ghost or dying from a poisoned blade in a set-up fencing match. If *Hamlet* were a game, as Bernstein says, it has to be rigged (2004b); Shakespeare's play is a *tragedy*. The play within a play is a *play*; the holodeck's simulation of reality is appealing because we are aware that the television screen is a precondition of its fictive seamlessness.

N4.19. My discussion of *Agrippa* draws on Kirschenbaum 2008, Liu 2004, Schwenger 1994, the documents collected by the Transcriptions Project for "The *Agrippa* Files" (http://agrippa.english.ucsb.edu), and personal correspondence with Kevin Begos, Jr.

N4.20. "between six and eight": The actual number of variants and copies published is unknown. There were two editions of the work, known as the deluxe and the small editions. They differ primarily in size and the layout of the DNA code (in single columns in the small edition), and in the complexity and cost of the paratextual apparatus used (method and materials for binding, boxing, etc.). No more than ninety-five of each edition were published, but known surviving copies of each edition are irregularly numbered; some planned copies of the work were never printed; viewable page counts and the number of aquatints in known copies of the deluxe edition also vary. Because elements of each of the copies were handmade or hand-finished, each copy is in this sense unique (Transcriptions Project 2005; Kirschenbaum 2008, 221–22).

N4.21. Ashbaugh's original idea was to print the overprints in a photosensitive ink that would fade to invisibility after exposure to light, but technical difficulties prevented this. The use of uncured print toner in some copies of *Agrippa* represented a gesture in this direction, although overprints printed in this way do not fade completely (Transcriptions Project 2005). "The concept of the disappearing book is older": As Schwenger 1994 proposes and Begos has confirmed, *Agrippa*'s self-consumption was inspired by Maurice Blanchot's and Stéphane Mallarmé's concepts of disappearing books-in-crisis. Ashbaugh's concept of page elements erased by exposure to light had been anticipated by Keith Smith in 1974 in his plan for *Book Number 50*, a "self-sacrificing book." Pages of the book (never constructed) would be made of film positives developed without fix, bound and presented in a light-tight box. On the exposure of each page to light, its image would blacken, thus protecting the transparencies beneath it from light, allowing the reader to see the next image when the page is turned, just before it blackens (K.A. Smith 2000, 103).

N4.22. A video incorporating footage of "The Transmission," a public broadcast of one playback of the poem on December 9, 2002, staged by the publisher, is available at http://agrippa.english.ucsb.edu/post/documents-subcategories/the-transmission/reagrippa.

N4.23. Letter from Kevin Begos, Jr., to Alan Liu, October 26, 2002, reproduced at http://www.english.ucsb.edu/faculty/ayliu/unlocked/begos/letter.html. Cited with permission.

N4.24. Though it is often claimed that these variants were produced by "hacking" *Agrippa*'s encryption program, Kirschenbaum (2008) has shown that they originated in a transcription of a surreptitiously recorded video transmission of a playing of the text. The "official" text of the poem is available online at Gibson's Web site, http://www.williamgibsonbooks.com/source/agrippa.asp.

N4.25. A CD-ROM based on *Agrippa* was planned but never completed or released. "An Interactive Multimedia Experience in Decay with Computer and CD-ROM" appears to have been conceived of as a slide show of photographs of the work and events surrounding its release, making no attempt to remodel it as an interactive text. (This was in fact proscribed by the project contract.) The project would not reproduce Gibson's poem. (Personal correspondence with Kevin Begos, Jr., November 3, 2006.) Cf. "A Contract for Never-Created CD-ROM of Agrippa," http://agrippa.english.ucsb.edu/contract-for-never-created-cd-rom-version-of-agrippaitem-d42-transcription.

N4.26. Maeda's five "Reactive Books" are: *The Reactive Square* (1995); *Flying Letters* (1996); *12 O'Clocks* (1997); *Tap, Type, Write* (1998); and *Mirror Mirror* (1999, never published). Initial releases of the first two works in the series were released with floppy disks bound within the codices, not mini-CDs. The entire series, including the unreleased *Mirror Mirror*, is described in the context of Maeda's other digital art objects and installations in Maeda 2000. Maeda 2005 includes a 10-minute video presentation of the series.

N4.27. "We say that print on paper has a certain something that cannot be realized on the computer display screen—a soul that stems from a physical existence. In the software that accompanies this printed edition, I attempt to refute this claim with ten *reactive* squares that seem to illustrate the contrary. Speak to them to reveal a soul that exists not in space but in time" (Maeda 1995).

N4.28. On Malevich and Suprematism, see (in addition to the texts I cite here) the essays collected in Petrova et al. 1991 and Drutt 2003.

N4.29. *White Square* is off-center on the canvas and rotated from its vertical axis about 12 degrees. This transformation marks an obvious contrast with the earlier painting, as Valliér observes (1975, 296), directing its structural principle outward in support of a blurring of the limit between the square and the field.

N4.30. "*Black Square* and *White Square*, those paradigmatic statements of Suprematism, have no inside. By being pure lack, these frameless pictures are themselves like frames. What Malevich discovered upon completing his first Suprematist painting is that nonobjectivity is uncontainable. The tabula rasa has indeed turned the tables. It made obvious that the frame does not protect the painting from its milieu, but the other way around. By framing the picture *in*, the world frames itself *out*" (Jakovljevic 2004, 28).

N4.31. "procedural and temporal": this is a point of contact between the model of interleaved surfaces I describe here and the "complex surfaces" described by electronic poet John Cayley (2005). For Cayley, a complex surface is one that "allows time to be reinstated as integral to all processes of writing and reading." He cites the example of Saul Bass's opening title sequence for Alfred Hitchcock's film *North by Northwest*, in which the words glide across, up and down an oblique grid, revealed later to be windows of an office block. Cayley observes that Bass's sequence "could only be performed in time," that is, the simulated time of the title sequence, with its dynamic movements and formal anticipation of the cross-country pursuit of the film's adventure, and the medial time of cinema (changing frames each ¼₄ second), by which the first kind of time is optically produced. Cayley is critical of a paper "flatland" that he finds surfaces of digital writing and reading have too often tried to emulate. His criticism is justified with regard to temporal dynamics in which he is most interested, although I think it neglects the plurality of surfaces evoked by printed forms.

N4.32. See Octavo's Web site at http://www.octavo.com for a complete catalogue of the editions and their features.

N4.33. In "The Dream of Irma's Injection," Freud dreams of a series of increasingly bizarre misdiagnoses made by himself and several colleagues of a patient's complaint of pains in her throat and abdomen. He concludes that the dream represents his wish that he should be acquitted of responsibility for the intractability of her symptoms. See Freud 1940–52, vols. 2–3, and 1955–66, vols. 4–5, chap. 2. Freud's interpretation cagily hints, and many critics have noted, that the dream's scenes of doctors percussing the patient's body and peering with alarm at the strange growths in her throat have definite if obscure sexual significance.

N4.34. It makes sense that in *Riven* this recursive opening should be mapped onto the terrain of the adventure. In *Myst*, Atrus, Achenar, and Sirrus (the father and his sons) are locked away in linking books and the mother's whereabouts are never described. In the sequel, the player's avatar travels inside the world of one of the books, in the Age of Riven, where Gehn (Atrus's tyrannical father) rules, and Catherine, the mother, has been secreted away by the rebel forces of the Moiety. In *Riven*, then, the avatar travels in the Age of the Mother; figures of her impenetrable mystery are marked everywhere in its natural and architectural landscapes.

N4.35. It is noteworthy also that these unreadable objects are marked as such by traces of a prior violence: in *Myst*, the books are torn and burned; in *Riven*, analogous openings in the landscape are carved or split. This is an old and familiar trope of the unreadable, and there are other ways of figuring the join of a reading crisis and a sexual crisis. See my discussion of such an alternative in Shelley Jackson's *Patchwork Girl*: ▶ 5.48.

N4.36. Wilson's (2002) and Wilson and Landoni's (2003) evaluations of electronic reading systems are based on this assumption.

N4.37. Here I have sidestepped problems of classification: what distinguishes works belonging to the categories "artist's book" and "children's book" from other books illustrated by or produced by fine artists or books that may be read by young readers? In the latter case, the term "children's book" seems primarily to describe the audience intended by an author or publisher. It has the disadvantage of excessive generality: that audience is at least as heterogeneous as any other, and the books themselves are more varied in design than their common rubric suggests, because it does not account for distinct traditions of method or operation. ("Pop-up books, mechanical books, picture books, board books"—each of these will have distinct grammatextual and paratextual characteristics that a proper study of the field must consider.)

In the former case, the precise meaning of the term "artist's book" has been contested for similar reasons (varied audience, even more varied methods and operations). Artisanal production techniques (many artist's books are one-off objects or published in limited numbers) and the contributions of the museum, gallery, and art journal cultures in which the books are circulated and collected make comprehensive definitions, especially those based on common aesthetic principles or audience conformity, unlikely. Drucker 1995 and Mœglin-Delcroix 1997 offer valuable discussions of this problem.

N4.38. The 1992 study by Hill et al. is a widely cited example. Chu et al. 2004 discuss a more recent application of these techniques.

N4.39. "onion": Barthes, "Le Style et son image" (1984, 141–51). "Dream of the Botanical Monograph": Freud, 1940–52, vols. 2–3; 1955–66, vol. 5, chap. 6. On Joyce and Jackson, see chapters 5 and 6 herein. Plucking may be the most elementary form of ex-foliation: in a brilliant decoding of the "Dream of the Botanical Monograph," Serge Leclaire identifies the point of origin of Freud's passion for book collecting in adolescence and early adulthood with Oedipal fantasy, "the scene of the defoliation of the mother-book" (Leclaire 1968, 45–49) ▶ 4.46.

N4.40. See Fitzgerald's 1996 review of *Throwing Apples* for *Emigre* magazine for a detailed discussion of the program and Earls's typography and poster design. Kirschenbaum 1997–98 stresses the "post-alphabetic" principles of Earl's design work.

N4.41. According to the book's frontispiece, Bachman was a professor of the Principle of Education at Ohio University and an assistant superintendent of the Cleveland Public Schools. *Great Inventors* is typical of popular science writing for young people of the era, with a heavy emphasis on the social and economic benefits of invention, and the inventors' hard labor, self-reliance, and eventual success. (A modestly revised edition of the text, retitled *The Story of Inventions* and including expanded discussions of aviation, telegraphy, and submarines, and new chapters on television, rocketry, and computing, is still in print and marketed to parents whose children are home-schooled.) Earls observes that he was drawn to the book by its "attitude": "I felt as if I had found a text profiling the kind of man I'd like to be 'when I grow up'—I have also been influenced quite a bit in my work by hip-hop braggadocio. With this in mind, I thought that the title of the book would speak directly to my own stature. How's that for humility?" (personal correspondence, September 5, 2006).

N4.42. Of William K——, Earls observes, "I believe he is my patron saint" (personal correspondence, September 5, 2006).

N4.43. The CD-ROM comes packaged with full-sized printed versions of the posters. The disk's soundtrack is also playable on standard audio CD equipment.

N4.44. See http://theapolloprogram.com.

N4.45. Once again, Earls's selection of pages from Bachman's book seems significant. The original pages are from a chapter on the development of electric engines. The verso and the top half of the recto close a discussion of batteries ("The battery is to-day the most common of electrical appliances. There are one or two in almost every home" [75]). The bottom half of the recto opens a discussion of magnetism ("Most boys at some time or other have owned a magnet . . ." [75]). These are *charged* terms; it seems not a reach to see them as metaphors for orders of visual-verbal condensation, discharge, and attraction of *Throwing Apples* as a whole.

N4.46. Earls has put to good use distinctive features of SuperCard, the multimedia authoring environment in which *Throwing Apples* was created. Like its predecessor HyperCard (released by Apple in 1987; SuperCard was released by Silicon Beach Software in 1989), SuperCard's underlying metaphor is of stacks of cards displayed in windows. Each card is composed of background and foreground layers of bit-mapped images (SuperCard also supports vector-based images in these layers), over which system controls or invisible mouse targets may be positioned. Mouse clicks or other user-instigated events on the screen may be captured by any or all of these targets and layers. (In relation to HyperCard, SuperCard significantly increases the number and kinds of events that may be captured, and the complexity of the message hierarchy by which they are processed.) The user may not always be able to discern which element in the interface responds to her actions, or which changes in the program have been produced in the response.

N4.47. *Eye Slingshot Lions* (CD-ROM, 1998) and *Catfish* (a 55-minute digital film by Earls, 2002) similarly eschew "good" HCI and graphic design conventions in favor of visual and aural cacophony and unpredictability.

N4.48. See Victor Shklovsky's famous characterization (1965) of *Tristram Shandy*.

5. Lexia Complexes

N5.01. Landow's proposition that literary and cultural theories of the late twentieth century "converged" with practices of computer hypertext, with "profound implications for literature, education, and politics" (1992, 2–3), strongly influenced humanist strains of new media criticism in the 1990s. Perhaps more than any other work of the period, *Hypertext* raised the profile of hypertext studies in literature and cultural studies programs and demonstrated the potential of the new media as a "laboratory" for critical-theoretical analysis.

In retrospect, convergences observed by Landow appear problematic. Some elements of the theoretical turn of the 1980s and 1990s may be recast in these terms; several authors (Jean Baudrillard, Jacques Derrida, and Friedrich Kittler) discussed implications of digital media for their research programs during that period or in the years since. It may be that a change in "the contemporary *episteme*" (Landow 1992, 2) of textuality was signaled by a congruence of terminologies ("link," "web," "network," "hyper-", etc.), as Landow contends. But it is not evident that authors he described in 1992 and 1997 as precursors to hypertext's "revolution in human thought" (2–3) meant to apply their arguments to the same objects of enquiry; few of these objects might in any case be subsumed within the digital field. A half-century into the digital and theoretical turns, their intersections remain incompletely defined.

In the third edition of the book, *Hypertext 3.0* (2006), Landow's enthusiasm for such crossings is notably attenuated. His justification for this change in emphasis seems to be not that the theorists have become less useful, but that they are now less fashionable ("The academic standing . . . of poststructuralism has also changed markedly since the first version of *Hypertext*, though in a way perhaps opposite to that of hypermedia. Whereas hypertext and other forms of digital media have experienced enormous growth, poststructuralism and other forms of critical theory have lost their centrality for almost everyone, it seems, but theorists of new media" [2006, xiii]). This I find more vexing than the fact that, having perhaps overstressed poststructuralist approaches, the first two versions of *Hypertext* stimulated too much everything-but-the-kitchen-sink theorizing by scholars writing in their wake. Indisputably, many of the writers of the theoretical turn can help us understand both the nascent new media of the period and the directions in which media may now be headed. We need only be discerning about which theories and which texts fit to genuinely productive ends.

The straw person that Landow next throws up—"one might claim to see a parallel between the dotcom bust and the general loss of academic standing by critical theory" (xiii–xiv)—he as quickly dismisses; coincidence and confluence are not the same (2006, 65–68), and I agree that there is no reason to confuse them in this case. A more likely correlation is that the euphoria of the dotcom era was yoked to refusals of critical thinking in the technical and commercial sectors. In the Academy, the perverse pleasures of refusal have sustained an anti-intellectual backlash against literary theory. If these are more than parallel phenomena, their common element is in their cultural-libidinal structure, not in the influence of one on the other.

N5.02. In contrast, the term *lexia* is seldom used by computer scientists. A June 2008 search of journal articles, magazines, newsletters, and conference proceedings included in the Association for Computing Machinery's Digital Library (available at: http://portal.acm.org/dl.cfm) found 9978 entries published since 1965 containing "hypertext" or "hypermedia" (Nelson first used the term "hypertext" in print in that year ▶2.01). Fifteen entries containing both "lexia" and "hypertext" or "hypermedia" were found in this corpus, less than 0.15 percent of the former number. At the time of the search, the Digital Library included more than 244,000 full-text articles and papers published since 1965. Titles and abstracts of the articles containing "lexia" were notably literary or artistic in their emphasis; most represented contributions of literary scholars who presented their work at one or more of the annual ACM conferences on hypertext in the mid-1990s and early 2000s. The Library is not a complete archive of publications in computer science—it is limited to only ACM-sponsored events and journals, and includes only works written in English—but it is the largest and most comprehensive full-text database of its kind. I think it probable that these proportions would be repeated in wider searches. (I am grateful to Bernard Rous, the Director of ACM's Electronic Publishing Program, for his assistance in compiling these statistics.)

N5.03. In his discussion of cybernetic literatures, *Cognitive Fictions*, Joseph Tabbi credits Nelson with having coined this use of *lexia* (2002, 121).

N5.04. I have not always held this position. See, for example, Harpold 1994.

N5.05. In these and other texts of this period—notably, his discussions of cultural "myth" in *Mythologies* (1957) and "Le Message photographique" ("The Photographic Message," 1982b), and the "fashion system" in *Système de la mode* (1967)—Barthes's model of connotation is based on one proposed by the Danish linguist Louis Hjelmslev. In Hjelmslev's elaboration on Saussure's semiology, called "glossematics," a linguistic system's plane of expression (E) is itself constituted by a linguistic system. Its relation (R) to a plane of content (C) composes a tiering or nesting of systems—

$$(E \ R \ C) \ R \ C$$

—in which the second plane of content (C) is *connotatively* derived from the first system (E R C) (see Barthes 1967, 38; Hjelmslev 1961, chap. 22; and Siertsema 1965, chap. 12). As in his other appropriations of Hjelmslev's and Saussure's terminology, Barthes pushes investigations of these operations in the direction of ideological structures. "As for the signified of connotation, its character is at the same time general, global, and diffuse. It is, if you will, an ideological fragment. The set of messages in French refers, for example, to the signified 'French'; a work can refer to the signified 'Literature'; these signifieds communicate closely with culture, knowledge [*savoir*], history—it is through them, one may say, that the world enters into the system" (1964a, 131). On glossematics, see Hjelmslev 1961, Siertsema 1965, Uldall 1967, and Ducrot and Todorov 1972. Barthes may have derived his use of *lexia* from Hjelmslev's use of it in a 1951 essay ("Outline of the Danish Expression System"). The essay was not translated from Danish (into English) until 1973, but Barthes's definitions of the term (1967, 249ff) seem too close to Hjelmslev's to be accidental.

N5.06. "L'Activité structuraliste" was first published in the journal *Lettres nouvelles* in 1963. It was reprinted in Barthes's *Essais critiques* (1964b).

N5.07. A similar rebinding of associationism to immanent structures of the archive informs Bush's descriptions of differences between Memex I, II, and III ▶ 1.45.

N5.08. In glossematics, *catalysis* is the inductive operation by which a linguist interpolates the presence of entities in the planes of expression or content on the basis of their *cohesion* (Danish: *konnexion*, literally, a determinate connection) with existing entities in those planes. See Hjelmslev 1961, chap. 19; and Siertsema 1965, 83, 190–98.

N5.09. "The commentator traces along the length of the text zones of reading, in order to observe the migration of meanings [*migration des sens*], the outcroppings of codes, the passage of citations. The lexia is only the wrapping of a semantic volume, the crest of the plural text, arranged like a berm of possible meanings . . . under the flux of discourse" (Barthes 1970, 20–21).

N5.10. In *Système de la mode*, Barthes observes that his description of the fashion system did not require that he review every magazine, newspaper, and advertisement related to fashion for the year that is the focus of his analysis, 1958–59. "What matters with regard to the semiological project is to constitute a corpus reasonably saturated by all the possible *differences* of vestimentary signs. . . . It is unimportant that these differences repeat themselves more or less, because that which determines meaning is not repetition, but difference. . . . The objective here is to distinguish the units, not count them" (1967, 21).

N5.11. Barthes's parsings of Balzac's text—sometimes "a few words, sometimes several sentences"—are guided by his discerning of variable-length isomorphisms between expression and content planes of the corpus. In contrast, segments of an artificial semiotic, such as the rules of a game, are conforming: a change in one plane is matched by a strictly corresponding change in the other (Siertsema 1965, 217). The role of nonconforming, isomorphic relations between expression and content in connotative operations of natural languages is clear.

N5.12. Some species of chance will obtain even in these crossings of nodes and lexias. The hypertext reader throws dice, but not without or before anticipating where she might be led; and not without another, logically prior, throw of the dice: her linguistic, narrative, and cultural competence. These, in effect, bring her to the moment of choice *before* the link is activated. See Bernstein 2000. On the relation of choice in hypertext reading and forms of identity that "precipitate" (Lacan's term) from its haste, see Harpold 1994.

N5.13. The intertexts multiply: Barthes's best-known assessment of Mallarmé's contribution to literary modernity is in his 1968 essay, "La Mort de l'auteur" ("The

Death of the Author," Barthes 1984b): "Mallarmé's entire poetics consists in suppressing the author to the benefit of writing (which is, as will be seen, to restore to the reader her place)." The essay opens with a brief discussion of Balzac's *Sarrasine*.

N5.14. Even so, as White observes, the relation of textual materiality to all this cutting and pasting remains poorly defined (2005, 36ff). The textual systems that "infinitely and tirelessly" traverse the Barthesian reader, he insists, must be activated in relation to a physical text, with specifiable attributes (typefaces, leading, margins, etc., to mention only attributes common to the most conventional printed texts). Their presence in the scene of structuralist activity would seem to bind the ideal text to a material *hic et nunc* with definite boundaries. Similarly, Barthes's writings about writing are characterized by a notable flatness of the spaces in which it occurs; he never writes at a desk, only at a table. The erotic corporeality of the text that Barthes celebrated is, Kopelson suggests (2004), oriented by an image-repertoire embodied in the author's workspace, but the workspace's corporeality *as a material space*—ordered or disordered container or store—is never acknowledged.

N5.15. Cf. Barthes 1970, sec. 4.

N5.16. "Dimensionality" in this context is applied along both paradigmatic and syntagmatic axes, and often moves from one to the other. According to Jakobson's famous formula (1960), this would constitute the "poetic" mechanism of the hypertext lexia.

N5.17. Here and elsewhere, I use "node" to describe the smallest integral unit of the textbase that may be linked to other units in a hypertext representation based on the link-node model. I prefer this term to "lexia" for reasons I describe in this chapter, and to other general terms that have been proposed ("component," "work," "object") because "node" seems the better compromise between formal abstraction and a suggestion of extensibility via network structures. ("Component" emphasizes a relation of inclusion. "Work" implies integrity. Using "object" would restrict the use of that valuable substantive in other contexts.) But as Whitehead has observed (2000), the names given to minimal units of hypertext systems have usually been driven by UI conventions ("card," "document," "window"); any name for this object carries with it a complex of associated, inconsistent meanings. The chief disadvantage of "node" is that it implies that link-node structures are the only kind of "multiple" text (M. Joyce 1991) that may be characterized as hypertext; other schemes for associating units of such a text have been proposed (▶ 4.20; see also Rosenberg 1994, 1996; Bernstein 2004b).

N5.18. This model of the lexia is similar to hypertext units David Kolb has termed "localities." These may span multiple nodes, and may be constituted by transitions between nodes. See Kolb 1997.

N5.19. The Expanded Books were a short-lived series published by The Voyager Company, the first commercial publisher of CD-ROM titles. Gardner's *Annotated Alice*, Michael Crichton's *Jurassic Park*, and Douglas Adams's *The Hitchhiker's Guide to the Galaxy* trilogy were the first three titles published. Based on Apple's HyperCard development environment, the layout of Expanded Books was modeled on the printed page (recto only), with the addition of full-text searching, bookmarking, linking, and embedded audio and animations.

N5.20. I am grateful to Edward White, who alerted me to the significance of Barthes's "Le Troisième Sens" in this context.

The other early essays on the semiotics of photography are "Le Message photographique" (1961) and "Rhétorique de l'image" (1964). The three essays are reprinted in order of their publication in the first section of *L'Obvie et l'obtus* (Barthes 1982a).

N5.21. Hazardous hopscotch ▶ 2.23: see my discussions of Lacan's semiotic grove ▶ 2.10, and Freud's 1899 "Screen Memories" essay, in which the French phrase *casser une branche d'un arbre* (to break the branch of a tree) is jokingly offered by Freud as a gloss of a German euphemism for masturbation, "to pull one off" (*sich einen ausreißen*) ▶ 7.70. Somewhere between these studied extremes lies Shelley Jackson's image of the heart roosting "like pheasants on high bone branches" ▶ 5.44.

N5.22. "Femininity," in *New Introductory Lectures*, Freud 1940–52, vol. 15; 1955–66, vol. 22.

N5.23. For critical responses to *Patchwork Girl*, see Hayles 2000 and 2002; M. Joyce 2000, 131–49; E. Joyce 2003; and Punday 2004. Except where they are noted, my discussion of Jackson's hypertext does not address substantive differences between releases for Macintosh and Windows platforms (compare, for example, ▶ Figure 2.02 and ▶ Figure 5.06). I take up the general problem of such differences in chapter 6.

N5.24. The two-window limit may be overridden by changing the preferences of the Windows Storyspace Reader, so that every node's window remains open when a link to another node is executed. The Mac OS version of *Patchwork Girl* includes no option to increase the number of concurrent open windows.

N5.25. Cf. Baetens 2001, 49–63, in particular, his observation that the use of diagrams and other schematic forms in literary works should not be assumed to be equivalent to the use of such instruments in scientific texts.

N5.26. Torjesen 1998. Descriptions of supplicants in prayer resembling the *orans* are also found in the Hebrew scriptures (Exodus 18:11–12) and in pre-Christian Roman literary sources (Cicero *Ad Familiares* 7.5; Virgil *Aeneid* 2.153; Apuleius *De Mundo* 33); some historians have observed variants of the *orans* in Egyptian iconography of Anubis and Horis. In these pre-Christian forms, the posture is almost always associated with male supplicants.

N5.27. "I am buried here. You can resurrect me, but only piecemeal. If you want to see the whole, you will have to sew me together yourself" (*Patchwork Girl*, {graveyard}).

N5.28. Moulthrop's *Victory Garden* ▶3.06 includes a similarly unreliable series of map-like graphics, resembling a cross between a topiary labyrinth and an integrated circuit board. (The obvious intertext here—again, we cross a lexial bridge—is the passage in Thomas Pynchon's *The Crying of Lot 49*, in which Oedipa Maas looks down on San Narciso, spread below her like a circuit board.) *Victory Garden* was published in the Storyspace Page Reader format, in which only one node may be viewed at a time, and in which the Storyspace Map View is hidden.

N5.29. See Gandelman's (1991, 111–30) discussion of the visual-textual trope of auto-flaying in Western art and literature. My sense is that Jackson's turn on this trope of dissection is congruent with the canny feminism of the text: the opening screen of *Patchwork Girl* seems to promise a peeling away of artifices to reveal a truth, if the reader wishes it, but then on multiple registers refuses that investigation. As Gandelman demonstrates (but does not acknowledge in these terms), the motif of the flayed man (or woman) is in its modern versions marked by a brutalizing of the motif object that is, more often than not, *feminized* by that brutality (124–30). In this respect, *Patchwork Girl*'s resistances to dissection constitute a knowing and even good-humored deflection of the surgeon's blade ▶4.46.

N5.30. A similar coalescing of biological substances into organ-like units characterizes the stories collected in Jackson's *The Melancholy of Anatomy* (2002). In stories with titles like "Egg," "Sperm," "Foetus," "Nerve," and "Cancer," the possibly lurid spectacle of errant fluids and tissues is short-circuited, on the one hand, by a wry narrative voice anticipated by *Patchwork Girl* and, on the other hand, by the activities of the body's overripe fruits, which seem more risible than alarming. "Once numerous, their herds raised a line of dust across the Great Plains, racing the locomotive. This opening sequence has become a cliché of film westerns: dust first, then a line of bobbing backs stretching across the screen. The nearby whistle of the train; some of the sperm cross the tracks, some turn, some scatter . . ." (43).

N5.31. The depth of colors shown on computer screens is measured in the number of data bits used to represent the shade of a single pixel. These are calculated in powers of 2, corresponding to the number of different colors that may be displayed at one time: 2^1 = one bit color (monochrome, usually black and white), 2^8 = 8-bit color (256 different colors), and so on. Into the late 1980s, most computer graphics subsystems displayed no more than 8-bit color; today, 16-bit ("thousands") or 32-bit ("millions") are the norm. (The 8-bit color standard is in fact unsupported on Mac OS X and disabled by default on Windows Vista systems.) While color depths higher than 32 bits are possible, they do not present optical advantages because 32-bit color already surpasses the number of discrete color gradations that the human eye can resolve.

N5.32. In 1995 the image is anachronistic, not because it is 1-bit, but because its bit depth alludes to a textual regime that is demoded. This effect is more marked in the Mac OS version of *Patchwork Girl*, since its interface elements (windows, navigational widgets, etc.) are also in 1-bit color. In the Windows version of the text, the black-and-white images are enframed with color widgets in shades of the Windows system palette.

N5.33. "I fingered her genitals and the lower part of her body, which struck me as very queer [*kurios* = 'curious' or 'singular']" (Freud 1940–52, 7:386; Freud 1955–66, 10:161).

N5.34. See Baum 1990. Shelley Jackson is the author and illustrator of three picture books for children and has illustrated several by other authors.

N5.35. In Storyspace, subordinate spaces and texts attached to a given space are said to be "inside" the parent space. In the user interface, this relation is depicted as a successive nesting of the windows associated with the spaces.

N5.36. Deena Larsen's *Samplers* (1998) uses a similar visual motif to associate the nine narrative threads composing the hypertext.

N5.37. An image of the Etruscan Chimera of Arezzo, scanned from a photograph from Feher, Naddaff, and Tazi's *Fragments for a History of the Human Body* (1989), is one of the few images in *Patchwork Girl* found in spaces deeper than the {her} series of nodes. (The image is located in a space titled {chimera}. A {footnote} node linked to it documents its provenance.) To my knowledge, it is the only graphic in *Patchwork Girl* that is not original to Shelley Jackson—an indirect sign, perhaps, of the image's function there as a textual chimera: not quite hers, no longer belonging to its unknown artist.

N5.38. On "agrammaticality," see Riffaterre 1978.

N5.39. Cf. *Tristram Shandy*'s narrative traceries—"the best line! say cabbage planters—is the shortest line, says *Archimedes*, which can be drawn from one given point to another . . ." (Sterne 1997, VI.xl: 392).

N5.40. This is reinforced by Jackson's ("Mary/Shelley") strategic, multiple interlacings of herself with the Patchwork Girl ("Herself") and her other protagonists. Jackson's semi/pseudo-autobiographical 1997 hypertext *"My Body"—a Wunderkammer* ("An autobiography, plus lies") resembles the {graveyard} sequence of *Patchwork Girl* (in which the history of each of the body parts sewn to make her whole is recounted): the opening reverse image of a naked woman (Jackson, holding a pad of paper in one hand and a pen in the other), mapped unpredictably and irregularly to interlinked anecdotes of the histories of the corresponding part, etc. Her 2006 print novel *Half-Life*, an alternate history of a post–World War II America populated by growing numbers of conjoined twins ("Twofers"), is a darkly witty meditation on the writer's work as her not-so-secret double. And this passage: "It has come to my attention that a young woman claiming to be the author of my being has been making appearances under the name of Shelley Jackson. It seems you have even invited her to speak tonight, under the misapprehension that she exists, that she is something besides a parasite, a sort of engorged and loathsome tick hanging off my side. May I say that I find this an extraordinary impertinence, and that if she would like to come forward, we shall soon see who is the author of whom . . ." ("Stitch Bitch," 526).

N5.41. Eco 1988, 258. The question is part of the title of one of the "admirable books" discovered by Pantagruel in the Abbey of St. Victor, Paris. "Whether the chimera, bombinating in the void, etc.," was debated—so the full title of the book indicates—for ten weeks at the Council of Constance (1414–18) (Rabelais 1994, *Pantagruel*, chap. 7). "Second intentions" is a scholastic formula for the accidental attributes of an object.

6. Allographs

N6.01. See, for example, Aarseth 1997; Bolter 1991 and 2001; Douglas 2000; Eskelinen 2001a; Harpold 1994; Hayles 2002; S. Johnson 1997; Landow 1997; Moulthrop 1989; and Punday 2004. In the criticism of the early and mid-1990s, few works of literary hypertext other than *Afternoon* are even discussed.

N6.02. Memmott 2000; Hayles 2002, 46–53. Hayles considerably expands her discussion of works embracing these new methods in 2008, 5–30.

N6.03. Storyspace is published by Eastgate Systems, Inc. Releases of the program before 1989, available only in versions for Mac OS, were authored by Jay David Bolter, Michael Joyce, and John Smith. Storyspace version 2.x for Mac OS and versions 1.x and 2.x for Windows were authored by Mark Bernstein. On the connections of early Macintosh hardware and software to the development of Storyspace, see Bernstein 2002; M. Joyce 1995, 31–35; and M. Joyce 1998c. Kirschenbaum 2008, 168–78, has the most complete discussion of the coevolution of Storyspace and *Afternoon*.

N6.04. More extreme is Eskelinen's proposal (2001a) that we should forget about literary hypertext because "dynamic textologies" have moved beyond early hypertext's narratological focus.

N6.05. "If a reader has no free movement, it is something [other than hypertext]. It is a maze. It is a kind of trap and a kind of prison. That is why I think the correct definition of hypertext is 'non-sequential text with *free user movement*.' If you cannot come and go as you please, that is not extended or generalized. If there is a hidden sequence, blocked pathways or irreversible movement, it should be called something else" (Nelson 1998, 63).

N6.06. As of June 2008, including Italian and German translations (Joyce 1993a,

2001b) and a 1998 JavaScript-based port,►N6.19 and excluding differences between Mac OS and Windows editions, nine major variants of *Afternoon* have been circulated privately or commercially since 1987. Most of these are noted in the colophon of the sixth edition (2007, identical to the colophon of the fifth edition, 2001), which reports differences between the first five editions. The majority of these are related to OS changes and to the correction of typographic and linking errors.

In the interest of a more precise nomenclature for identifying the variants, I will use the term *version* to mean an executable presentation of the work specific to an OS, in much the same way that that term is widely used to describe different versions of system or application software. Different versions of *Afternoon* may not be computationally compatible and may incorporate content and program features or limitations specific to the OS for which they were produced. It is possible to migrate Mac OS Storyspace textbases to the Windows Storyspace editor, from which they can be published in Windows-compatible editions, and vice versa, but some elements of the original files—for example, graphic images embedded in writing spaces—cannot be migrated directly, since they are based on formats specific to each OS (Eastgate Systems, Inc. 2001a, 2001b). In this scheme, successive versions are incrementally numbered (1.0, 2.0, etc.); a "dot-x" version (1.x, 2.x) indicates a grouping of minor iterations of the same whole-number version.

I will use the term *edition* to mean a numbered iteration of the textbase of *Afternoon*, that is, the structured database of nodes, links, and other computational data from which a Storyspace reading program generates a sequence in response to user input. Successive editions are indicated by whole-number increments. Edition numbers for different versions of the text may be identical, even though they are not computationally compatible and may differ substantially in appearance and functionality. Where necessary, I will identify an edition also by OS and version, so as to more clearly distinguish between them: for example, *Afternoon*, 5th ed. for Windows and *Afternoon*, 5th ed. for Mac OS (Joyce 2001a). I ignore a further distinction that applies to all editions of *Afternoon* for Windows, in which the data file corresponding to the edition and application file corresponding to the version of the reader program are stored as discrete objects on the user's computer. In those cases, I use a single version-edition descriptor, for example, "the Windows Storyspace Reader 1.3, 4th ed."

I will use the term *release* to mean a published version or edition differing from other versions and editions by the medium in which it is distributed (generally speaking, floppy disk or CD-ROM).

An *instance* means a specific, concrete presentation of a version, edition, and release, as it is instantiated within a specific computing framework, by which I mean an OS and its UI. This term could sustain even finer granularities: reading *Afternoon* in Storyspace for Macintosh 1.x, 3rd ed. under Mac OS 6.0.7 is different from reading the same version and edition under Mac OS 9, in that these versions of the Mac OS present that document with different uses of color and window- and widget styles. In general, I will not observe such minor in-platform distinctions, so as to limit the number of variables for which I have to account in order to associate variants of *Afternoon* with variants of the OSs on which it may be or may have been read. In principle, every combination of operating system version, program version, and edition may produce distinguishable effects in a given reading.

This version/edition/release/instance scheme is more limited than one proposed by Kirschenbaum (2002; 2008, 188–89) and thus may be less useful than his with regard to works other than *Afternoon*. He distinguishes between a text's *layer, version, release, object, state, instance,* and *copies* that may be made of any *instance*. My use of the terms *version* and *edition* overlap with his terms *layer* ("all elements of an electronic work that are both computationally compatible and functionally integrated" [Kirschenbaum 2002, 46]) and *version* ("each *layer* of a work should be marked by a whole-number incremental increase in the *version* number" [46]), but they are not synonymous. I find connotations of his term *layer* difficult to expunge from my description of the GUI's language of enclosure and interiority. I believe my uses of *version* and *edition* to be more supple in the case of *Afternoon*, where iterative changes to the textbase and the program must be considered, sometimes together, sometimes distinctly. Kirschenbaum's discussions (2002, 2008) of the avant-textes, variants, and versions of *Afternoon* represent to my knowledge the only sustained discussion of differences between the Mac OS and Windows releases before mine. I am indebted to his careful review of the work's publication history.

N6.07. The commercial publication of Storyspace documents is most often in formats that block the reader from changing any aspect of the text, and in some cases from displaying selected views of its structure or accessing navigation functions available in editable Storyspace documents. Versions of Storyspace for Macintosh prior to version 2.0 accomplished this control of the reader's access to the text by allowing the author to save documents in one of three formats that bundled a subset of program code with the document, the Easy Reader, the Page Reader (in later versions known as the Readingspace Reader), and the Storyspace Reader. Each document thus saved became a stand-alone application; the reader did not need an additional program in order to read the document. (See Bolter et al. 1993. This was a common technique of hypermedia and multimedia applications of the early 1990s.) All versions of Storyspace for Windows and version 2.x and later for Macintosh 2.x use a different approach: documents may be saved in a special format and distributed with a separate, stripped-down "Reader" version of Storyspace that lacks most editing functions; which functions will be available to the reader is determined when the document is saved in the Reader format (Eastgate Systems, Inc. 1999, 2001a, 2001b).

These two solutions to the problem of controlling access to program code—driven as much by concerns about software piracy as by management of the reader's encounters with the text—produce subtly different conditions for use. Whereas the Macintosh reader of *Afternoon* (which was until 2007 [▶ 6.50] published in the older 1.x Page Reader format) opens an *application* on her computer called *Afternoon*, the Windows reader opens a *document* called *Afternoon*, which is run by an application called *Storyspace Reader*.

In the following discussion, I use the lowercase form of the word "reader" to indicate the human subject who *reads* the hypertext, the uppercase form ("Reader") to indicate the computer *programs* used by that subject.

N6.08. Aarseth 1997 is a notable exception.

N6.09. Storyspace does not impose in-text markers on the visual presentation of links; authors may elect to signal a link's presence (with a change in typeface or -style or a graphic, for example), but they are not obliged to do so. The user may temporarily highlight unmarked links in the current node by pressing a keyboard "shortcut" (Command-Option on Mac OS, Control on Windows). Mac OS users may also display a list of links to and from the current node by clicking on the palette button resembling an open book. This list is seldom helpful to novice readers, since most of the link names are cryptic (perhaps named according to a mnemonic system used by Joyce when composing the text?). See Weinrich, Obendorf, and Lamersdorf 2001 for an overview of methods for signaling the presence of links in hypertext.

N6.10. In the interest of full disclosure, see Harpold 1991, 1994.

N6.11. "The concept of cybertext focuses on the mechanical organization of the text, by positing the intricacies of the medium as an integral part of the literary exchange. However, it also centers attention on the consumer, or user, as a more integrated figure than even reader-response theorists would claim. The performance of their reader takes place all in his head, while the user of cybertext also performs in an extranoematic sense. During the cybertextual process, the user will have effectuated a semiotic sequence, and this selective movement is a work of physical construction that the various concepts of 'reading' do not account for. This phenomenon I call *ergodic*, using a term appropriated from physics that derives from the Greek words *ergon* and *hodos*, meaning 'work' and 'path'" (Aarseth 1997, 1).

N6.12. Ryan proposes a similar characterization of the excesses of the first wave: "The traditional length of [the novel] motivated hypertext authors to start right away with large compositions that made unreasonable demands on the reader's concentration. Instead of being gently initiated into point-and-click interactivity, readers were intimidated by the forbidding complexity of a maze they had no fair chance of mastering. With the arrogance typical of so many avant-garde movements, hypertext authors worked from the assumption that audiences should be antagonized and stripped of any sense of security, rather than cajoled into new reading habits. [The] model of the novel created a pattern of expectations that subordinated local meaning to a global narrative structure, and even though this structure hardly ever materialized, its pursuit distracted readers from the poetic qualities of the individual lexias" (Ryan 2001b, 265). Ryan's use of the term "interactive" here is specific to a more general argument ("the interactive text is a machine fueled by the input of the user" [210]): the reader of the interactive text is tasked with reconstructing coherence from fractious narrative and semiotic data presented to her (242–70). Her complaint with regard to the first wave is that it presents too few or inconsistent bases for that process. The early hypertexts represented interesting and valuable models for dismantling narrative conventions, she observes, but at the price of readerly satisfaction except of the most formalist kind.

N6.13. See, for example, Eskelinen 2001a, 2001b, 2004 and Frasca 2003. For counterarguments, see Ryan 2001a, 2006 and Harpold 2005, 2008. The texts and discussion threads collected in Wardrip-Fruin and Harrigan 2008 represent a broad survey of the ludology/narratology debates.

N6.14. Re "second intentions" ▶ 5.60.

N6.15. I take up differences introduced in the sixth edition of *Afternoon*, Mac OS (2007) in ▶ 6.50. Until then, most of my observations apply to the first through fifth editions.

N6.16. The Macintosh Reader's floating palette includes one button missing from the Windows Reader's toolbar, used to print the current node. That function has been moved to a menu of the Windows Storyspace Reader.

N6.17. Storyspace *keywords* are textual metadata attached to writing spaces and are commonly used to associate spaces that are not linked directly. Support for keywords, absent from earlier versions of Storyspace for Macintosh, was added in Version 2.0. *Afternoon* includes no keywords on either platform.

N6.18. The multiplying of frames is the most significant difference between windowing models of the two versions. Releases of *Afternoon* for Mac OS adhere to the OS's window model, known as "Single Document Interface" (SDI) (Apple Computer, Inc. 1992, 2005, 2008). In SDI, document windows are managed independently by the OS, and in most cases may be resized and repositioned anywhere within the confines of the screen. In contrast, Windows releases adhere to a "Multiple Document Interface," or MDI, at one time the preferred model for Windows applications and still common on that platform (Microsoft Corporation 1995, 2005, 2008). In MDI, document ("child") windows belonging to the same application are displayed within a shared application ("parent") window. Multiple child windows may be opened and arranged in z-order within the parent window and may overlap with or even obscure other child windows. Each is confined to the region of the screen defined by the parent; when it is moved or resized, the child windows may be resized or repositioned, or may be cropped. The reader of *Afternoon* under Windows is always aware that the document window resides within an application window, whereas on the Macintosh, the application window effectively coincides with the limits of the screen. The Macintosh (SDI) model seems the visually shallower of the two, especially when a fixed window size matches the contours of the screen, as when the classic release is viewed on hardware of that period. Under the Windows (MDI) model, the frame of the application window appears to install a layer between the document windows and the deepest background of the screen that is not present in the Macintosh model.

N6.19. In 1998, two further variants of *Afternoon* were created for *Postmodern American Fiction: A Norton Anthology* (Geyh, Leebron, and Levy 1998). A selection of nodes of the hypertext, possibly corresponding to the sequence of a specific reading, is reprinted in the *Anthology* under the rubric "FROM *afternoon, a story*" (Joyce 1998a). A "special web edition" of the hypertext was also prepared for the *Anthology*'s companion Web site (Joyce 1998b). Using a JavaScript browsing engine written by Justin Edelson, this edition restricts readings to "no more than fifteen pages (or lexia to use George Landow's term for hypertext screens), and, more importantly[,] allows readers on the world wide web to experience the distinctive hypertextual 'smart links' which characterize this pioneer hyperfiction." Visual traits of the *Norton* Web edition—text and background colors, window sizes, and so on, designed by Jason Lucas—differ substantially from those of the standalone Mac OS and Windows editions. The navigational apparatus is minimal, closer in that sense to the Mac OS editions. And copyright restrictions (the limit to 15 nodes) introduce entirely new forms of constraint, recasting the text's segmentations in anthological terms. On the history of the port and the design compromises it entailed, see Kirschenbaum 2008, 191–96.

N6.20. These elements of the UI are, in other words, database structures, collections that are unordered or ordered in ways that are of little or no interest to human readers until a specific ordering is needed. On the more general significance of database logic in new media forms, see Manovich 2001, esp. 218–43, and Manovich 2005.

N6.21. In a footnote to her analysis of Joyce's *Twelve Blue* (1996b) ▶3.45, Ryan observes, "*Twelve Blue*, unlike *afternoon*, does not offer a dictionary of all segments" (Ryan 2001b, 367n1). It must be the case that she refers here to Windows versions of *Afternoon*, since no "dictionary" of spaces is available in the Mac OS versions, because they lack the Find function. Her characterization of the reader's lack of access to a comprehensive list of segments is true of both *Twelve Blue* and the classic version of *Afternoon*.

N6.22. Moulthrop (1991b) paid homage to Douglas's discovery by including an unlinked node in *Victory Garden* ▶3.06. Titled {Janespace}, it cannot be viewed in Macintosh versions but is easily accessed in Windows versions.

N6.23. In the first edition of *Afternoon*, the {Jung} space was titled but included no text. (Kirschenbaum 2002 includes a screenshot of the empty space.) The first and second lines shown in ▶ Figure 6.05, citing Jung's *Man and His Symbols* and acknowledging Douglas's discovery, were added by Joyce to the second edition. The following sentence and the quote from *The Satanic Verses* were added in the third edition (personal correspondence with M. Joyce, February 8, 1994).

N6.24. While completing the manuscript of this chapter I discovered Kirschenbaum's studies of *Afternoon*'s variants (2002, 2008—the latter was published as this book was in press). Reading excerpts of his correspondence with Michael Joyce regarding {Jung}, dated May 18, 1999, I recalled my 1994 e-mail exchange with Joyce on that subject. When I compared my copy of the correspondence to Kirschenbaum's, they were identical in nearly all respects: Joyce must have cut and pasted portions of the earlier e-mail message into the later one. (Or perhaps he cut and pasted the message to me from another communication with someone else?) I claim no privilege in repeating these lines here; it seems more prudent to acknowledge their free circulation within a small community of scholars. More interesting perhaps is the instability that this doubling raises in relation to the two or three archives involved: (1) my notes for an early article that, after a decade stored in the digital equivalent of a desk drawer, morphed into this chapter; (2) Joyce's archive: how long did he keep a copy of these observations? does he still keep a copy? has he passed copies to others?; (3) Kirschenbaum's archive, the citation of which reminded me of my notes, which I had forgotten until I read it there. "IF I have anything to offer, it might be that the copy-and-paste nature of my {Jung} node responses to you and Matt do not mark an attempt at maintaining an orthodoxy but rather that computer files (and specifically my ridiculously over-sized Eudora mailboxes) more and more function as my memory" (personal correspondence with M. Joyce, June 28, 2007). Trails and trails of trails.

N6.25. Personal correspondence with M. Joyce, February 8, 1994.

N6.26. Here also the upgrade path has blocked some paths of investigation. The 1987 and 1989 (first and second) editions of *Afternoon* may be opened with versions of the Mac OS Storyspace editor up to version 1.5. Later versions of the editor appear to incorrectly parse documents created with the earliest versions. Unfortunately, versions of Storyspace before 1.7 are unstable on more recent iterations (9 and X) of the Mac OS. The program can be used reliably only with Apple hardware and OSs released prior to mid-1999. Editions of *Afternoon* created before the fourth edition cannot be transferred reliably to any version of the Windows Storyspace editor.

N6.27. Bernstein observes that the very presence of this yes/no option in *Afternoon*—the user may elect *not* to "hear about it," though she will by that choice still remain within the branching logic of the text—represents a significant break with computer game conventions (2002, 176).

N6.28. This technique is often used by Storyspace writers of the first wave. It is used with particular effectiveness in Tim McLaughlin's "philatelic novel," *Notes to-*

ward Absolute Zero (1993), in which changes in typeface and margin widths are associated with separate voices and threads of the collagist narrative.

N6.29. "If the window is made very large": I stress this point because I have observed that Windows users often maximize document window sizes as a matter of course. In the case of a work such as *Afternoon*, opening the window to the dimensions of a contemporary monitor when it was composed for those of a much smaller visual field appreciably changes the text's presentation.

N6.30. Personal correspondence with M. Joyce, August 23, 2006.

N6.31. Joyce has not kept to this limitation in other published hypertexts created with Storyspace. For example, most of the nodes of *Twilight, a Symphony* (1996c) are resizable and include scrolling text fields. Some, however, are displayed in fixed-sized windows without scrolling text, suggesting that these differences in window and text field styles may be significant. *Twilight* is also noteworthy for extensive variations in typeface and -color, and for being available only for Mac OS, because of its uses of typefaces and QuickTime elements that could not be ported to a Windows version (personal correspondence with M. Joyce, June 28, 2007).

Larger screens were not uncommon on Macintosh systems in 1989, but most users at the time were still working on single-monitor systems in the classic configuration. A default window size within these dimensions may have been justified by market considerations. The size of text window(s) in the Windows releases of *Afternoon* has never been so limited, though the application window's default size appears to have been set to dimensions appropriate to a monitor of 800 × 600 pixels, a typical configuration on Windows machines in 1992.

The first three editions of the Macintosh release are strictly 1-bit (black and white) applications. (The fifth and sixth editions included new color desktop icons, but the colors of other interface elements were unchanged, apart from OS-determined elements of the sixth edition.) The text of the Windows releases is also black and white, but other elements of the interface have always been in the palette of the Windows GUI, in keeping with the predominance of color in GUIs by 1992.

N6.32. Cf. the analogous erasure of borders in Kazimir Malevich's black-and-white *Squares* ▶ 4.30.

N6.33. Which is not to say that there can be no evidence of Joyce's decisions; only that it will be hard to locate. Perhaps the most careful examination of every instance of *Afternoon* among the hundreds of floppy disks included in the *fonds* of the Michael Joyce Papers[N0.18] might uncover variants that indicate his compositional choices with regard to the boundaries of the 512K screen. (Kirschenbaum 2008, Stollar 2006, and Stollar and Kiehne 2006, which represent the most complete examinations of the *fonds* to date, do not address problems of this kind.) My assumption is that those choices were made as the edges of screen anticipated or imposed them, and therefore are unlikely to have been recorded in a direct way. It may be possible to find their traces at the archive's lower levels, because storage media can retain portions or even all of a deleted file under some circumstances; the manner in which early versions of Storyspace managed file changes could make this difficult or impossible to discover. The archaeology of variants in cases such as these drifts into the minutest problems of digital forensics.

N6.34. The feature set of Storyspace Reader 2.5.x for Mac OS is not appreciably changed from earlier versions, apart from the new ability to resize node windows. Other changes are more subtle. A larger default size is used for the body text and the window frame and elements of the navigation palette and Link dialog are in the Mac OS X color scheme, giving this edition a more open and modern look.

N6.35. Joyce began writing *Afternoon* in 1987. The third edition, the first to be commercially published, was released in 1989. The composition and early dissemination of *Afternoon* occurred during the period of the Mac OS's change from a unitasking to a (cooperative) multitasking model, and the development of interface techniques associated with it (overlapping windows grouped by application, reorderable by user selection, etc.). But Joyce's text resists incursions of a conceptual regime figured by these techniques: it refuses efforts to recast its narrative structure as depths beyond the document window; it enforces strictly modal and serial access to regions of the screen under its control. If we assume that most early readers encountered it on the 9-inch monitor of the unitasking "classic" Macintosh computer ▶ 0.08, the regions under *Afternoon*'s control *were equivalent to* the whole of the screen. Under a multitasking version of the OS on the same hardware, this is only a little changed; *Afternoon* continues to control the screen while it is the active application. In these conditions, the work's visual and procedural flatness presented medially bound resistances to metaphors of discovery and investigation of depth. This resistance of depth was, in contrast, weakened considerably in Windows releases five years later, after important shifts in the baseline features of the most popular GUIs. The Windows version is, unambiguously, the more contemporary of the two in its appearance and feature set.

N6.36. Studies by Andersen (1997) and Sieckenius de Souza (2005) of the semiotics of human-computer interaction represent, albeit indirectly, the most important book-length contributions to this problem. Several of the essays collected in Andersen, Holmqvist, and Jensen 1993 are also useful in this regard. Rau's brief article (1999) surveys problems of definition that may be applied more generally to include digital literary texts, but proposes only that this is a field in need of investigation. Ricardo 1998 presents a model of second-order textual patterns of digital texts that he calls "paratexts," but he means by this something different from Genette's term, closer to diagrammatic grammatexts of hypertexts, which he proposes to extract by statistical methods. Stanitzek 2005 is an excellent recent statement of the difficulty of formulating paratext taxonomies in media.

N6.37. Mallarmé 1945. Some "Read Me" files of this kind are published separately and later matched to the texts whose method they explain—for example, Edgar Allan Poe's "The Philosophy of Composition" (1846) and Raymond Roussel's *Comment j'ai écrit certains de mes livres* (1935).

N6.38. See, for example, Cayley 2004, Cayley and Eskelinen 2001, Eskelinen 2001a, Glazier 2001, and Rosenberg 1996, 2001.

N6.39. A deep and thorough documentation of variants is an important precondition for preservation of digital texts (Liu et al. 2005; Kirschenbaum 2008). In addition to the vagaries of application version, file formats, and operating system, they note as difficulties for the long-term preservation, migration, and analysis of digital texts that accidental attributes of structure (such as the Janespace) represent a particular problem. Such elements may not be addressable by descriptions of function; they may be unrecognized by the text's creators (Marshall and Golovchinsky 2004).

N6.40. Cf. McGann's discussion (2001, 205) of the injunctive character of textuality itself. What could be more injunctive in this way than the question of *Afternoon*'s narrator: "do you want to hear about it?" or the opening, allographic instructions to "read at depth"?

N6.41. "Most writers—poets in especial—prefer having it understood that they compose by a species of fine frenzy—an ecstatic intuition—and would positively shudder at letting the public take a peep behind the scenes, at the elaborate and vacillating crudities of thought—at the true purposes seized only at the last moment—at the innumerable glimpses of idea that arrived not at the maturity of full view—at the fully-matured fancies discarded in despair as unmanageable—at the cautious selections and rejections—at the painful erasures and interpolations—in a word, at the wheels and pinions—the tackle for scene-shifting—the step-ladders, and demon-traps—the cock's feathers, the red paint and the black patches, which, in ninety-nine cases out of a hundred, constitute the properties of the literary histrio" (Poe 2003 [1846], 430).

7. Reading Machines

N7.01. After having been pestered for nearly three decades by readers seeking an answer to the Mad Hatter's riddle (which was never meant to have one), Carroll proposed this response in his preface to the 1896 edition of *Alice*. The misspelled "nevar" ("raven" backwards) was silently corrected by the printer in the next and subsequent editions, making Carroll's response seem more nonsensical than it was (Crutch 1976).

N7.02. Libeskind 1991, 37–49. Libeskind's wheel was destroyed in a gallery fire in the mid-1990s (Mathews and Brotchie 1998, 177–78). Hall 1970 includes several photographs of another working scale model of Ramelli's wheel created by Dante Gnudi.

N7.03. For books as tables, see Italian sculptor Livio de Marchi's *Casa di Libri N° 1*, a wooden sculpture in the shape and size of a small house. The house is outfitted with furniture whose parts resemble large books (see http://www .liviodemarchi.com/casauk.htm).

N7.04. More ambiguous, seriocomic versions of this scene: Gulliver, traversing the 25-foot-high pages of Brobdingnagian books with "a moveable pair of stairs" that allows him to walk the length of each line before descending to read the one below it (Swift 1957–69, book 2, chap. 7); in Jules Verne's unpublished 1863 novel, *Paris au XXe siècle*, the *Grande Livre* of the bank Casmodage et Cie, on whose 3-meter-high pages the secretary writes out each day's transactions, moving up and down the page with the aid of a revolving staircase.

N7.05. In a later chapter, Tschichold complains of the fashion of square-shaped books "among people who fancy themselves to be ultramodern" (1991, 166).

N7.06. Stoicheff and Taylor observe that the page's predominant format—generally rectangular, vertically oriented, in a 5:8 ratio—has remained remarkably consistent for at least two millennia (2004b, 3–9). They speculate that several material and cultural factors are responsible for this, including "anatomical practicality" (the "rectangular and vertical space of the human hand" was easily translated onto the visual field of clay and wax tablets, and later to units of scrolls and the individual leaves of the codex) and the aesthetic appeal of the ratio, as it matches the Golden Section. See also Tschichold 1991, 36–64.

N7.07. Perhaps the simplest requirement is that it should be readable. Reading should not be perilous to the operator: Lucas Samaras's "garbage" and "pinned" books of the early 1960s, stuffed with trash and glass shards or encrusted with straight pins, knife blades, scissors, and razor blades would be off-putting to all but the most determined bibliophiles (Levin 1975). Reading should be possible, in that the mechanism should permit it: Maurizio Nannucci's *Universum* (1969), leather-bound in the classic codex form, has a second spine in place of the foreedge. It cannot be opened—"[it is] a Janus-faced, two-headed creature—but one which always looks inside on itself, its contents sealed against intrusion" (Drucker 1995, 178). The uncut form of Roussel's *Nouvelles Impressions d'Afrique* represents a variant of Nannucci's *Universum*, more pliable, a little less resistant to discovery of its interiors ▶ 7.28.

N7.08. Clark 1977, 294–95; Hall 1970, 391. Horizontal wheels appear often in paintings and drawings of the scholar's study, including several depictions of Saint Jerome at work, as in ▶ Figure 1.03.

N7.09. Ramelli's design was known in China by the early seventeenth century; Needham and Wang (1965, 548) reproduce an illustration from a Chinese text of the period that is obviously (although inaccurately) based on Ramelli's engraving.

Needham speculates that the Chinese wheels may have been introduced to the West through Arab contacts with the East. Goodrich 1942, noting differences in the size and principal uses of the Chinese and European devices, doubts a direct influence. Hall 1970 proposes that reading-wheel technologies were independently developed in China and Europe.

N7.10. Ramelli's reputation as a military engineer was considerable. He was called to France by the Duke of Anjou, later Henry III, and participated in the 1572 siege of La Rochelle (Ramelli 1976, 13).

N7.11. In an analysis of Gabriel Harvey's marginalia in political and historical texts he read for the Earl of Leicester in 1580, Lisa Jardine and Anthony Grafton find that the annotations traverse the texts in such a way that unexpected "cohesiveness" emerges from the fray. "In addition to the richness and density of annotation throughout them, there is persistent echoing of sentiments from one book to another; recognizable continuity of handwriting, to the extent that we can sometimes hazard a guess as to which book succeeded which other in the circulating process of reading and annotation" (1990, 51). They conjecture that Harvey used a mechanical aid similar to Ramelli's wheel to facilitate moving between texts, though they give no evidence for why it must have been vertically oriented, like Ramelli's device. Their conjecture suggests that the wheel's mnemonic circuits may be, in a sense, reversed—which is not to say, literally (that is obvious: the wheel can always turn in both directions of the clock), but philologically or genetically, thus enabling the retrospective reconstruction of a reading history from the products of its rotations.

N7.12. On Camillo's theater, see Yates 1974.

N7.13. Each of Libeskind's lessons shows the formal influences of Tatlin's design for the *Monument to the Third International* (1920, never built), a massive tower in iron, glass, and steel, which was to incorporate three geometric units rotating respectively on annual, daily, and hourly cycles.

N7.14. The eight "words" were: ideas, energia, created being, power, subject, spirit, will to power, and being. Libeskind (1991, 48–49) shows examples of the fractured texts made from them, for example: "*Eingc Rea*. T. Edbe in gcr eated b ei ngc treat edb ei ng . . ." Libeskind's decision that there should be eight books and lecterns on the wheel represents something of a mystery: "Someone . . . asked me, 'Why eight books?' I discovered why while reading *Don Quixote*. You've read about the great knight, Don Quixote in his paper visor, going to fight against the injustice of the whole world. Cervantes says that Don Quixote met only one gentleman in his travels in Spain. In all his time (because he was old by the time he died) he met only *one* gentleman. He said it was the gentleman in green; he was a gentleman because he travelled with a satchel of only eight books. Clearly Cervantes already had more than eight books in the sixteenth century, and I certainly have more than eight books in my library. I made this project in order to get rid of my books, because I decided that I, too, like the good knight, should reduce my library" (Libeskind 1991, 40).

But Diego Miranda, "the gentleman in green" of Cervantes's novel, observes to Quixote that he owns six dozen books, and seems to carry none of them with him (Part 2, chaps. 16–18). The need to "reduce" one's library—that is, to compress its sprawl (Bush) and rationalize its disorders but preserve the possibility of recovering them (Nelson)—is, as we have seen, an exemplary motive of the reading machine. Libeskind's specific justification for this aspect of his design may involve a mistaken recollection or a confusion about his source texts.

N7.15. This is one of the wheel's anticipations of cinematic form, in that it immobilizes its user's body in securing for her a more dynamic field of representation. Cf. Manovich 2001, 103–11.

N7.16. Such complexity and contingency applies even to ostensibly objective methods of classification (by author's name, title, subject, Dewey Decimal or Library of Congress number, etc.); each must have its own basis particular to the owner, and each must account for the irregular and the one-off. Any system—even no system (remember the disorder of Jerome's cell ▶ 1.18)—will be marked by signatures of a reading history; in that respect it has its reasons (Perec 1985, 41; Petroski 1999, 233–52).

N7.17. This principle also determines the wheel's narrative potential, for within the course of its circuits, momentary confusions and inconsistencies can be held in abeyance, temporarily set aside in the reader's mental store, until a path is discovered along which they may be rejoined or motivated. (It remains possible that some loose ends will represent completely unfruitful collations, of no value to the reader. But then they do not constitute parts of a narratively meaningful product.) Marie-Laure Ryan has proposed a model of multivariant narrative along these lines (Ryan 2004, 2005, 2006).

N7.18. Such a segmentation into pages may not produce effects of dislocation or interruption. Jack Kerouac typed the first draft of *On the Road* (1951, published in 1957) in a single paragraph, on ten 12-foot rolls of paper that he taped together to form a continuous scroll. Juan Benet composed his novel *Una meditación* (1969) on an apparatus combining a single roll of paper, a typewriter, and a mechanism that prevented him from reversing the roll as he typed (his first draft was his final; Manguel 2004, 28). But Kerouac's text was substantially edited before publication, and both novels were published as conventional codices. The reader is able to move through these texts in more than two directions, whereas Kerouac was, at least locally, constrained to only two. Benet could only move in something closer to one and a half directions, the fraction corresponding to the carriage returns of his typewriter.

N7.19. The sonnets are in a modified Sicilian form: an octave composed of two cross-rhymed quatrains (*abab abab*), followed by a sestet in which the first and second line of each tercet are rhymed, and the third rhymes with the corresponding third of the other tercet (*ccd eed*). The lines are alexandrines (twelve syllables) and the initial rhymes of each quatrain and tercet are feminine. Queneau's attention to details such as these is mandated by the rigorous method of the sonnet machine. If each line can be substituted for the corresponding line of the nine remaining sonnets, then it must adhere to a versification specific to that position. These strictly formal constraints must logically precede the problem of fitting the line semantically to the others.

N7.20. Massin's design captures a substructure of the textbase incidental to the support of compatible sonnet sequences. As Mathews and Brotchie observe, when the reader folds a paper strip, she reveals or obscures a corresponding line that matches it in meter and rhyme, "rhyming, as it were, three-dimensionally" (1998, 14). Riffling the pages of the book so that its strips are held open like a fractured fan, as in ▶ Figure 7.03, we observe another aspect of its three-dimensionality: the strips describe trajectories in a textual field, as a set of digraphs (▶ Figure 5.03) or a twingle (▶ Figure 2.04).

N7.21. Roussel's book was published at his expense in 1932 by Lemerre. Fassio appears to have constructed a working model of his reading wheel before 1954, as a photograph of it appears in his essay of that year on Alfred Jarry and the College of Pataphysics (Fassio 1954). The first detailed description of the wheel appeared a decade later, in a text by François Caradec based on Fassio's notes (Fassio and Caradec 1964).

N7.22. Because my chief emphasis is on Fassio's device for reading Roussel's text, my description of the poem and its presentation is necessarily summary. See Roussel 2004a for Ian Monk's excellent introduction to his English translation of *Nouvelles Impressions* and Roussel 2004b for Jacques Sivan's extended postface to the 2004 Al Dante edition for detailed treatments of its mechanisms. My description of the poem's parenthetical system and verse scheme follows Monk's.

N7.23. Like Queneau's sonnet machine, the verse of *Nouvelles Impressions* is alexandrines, in rhyming couplets with alternating masculine and feminine rhymes. This is a canonical form of modern French poetry, but it cannot be a simple coincidence that the two works resemble one another in this regard: each author has chosen a verse form that is both classic and particularly unforgiving in modern French. Monk observes that Roussel made his labors in this respect all the greater: fantastically, he seems to have used a pattern of *bouts rimés* (forced rhymes), beginning with a list of rhyming terms at the ends of lines and constructing the rest of the lines backwards from the rhyme (Roussel 2004a, 7).

N7.24. Fassio chose a different color scheme, apparently for its legibility in the context of the reading wheel, but also preserved the parenthetical markers.

N7.25. See Sivan, "Proposition de lecture des illustrations," postface to Roussel 2004b, 321–38; and Reggiani 2004, 38–41.

N7.26. Most books are printed on sheets of paper much larger than the size of the finished page. *Imposition* is the process of arranging the images of pages prior to printing so that the sheets may be folded, bound, and trimmed with the pages in the correct orientation and sequence.

N7.27. Roussel's indication to Zo for image number 28—exactly in the book's center—suggests that this is how he intended it to be read: "A man sitting by a table on which a book is positioned vertically; he separates two of the uncut leaves to read a passage." The 1985 re-edition of the poem by J.-J. Pauvert displaces the images to an appendix after the poem's end. Roussel's calculated interleaving of image and text is undone by this change (Roussel 2004a, 8–10).

N7.28. On the manicule, also known as a "fist," the pointing figure used since early modernity for textual emphasis and readerly direction, ☞Sherman 2005.

N7.29. Related to this change in the folding scheme is a division of the text forced on Fassio by the wheel's mechanical limits. When a segment of the text is too long to fit on a card, it is run over onto other cards, since this is the only practical way to ensure that rotations of the wheel are not tripped up by very long segments.

N7.30. ▶ 4.45.

N7.31. "It is, we see, once more a question of external and internal [*wieder eine Frage des Aussen und Innen*]" ("Negation," in Freud 1940–52, 14:13; 1955–66, 19:237).

N7.32. On the development of the Star, see D.C. Smith et al. 1982 and J. Johnson 1995.

N7.33. These and similar print and television advertisements are collected in Wichary 2008.

N7.34. S. Johnson 1997, 42–75, summarizes these debates in the popular press. Friedberg 2006, 344n114, cites a 1994 column by Umberto Eco for the Italian newsweekly *L'Espresso* that compared debates between partisans of the Mac OS and MS-DOS to doctrinal disputes between Catholics (Mac OS users) and Protestants (MS-DOS users). The Macintosh's GUI, Eco observed, is "catechistic: the essence of revelation is dealt with via simple formulae and sumptuous icons," whereas MS-DOS allows its users to freely interpret scripture, but "imposes a subtle hermeneutics upon the user, and takes for granted the idea that not all can reach salvation."

N7.35. Stephenson 1999 is typical of residual support for, and inconsistent counter-propositions concerning, the command line. Raskin's promotion of a mixed command line–GUI scheme he called the "human environment" (2000) represents a unique and scrupulous middle position with regard to these debates.

N7.36. Engelbart's NFS and Sutherland's Sketchpad included interface elements that anticipated later GUI forms (Engelbart and English 1968; Sutherland 1988; Barnes 1997).

N7.37. This perception of potential structure is distinct from, though perhaps related to, the apparent inability of the human visual system to long abide uniform visual fields. Neurologically and photochemically, sighted humans are primed to discern visual structure even when none is objectively present, or to react with anxiety and fear to its absence, as polar explorers confronted by "whiteout" phenomena, and subjects of *ganzfeld* sensory deprivation experiments have found (Elkins 2000, 238–42). The computer screen will never approach the total blankness of such fields, because its boundaries are easily discerned (when its emptiness is too much for her, the user may avert her eyes), and it is potentially reflective: the faintest double of herself and her surroundings are reflected back from its surface, especially from the solid black regions of early command-line systems.

N7.38. See Goldberg 2002 for an insightful analysis of the critical-philosophical bases of the UI elements of Director.

N7.39. A graphic front end for Windows 3.0, Bob depicted a crudely rendered house outfitted with multiple rooms, furnishings, and objects suited to common user tasks, such as a calendar, checkbook, and letter cubby. Room layouts and color schemes could be changed ("decorated") to create personalized milieus for the user, who was also free to change the locations of furnishings and objects. But the paradigm was inconsistently realized. Many screen objects were purely ornamental (curtains on a window, the pattern or color of a carpet) and could not be altered; the program's back end was liable to intrude on the conceit of the front end in awkward ways. (For example, to identify which objects were associated with computer tasks, the user pressed the F1 key.) Touted as a user-friendly alternative to the mysteries of MS-DOS—"Bob makes your computer as comfortable as an old shoe"—the program was quickly withdrawn from the market because of poor sales and ridicule in the computing press. Microsoft has removed nearly all evidence of Bob's existence from their corporate literature, and its only legacy are the annoying "social" guides of Microsoft Office 97–2003 ("Clippy" and friends, introduced in Bob), a feature that many users disabled after a first encounter. Rowley 1995, essentially a manual for a program that claimed no manual was required, may be the only complete documentation of Bob's features. Winograd's brief article (1996) appears to be the only serious treatment of Bob in HCI design literature.

N7.40. "Keyboards": Magic Cap users entered text in the device with an on-screen "soft" keyboard or by drawing in "digital ink" directly on its surface.

N7.41. The Windows 95 port (▶ Figure 7.07) illustrates potential conflicts of screen grammatexts when different OS idioms coincide. In its Windows incarnation, Magic Cap's realist tropes (the Desk surface, the office cubicle, hallways, rooms, etc.) are, literally, framed by elements of Microsoft's GUI, which adheres less consistently (if it may be said to adhere at all) to realist methods.

N7.42. *Telecards*: Magic Cap devices were capable of sending postcard-like messages in which were embedded program code to facilitate interactions between the user's and receiver's communicators. These were written in a proprietary network language called Telescript, the basis of AT&T's short-lived network for pagers and handheld devices, PersonalLink (General Magic, Inc. 1995).

N7.43. The digital simulacrum of the book reduced to a bag of words ▶ 4.48: "The Library is filled with books that really look and act like the books you're used to; it even has a card catalog that maintains an inventory of the books there. Of course, these are electronic replicas of books, with no paper to tear and no jackets to lose, only information-filled pages" (Knaster 1994, 224).

N7.44. General Magic had forecast that buildings along the street (Magic Cap's "Downtown") would serve as portals for an expanding network of service providers and online merchants—a tamer, more vendor-friendly version of the virtual corridors of Stephenson's Metaverse (1993). Only a few such services were ever made available to users.

N7.45. Lacan 1961–62, "Séminaire IX: Identification" (December 20, 1961, and January 10, 1962). As of this writing, Seminar IX has not been published in an official transcription. I rely here on an unofficial transcript (the "version rue CB"), available online at http://new.lutecium.org. Lacan's use of the term *marque* throughout this passage is a several-layered play on words, as the term means both a stroke or a grapheme (a "mark") and a brand-name (as in "trademark"). For Kripke's critique of descriptivism, see Kripke 1980.

N7.46. "Traveling shot," ▶ 1.32.

N7.47. Cf. Kittler 1997, 150: "There would be no software if computer systems were not surrounded by an environment of everyday languages."

N7.48. Lacan 1978, 63.

N7.49. See Bolter and Gromala 2003 for a version of this argument cast in terms of an "oscillation" in the most effective GUI designs between "transparency" and "reflectivity" of the UI's surfaces.

N7.50. Thus, the subject of usability is a Cartesian subject—not with respect to the promised autarchy of Descartes's *cogito*, but because that affirmation requires another, less often acknowledged prop: the belief in the goodness of an Other beyond thought—God—who guarantees the validity of knowledge. Cf. Verhaeghe 2002.

N7.51. On this cognitive strategy of "the cult of order and reason," see Leclaire 1971, 53.

N7.52. Conversely, the Windows user may elect to embrace the precariousness of her condition. Another popular enhancement to Windows allows the user to save her screen with the image of a mock BSOD ("amaze your friends and scare your enemies!"). Available at: http://technet.microsoft.com/en-us/sysinternals/bb897558.aspx.

N7.53. Freud 1940–52, 1:531–54; 1955–66, 3:303–22. As Friedberg (2006, 17) notes, Strachey's translation of *Deckerinnerungen* as *"screen* memories"—when Freud in 1899 did not mean to suggest by *Decke,* "cover" or "blanket," a projection surface—has resulted in a drift of the term toward metaphors of projection such as the one I imply here. In defense of my abuse of Freud's metaphor I would propose that this double operation of projecting and covering is achieved by the GUI screen's conjuring away of the real limits of reading, even as it depends on their determination of its symbolic structure. In this sense, the screen shows (projects) by screening (blocking) what it cannot show directly.

N7.54. "The most seductive part of the whole subject for a young scapegrace [*nichts-nutzigen Jüngling*] is the picture of the marriage night. (What does he care about what comes afterwards?)" (Freud 1940–52, 1:547; 1955–66, 3:316).

N7.55. The twin towers of the World Trade Center appear twice in Madonna's music video, between the 2:30 and 2:40 marks.

Bibliography

Aarseth, Espen J. 1997. *Cybertext: Perspectives on Ergodic Literature.* Baltimore, Md.: Johns Hopkins University Press.

Adler, Jeremy, and Ulrich Ernst. 1990. *Text als Figur: Visuelle Poesie von der Antike bis zur Moderne.* Weinheim, Germany: Herzog August Bibliothek.

Akscyn, Robert M., Donald L. McCracken, and Elise A. Yoder. 1988. "KMS: A Distributed Hypermedia System for Managing Knowledge in Organizations." *Communications of the ACM* 31 (7): 820–35.

Allen, Thomas. 2007. *Uncovered.* Edited by Chip Kidd. New York: Aperture Foundation.

Andersen, Peter Bøgh. 1997. *A Theory of Computer Semiotics: Semiotic Approaches to Construction and Assessment of Computer Systems.* 2nd ed. Cambridge, Eng.: Cambridge University Press.

Andersen, Peter Bøgh, Berit Holmqvist, and Jens F. Jensen, eds. 1993. *The Computer as Medium.* Cambridge, Eng.: Cambridge University Press.

Anzieu, Didier. 1988. *L'Auto-analyse de Freud et la découverte de la psychanalyse.* 3rd ed. Paris: Presses Universitaires de France.

Apple Computer, Inc. 1992. *Macintosh Human Interface Guidelines.* Reading, Mass.: Addison-Wesley.

———. 2005. *Apple Human Interface Guidelines (Tiger).* Cupertino, Calif.: Apple Computer, Inc. Available at: http://developer.apple.com/documentation/LegacyTechnologies/UserExperience-date.html.

———. 2008. *Apple Human Interface Guidelines (Leopard).* Cupertino, Calif.: Apple Computer, Inc. Available at: http://developer.apple.com/documentation/UserExperience/index.html.

"The Atomic Age." 1945. *Life* 19 (8) (August 20): 32.

Bachelard, Gaston. 1964. *La Poétique de l'espace.* 4th ed. Paris: Presses Universitaires de France.

Bachman, Frank P. 1918. *Great Inventors and Their Inventions.* New York, Cincinnati, Chicago: American Book Company.

Baetens, Jan. 2001. *Le Texte comme espace: Études grammatextuelles.* Berlin: Weidler.

Baran, Paul. 1962. "On Distributed Communications Networks." Rand Paper P-2626. Santa Monica, Calif.: Rand Corporation. Available at: http://www.rand.org/pubs/papers/P2626.

Bardini, Thierry. 2000. *Bootstrapping: Douglas Engelbart, Coevolution, and the Origins of Personal Computing.* Stanford, Calif.: Stanford University Press.

Barnes, Susan B. 1997. "Douglas Carl Engelbart: Developing the Underlying Concepts for Contemporary Computing." *IEEE Annals of the History of Computing* 19 (3): 16–26.

Barthes, Roland. 1957. *Mythologies.* Paris: Éditions du Seuil.

———. 1964a. "Éléments de sémiologie." *Communications* 4:91–135.

———. 1964b. *Essais critiques.* Paris: Éditions du Seuil.

———. 1964c. "L'Activité structuraliste." In Barthes 1964b, 215–18.

———. 1964d. "Rhétorique de l'image." *Communications* 4:40–51.

———. 1967. *Système de la mode.* Paris: Éditions du Seuil.

———. 1970. *S/Z.* Paris: Éditions du Seuil.

———. 1973. *Le Plaisir du texte.* Paris: Éditions du Seuil.

———. 1982a. *L'Obvie et l'obtus.* Paris: Éditions du Seuil.

———. 1982b. "Le Message photographique." In Barthes 1982a, 9–24.

———. 1982c. "Le Troisième sens." In Barthes 1982a, 43–61.

———. 1984a. *Le Bruissement de la langue.* Paris: Éditions du Seuil.

———. 1984b. "La Mort de l'auteur." In Barthes 1984a, 61–67.

Battles, Matthew. 2004. *Library: An Unquiet History.* New York: W.W. Norton.

Baum, L. Frank. 1990 [1913]. *The Patchwork Girl of Oz.* New York: Dover Publications.

Bearman, David. 1999. "Reality and Chimeras in the Preservation of Electronic Records." *D-Lib Magazine* 5 (4). Available at: http://www.dlib.org/dlib/april99/bearman/04bearman.html.

Beiguelman, Giselle. 2004. *//**Code_UP.* Available at: http://container.zkm.de/code_up.

Benedikt, Michael, ed. 1991. *Cyberspace: First Steps.* Cambridge, Mass.: MIT Press.

Benjamin, Walter. 1968a. *Illuminations: Essays and Reflections.* Translated by Harry Zohn. New York: Harcourt, Brace & World.

———. 1968b. "Unpacking My Library." In Benjamin 1968a, 59–67.

Berners-Lee, Tim. 1989. "Information Management: A Proposal." Geneva, Switzerland: CERN. Available at: http://www.w3.org/History/1989/proposal.html.

———. 1999. *Weaving the Web: The Original Design and Ultimate Destiny of the World Wide Web by Its Inventor.* San Francisco: HarperSanFrancisco.

Bernfeld, Siegfried. 1946. "An Unknown Autobiographical Fragment by Freud." *American Imago* 4 (1): 3–19.

Bernstein, Mark. 2000. "More than Legible: On Links That Readers Don't Want to Follow." In *Hypertext '00*, 216–17. San Antonio, Tex.: Association for Computing Machinery.

———. 2002. "Storyspace 1." In *Hypertext '02*, 172–81. College Park, Md.: Association for Computing Machinery.

———. 2004a. "*Lust*, Touch, Metadata: Meaning and the Limits of Adaptation." In *Hypertext '04*, 36–37. Santa Cruz, Calif.: Association for Computing Machinery.

———. 2004b. "Mein Freund Hamlet / My Friend Hamlet." In Block, Heibach, and Wenz 2004, 134–51.

Bernstein, Mark, David E. Millard, and Mark J. Weal. 2002. "On Writing Sculptural Hypertext." In *Hypertext '02*, 65–66. College Park, Md.: Association for Computing Machinery.

Birkerts, Sven. 1994. *The Gutenberg Elegies: The Fate of Reading in an Electronic Age*. Boston: Fawcett Columbine.

———. 1996. "'The Fate of the Book.'" In *Tolstoy's Dictaphone: Technology and the Muse*, edited by Sven Birkerts, 189–90. St. Paul, Minn.: Graywolf Press.

Blavier, André. 2000. *Les Fous littéraires*. Revised ed. Paris: Éditions des Cendres.

Block, Friedrich W., Christiane Heibach, and Karin Wenz, eds. 2004. *p0es1s: Ästhetik digitaler Poesie / The Aesthetics of Digital Poetry*. Ostfildern-Ruit, Germany: Hatje Cantz Verlag.

Blow Out. 1981. Directed by Brian De Palma. 35 mm, 108 min. Cinema 77.

Blowup. 1966. Directed by Michelangelo Antonioni. 35 mm, 111 min. Bridge Films and Metro-Goldwyn-Mayer.

Bogost, Ian, and Nick Montfort. 2008. "Platform Studies." Available at: http://platformstudies.com.

Bolt, Robert A. 1980. "Put-That-There: Voice and Gesture at the Graphics Interface." *Computer Graphics* 15 (3): 262–70.

Bolter, Jay David. 1984. *Turing's Man: Western Culture in the Computer Age*. Chapel Hill: University of North Carolina Press.

———. 1991. *Writing Space: The Computer, Hypertext, and the History of Writing*. Hillsdale, N.J.: Lawrence Erlbaum.

———. 2001. *Writing Space: Computers, Hypertext, and the Remediation of Print*. 2nd ed. Hillsdale, N.J.: Lawrence Erlbaum.

Bolter, Jay David, and Diane Gromala. 2003. *Windows and Mirrors: Interaction Design, Digital Art, and the Myth of Transparency*. Cambridge, Mass.: MIT Press.

Bolter, Jay David, and Richard Grusin. 1999. *Remediation: Understanding New Media*. Cambridge, Mass.: MIT Press.

Bolter, Jay David, Michael Joyce, John B. Smith, and Mark Bernstein. 1993. *Getting Started with Storyspace*. Cambridge, Mass.: Eastgate Systems, Inc.

Boothby, Richard. 2001. *Freud as Philosopher: Metapsychology after Lacan*. New York: Routledge.

Borges, Jorge Luis. 1972. *A Universal History of Infamy*. Translated by Norman Thomas di Giovanni. New York: Dutton.

Bright, Betty. 2005. *No Longer Innocent: Book Art in America, 1960–1980*. New York: Granary Books.

Brown, Peter J. 1986. "Viewing Documents on a Screen." In *CD-ROM: The New Papyrus*, edited by Steve Lambert and Suzanne Ropiequet, 175–84. Redmond, Wash.: Microsoft Press.

———. 1987. "Turning Ideas into Products: The Guide System." In *Hypertext '87*, 33–40. Chapel Hill, N.C.: Association for Computing Machinery.

Burke, Colin. 1991. "A Practical View of Memex: The Career of the Rapid Selector." In Nyce and Kahn, 1991a, 145–64.

Bush, Vannevar. 1929. *Operational Circuit Analysis*. New York: John Wiley & Sons.

———. 1945a. "As We May Think." *The Atlantic* [*The Atlantic Monthly*] 176 (1) (July): 101–8.

———. 1945b. "As We May Think." Illustrated by Alfred D. Crimi. *Life* 19 (11) (September 10): 112–24.

———. 1945c. "Justifying Typewriter." U.S. Patent 2,379,862, filed July 31, 1942, and issued July 10, 1945.

———. 1967. *Science Is Not Enough*. New York: William Morrow.

———. 1991a. "As We May Think." In Nyce and Kahn 1991a, 85–110.

———. 1991b. "Memex II." In Nyce and Kahn 1991a, 165–84.

———. 1991c. "Memex Revisited." In Nyce and Kahn 1991a, 197–216.

Callihan, John C., ed. 1982. *An Anthology of American Classics: A Quarter of a Century of Limited Editions Published for Friends of Westvaco at Christmastime, 1958–1982*. Book design by Bradbury Thompson. New York: Westvaco, Inc.

Camille, Michael. 2004. *Image on the Edge: The Margins of Medieval Art*. London: Reaktion Books, Ltd.

Caradec, François. 1964. "La Machine à imprimer Roussel, ou l'impression des impressions." *Bizarre* 34/35:58–62.

Card, Stuart K., George G. Robertson, and William York. 1996. "The Web-Book and the Web Forager: An Information Workspace for the World-Wide-Web." *CHI '96 Conference Proceedings*, 111–17. New York: Association for Computing Machinery.

Carrión, Ulises. 1993. "The New Art of Making Books." In *Artists' Books: A Critical Anthology & Sourcebook*, edited by Joan Lyons, 31–43. Rochester, N.Y.: Visual Studies Workshop.

Carroll, Lewis. 1991. *The Complete Annotated Alice*. Edited by Martin Gardner. Santa Monica, Calif.: The Voyager Company.

Carruthers, Mary. 1998. *The Craft of Thought: Meditation, Rhetoric, and the Making of Images, 400–1200*. New York: Cambridge University Press.

Cayley, John. 2003. "Digital Wen: On the Digitization of Letter- and Character-Based Systems of Inscription." In *Reading East Asian Writing: The Limits of Literary Theory*, edited by Michel Hockx and Ivo Smits, 277–94. London: Routledge Curzon.

———. 2004. "Der Code ist nicht der Text (es sei denn, er ist der Text) / The Code Is Not the Text (Unless It Is the Text)." In Block, Heibach, and Wenz 2004, 287–305.

———. 2005. "Writing on Complex Surfaces." *dichtung-digital* 2/2005. Available at: http://www.dichtung-digital.org/2005/2-Cayley.htm.

Cayley, John, and Markku Eskelinen. 2001. "In the Event of the Text." In Eskelinen and Koskimaa 2001, 86–99.

Cervantes Saavedra, Miguel de. 1950. *The Adventures of Don Quixote*. Translated by J.M. Cohen. New York: Penguin Books.

Charraud, Nathalie. 1997. *Lacan et les mathématiques*. Paris: Anthropos.

Christensen, Inger. 1981. *Alfabet*. Copenhagen, Denmark: Gyldendal.

———. 2001. *Alphabet*. Translated by Susanna Nied. New York: New Directions.

Christin, Anne-Marie. 2000. *Poétique du blanc. Vide et intervalle dans la civilisation de l'alphabet*. Louvain-Paris: Éditions Peeters-Vrin.

Chu, Yi-Chun, David Bainbridge, Matt Jones, and Ian H. Witten. 2004. "Realistic Books: A Bizarre Homage to an Obsolete Medium?" In *ACM/IEEE-CS Joint Conference on Digital Libraries*, 78–86. Tucson, Ariz.: Association for Computing Machinery.

Cicero. 1979. *De Oratore, Books I–II*. Translated by E.W. Sutton and H. Rackham. Cambridge, Mass.: Harvard University Press.

Clark, John Willis. 1977 [1909]. *The Care of Books: An Essay on the Development of Libraries and Their Fittings, from the Earliest Times to the End of the Eighteenth Century*. Norwood, Pa.: Norwood Editions.

Conklin, Jeff. 1987. "Hypertext: An Introduction and Survey." *IEEE Computer* 20 (9): 17–41.

Coover, Robert. 1992. "The End of Books." *New York Times Book Review*, June 21, 1, 23–25.

———. 2000. "Literary Hypertext: The Passing of the Golden Age." *Feed*. February 8. Formerly available at: http://www.feedmag.com/document/d0291lofi.html.

Cortázar, Julio. 1963. *Rayuela*. Buenos Aires, Argentina: Sudamerica.

———. 1966. *Hopscotch*. Translated by Gregory Rabassa. New York: Random House.

Cottom, Daniel. 1999. "The Work of Art in the Age of Mechanical Digestion."
    Representations 66:52–74.

Crane, Stephen. 1968. *The Red Badge of Courage: An Episode of the American
    Civil War.* Edited by Jean A. Bradnick. Book design by Bradbury Thompson.
    New York: West Virginia Pulp and Paper Company.

Crimi, Alfred D. 1977. *The Art of Abstract Dimensional Painting.* New York:
    M. Grumbacher.

———. 1987. *Crimi: A Look Back—A Step Forward. My Life Story.* Staten
    Island, N.Y.: Center for Migration Studies.

Crutch, Denis. 1976. "A Note on the Hatter's Riddle." *Jabberwocky* 5 (1): 32.

Cyan, Inc. 1993. *Myst* (Mac OS). Novato, Calif.: Brøderbund Software.

———. 1997. *Riven* (Mac OS). Novato, Calif.: Brøderbund Software.

———. 2000. *realMyst* (Mac OS and Windows). El Segundo, Calif.: Mattel
    Interactive.

Davis, Whitney. 1995. *Drawing the Dream of the Wolves: Homosexuality,
    Interpretation and Freud's "Wolf-Man."* Bloomington: Indiana University
    Press.

Debray-Genette, Raymond. 1988. *Métamorphoses du récit: Autour de Flau-
    bert.* Paris: Éditions du Seuil.

Deppman, Jed, Daniel Ferrer, and Michael Groden, eds. 2004. *Genetic Criti-
    cism: Texts and Avant-textes.* Philadelphia: University of Pennsylvania
    Press.

Derrida, Jacques. 1967. "Freud et le scène de l'écriture." In *L'Écriture et la dif-
    férence,* 293–340. Paris: Éditions du Seuil.

———. 1972. "La Pharmacie de Platon." In *La Dissemination.* Paris: Éditions
    du Seuil.

———. 1978. "Cartouches." In *La Verité en peinture.* Paris: Flammarion.

———. 1995. *Mal d'archive: Une Impression freudienne.* Paris: Éditions
    Galilée.

———. 2001. "La Machine à traitement de texte." In *Papier Machine: Le Ru-
    ban de machine à écrire et autres réponses,* 151–66. Paris: Éditions Galilée.

Douglas, Jane Yellowlees. 2000. *The End of Books—or Books without End?:
    Reading Interactive Narratives.* Ann Arbor: University of Michigan Press.

Drucker, Johanna. 1995. *The Century of Artists' Books.* New York: Granary
    Books.

———. 1996. *The Visible Word: Experimental Typography and Modern Art,
    1909–1923.* Chicago: University of Chicago Press.

———. 1998. "Language as Information: Intimations of Immateriality." In *Fig-
    uring the Word: Essays on Books, Writing, and Visual Poetics,* 213–20.
    New York: Granary Books.

Drutt, Matthew, ed. 2003. *Kazimir Malevich: Suprematism.* New York: Solo-
    mon R. Guggenheim Foundation.

Ducrot, Oswald, and Tzvetan Todorov. 1972. *Dictionnaire encyclopédique des
    Sciences du langage.* Paris: Éditions du Seuil.

Duguid, Paul. 1996. "Material Matters: The Past and Futurology of the Book." In *The Future of the Book*, edited by Geoffrey Nunberg, 63–102. Berkeley: University of California Press.

Earls, Elliott Peter. 1995. "WD40™: A Toolkit in a Can®, or, the Importance of *David Holzman's Diary*." *Emigre* 35.

———. 1996. *Throwing Apples at the Sun*. CD-ROM. Sacramento, Calif.: Emigre.

———. 1998. *Eye Slingshot Lions*. CD-ROM. The Apollo Program.

———. 2002. *Catfish*. DVD. Sacramento, Calif.: Emigre.

Eastgate Systems, Inc. 1999. *User's Manual, Storyspace for Windows, Version 1.75*. Cambridge, Mass.: Eastgate Systems, Inc.

———. 2001a. *User's Manual, Storyspace for Macintosh, Version 2.0*. Cambridge, Mass.: Eastgate Systems, Inc.

———. 2001b. *User's Manual, Storyspace for Windows, Version 2.0*. Cambridge, Mass.: Eastgate Systems, Inc.

Eco, Umberto. 1988. "An *Ars Oblivionalis*? Forget It!" Translated by Marilyn Migiel. *PMLA* 103 (3): 254–61.

Elkin, Tobi. 2001. "Opening Windows." *Advertising Age* 72 (41) (October 8): 10.

Elkins, James. 2000. *How to Use Your Eyes*. New York: Routledge.

Engelbart, Douglas C. 1986. "The Augmented Knowledge Workshop." *ACM Conference on the History of Personal Workstations*, 73–83. Palo Alto, Calif.: Association for Computing Machinery.

Engelbart, Douglas C., and William K. English. 1968. *A Research Center for Augmenting Human Intellect* (QuickTime™ streaming video). Menlo Park, Calif.: Stanford Research Institute. Available at: http://www.invisible revolution.net/68-demo.html.

Engler, Rudolf. 2004. "The Making of the *Cours de linguistique générale*." In *The Cambridge Companion to Saussure*, edited by Carol Sanders, 47–58. Cambridge, Eng.: Cambridge University Press.

Eskelinen, Markku. 2001a. "(Introduction to) Cybertext Narratology." In Eskelinen and Koskimaa 2001, 52–68.

———. 2001b. "The Gaming Situation." *Game Studies* 1 (1). Available at: http://www.gamestudies.org/0101/eskelinen.

———. 2004. "Six Problems in Search of a Solution: The Challenge of Cybertext Theory and Ludology to Literary Theory." *dichtung-digital* 3/2004. Available at: http://www.dichtung-digital.org/2004/3-Eskelinen.htm.

Eskelinen, Markku, and Raine Koskimaa, eds. 2001. *Cybertext Yearbook 2000*. Jyväskylä, Finland: Research Centre for Contemporary Culture.

Esposito, Joseph J. 2003/2005. "The Processed Book." *First Monday* 8 (3) (March 3, 2003; October 23, 2005). Available at: http://firstmonday.org/ issues/issue8_3/esposito/index.html.

Evans, Dylan. 1996. *An Introductory Dictionary of Lacanian Psychoanalysis*. New York: Routledge.

Fassio, Juan-Esteban. 1954. "Alfred Jarry y el Colegio de Patafísica." *Letra y línea* 4:2–5.

Fassio, Juan-Esteban, and François Caradec. 1964. "La Machine à lire Roussel, ou la machine à lire *Les Nouvelles Impressions d'Afrique*." *Bizarre* 34/35:63–66.

Ferrer, Daniel. 1998. "Le Matériel et le virtuel: Du paradigme indiciaire à la logique des mondes possibles." In *Pourquoi la critique génétique? Méthodes, théories*, edited by Michel Contat and Daniel Ferrer, 11–30. Paris: Éditions du Centre National de la Recherche Scientifique.

Fink, Bruce. 2002. "Knowledge and Science: Fantasies of the Whole." In Glynos and Stavrakakis 2002, 167–78.

———. 2004. *Lacan to the Letter: Reading Écrits Closely*. Minneapolis: University of Minnesota Press.

Fitzgerald, Kenneth. 1996. "The Angel Is My Floating Point!" *Emigre* 39:34–44.

Frasca, Gonzalo. 2003. "Simulation versus Narrative: Introduction to Ludology." In *The Video Game Theory Reader*, edited by Mark J.P. Wolf and Bernard Perron, 221–36. New York: Routledge.

Freud, Sigmund. 1940–52. *Gesammelte Werke, chronologisch geordnet*. Edited by Anna Freud. 18 vols. London: Imago Publishing.

———. 1954. *The Origins of Psychoanalysis. Letters to Wilhelm Fliess, Drafts and Notes, 1887–1902*. Edited by Marie Bonaparte, Anna Freud, and Ernst Kris. Translated by Eric Mosbacher and James Strachey. New York: Basic Books.

———. 1955–66. *Standard Edition of the Complete Psychological Works of Sigmund Freud*. Edited by James Strachey. Translated by James Strachey, Anna Freud, Alix Strachey, and Alan Tyson. 24 vols. London: Hogarth Press.

———. 1987. *Gesammelte Werke, Nachtragsband. Texte aus den Jahren 1885 bis 1938*. Edited by Angela Richards and Ilse Grubrich-Simitis. Frankfurt am Main: S. Fischer Verlag.

Friedberg, Anne. 2006. *The Virtual Window: From Alberti to Microsoft*. Cambridge, Mass.: MIT Press.

Fuller, Matthew, ed. 2008. *Software Studies: A Lexicon*. Cambridge, Mass.: MIT Press.

Gamwell, Lynn, and Mark Solms, eds. 2006. *From Neurology to Psychoanalysis: Sigmund Freud's Neurological Drawings and Diagrams of the Mind*. Binghamton: Binghamton University Art Museum, State University of New York.

Gandelman, Claude. 1991. *Reading Pictures, Viewing Texts*. Bloomington: Indiana University Press.

Gass, William H. 1991. *On Being Blue: A Philosophical Inquiry*. New York: David R. Godine.

Gaudreault, André. 1988. *Du Littéraire au filmique: Système du récit.* Paris: Méridiens Klincksieck.

General Magic, Inc. 1995. *Magic Cap™ Complete.* Reading, Mass.: Addison-Wesley.

Genette, Gérard. 1976. *Mimologiques: Voyage en Cratylie.* Paris: Éditions du Seuil.

———. 1987. *Seuils.* Paris: Éditions du Seuil.

Gentner, Don, and Jakob Nielsen. 1996. "The Anti-Mac Interface." *Communications of the ACM* 39 (8): 70–82.

Geyh, Paula, Fred G. Leebron, and Andrew Levy, eds. 1998. *Postmodern American Fiction: A Norton Anthology.* New York: W. W. Norton.

Gibson, William, Dennis Ashbaugh, and Kevin Begos, Jr. 1992. *Agrippa (A Book of the Dead).* New York: Kevin Begos Publishing.

Glazier, Loss Pequeño. 2001. *Digital Poetics: The Making of E-Poetries.* Tuscaloosa: University of Alabama Press.

———. 2004. "Der konditionale Texte: Zur Verortung der 'Poesie' in digitaler Poesie / The Conditional Text: Siting the 'Poetry' in E-Poetry." In Block, Heibach, and Wenz 2004, 57–77.

Glynos, Jason, and Yannis Stavrakakis, eds. 2002. *Lacan and Science.* London: Karnac Books.

Goldberg, David. 2002. "EnterFrame: Cage, Deleuze and Macromedia Director." *Afterimage* 30 (1): 8–9.

Goodrich, L. Carrington. 1942. "The Revolving Book-Case in China." *Harvard Journal of Asiatic Studies* 7 (2): 130–61.

Granger, Stewart. 2000. "Emulation as a Digital Preservation Strategy." *D-Lib Magazine* 6 (10). Available at: http://www.dlib.org/dlib/october00/granger/10granger.html.

Greene, Roland. 1992. "The Concrete Historical." *The Harvard Library Bulletin*, n.s., 3 (2): 9–18.

Grigg, Russell. 1998. "Le Nom propre, c'est le signifiant à l'état pur." *La Cause freudienne* 39:125–28.

Grimm, Reinhold. 1978. "Marc Saporta: The Novel as Card Game." Translated by Helene Scher. *Contemporary Literature* 19 (3): 280–99.

Groensteen, Thierry. 2003. "Un Premier bouquet de contraintes." *Oubapo* 1:13–59.

Halasz, Frank G. 1988. "Reflections on NoteCards: Seven Issues for the Next Generation of Hypermedia Systems." *Communications of the ACM* 31 (7): 836–52.

Hall, Bert S. 1970. "A Revolving Bookcase by Agostino Ramelli." *Technology and Culture* 11 (3): 389–400.

Hanebutt-Benz, Eva-Maria. 1985. *Die Kunst des Lesens. Lesemöbel und Lesverhalten vom Mittelalter biz zur Gegenwart.* Frankfurt am Main: Museum für Kunsthandwerk.

Harpold, Terry. 1991. "The Contingencies of the Hypertext Link." *Writing on the Edge* 2 (2): 126–38.

———. 1994. "Conclusions." In *Hyper/Text/Theory*, edited by George P. Landow, 189–222. Baltimore, Md.: Johns Hopkins University Press.

———. 2003. "Hypertext." In *Glossalalia*, edited by Julian Wolfreys, 113–26. Edinburgh: Edinburgh University Press.

———. 2005. "Digital Narrative." In *Routledge Encyclopedia of Narrative Theory*, edited by David Herman, Manfred Jahn, and Marie-Laure Ryan, 108–12. New York: Routledge.

———. 2008. "Screw the Grue: Mediality, Metalepsis, Recapture." In *Playing the Past: History and Nostalgia in Video Games*, edited by Zach Whalen and Laurie Taylor, 91–108. Nashville, Tenn.: Vanderbilt University Press.

Hayles, N. Katherine. 1999. *How We Became Posthuman: Virtual Bodies in Cybernetics, Literature, and Informatics*. Chicago: University of Chicago Press.

———. 2000. "Flickering Connectivities in Shelley Jackson's *Patchwork Girl*: The Importance of Media-Specific Analysis." *Postmodern Culture* 10 (2). Available at: http://muse.jhu.edu/journals/postmodern_culture/toc/pmc10.2.html.

———. 2002. *Writing Machines*. Cambridge, Mass.: MIT Press.

———. 2005. *My Mother Was a Computer: Digital Subjects and Literary Texts*. Chicago: University of Chicago Press.

———. 2007. "Electronic Literature: What Is It?" College Park, Md.: Electronic Literature Organization. Available at: http://eliterature.org/pad/elp.html.

———. 2008. *Electronic Literature: New Horizons for the Literary*. Notre Dame, Ind.: University of Notre Dame Press.

Hayles, N. Katherine, Nick Montfort, Scott Rettberg, and Stephanie Strickland, eds. 2006. *Electronic Literature Collection, Volume 1*. College Park, Md.: Electronic Literature Organization. Available at: http://collection.eliterature.org.

Heidegger, Martin. 1977. "The Age of the World Picture." In *The Question Concerning Technology and Other Essays*, 115–54. New York: Harper Torchbooks.

Heim, Michael. 1993. *The Metaphysics of Virtual Reality*. New York: Oxford University Press.

Higgins, Dick. 1987. *Pattern Poetry: Guide to an Unknown Literature*. Albany: State University of New York Press.

Hill, William, James Hollan, Dave Wrobleski, and Tim McCandless. 1992. "Edit Wear and Read Wear." In *CHI '92 Conference Proceedings*, Monterey, Calif., 3–9. Reading, Mass.: Addison-Wesley.

Hilton, Nelson. 1995. *Lexis Complexes: Literary Interventions*. Athens: University of Georgia Press.

Hjelmslev, Louis. 1961. *Prolegomena to a Theory of Language*. Translated by Francis J. Whitfield. Madison: University of Wisconsin Press.

———. 1973 [1951]. "Outline of the Danish Expression System with Special Reference to the *Stød*." In *Essais linguistiques II*, edited by Niels Ege, Eli Fischer-Jorgensen, Knud Togeby, and Francis J. Whitfield, 247–66. Copenhagen, Denmark: Nordisk Sprog- og Kulturforlag.

Horæ Beatæ Mariæ ad usum Romanum (France, 1524). 1999. Edited by Christopher De Hamel. Translated by Glenn Gunhouse, Pamela Morgan, and Karma Pippin. Oakland, Calif.: Octavo.

Hutchins, Edwin L., James D. Hollan, and Donald A. Norman. 1986. "Direct Manipulation Interfaces." In *User Centered System Design: New Perspectives on Human-Computer Interaction*, edited by Donald A. Norman and Stephen W. Draper, 87–124. Hillsdale, N.J.: Lawrence Erlbaum.

Infocom, Inc. 1983. *Zork I: The Great Underground Empire.* Cambridge, Mass.: Infocom, Inc.

Jackson, H. J. 2001. *Marginalia: Readers Writing in Books.* New Haven, Conn.: Yale University Press.

Jackson, K. David, Eric Vos, and Johanna Drucker, eds. 1996. *Experimental —Visual—Concrete: Avant-Garde Poetry since the 1960s.* Amsterdam: Rodopi.

Jackson, Shelley. 1995a. *Patchwork Girl; or, a Modern Monster.* 1st ed. (Mac OS). Cambridge, Mass.: Eastgate Systems, Inc.

———. 1995b. *Patchwork Girl; or, a Modern Monster.* 1st ed. (Windows). Cambridge, Mass.: Eastgate Systems, Inc.

———. 1997. *"My Body"—a Wunderkammer.* Available at: http://www.altx.com/thebody.

———. 1998. "Stitch Bitch." *Paradoxa* 4:526–38.

———. 2002. *The Melancholy of Anatomy.* New York: Anchor Books.

———. 2006. *Half Life: A Novel.* New York: HarperCollins.

Jakobson, Roman. 1960. "Closing Statement: Linguistics and Poetics." In *Style in Language*, edited by Thomas A. Sebeok, 350–77. Cambridge, Mass.: MIT Press.

———. 1971 [1965]. "Quest for the Essence of Language." In *Selected Writings, Volume 2*, 345–59. The Hague: Mouton.

Jakovljevic, Branislav. 2004. "Unframe Malevich! Ineffability and Sublimity in Suprematism." *Art Journal* 63 (3): 18–31.

Jameson, Fredric. 1992. *Postmodernism, or, The Cultural Logic of Late Capitalism.* Durham, N.C.: Duke University Press.

Jardine, Lisa, and Anthony Grafton. 1990. "'Studied for Action': How Gabriel Harvey Read His Livy." *Past and Present* 129:30–78.

Jay, Ricky. 2001. "The Automaton Chess Player, The Invisible Girl & The Telephone." In *Jay's Journal of Anomalies*, 147–62. New York: Farrar, Straus and Giroux.

Johnson, George. 1992. *In the Palaces of Memory: How We Build the Worlds inside Our Heads.* New York: Vintage.

Johnson, Jeff, Teresa L. Roberts, William Verplank, David C. Smith, Charles

H. Irby, Marian Beard, and Kevin Mackey. 1995. "The Xerox Star: A Retrospective." In *Readings in Human-Computer Interaction: Toward the Year 2000*, edited by Ronald M. Baecker, Jonathan Grudin, William A.S. Buxton, and Saul Greenberg, 2nd ed., 53–70. San Francisco: Morgan Kaufman Publishers.

Johnson, Ronald. 1977. *Radi Os OI–OIV*. Berkeley, Calif.: Sand Dollar.

———. 2005. *Radi Os OI–OIV*. Chicago, Ill.: Flood Editions.

Johnson, Steven. 1997. *Interface Culture: How New Technology Transforms the Way We Create and Communicate*. San Francisco: HarperSanFrancisco.

Jolly, Penny Howell. 1983. "Antonello da Messina's *Saint Jerome in His Study*: An Iconographic Analysis." *Art Bulletin* 65 (2): 238–53.

Joyce, Elizabeth. 2003. "Sutured Fragments: Shelley Jackson's *Patchwork Girl* in Piecework." In *Close Reading New Media: Analyzing Electronic Literature*, edited by Jan Van Looy and Jan Baetens, 39–52. Leuven, Belgium: Leuven University Press.

Joyce, Michael. 1987. *Afternoon, a Story*. 1st ed. (Mac OS). Privately circulated digital document.

———. 1988. "Siren Shapes: Exploratory and Constructive Hypertexts." *Academic Computing* 3 (4): 10–14, 37–42.

———. 1989. *Afternoon, a Story*. 2nd ed. (Mac OS). Privately circulated digital document.

———. 1990. *Afternoon, a Story*. 3rd ed. (Mac OS). Cambridge, Mass.: Eastgate Systems, Inc.

———. 1991. "Selfish Interaction or Subversive Texts and the Multiple Novel." In *Hypertext/Hypermedia Handbook*, edited by Emily Berk and Joseph Devlin, 79–92. New York: McGraw-Hill/Intertext.

———. 1992a. *Afternoon, a Story*. 4th ed. (Windows). Cambridge, Mass.: Eastgate Systems, Inc.

———. 1992b. *Afternoon, a Story*. 5th ed. (Mac OS). Cambridge, Mass.: Eastgate Systems, Inc.

———. 1993a. *Pomeriggio [Afternoon]* (Mac OS). Translation of Joyce 1992b by Alearda Pandolfi, Filippo Soresi, and Walter Vannini. Bologne and Rome: Elettrolibri.

———. 1993b. "La rivalsa della narrativa sulla televisione." *Il Sole 24 Ore* (Milan), July 18.

———. 1995. *Of Two Minds: Hypertext Pedagogy and Poetics*. Ann Arbor: University of Michigan Press.

———. 1996a. "(Re)placing the Author: 'A Book in the Ruins.'" In *The Future of the Book*, edited by Geoffrey Nunberg, 273–93. Berkeley: University of California Press.

———. 1996b. *Twelve Blue*. Cambridge, Mass.: Eastgate Systems, Inc. Available at: http://www.eastgate.com/TwelveBlue/Welcome.html.

————. 1996c. *Twilight, a Symphony.* 1st ed. (Mac OS). Cambridge, Mass.: Eastgate Systems, Inc.

————. 1998a. "From *Afternoon, a Story.*" In Geyh, Leebron, and Levy 1998, 576–80.

————. 1998b. *Afternoon, a Story.* JavaScript port of Joyce 1992b by Justin Edelson. New York: W. W. Norton. Formerly available at: http://www.wwnorton.com/college/english/pmaf/hypertext/aft/index.html.

————. 1998c. "New Stories for New Readers: Contour, Coherence and Constructive Hypertext." In *Page to Screen: Taking Literacy into the Electronic Era,* edited by Ilana Snyder, 163–82. New York: Routledge.

————. 2000. *Othermindedness: The Emergence of Network Culture.* Ann Arbor: University of Michigan Press.

————. 2001a. *Afternoon, a Story.* 5th ed. (Mac OS and Windows). Cambridge, Mass.: Eastgate Systems, Inc.

————. 2001b. *Nachmittags, eine Geschichte [Afternoon, a Story]* (Mac OS). Translation of Joyce 1992b by Doris Köhler and Rolf D. Krause. Cambridge, Mass.: Eastgate Systems, Inc.

————. 2007. *Afternoon, a Story.* 6th ed. (Mac OS and Windows). Cambridge, Mass.: Eastgate Systems, Inc.

Jung, Carl G., and M.-L. Von Franz, eds. 1968. *Man and His Symbols.* New York: Random House.

Jussim, Estelle, Gus Hayafas, and Harold E. Edgerton. 1987. *Stopping Time: The Photographs of Harold Edgerton.* New York: Harry N. Abrams.

Kahn, Paul, and James M. Nyce. 1991. "The Idea of a Machine: The Later Memex Essays." In Nyce and Kahn 1991a, 113–44.

Kendall, Robert. 1998. "The Hypertexts of Yesteryear." *SIGLINK Newsletter* 7 (1–2): 12–15.

Kirschenbaum, Matthew. 1997–98. "Machine Visions: Towards a Poetics of Artificial Intelligence." *Electronic Book Review* 6. Available at: http://www.altx.com/EBR/EBR6.

————. 2002. "Editing the Interface: Textual Studies and First Generation Electronic Objects." In *TEXT 14,* edited by W. Speed Hill, Edward M. Burns, and Edward Shillingsburg, 15–51. Ann Arbor: University of Michigan Press.

————. 2008. *Mechanisms: New Media and the Forensic Imagination.* Cambridge, Mass.: MIT Press.

Kittler, Friedrich A. 1997. *Literature, Media, Information Systems: Essays.* Edited by John Johnston. Amsterdam: G+B Arts International.

————. 1999. *Gramophone, Film, Typewriter.* Translated by Geoffrey Winthrop-Young and Michael Wutz. Stanford, Calif.: Stanford University Press.

Klima, Stefan. 1998. *Artists Books: A Critical Survey of the Literature.* New York: Granary Books.

Knaster, Barbara. 1994. *Presenting Magic Cap™: A Guide to General Magic's Revolutionary Communicator Software*. Reading, Mass.: Addison-Wesley.

Kolb, David. 1997. "Discourse across Links." In *Philosophical Perspectives on Computer-Mediated Communication*, edited by Charles Ess, 15–26. Albany: State University of New York Press.

Kopelson, Kevin. 2004. *Neatness Counts: Essays on the Writer's Desk*. Minneapolis: University of Minnesota Press.

Koyaanisqatsi: Life out of Balance. 1982. Directed by Godfrey Reggio. Music by Philip Glass. 35 mm, 87 min. New Cinema / Island Alive.

Kripke, Saul. 1980. *Naming and Necessity*. Cambridge, Mass.: Harvard University Press.

Labbie, Erin Felicia. 2006. "The Quadrangle, the Hard Sciences, and Nonclassical Thinking." In *Lacan's Medievalism*, 146–89. Minneapolis: University of Minnesota Press.

Lacan, Jacques. 1957. "L'Instance de la lettre dans l'inconscient ou la raison depuis Freud." In *La Psychanalyse 3 (La Psychanalyse et sciences de l'homme)*, edited by Juliette Favez-Boutonier, 47–81. Paris: Presses Universitaires de France.

———. 1961–62. "Le Séminaire IX: Identification." Unedited transcripts of Nov. 15, 1961–June 27, 1962 ("Version rue CB"). Available at: http://new .lutecium.org.

———. 1966. *Écrits*. Paris: Éditions du Seuil.

———. 1973. *Le Séminaire XI: Les Quatres Concepts fondamentaux de la psychanalyse*. Edited by Jacques-Alain Miller. Paris: Éditions du Seuil.

———. 1975. *Le Séminaire I: Les Écrits techniques de Freud*. Edited by Jacques-Alain Miller. Paris: Éditions du Seuil.

———. 1978. *Le Séminaire II: Le Moi dans la théorie de Freud et dans la technique de la psychanalyse*. Edited by Jacques-Alain Miller. Paris: Éditions du Seuil.

———. 1981. *Le Séminaire III: Les Psychoses*. Edited by Jacques-Alain Miller. Paris: Éditions du Seuil.

———. 1991a. *Le Séminaire VIII: Le Transfer*. Edited by Jacques-Alain Miller. Paris: Éditions du Seuil.

———. 1991b. *Le Séminaire XVII: L'Envers de la psychanalyse*. Edited by Jacques-Alain Miller. Paris: Éditions du Seuil.

———. 1994. *Le Séminaire IV: La Relation d'objet*. Edited by Jacques-Alain Miller. Paris: Éditions du Seuil.

———. 1998. *Le Séminaire V: Les Formations de l'inconscient*. Edited by Jacques-Alain Miller. Paris: Éditions du Seuil.

———. 2002. *789 Néologismes de Jacques Lacan*. Edited by Yan Pélissier, Marcel Bénabou, Dominique de Liège, and Laurent Cornaz. Paris: Épel.

———. 2006. *Écrits*. Translated by Bruce Fink. New York: W. W. Norton.

Landow, George P. 1992. *Hypertext: The Convergence of Contemporary*

Critical Theory and Technology. Baltimore, Md.: Johns Hopkins University Press.

———. 1997. *Hypertext 2.0: The Convergence of Contemporary Critical Theory and Technology*. Baltimore, Md.: Johns Hopkins University Press.

———. 2006. *Hypertext 3.0: Critical Theory and New Media in an Era of Globalization*. Baltimore, Md.: Johns Hopkins University Press.

Lapacherie, Jean-Gérard. 1982. "Écriture et lecture du calligramme." *Poétique* 50:194–202.

———. 1984. "De la grammatextualité." *Poétique* 59:283–94.

———. 1990. "Poly-, hétéro, exo-graphies." *Poétique* 84:395–410.

———. 1994. "Typographic Characters: Tension between Text and Drawing." Translated by Anna Lehmann. *Yale French Studies* 84:63–77.

Larsen, Deena. 1998. *Samplers*. Cambridge, Mass.: Eastgate Systems, Inc.

Laurel, Brenda, ed. 1990. *The Art of Human-Computer Interface Design*. Reading, Mass.: Addison-Wesley.

Lebrave, Jean-Louis. 1994. "Hypertextes, mémoires, écriture." *Génésis* 5:9–24.

Leclaire, Serge. 1968. *Psychanalyser: Un Essai sur l'ordre de l'inconscient et la pratique de la lettre*. Paris: Éditions du Seuil.

———. 1971. *Démasquer le réel*. Paris: Éditions du Seuil.

Leung, Y.K., and M.D. Apperley. 1994. "A Review and Taxonomy of Distortion-Oriented Presentation Techniques." *ACM Transactions on Computer-Human Interaction* 1 (2): 126–60.

Levin, Kim. 1975. *Lucas Samaras*. New York: Harry N. Abrams.

Libeskind, Daniel. 1991. *Countersign*. London: Academy Editions.

Liestøl, Gunnar, Andrew Morrison, and Terje Rasmussen, eds. 2003. *Digital Media Revisited: Theoretical and Conceptual Innovation in Digital Domains*. Cambridge, Mass.: MIT Press.

Liu, Alan. 2004. *The Laws of Cool: Knowledge Work and the Culture of Information*. Chicago: University of Chicago Press.

Liu, Alan, David G. Durand, Nick Montfort, Merrilee Proffitt, Liam R.E. Quin, Jean-Hugues Réty, and Noah Wardrip-Fruin. 2005. "Born-Again Bits: A Framework for Migrating Electronic Literature (v. 1.1)." College Park, Md.: Electronic Literature Organization. Available at: http://eliterature.org/pad/bab.html.

Luria, A.R. 1987. *The Mind of a Mnemonist: A Little Book about a Vast Memory*. Translated by Lynn Solotaroff. Cambridge, Mass.: Harvard University Press.

"A Machine That Thinks." 1945. *Time* 47 (4) (July 23).

Maeda, John. 1995. *The Reactive Square*. Tokyo: Digitalogue.

———. 2000. *Maeda @ Media*. New York: Rizzoli.

———. 2005. "Reactive Books, 1994–1999." Available at: http://www.maedastudio.com/2004/rbooks2k/index.php?category=all&next=2005/timestable&prev=2002/technology&this=reactive_books.

Mallarmé, Stéphane. 1945. *Œuvres complètes.* Paris: Gallimard.

Manguel, Alberto. 2004. "Turning the Page." In Stoicheff and Taylor 2004a, 27–36.

Mannoni, Octave. 1969. "Je sais bien, mais quand même . . ." In *Clefs pour l'imaginaire, ou l'autre scène,* 9–33. Paris: Éditions du Seuil.

Manoff, Marlene. 2006. "The Materiality of Digital Collections: Theoretical and Historical Perspectives." *Portal: Libraries and the Academy* 6 (3): 311–25.

Manovich, Lev. 2001. *The Language of New Media.* Cambridge, Mass.: MIT Press.

———. 2005. *Soft Cinema: Navigating the Database.* Cambridge, Mass.: MIT Press.

Marion, Philippe. 1993. *Traces en cases: Travail graphique, figuration narrative et participation du lecteur. Essai sur la bande dessinée.* 2 vols. Louvain-la-Neuve, Belgium: Academia.

Marshall, Catherine C., and Gene Golovchinsky. 2004. "Saving Private Hypertext: Requirements and Pragmatic Dimensions for Preservation." In *Hypertext '04,* 130–38. Santa Cruz, Calif.: Association for Computing Machinery.

Mathews, Harry, and Alastair Brotchie, eds. 1998. *Oulipo Compendium.* London: Atlas Press.

Mathieu, Marc-Antoine. 2004. *Julius Corentin Acquefacques, prisonnier des rêves.* Vols. 1–5. Paris: Éditions Delcourt.

McCaffery, Steve. 2002. "Corrosive Poetics: The Relief Composition of Ronald Johnson's *Radi Os.*" *Pretexts* 11 (2): 121–33.

McCay, Winsor. 2005 [1905–1910]. *Little Nemo in Slumberland, So Many Splendid Sundays, 1905–1910.* Edited by Peter Maresca. Palo Alto, Calif.: Sunday Press Books.

McDaid, John. 1993. *Uncle Buddy's Phantom Funhouse.* Cambridge, Mass.: Eastgate Systems, Inc.

McGann, Jerome. 1991. *The Textual Condition.* Princeton, N.J.: Princeton University Press.

———. 1993. *Black Riders: The Visible Language of Modernism.* Princeton, N.J.: Princeton University Press.

———. 2001. *Radiant Textuality: Literature after the World Wide Web.* New York: Palgrave.

McLaughlin, Tim. 1995. *Notes toward Absolute Zero.* 1st ed. (Mac OS). Cambridge, Mass.: Eastgate Systems, Inc.

Mead, Pamela, and Chris Pacione. 1996. "Time and Space." *Interactions* 3 (2): 69–77.

"Mechanical Brains." 1944. *Life* 16 (4) (January 24): 66–67, 69–70, 72. Illustrated by Alfred D. Crimi.

Memmott, Talan. 2000. *Lexia to Perplexia.* Available at: http://trace.ntu.ac.uk/newmedia/lexia.

Microsoft Corporation. 1995. *The Windows® Interface Guidelines for Software Design*. Redmond, Wash.: Microsoft Press.

———. 2005. "Windows User Interface (Windows XP)." Available at: http://msdn.microsoft.com/en-us/library/default.aspx.

———. 2008. "Windows User Interface (Windows Vista)." Available at: http://msdn.microsoft.com/en-us/library/default.aspx.

Miles, Adrian. 2001. "Hypertext Structure as the Event of Connection." In *Hypertext 2001*, 61–68. Århus, Denmark: Association for Computing Machinery.

Milner, John. 1996. *Kazimir Malevich and the Art of Geometry*. New Haven, Conn.: Yale University Press.

Mindell, David A. 2002. *Between Human and Machine: Feedback, Control, and Computing before Cybernetics*. Baltimore, Md.: Johns Hopkins University Press.

Mœglin-Delcroix, Anne. 1997. *Esthétique du livre artiste (1960/1980)*. Paris: Jean-Michel Place / Bibliothèque Nationale de France.

Montfort, Nick. 2000. *Ad Verbum*. Available at: http://www.nickm.com/if/adverbum_web.html.

———. 2003. *Twisty Little Passages: An Approach to Interactive Fiction*. Cambridge, Mass.: MIT Press.

Montfort, Nick, and Ian Bogost. 2008. *Video Computer System: The Atari 2600 Platform*. Cambridge, Mass.: MIT Press.

Montfort, Nick, and Noah Wardrip-Fruin. 2004. "Acid-Free Bits (v. 1.0)." College Park, Md.: Electronic Literature Organization. Available at: http://eliterature.org/pad/afb.html.

Moulthrop, Stuart. 1989. "Hypertext and 'the Hyperreal.'" In *Hypertext '89*, 259–67. Pittsburgh, Pa.: Association for Computing Machinery.

———. 1991a. "Toward a Paradigm for Reading Hypertexts: Making Nothing Happen in Hypermedia Fiction." In *Hypertext / Hypermedia Handbook*, edited by Emily Berk and Joseph Devlin, 165–78. New York: McGraw-Hill/Intertext.

———. 1991b. *Victory Garden*. 1st ed. (Mac OS). Cambridge, Mass.: Eastgate Systems, Inc.

Mullet, Kevin, and Darrell Sano. 1995. *Designing Visual Interfaces: Communication-Oriented Techniques*. Mountain View, Calif.: Sun Microsystems.

Murray, Janet H. 1997. *Hamlet on the Holodeck: The Future of Narrative in Cyberspace*. Cambridge, Mass.: MIT Press.

Myers, Brad A. 1998. "A Brief History of Human-Computer Interaction Technology." *Interactions* 5 (2): 44–54.

Nancy, Jean-Luc, and Philippe Lacoue-Labarthe. 1973. *Le Titre de la lettre (Une lecture de Lacan)*. Paris: Éditions Galilée.

Needham, Joseph, and Ling Wang. 1965. *Science and Civilization in China, Vol. 4: Physics and Physical Technology. Part II: Mechanical Engineering*. Cambridge, Eng.: Cambridge University Press.

Nelson, Theodor Holm. 1965. "A File Structure for the Complex, the Changing and the Indeterminate." *Association for Computing Machinery, 20th
National Conference*, vol. P-65:84–100. Cleveland, Ohio: ACM Publications.

———. 1974. *Computer Lib / Dream Machines*. South Bend, Ind.: The Dis-
tributors.

———. 1975. "Data Realms and Magic Windows." *Meeting of the Association
of Computer Programmers and Analysts (ACPA)*, 23–26.

———. 1987a. "All for One and One for All." In *Hypertext '87*, v–vii. Chapel
Hill, N.C.: Association for Computing Machinery.

———. 1987b. *Literary Machines 87.1*. Edinburgh: OWL International.

———. 1990a. *Literary Machines 90.1*. Sausalito, Calif.: Mindful Press.

———. 1990b. "The Right Way to Think about Software Design." In Laurel
1990, 235–43.

———. 1991. "As We Will Think." In Nyce and Kahn 1991a, 245–60.

———. 1992. "Opening Hypertext: A Memoir." In *Literacy Online: The Promise (and Peril) of Reading and Writing with Computers*, edited by Myron C.
Tuman, 43–57. Pittsburgh, Pa.: University of Pittsburgh Press.

———. 1995. "Xanks and No, Xanks." Available at: http://www.wired.com/
wired/archive/3.09/rants.html.

———. 1997. *The Future of Information: Ideas, Connections, and the Gods
of Electronic Literature*. Tokyo: ASCII Corporation. Available at: http://
xanadu.com.au/ted/INFUTscans/INFUTscans.html.

———. 1998. "What's on My Mind." International Conference on Wearable
Computing (ICWC). Fairfax, Va. Available at: http://www.xanadu.com.au/
ted/zigzag/xybrap.html.

———. 1999a. "Welcome to Zigzag®." Available at: http://www.xanadu.com/
zigzag/tutorial/ZZwelcome.html.

———. 1999b. "Xanalogical Structure, Needed Now More than Ever: Parallel
Documents, Deep Links to Content, Deep Versioning, and Deep Re-Use."
ACM Computing Surveys 31.4es.

———. 2002. "Xanadu® Technologies—An Introduction." Available at: http://
xanadu.com/tech.

Newell, Peter. 2001a [1908]. *The Hole Book*. Boston: Tuttle Publishing.

———. 2001b [1912]. *The Rocket Book*. Boston: Tuttle Publishing.

NeXT Computer, Inc. 1992. *NeXTSTEP User Interface Guidelines, Release 3*.
Reading, Mass.: Addison-Wesley.

Nielsen, Jakob. 1995. *Multimedia and Hypertext: The Internet and Beyond*.
Boston: AP Professional.

Norman, Donald. 1993. *Things That Make Us Smart: Defending Human Attributes in the Age of the Machine*. Reading, Mass.: Addison-Wesley.

———. 1994. *Defending Human Attributes in the Age of the Machine*. Santa
Monica, Calif.: The Voyager Company.

———. 1998. *The Invisible Computer: Why Good Products Can Fail, the Per-*

sonal Computer Is So Complex, and Information Appliances Are the Solution. Cambridge, Mass.: MIT Press.

Nufer, Doug. 2004 [2002]. *Never Again.* New York: Four Walls Eight Windows.

Nyce, James M., and Paul Kahn, eds. 1991a. *From Memex to Hypertext: Vannevar Bush and the Mind's Machine.* New York: Academic Press.

———. 1991b. "A Machine for the Mind: Vannevar Bush's Memex." In Nyce and Kahn 1991a, 39–66.

Oinas-Kukkonen, Henry. 2007. "From Bush to Engelbart: 'Slowly, Some Little Bells Were Ringing.'" *IEEE Annals of the History of Computing* 29 (2): 31–39.

Olson, Mary C. 2003. *Fair and Varied Forms: Visual Textuality in Medieval Illuminated Manuscripts.* New York: Routledge.

Oren, Tim. 1991. "Memex: Getting Back on the Trail." In Nyce and Kahn 1991a, 319–38.

Owens, Larry. 1991. "Vannevar Bush and the Differential Analyzer: The Text and Context of an Early Computer." In Nyce and Kahn 1991a, 3–38.

Paraye, Marc. 1998. "*La Disparition*: Ah, le livre sans e! *El Secuestro*: Euh . . . un livre sans a?" *Formules* 2.

Perec, Georges. 1974. *Espèces d'espaces.* Paris: Éditions Galilée.

———. 1985. *Penser/Classer.* Edited by Maurice Olender. Paris: Hachette.

———. 1986 [1969]. *La Disparition: Roman.* Paris: Denoël.

———. 1989. *L'Infra-ordinaire.* Paris: Éditions du Seuil.

———. 1994. *A Void.* Translated by Gilbert Adair. New York: HarperCollins.

———. 1997. *El Secuestro.* Translated by Marisol Arbués, Mercè Burrel, Marc Parayre, Hermes Salceda, and Regina Vega. Barcelona, Spain: Anagrama.

Petroski, Henry. 1999. *The Book on the Bookshelf.* New York: Alfred A. Knopf.

Petrova, Evgeniya, Charlotte Douglas, Irina Vakar, Evgeny Kovtun, Dmitry Sarabianov, Irina Karasik, and Kazimir Malevich. 1991. *Malevich: Artist and Theoretician.* Translated by Sharon McKee. Moscow: Avant-Garde.

Phillips, Tom. 2005. *A Humument: A Treated Victorian Novel.* 4th ed. London: Thames and Hudson.

Plotnitsky, Arkady. 2002. "Versions of the Irrational: The Epistemology of Complex Numbers and Jacques Lacan's Quasi-Mathematics." In *The Knowable and the Unknowable: Modern Science, Nonclassical Thought, and the "Two Cultures,"* 109–56, 261–73. Ann Arbor: University of Michigan Press.

Poe, Edgar Allan. 2003 [1846]. "The Philosophy of Composition." In *The Fall of the House of Usher and Other Writings,* edited by David Galloway, 430–42. New York: Penguin Books.

Postman, Neil. 1986. *Amusing Ourselves to Death.* New York: Penguin Books.

Proust, Marcel. 1999. *À la recherche du temps perdu.* Edited by Jean-Yves Tadié. Paris: Gallimard.

Punday, Daniel. 2004. "Involvement, Interruption, and Inevitability: Melancholy as an Aesthetic Principle in Game Narratives." *SubStance* 33 (3): 80–107.

Queneau, Raymond. 1950. "Délire typographique." In *Bâtons, chiffres et lettres*, 191–96. Paris: Gallimard.

———. 1961. *Cent mille milliards de poèmes*. Book design by Massin. Paris: Gallimard.

Rabelais, François. 1994. *Les Cinq livres: Gargantua, Pantagruel, Le Tiers livre, Le Quart livre, Le Cinqième livre*. Edited by Jean Céard, Gérard Defaux, and Michel Simonin. Paris: Librairie Générale Française.

Ramelli, Agostino. 1588. *Le diverse et artificiose machine del Capitano Agostino Ramelli*. Paris: In case del Autore. Available at: http://cnum.cnam.fr/SYN/fDY3.html.

———. 1976. *The Various and Ingenious Machines of Agostino Ramelli*. Translated by Martha Teach Gnudi. Edited by Martha Teach Gnudi and Eugene S. Ferguson. Baltimore, Md.: Johns Hopkins University Press.

Raskin, Jef. 2000. *The Humane Interface: New Directions for Designing Interactive Systems*. Reading, Mass.: Addison-Wesley.

Rasula, Jed, and Steve McCaffery, eds. 1998. *Imagining Language: An Anthology*. Cambridge, Mass.: MIT Press.

Rau, Anja. 1999. "Towards the Recognition of the Shell as an Integral Part of the Digital Text." In *Hypertext '99*, 119–20. Darmstadt, Germany: Association for Computing Machinery.

"Ray of Light." 1998. Directed by Jonas Åkerlund. Music and lyrics by Dave Curtiss, Christine Leach, Madonna, Clive Muldoon, and William Orbit. Music video, 5:03 min. Los Angeles: Oil Factory, Inc.

Reggiani, Christelle. 2004. "Des livres d'images: Statuts textuels de l'image roussellienne." In *Raymond Roussel 2*, edited by Anne-Marie Amiot and Christelle Reggiani, 23–46. Paris: Lettres modernes Minard.

Ricardo, Francisco J. 1998. "Stalking the Paratext: Speculations on Hypertext Links as a Second Order Text." In *Hypertext '98*, 142–51. Pittsburgh, Pa.: Association for Computing Machinery.

Rice, Eugene F., Jr. 1985. *Saint Jerome in the Renaissance*. Baltimore, Md.: Johns Hopkins University Press.

Riffaterre, Michael. 1978. *Semiotics of Poetry*. Bloomington: Indiana University Press.

Riskin, Jessica. 2003. "The Defecating Duck, or, the Ambiguous Origins of Artificial Life." *Critical Inquiry* 29 (4): 599–633.

Rosenberg, Jim. 1992. "Intergrams." *Eastgate Quarterly Review of Hypertext* 1 (1).

———. 1994. "Navigating Nowhere / Hypertext Infrawhere." *SIGLINK Newsletter* 3 (3): 16–19.

———. 1996. "The Structure of Hypertext Activity." In *Hypertext 1996*, 22–30. Bethesda, Md.: Association for Computing Machinery.

———. 2000. "A Prosody of Space/Non-Linear Time." *Postmodern Culture* 10 (3).

———. 2001. "And *And*: Conjunctive Hypertext and the Structure Acteme Juncture." In *Hypertext 2001*, 51–60. Århus, Denmark: Association for Computing Machinery.

Rossi, Paolo. 2000. *Logic and the Art of Memory: The Quest for a Universal Language*. Translated by Stephen Clucas. Chicago: University of Chicago Press.

Rothenberg, Jeff. 1999. *Avoiding Technological Quicksand: Finding a Viable Foundation for Digital Preservation (CLIR Report 77)*. Washington, D.C.: Council on Library and Information Resources.

Rothenberg, Jeff, and Tora K. Bikson. 1999. *Carrying Authentic, Understandable and Usable Digital Records through Time*. Santa Monica, Calif.: RAND Corporation.

Rothenberg, Jerome, and Steven Clay. 2000. *A Book of the Book: Some Works & Projections about the Book & Writing*. New York: Granary Press.

Roussel, Raymond. 1979 [1935]. *Comment j'ai écrit certains de mes livres*. Paris: Gallimard.

———. 1985 [1932]. *Nouvelles Impressions d'Afrique*. Paris: J.-J. Pauvert.

———. 2004a [1932]. *New Impressions of Africa*. Edited and translated by Ian Monk. London: Atlas Press.

———. 2004b [1932]. *Nouvelles Impressions d'Afrique. Mise en couleurs et postface de Jacques Sivan*. Paris: Éditions Al Dante / Éditions Léo Scheer.

Rowley, Barbara. 1995. *At Home with Microsoft Bob™: Ideas and Activities for Getting the Most from Your Home PC*. Redmond, Wash.: Microsoft Press.

Rushdie, Salman. 2000. *The Satanic Verses*. New York: Picador USA.

Ryan, Marie-Laure. 2001a. "Beyond Myth and Metaphor: The Case of Narrative in Digital Media." *Game Studies* 1 (1). Available at: http://www.gamestudies.org/0101/ryan.

———. 2001b. *Narrative as Virtual Reality: Immersion and Interactivity in Literature and Electronic Media*. Baltimore, Md.: Johns Hopkins University Press.

———. 2004. "Multivariant Narratives." In *A Companion to Digital Humanities*, edited by Susan Schreibman, Ray Siemens, and John Unsworth, 415–30. Malden, Mass.: Blackwell.

———. 2005. "Narrative and the Split Condition of Digital Textuality." In *Videogame, Player, Text*, edited by Barry Atkins and Tanya Krzywinska. Manchester, Eng.: Manchester University Press.

———. 2006. *Avatars of Story*. Minneapolis: University of Minnesota Press.

Saporta, Marc. 1962. *Composition no. 1, roman*. Paris: Éditions du Seuil.

———. 1963. *Composition No. 1: A Novel*. Translated by Richard Howard. New York: Simon and Schuster.

Saussure, Ferdinand de. 1982 [1916]. *Cours de linguistique générale*. Edited by

Charles Bally, Albert Sechehaye, Albert Riedlinger, and Tullio de Mauro. Paris: Payot.

Schaff, Philip, ed. 1956. *A Select Library of the Nicene and Post-Nicene Fathers of the Christian Church*. First series. Vol. 1: *The Confessions and Letters of St. Augustin, with a Sketch of His Life and Work*. Grand Rapids, Mich.: Wm. B. Eerdmans.

Schilit, Bill N., Morgan N. Price, Gene Golovchinsky, Kei Tanaka, and Catherine C. Marshall. 1999. "As We May Read: The Reading Appliance Revolution." *IEEE Computer* 32 (1): 65–73.

Schwenger, Peter. 1994. "*Agrippa*, or, The Apocalyptic Book." In *Flame Wars: The Discourse of Cyberculture*, edited by Mark Dery, 61–70. Durham, N.C.: Duke University Press.

Selinger, Eric. 1992. "'I Composed the Holes': Reading Ronald Johnson's *Radi Os*." *Contemporary Literature* 33 (1): 46–73.

Sherman, William H. 2005. "Toward a History of the Manicule." In *Owners, Annotators and the Signs of Reading,* edited by Robin Myers, Michael Harris, and Giles Mandelbrote, 19–48. New Castle, Del., and London: Oak Knoll Press and The British Library.

Shklovsky, Victor. 1965. "Sterne's *Tristram Shandy*: Stylistic Commentary." In *Russian Formalist Criticism: Four Essays*, edited and translated by L.T. Lemon and M.J. Reis. Lincoln: University of Nebraska Press.

Shneiderman, Ben. 1987 [1983]. "Direct Manipulation: A Step beyond Programming Languages." In *Readings in Human-Computer Interaction: A Multidisciplinary Approach*, edited by Ronald M. Baecker and William A.S. Buxton, 461–67. San Francisco: Morgan Kaufman Publishers.

Sieckenius de Souza, Clarisse. 2005. *The Semiotic Engineering of Human-Computer Interaction*. Cambridge, Mass.: MIT Press.

Siertsema, Bertha. 1965. *A Study of Glossematics: Critical Survey of Its Fundamental Concepts*. The Hague: Martinus Nijhoff.

Smith, David Canfield, Charles Irby, Ralph Kimball, and Bill Verplank. 1982. "Designing the Star User Interface." *Byte* 7 (4): 242–82.

Smith, Keith A. 2000. *Two Hundred Books by Keith Smith: An Anecdotal Bibliography (Book 200)*. Rochester, N.Y.: Keith Smith Books.

———. 2003. *Structure of the Visual Book (Book 95)*. 4th ed. Rochester, N.Y.: Keith Smith Books.

———. 2004. *Text in the Book Format (Book 120)*. 3rd ed. Rochester, N.Y.: Keith Smith Books.

Sokal, Alan D., and Jean Bricmont. 1998. *Fashionable Nonsense: Postmodern Intellectuals' Abuse of Science*. New York: Picador USA.

Spence, Jonathan D. 1994. *The Memory Palace of Matteo Ricci*. New York: Viking.

Stallabrass, Julian. 1995. "Empowering Technology: The Exploration of Cyberspace." *New Left Review* 211:3–32.

Standage, Tom. 2002. *The Turk: The Life and Times of the Famous Eighteenth-Century Chess-Playing Machine.* New York: Walker & Co.

Stanitzek, Georg. 2005. "Texts and Paratexts in Media." Translated by Ellen Klein. *Critical Inquiry* 32 (1): 27–42.

Starobinski, Jean. 1971. *Les Mots sous les mots: Les Anagrammes de Ferdinand de Saussure.* Paris: Gallimard.

Stefans, Brian-Kim. 2003. *Fashionable Noise: On Digital Poetics.* Berkeley, Calif.: Atelos Press.

Stephenson, Neal. 1993. *Snow Crash.* New York: Bantam Books.

———. 1999. *In the Beginning Was the Command Line.* New York: Avon Books.

Sterne, Laurence. 1997 [1759–67]. *The Life and Opinions of Tristram Shandy, Gentleman.* Edited by Melvyn New and Joan New. New York: Penguin.

Stoicheff, Peter, and Andrew Taylor, eds. 2004a. *The Future of the Page.* Toronto: University of Toronto Press.

———. 2004b. "Architectures, Ideologies, and Materials of the Page." In Stoicheff and Taylor 2004a, 3–26.

Stollar, Catherine. 2006. "When Not All Papers Are Paper: A Case Study in Digital Archivy." *Provenance* 24:23–35.

Stollar, Catherine, and Thomas Kiehne. 2006. "Guarding the Guards: Archiving the Electronic Records of Hypertext Author Michael Joyce." Annual conference of the Society of American Archivists.

Storkerson, Peter, and Janine Wong. 1997. "Hypertext and the Art of Memory." *Visible Language* 31 (2): 126–57.

Sutherland, Ivan E. 1988. "Sketchpad: A Man-Machine Graphical Communication System." In *Twenty-Five Years of Electronic Design Automation,* 507–24. New York: Association for Computing Machinery.

Swales, Peter J. 1982. "Freud, Minna Bernays, and the Conquest of Rome." *New American Review* 1 (2/3): 1–23.

———. 2003. "Freud, Death and Sexual Pleasures: On the Psychical Mechanism of Dr. Sigm. Freud." *Arc de Cercle* 1 (1): 5–74.

Swift, Jonathan. 1957–69 [1726, 1735]. *Gulliver's Travels. The Prose Works of Jonathan Swift, Vol. 11.* Edited by Herbert Davis. Oxford: Blackwell.

Tabbi, Joseph. 2002. *Cognitive Fictions.* Minneapolis: University of Minnesota Press.

———. 2007. "Toward a Semantic Literary Web: Setting a Direction for the Electronic Literature Organization's Directory." College Park, Md.: Electronic Literature Organization. Available at: http://eliterature.org/pad/slw.html.

Thompson, Bradbury. 1988. *The Art of Graphic Design, with Contributions by Noteworthy Designers, Critics, and Art Historians.* New Haven, Conn.: Yale University Press.

Torjesen, Karen Jo. 1998. "The Early Christian *Orans*: An Artistic Representation of Women's Liturgical Prayer and Prophecy." In *Women Preachers and Prophets through Two Millennia of Christianity*, edited by Beverly Mayne Kienzle and Pamela J. Walker, 42–56. Berkeley: University of California Press.

Tory, Geofroy. 2003 [1529]. *Champ fleury*. Edited by Kay Amert. Translated by George B. Ives. Oakland, Calif.: Octavo.

Transcriptions Project. 2005. "The *Agrippa* Files." Available at: http://agrippa .english.ucsb.edu.

Trigg, Randall H. 1991. "From Trailblazing to Guided Tours: The Legacy of Vannevar Bush's Vision of Hypertext Use." In Nyce and Kahn 1991a, 353–67.

Tschichold, Jan. 1975. *Ausgewählte Aufsätze über Fragen der Gestalt des Buches und der Typographie*. Basel, Switzerland: Birkhäuser Verlag.

———. 1991. *The Form of the Book: Essays on the Morality of Good Design*. Translated by Hajo Hadeler. Vancouver, B.C.: Hartley & Marks.

Tupitsyn, Margarita, and Victor Tupitsyn. 2002. *Malevich and Film*. New Haven, Conn.: Yale University Press and Funação Centro Cultural de Belém.

Uldall, Hans Jørgen. 1967. *Outline of Glossematics: A Study in the Methodology of the Humanities with Special Reference to Linguistics*. Copenhagen, Denmark: Nordisk Sprog- og Kulturforlag.

Ulmer, Gregory L. 1989. *Teletheory: Grammatology in the Age of Video*. New York: Routledge.

———. 1991. "Grammatology Hypermedia." *Postmodern Culture* 1 (2). Available at: http://muse.jhu.edu/journals/postmodern_culture/v001/1.2ulmer .html.

———. 1997. "A Response to *Twelve Blue* by Michael Joyce." *Postmodern Culture* 8 (1). Available at: http://muse.jhu.edu/journals/postmodern_ culture/v008/8.1ulmer.html.

Valéry, Paul. 1957. *Œuvres*. Edited by Jean Hytier. 2 vols. Paris: Éditions Gallimard.

Valliér, Dora. 1975. "Malevitch et le modèle linguistique en peinture." *Critique* 334:284–96.

———. 1979. "Le Blanc et le noir dans l'art abstrait." In *A Semiotic Landscape / Panorama sémiotique*, edited by Seymour Chatman, Umberto Eco, and Jean-Marie Klinkenberg, 825–29. The Hague and New York: Mouton.

Van Dam, Andries. 1997. "Post-WIMP User Interfaces." *Communications of the ACM* 40 (2): 63–67.

Van Haute, Philippe. 2003. *Against Adaptation: Lacan's "Subversion" of the Subject*. Translated by Paul Crowe and Miranda Vankerk. New York: The Other Press.

Veith, Richard H. 2006. "Memex at 60: Internet or iPod?" *Journal of the American Society for Information Science and Technology* 57 (9): 1233–42.

Verhaeghe, Paul. 2002. "Causality in Science and Psychoanalysis." In Glynos and Stavrakakis 2002, 119–46.

Verne, Jules. 1996. *Paris au XXe siècle.* Paris: LGF.

Virilio, Paul. 1981. "La Troisième fenêtre: Entretien avec Paul Virilio." *Cahiers du Cinéma* 322:35–40.

———. 1984. *Guerre et cinéma I. Logistique de la perception.* Paris: Cahiers du Cinéma.

Viscomi, Joseph. 1997. "The Evolution of *The Marriage of Heaven and Hell.*" *Huntington Library Quarterly* 58 (3–4): 281–344.

Vita et transitus Santi Hieronymi / La Vie, mors et miracles du glorieux Saint Jherome translates de latin en françoys. France, 1515. Harold B. Lee Library, Brigham Young University, MS 091 H532.

Walker, Jill. 1999. "Piecing Together and Tearing Apart: Finding the Story in *afternoon.*" In *Hypertext '99,* 111–17. Darmstadt, Germany: Association for Computing Machinery.

Walker, John. 1994. "Xanadu" and "Farewell, Xanadu." In *The Autodesk File.* 4th ed. Available at: http://www.fourmilab.ch/autofile.

Wardrip-Fruin, Noah. 2004. "What Hypertext Is." In *Hypertext 2004,* 126–27. Santa Cruz, Calif.: Association for Computing Machinery.

———. 2005. "Playable Media and Textual Instruments." *Dichtung-digital* 1/2005. Available at: http://www.dichtung-digital.org/2005/1/Wardrip-Fruin.htm.

Wardrip-Fruin, Noah, David G. Durand, Brion Moss, and Elaine Froehlich. 2004. *Regime Change.* New York: New Radio and Performing Arts. Available at: http://www.turbulence.org/Works/twotxt/index.htm.

Wardrip-Fruin, Noah, and Pat Harrigan. 2008. "First Person." *Electronic Book Review.* Available at: http://www.electronicbookreview.com/thread/firstperson.

"The War Ends." 1945. *Life* 19 (8) (August 20): 25–31.

Warner, Marina. 1989. "Signs of a Fifth Element." In *The Tree of Life: New Images of an Ancient Symbol,* edited by Roger Malbert, 7–47. London: South Bank Centre.

Weinreich, Harald, Harmut Obendorf, and Winfried Lamersdorf. 2001. "The Look of the Link—Concepts for the User Interface of Extended Hyperlinks." In *Hypertext 2001,* 19–28. Århus, Denmark: Association for Computing Machinery.

Weiss, Christina. 1984. *Seh-Texte: Zur Erweiterung des Textbegriffes in konkreten und nach-konkreten Texten.* Zirndorf, Germany: Verlag für moderne Kunst.

Whalen, Zach. 2008. "The Videogame Text: Typography and Textuality." PhD diss., University of Florida, Gainesville.

White, Glyn. 2005. *Reading the Graphic Surface: The Presence of the Book in Prose Fiction.* Manchester, Eng.: Manchester University Press.

Whitehead, Jim. 2000. "As We Do Write: Hyper-terms for Hypertext." *ACM SIGWEB Newsletter* 9 (2–3): 8–18.

Wichary, Marchin. 2008. "GUIdebook: Graphical User Interface Gallery." Available at: http://www.guidebookgallery.org.

Wickware, Francis Sill. 1945. "Manhattan Project: Its Scientists Have Harnessed Nature's Basic Force." *Life* 19 (8) (August 20): 91–95, 100–111.

Wilson, Ruth. 2002. "Electronic Books for Technical Learning: The 'Look and Feel' of an EBook: Considerations in Interface Design." In *ACM Symposium on Applied Computing*, 530–34. Madrid: Association for Computing Machinery.

Wilson, Ruth, and Monica Landoni. 2003. "Evaluating the Usability of Portable Electronic Books." In *ACM Symposium on Applied Computing*, 564–68. Melbourne, Fla.: Association for Computing Machinery.

Winograd, Terry. 1996. "Microsoft© Bob™." In *Bringing Design to Software*, edited by Terry Winograd, 146–50. Reading, Mass.: Addison-Wesley.

Wolf, Gary. 1995. "The Curse of Xanadu." *Wired* 3 (06): 137–52, 94–202.

Woolf, S.J. 1945. "Dr. Bush Sees a Boundless Future for Science / The OSRD Director Holds That We Have the Knowledge to Build a New and Better World." *New York Times*, September 2, 72, 104.

Yankelovich, Nicole, Bernard J. Haan, Norman K. Meyrowitz, and Steven M. Drucker. 1988. "Intermedia: The Concept and the Construction of a Seamless Information Environment." *IEEE Computer* 21 (1): 81–83, 90–96.

Yates, Francis A. 1974. *The Art of Memory*. Chicago: University of Chicago Press.

Zachary, G. Pascal. 1997. *Endless Frontier: Vannevar Bush, Engineer of the American Century*. New York: Free Press.

Zali, Anne, and Lucile Trunel, eds. 1999. *L'Aventure des écritures. La Page*. Paris: Bibliothèque Nationale de France.

Žižek, Slavoj. 1989. *The Sublime Object of Ideology*. London: Verso.

Žižek, Slavoj, Ulrich Gutmair, and Chris Flor. 1998. "Hysteria and Cyberspace." *Telepolis* (October 7). Available at: http://www.heise.de/tp/english/inhalt/co/2492/1.html.

Permissions and Trademarks

Portions of chapters 1 and 2 were previously published as "Hypertext," in *Glossalalia*, edited by Julian Wolfreys (Edinburgh: Edinburgh University Press, 2003).

Extended citations in chapter 2 appeared in Vannevar Bush's essay "As We May Think," *The Atlantic* [*The Atlantic Monthly*] 176 (1) (July 1945). Reprinted with permission.

An excerpt in chapter 4 appeared in Peter Newell's *The Rocket Book* (New York: Harper and Brothers, 1912).

Except where noted otherwise, all screen captures and translations from natural languages are the work of the author.

Acrobat®, Director®, Flash™, Photoshop®, and Shockwave™ are registered trademarks or trademarks of Adobe Systems, Inc.

Apple®, Aqua®, Final Cut Pro®, HyperCard®, iMac®, iPhone™, iPod®, Leopard™, Macintosh®, Mac OS®, Power Mac®, QuickTime®, Safari™, and Tiger™ are trademarks of Apple Computer, Inc., registered in the United States and other countries.

Google Docs™ is a trademark of Google.

Guide™ is a trademark of InfoAccess, Inc.

Holodeck™ is a trademark of Paramount Pictures Corporation.

Intel® and Core™2 Duo are registered trademarks or trademarks of Intel Corporation in the United States and other countries.

JavaScript™ is a registered trademark of Sun Microsystems, Inc.

Magic Cap™ is a trademark of General Magic, Inc. and Intellectual Ventures, LLC.

Microsoft®, Microsoft Bob™, Windows®, Windows XP™, Windows Vista™, Microsoft Word®, and Virtual PC® are registered trademarks or trademarks of Microsoft Corporation in the United States and/or other countries.

Mini vMac is copyright © 2007 by Paul C. Pratt, and is distributed under the terms of the GNU General Public License, version 2.

Motorola™ is a registered trademark of Motorola, Inc.

Myst™ and Riven™ are trademarks of Brøderbund Software, Inc., and Cyan, Inc.

Octavo Editions™ is a trademark of Octavo.

Parallel Textface™, SilverStand™, Stretchtext™, Xanadu™, and ZigZag® are registered trademarks of or copyrighted by Theodor Holm Nelson and/or Project Xanadu.

Parallels® and Parallels® Desktop are registered trademarks of Parallels, Inc.

Post-it® is a registered trademark of 3M Corporation.

PowerPC® is a registered trademark of IBM Corporation.

Rolodex® is a registered trademark of the Insilco Corporation.

Storyspace™ is a trademark of Eastgate Systems, Inc.

SuperCard® is a registered trademark of Solutions Etcetera.

UNIX® is a registered trademark of The Open Group.

Visi On™ is a trademark of VisiCorp.

Voyager Expanded Book™ is a trademark of The Voyager Company.

All other trademarks are the property of their respective owners.

Index

Entries are keyed to paragraph, figure, and note numbers. For a description of the paragraph numbering scheme used, see note at bottom of page 1.

Terry Harpold
is associate professor of English and film and
media studies at the University of Florida.